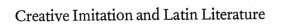
Creative Imitation and Latin Literature

Creative Imitation and Latin Literature

EDITED BY

DAVID WEST &
TONY WOODMAN

THE UNIVERSITY OF NEWCASTLE UPON TYNE

CAMBRIDGE UNIVERSITY PRESS

CAMBRIDGE

LONDON · NEW YORK · MELBOURNE

Published by the Syndics of the Cambridge University Press
The Pitt Building, Trumpington Street, Cambridge CB2 1RP
Bentley House, 200 Euston Road, London NW1 2DB
32 East 57th Street, New York, NY 10022, USA
296 Beaconsfield Parade, Middle Park, Melbourne 3206, Australia

First published 1979

Printed in Great Britain
at the Alden Press, Oxford

Library of Congress Cataloguing in Publication Data

Main entry under title:

Creative imitation and Latin literature.

Bibliography: p.
Includes indexes.
1. Latin literature – Criticism and interpretation – Addresses, essays,
lectures. I. West, David Alexander. II. Woodman, Anthony John.
PA6011.C7   470′.9   79–1181
ISBN 0 521 22668 6

CONTENTS

Contents

CONTRIBUTORS

DAVID BAIN. Lecturer in Greek and Latin in the University of Manchester and author of *Actors and audience: a study of asides and related conventions in Greek drama* (1977)

FRANCIS CAIRNS. Professor of Latin in the University of Liverpool; author of *Generic composition in Greek and Roman poetry* (1972) and *Tibullus: a Hellenistic poet at Rome* (1979)

IAN M. LE M. DU QUESNAY. Lecturer in Latin in the University of Birmingham, at present preparing a book on Virgil's *Eclogues* and a commentary on Tibullus 1

K. W. GRANSDEN. Reader in English and Comparative Literature in the University of Warwick and author of *Virgil: Aeneid VIII* (1977); author of the chapter on Homer in the forthcoming *Legacy of Greece*, and at present preparing a commentary on *Aeneid* 11

E. J. KENNEY, F.B.A. Kennedy Professor of Latin in the University of Cambridge; editor of Ovid, *Amores, Ars amatoria, Remedia amoris* (1961) and with Mrs P. E. Easterling of *Ovidiana Graeca* (1965), and author of *Lucretius: De rerum natura III* (1971) and *The classical text* (1974, Sather Classical Lectures)

C. W. MACLEOD. Student and Tutor of Christ Church, Oxford; author of articles on many writers including Aeschylus, Catullus, Horace and Thucydides, and at present preparing a commentary on *Iliad* 24

NIALL RUDD. Professor of Latin in the University of Bristol; author of *The Satires of Horace* (1966) and *Lines of enquiry* (1976), and with E. Courtney of *Juvenal: Satires 1, 3 and 10* (1977)

D. A. RUSSELL, F.B.A. Fellow of St John's College and Reader in Classical Literature in the University of Oxford; editor of '*Longinus*'

On the sublime (1964) and author of *Plutarch* (1972), and (with M. Winterbottom) of *Ancient literary criticism* (1972); editor (with N. G. Wilson) of 'Menander Rhetor' (in the press)

DAVID WEST. Professor of Latin in the University of Newcastle upon Tyne; author of *Reading Horace* (1967) and *The imagery and poetry of Lucretius* (1969)

TONY WOODMAN. Reader in Latin Literature in the University of Newcastle upon Tyne and author of *Velleius Paterculus: the Tiberian narrative* (1977)

The editors wish to thank the staff of the Cambridge University Press for the patience, kindness and care which they have shown over this book.

PROLOGUE

This book is a sequel to *Quality and pleasure in Latin poetry* but has a narrower focus. At the suggestion of one of our contributors it is devoted to literary imitation, a subject so fundamental to Latin literature that it seemed to deserve a study to itself.

After an introductory survey of the ancient view of *imitatio*, each contributor has analysed a passage in detailed comparison with its literary antecedent(s). As in our previous volume, contributors have been left free to choose their own passages and to devise their own approach. The result is again a varied collection of essays. Some have compared Latin poetry with Greek antecedents, some with Latin antecedents; some have investigated self-imitation, some the relationship between English poetry and Latin – for we should remember that other literatures were inspired by Latin in much the same way as Latin itself was inspired by Greek.

Contributors have tried to make their essays as wide as possible in their appeal, useful to both students and scholars alike: they have freely referred to other discussions and critiques where appropriate, and technical terms, except the most common, have been explained.

We as editors have again tried to summarize in an epilogue the issues raised by the contributors. We hope that these essays will help readers to apprehend the richness, impetus and creative originality of this literary process. *Imitatio* is neither plagiarism nor a flaw in the constitution of Latin literature. It is a dynamic law of its existence.

D.A.W., A.J.W.

I

D. A. Russell

DE IMITATIONE

One of the inescapable features of Latin literature is that almost every author, in almost everything he writes, acknowledges his antecedents, his predecessors – in a word, the tradition in which he was bred. This phenomenon, for which the technical terms are *imitatio* or (in Greek) *mimēsis*, is not peculiar to Latin; the statement I have just made about Latin writers would also be true very generally of Greek. In fact, the relationship between the Latin genres and their Greek exemplars may best be seen as a special case of a general Greco-Roman acceptance of imitation as an essential element in all literary composition. Of course, the business of translation was difficult, and victory over the *patrii sermonis egestas* a notable thing.[1] The boast of having given Rome her own *Aeolium* or *Ascraeum carmen* was made with justifiable pride.[2] But we must not make too much of this. The *exemplaria Graeca* of Horace (*Ars poetica* 268–9) were to be thumbed night and day not because they were Greek but because they were good. Horace (ibid. 132ff.) warns the would-be poet against slavish copying of tradition:

> nec uerbo uerbum curabis reddere, fidus
> interpres, nec desilies imitator in artum
> unde pedem proferre pudor uetet aut operis lex.

> *Nor will you take pains to render word for word, like a scrupulous interpreter, or jump down, as you imitate, into some little hole from which shame or the rules of the work won't let you escape.*

He is not thinking here primarily of the translator, but, as the context makes clear, of any poet who lacks the power to make what he inherits his own, whether he is writing in the same language or a different one. And the poet cannot help being *imitator*; that is his inevitable status. What he can avoid is getting into impossible situations through the meticulous adherence to verbal and superficial features of his model.

In another place (*Epistles* 1.19.19) Horace attacks his own *imitatores* as 'a pack of slaves', *seruum pecus*: he is not here condemning them because they copied him, which might of course be flattering, but because they did so in superficial and trivial respects.

The traditional character of classical Greek literature needs no exposition here. It can be seen not only within genres like epic and tragedy, but also between genres, where it tends naturally to be a matter of content rather than of form. Aeschylus, we recall, called his plays τεμάχη, 'slices', of Homer's great banquets (Athenaeus, *Dipnosophistae* 7.348e). That poetry had a language, or rather several languages, of its own, was accepted and not questioned. Aristotle, despite the fundamental quality of his thinking about poetry, took these traditional characteristics of the *technē* for granted. He defined the differentia of the language of poetry as elevation (λέξιν ... μὴ ταπεινήν) and examined its use of archaic and foreign words and freshly invented compounds (*Poetics* 1458a). He also rationalized the tragedians' restricted range of plots, alleging that it was only the stories of certain families that were suitable for the proper effect of tragedy (*Poetics* 1454a). Comedy also was very 'imitative'; scenes and characters were freely borrowed and improved, and it is easy to see that Plautus and Terence played the game on much the same terms, language apart, as their Greek predecessors.[3] All this was in the age of classical Attic literature. The Hellenistic period which followed, with its blend of changing ideas and archaic forms, gave quite a new perspective to the use of models and tradition. It turned it into a matter not so much of continuity as of revival: *mimēsis* became μίμησις τῶν ἀρχαίων, 'imitation of the ancients', no longer simply of one's predecessors. Callimachus' praise of Aratus gives the new ideal in concise form:

> Ἡσιόδου τό τ᾽ ἄεισμα καὶ ὁ τρόπος· οὐ τὸν ἀοιδῶν
> ἔσχατον, ἀλλ᾽ ὀκνέω μὴ τὸ μελιχρότατον
> τῶν ἐπέων ὁ Σολεὺς ἀπεμάξατο· χαίρετε λεπταὶ
> ῥήσιες, Ἀρήτου σύμβολον ἀγρυπνίης.　　(*Epigram* 27)

Hesiod's is the song and the manner; the man from Soloi has reproduced not the worst of poets, and I suspect he has hit off the sweetest part of his verses. Hail, ye delicate utterances, token of Aratus' wakeful nights!

In other words, one should mould oneself on the ancients, choose a good model, and select his best features.

But already in Hellenistic times, and still more under the Roman domination, there was an ingredient in Greek *mimēsis* which was present only in a much weaker form in Latin: linguistic archaism. It is true that Latin developed, both for poetry and for many kinds of prose, a literary language which diverged widely from the vernacular and was maintained by educational effort from generation to generation. But this tendency was very much stronger in Greek, and indeed has remained strong almost to the present day. During the whole period in which Greek and Latin literature existed and developed side by side – say from 200 B.C. to A.D. 400 – Greek poets continued to write in their ancient dialects and with their ancient techniques, making no concession to linguistic changes, except at the very end of the period, when accentual rules began to be observed. Prose went through a slightly different development. In Hellenistic times, to judge from our scanty remains, there was a good deal of innovation, especially in vocabulary; but a reaction followed, and critics like Dionysius of Halicarnassus, who lived and worked at Rome under Augustus, violently attacked the stylistic standards of their immediate predecessors, and advocated a return to the manner of the fourth-century Attic classics, from Thucydides to Demosthenes. Linguistic *mimēsis* of these models thus became an essential element in rhetorical teaching. We find the corpus of acceptable models referred to as 'the books', *ta biblia* ([Dionysius] *Ars rhetorica* 298.1) – an interesting pagan parallel to the Jewish and Christian term for the scriptures. The rhetorical culture of the first four centuries of our era was indeed a civilization of 'the books'.

The term *mimēsis* and its cognates, destined to play so vital a part in the classicizing poetics and rhetoric of Hellenistic and Roman times, had entered the world of literary theory in a different sense. These were the words by which it was usual to describe not the relationship between one work of literature and another, but the relationship between literature, or any other representational art, and the world. The basic sense of *mimeisthai* is apparently 'to mimic', as when one mimics bird-song or assumes an alien dialect; and it was easy enough for Plato (as in the tenth book of the *Republic*) to represent poetry, because it is a 'mimetic art', as the purveyor of psychologically dangerous illusions. Nor perhaps was it too difficult for Aristotle to answer this by pointing out that mimicry and copying are roads to knowledge (as they evidently are for children), and that poets need to have some generalized understanding of character and emotion if they are to produce anything worth-while.

3

D. A. Russell

Now it is, I suspect, natural to think that the sense of *mimēsis* in which the philosophers tried to use it to describe the kind of human activity of which literature is an instance has nothing to do with the imitation of one author by another. It is surely just a homonymous use of the word. But I fear this may be too simple. Of course, the notion of literary copying is perfectly well conveyed by *mimēsis* and its cognates in their everyday sense. But once these terms had been used in an attempt to explain what in general poetry does and is, their later literary uses could not fail to be affected by the associations they had thus acquired. Words have this sort of power to influence ways of thinking. At any rate, there are features in the Hellenistic and Roman concept of literary imitation which strongly recall the apparently homonymous use of these terms in general poetic theory. The analogy between the mimetic relationship of works of literature to each other and their mimetic relationship to the outside world proved suggestive. In one sense, all poets were *imitatores*, in another this was true only of those who did not (like Homer) stand at the beginning of a tradition. It was possible even to play with the two senses. In the line of the *Ars poetica* quoted above – *nec desilies imitator in artum* (133) – it is difficult to believe that Horace did not mean us to have both senses in mind. Again, there is the assumption sometimes made that the copy is bound to be inferior to the model. Plato had always emphasized this; for him, the product of imitation (the *mimēma*) was less 'real', just as the visible world was less 'real' than the world of Forms on which the creator modelled it. So in literature also, *semper citra ueritatem est similitudo* (Seneca, *Controuersiae* 1 *praefatio* 6; cf. Quintilian, *Institutio oratoria* 10.2.11), a reflection which naturally struck a responsive chord in generations habitually looking back to a greater past. However, there were at all periods those who did not despair of surpassing their predecessors. They had to think of countervailing considerations. Acquiescence in inferiority is an impossible attitude. Nor indeed was it at all common: even Statius' farewell to his *Thebaid* (12.816–17) –

> nec tu diuinam Aeneida tempta
> sed longe sequere et uestigia semper adora

> *make no assault on the divine Aeneid, but follow at a distance, and worship its footsteps –*

is coupled with a proud assertion of posthumous fame. Commoner by far is the hope of improving on the models. There seemed to be plenty

4

of evidence in the history of literature that this could be done. As
Philodemus wrote:[4]

πολλάκις τοὺς εἰληφότας ἀμείνους τῶν προκεχρημένων,
ἂν τὸ ποιητικὸν ἀγαθὸν μᾶλλον εἰσενέγκωνται.

[*We often find in the treatment of myth*] *that those who take over
a story are better than its previous users, if they make a greater
contribution of poetical excellence.*

There is thus no reason to despair if you find you have many predecessors:

condicio optima est ultimi: parata uerba inuenit, quae
aliter instructa nouam faciem habent. (Seneca, *Epistulae* 79.6)

*The last comer is best placed. He finds the words to hand;
differently arranged, they take on a new look.*

We shall see more of this attitude later; but what Seneca says in that
sentence to Lucilius – which is meant to encourage him to write about
Etna – is of some considerable significance. The novelty which the
'last comer' can seek lies not in the subject, nor even in the words,
but in the mysterious 'arrangement' (σύνθεσις, *compositio*) which
for many ancient critics was the most decisive, and most difficult
to analyse, of the elements of literature.

The extant theoretical discussions of *imitatio*, of which we must now
take account, make two central points. One is that the true object of
imitation is not a single author, but the good qualities abstracted from
many. Only the late second-century rhetor Hermogenes says something different; his elaborate argument to show that all virtues and
excellences are to be found in Demosthenes is well worth study.[5] The
second point, related to the first, is that the *imitator* must always pene-
trate below the superficial, verbal features of his exemplar to its spirit
and significance. The analogy between these points and those made by
Aristotle in his account of general poetic *mimēsis* is, I think, clear: in
Aristotelian theory, all poetry deals in generalities (*Poetics* 1451b7),
and requires not only verbal skill but, more importantly, understanding
of character and plot.

We have two fairly extensive treatments of *imitatio*, both rhetorical,
and closely related to each other. Dionysius of Halicarnassus wrote
three books on the subject: the first discussed the nature of the process,

5

the second listed desirable models, the third explained how it should be done. We have some fragments of the first, a good deal of the second (which is the source of Quintilian's list of desirable Greek models), nothing of the third. It is to Dionysius that we owe the anecdote which purports to demonstrate the benefits of collecting good features from a range of models:

> The story goes that a farmer, who was an ugly man, became afraid of fathering children who took after him. Fear, however, taught him a technique of having handsome offspring. He showed his wife some beautiful pictures, and got her into the habit of looking at them. He then went to bed with her, and succeeding in begetting good-looking children.
>
> (*De imitatione* fr. VI, p. 203)[6]

Better known than Dionysius is of course Quintilian's detailed list of useful authors, and the accompanying general reflections (*Institutio oratoria* 10.1–2). For the Greek material, he relies almost word for word on Dionysius, and is very much himself the *fidus interpres*; in the Latin part of the chapter, on the other hand, he airs his own views, especially his dislike of Seneca, whom he reserves for a place of dishonour at the end. His general theory is on the lines we should expect, and he may well be more heavily dependent on the lost parts of Dionysius' treatise than we can tell. *Imitatio*, says Quintilian, is a necessity for most of us, since very few have the natural abilities to enable them to equal the classical models.[7] But it is not enough; if there were nothing else, *nihil fuisset inuentum*. In fact many vital qualities of an orator – invention, spirit, personality – are no more attainable by *imitatio* than they are by any other technique of the *ars*. Nor is successful *imitatio* a mechanical affair. It needs critical intelligence, an understanding of *why* the model is so good. It needs a capacity for abstracting from literature of all kinds the common quality (*commune*) which is going to be of use. It needs the power to comprehend thoroughly not only the words of the models but their purposes and methods. The *perfectus orator* will not follow in anyone's footsteps; he will rise on his predecessors' achievements to supply their deficiencies.

Dionysius and Quintilian thus share a concept of *imitatio* consistent with a certain confidence in literary progress – Dionysius was aggressively optimistic about his own generation[8] – and immune to the cruder attacks that could be made on a mere technique of reproduction. Both, however, are concerned exclusively with the teaching of rhetoric, and particularly with the acquisition of verbal facility. And neither – in the texts we possess – gives us examples of good and bad *imitatio*. They thus assert their case without advancing evidence. To supplement them, we must turn elsewhere. But where?

An obscure and despised Greek writer named Dorion composed a *Metaphrasis of Homer* in which he wrote of the rock the Cyclops hurled into the sea ὄρους ὄρος ἀποσπᾶται ('from mountain mountain is wrenched'), and καὶ χειρία βάλλεται νῆσος ('and, gripped in the hand, is thrown an island'). It was the view of Maecenas, according to the elder Seneca (*Suasoriae* 1.12),[9] that these passages, which were *corrupta* and *tumida*, were to be contrasted with the *magna et sana* of Virgil's adaptations, viz. *haud partem exiguam montis* (*Aeneid* 10.128) and *credas innare reuolsas* | *Cycladas* (*Aeneid* 8.691–2). Maecenas is evidently defending Virgil against a charge of *tumor*, 'bombast', by setting his *sententiae* against the obviously grosser ones of Dorion. But his arguments are unimpressive. In the first instance, we are told, he praised Virgil for 'keeping size in mind without ill-advisedly departing from credibility' – by changing the whole mountain into 'no small part' of one. In the second, *non dicit hoc fieri sed uideri*, i.e. Virgil replaces a statement of fact by one of visual impression, so that the hyperbole disappears. Successful *imitatio* thus improves on its 'models' by correcting faults like bombast or unrealistic hyperbole. Maecenas was a great patron; this anecdote gives no very favourable notion of his capacity as a critic.

Most of the Latin examples of this kind of criticism relate (like this one) to Virgil, about whom a large literature gathered from an early date. We have for instance the remarks of the grammarian Valerius Probus on the resemblances between Homer's comparison of Nausicaa with Artemis (*Odyssey* 6.102ff.), and Virgil's simile of Artemis and Dido (*Aeneid* 1.498ff.).[10] 'In Homer', said Probus (or so his pupils reported),

> 'the girl Nausicaa, playing about in a solitary place with girls of her own age, is correctly and appropriately compared with Diana hunting in the mountain ridges among goddesses of the wild; but what Virgil did was in no way appropriate, because Dido, walking in the centre of the city among the Tyrian lords, with dignified dress and gait, "intent on the work and the kingdom to come" (as he says himself), is incapable of filling any of the points of comparison that suit the sport and hunting of Diana. Secondly, Homer frankly and honourably

7

asserts Diana's enthusiasm and pleasure in the hunt; Virgil on the other hand says nothing about her hunting, but only makes her carry a quiver on her shoulder, like a load or a piece of luggage . . .'

He went on to point the contrast between Homer's simple expression of sincere joy γέγηθε δέ τε φρένα Λητώ ('and Leto rejoices in her heart') and the half-hearted pleasure of Virgil's Latona: *Latonae tacitum pertemptant gaudia pectus.*

What concerns us here is not so much the validity of Probus' arguments, as their nature and presuppositions. They are polemical, and consistency is not to be expected. The first rests on the notion of *decorum*: the essence of it is that this simile was not suitable for Dido, who is a more dignified personage than Nausicaa. The second and third, on the other hand, complain of a loss of the very vivacity which the first argument regards as inappropriate. There seems to be little perception here of the subtlety with which Virgil has tried to make the simile *priuati iuris*,[11] or of the positive value of the refinements he has added. We may prefer Homer, as Probus obviously did; but we must find better reasons.

There are many such critiques to be found in Gellius and Macrobius. The second-century sophist Favorinus of Arles takes the descriptions of an eruption of Etna in Virgil (*Aeneid* 3.570ff.) and in Pindar (*Pythian* 1.21ff.), and comes down heavily in Pindar's favour.[12] The criticism resembles that of Probus – on whom indeed it has been thought to depend – and is partly factual, partly stylistic. Pindar distinguishes the smoke seen by day from the fire seen by night; Virgil confounds the two. In describing a cloud as *turbine fumantem piceo et candente fauilla*, Virgil must be guilty of one of two errors: either a vulgar misuse of *candens* for 'hot', or a self-contradiction between the 'white-hot' ash and the 'pitchy' whirling smoke. That Pindar's description is more vivid and precise would, I suppose, be our common feeling; but once again, the kind of sharpness with which the grammarian establishes his point falls far short of any proper discussion of the *mimēsis*. So too in some cases where Virgil is said to have improved on his model. Homer had written (*Iliad* 16.33ff.):

γλαυκὴ δέ σε τίκτε θάλασσα,
πέτραι τ' ἠλίβατοι, ὅτι τοι νόος ἐστιν ἀπήνης

and it was the grey sea that bore you, and the towering rocks, so remorseless is your heart.

Virgil in his adaptation (*Aeneid* 4.365ff.) adds a new idea: *Hyrcanaeque admorunt ubera tigres.* Why did he do this? Because, Favorinus tells us,[13] character is the product of *nutricatio* as well as of birth. Homer's *criminatio morum* is thus defective in a respect which Virgil supplied. The defect is both ignorance of a truth of ethics and failure to apply the rule of rhetoric which expects *vituperatio* (ψόγος), like *laus* (ἐγκώμιον), to cover not only birth (γένεσις) but upbringing (ἀνατροφή). A somewhat better example is the comparison between *Aeneid* 1.198ff. and *Odyssey* 12.108.[14] Here, Virgil's encouragement of his shipwrecked companions is represented as rhetorically more effective than Odysseus' corresponding speech.

> Ulysses reminded his friends of one trouble [the Cyclops], Aeneas encourages his men to hope for an end to their present woes by alluding to the issue of two episodes [Scylla and Cyclops]. Ulysses says somewhat obscurely καί που τῶνδε μνήσεσθαι ὀίω ('I am sure you will remember these happenings'), Aeneas more plainly *forsan et haec olim meminisse iuuabit*, 'it will give you pleasure one day to remember even this'. But the addition which the Roman poet has made marks a more potent consolation. Aeneas heartens his men not only by an example which illustrates escape, but by the hope of future happiness, promising them not only *sedes quietas* as a result of their hardships, but also *regna*.

This is perhaps as satisfactory an example of these comparisons as we can find; and it shall close this brief selection.[15] The criteria of realism, moral appropriateness, and grammatical correctness strike us inevitably as superficial and unhelpful. The more detailed rhetorical analysis of the last example raises hopes of something more perspicacious. But on the whole, if this were the best that we could learn from the ancient critics about the criteria for judging *mimēsis*, we might as well follow our own poor wits. Fortunately, there is something which is at least a little better.

'Longinus' opens the subject of *mimēsis* at 13.2, and devotes the rest of chapters 13 and 14 to it. He is here listing ways of achieving 'sublimity' of thought; questions of style and diction are to come later. Plato showed the way; and for us too ἡ τῶν ἔμπροσθεν μεγάλων συγγραφέων καὶ ποιητῶν μίμησίς τε καὶ ζήλωσις ('*mimēsis* and *zēlōsis* of the great prose-writers and poets of old') is 'a road to the sublime'.

Why these two terms, *mimēsis* and *zēlōsis?* They correspond to *imitatio* and *aemulatio* in Latin. The question inevitably arises whether there is any difference between them, for it is natural to think that they may represent essentially different attitudes, the one more negative, the other more independent. Now we do find a sharp distinction made in the fragments of Dionysius' treatise on *mimēsis* (p. 200 Usener–Radermacher), if we can trust our reports of what he said:

μίμησίς ἐστιν ἐνέργεια διὰ τῶν θεωρημάτων ἐκματτομένη τὸ παράδειγμα· ζῆλος δὲ ἐστιν ἐνέργεια ψυχῆς πρὸς θαῦμα τοῦ δοκοῦντος εἶναι καλοῦ κινουμένη.[16]

Mimēsis is an activity reproducing the model by means of theoretical principles. Zēlos is an activity of the mind, roused to admiration of something believed to be beautiful.

It is clear that for Dionysius *zēlos* is at any rate the more spontaneous of the two, the less amenable to rule. But it is important to remember that both are means to the same end; they are not exclusive, they complement each other, rather like *ars* and *ingenium* in Horace's account of their function in poetry:

alterius sic
altera poscit opem res et coniurat amice.[17]

And it is clear that in 'Longinus' also the two terms represent aspects of the same process. He later (13.4) expounds it further, and commends a healthy 'strife' between imitator and model. What he says in that connection refers to the whole complex idea of '*mimēsis–zēlōsis*', not to *zēlōsis* without its partner. It is thus wrong, or at least false in terms of this evidence, to treat 'imitation' and 'emulation' as fundamentally different, the one passive and negative, the other positive and original. Professor Brink rightly says[18] that 'in one sense ... no literature is more imitative than Augustan poetry, in another none is more creative than Virgil's or Horace's work'. It would be wrong to connect the 'creative' element here with *aemulatio*, and the 'imitative' with *imitatio*. The two always complement each other; the process they denote may be either well or badly done, and the difference lies, not in more or less *mimēsis* or more or less *zēlōsis*, but in the choice of object, the depth of understanding, and the writer's power to take possession of the thought for himself.

We noticed that 'Longinus' introduces his recommendation of *mimēsis* by the instance of Plato, who, he says, himself 'broke a lance' with Homer, as Stesichorus, Archilochus and Herodotus had done before him. A powerful argument for the practice of *mimēsis* is thus the example of the great classical writers themselves. This is a common idea. Horace uses it in *Epistles* 1.19 to defend his own work.[19] Quintilian (10.1.69) discusses Menander's dependence on Euripides, whom 'he admired, as he often testifies, and followed most of all'. Dionysius elaborated a whole history of the relationships between the Attic orators. Others regarded Demosthenes' *De corona* as based on Plato's *Apology*,[20] and so on. Once this had been accepted as historical fact, the status of the contemporary writer was raised. He could be seen as in some sense competing with the great classics in a repeat performance of the competitions they had held among themselves in the old days. 'Longinus' at least seems to hold out no great hopes. The best he expects is honourable defeat; the noblest of contests is one in which 'it is no disgrace to be beaten by one's forerunners' (13.4). His advice is really directed to effecting such self-improvement as is possible in a degenerate age, and it is clear enough from the general moral tendency of his work how he thought this could be done. It is, I think, very significant that what he says corresponds so closely with what the philosopher Epictetus[21] advises in the sphere of ethics: ask yourself what some great hero would have done or said, and then do or say likewise. This is the way to think of posterity, and so avoid limiting one's vision to the petty concerns of the present.

It is clear that *mimēsis*, for 'Longinus', is no mere mechanical skill or easily teachable technique. He emphasizes this further by associating it with the most powerful group of metaphors available for expressing the mystery and wonder of literary composition: the metaphors of inspiration and prophecy. Mysterious effluences (ἀπόρροιαι) of the ancients' grandeur enter our hearts and inspire us, just as Apollo inspires the Delphic priestess. So far as we know, this way of looking at *mimēsis* is original; it is certainly a far cry from Dionysius and his ill-favoured farmer.

Elevating as all this is, it does not explain the rationale of 'Longinus'' next important assertion, namely that the process is not κλοπή, theft or plagiarism.[22] Whatever 'Longinus' means by the corrupt or obscure phrase that follows,[23] he does not make explicit the essential distinction between κλοπή and legitimate imitation. We must, however, consider what this was, for there was an extensive literature on plagiarism in antiquity, and it was a common charge thrown in controversy.[24] But how could the complaint of borrowed feathers really make sense

in a literature which was so thoroughly 'imitative' and traditional?
Terms of polemic and abuse of course often have very little real content, and perhaps whether a particular borrowing was to be called
furtum or not depended on the prejudice of the critic. It was the
obtrectatores Vergilii who were responsible for the lists of his 'thefts'.
Nevertheless, it is reasonable to expect that there were some criteria
which common opinion would accept. For one thing, it is clear that
the borrowing had to be acknowledged. Cicero (*Brutus* 76) apostro-
phizes Ennius:

> A Naevio uel sumpsisti multa, si fateris, uel, si negas,
> surripuisti.

> *There are many things from Naevius that you either 'took over'
> – if you confess it – or 'pinched' – if you deny it.*

So also the elder Seneca (*Suasoriae* 3.7) observes that Ovid took things
from Virgil

> non subripiendi causa sed palam mutuandi, hoc animo ut
> uellet agnosci,

> *not to pinch them, but to borrow openly, with the intention of
> being recognized.*

But how is this acknowledgement to be made? Not in footnotes, as
with Gray's *Pindarick Odes* or Eliot's *The Waste Land*, but by making
it clear by the tenor of your writing that you are working in a certain
tradition, and are fully aware of the resources of your medium, which
you assume also to be known to your readers. This is how Alexandrian
and Augustan poets worked. They assumed in the reader a sufficient
understanding of Alcaeus or Hesiod or Theocritus to feel sure that
he would not bring a charge of κλοπή out of pedantic half-knowledge,
and would know when the *mimēsis* had been successfully executed.
Quintilian in a passage already quoted (10.1.69) clearly attributes this
sort of tacit acknowledgement to Menander, when he alleges that that
poet *saepe testatur*, 'often testifies to', his admiration for Euripides.

But acknowledgement, of course, must be combined with appropriation: a paradoxical but essential point. You must make the thing
'your own', *priuati iuris* (Horace, *Ars poetica* 131), and the way to do
this is to select, to modify, and at all costs to avoid treading precisely
and timidly in the footprints of the man in front.

What then makes *imitatio* successful? It is not simply a matter of avoiding κλοπή. It would be possible to fulfil the conditions of acknowledgement and appropriation, and still fail to achieve an acceptable result. 'Longinus' takes us further towards a definition of the relevant criteria than any other ancient critic, certainly much further than the censors and defenders of Virgil whom we have been sampling. adIn 16.3, in the course of his introductory discourse on figures, he adduces these lines of the comic poet Eupolis:

οὐ γὰρ μὰ τὴν Μαραθῶνι τὴν ἐμὴν μάχην
χαίρων τις αὐτῶν τοὐμὸν ἀλγυνεῖ κέαρ

By Marathon, by my battle,
Not one of them shall safely grieve my heart!

This, 'Longinus' tells us, was said to be the 'seed' – σπέρμα, surely a better metaphor than 'source' – of the famous oath in Demosthenes' *De corona* (218) 'by those who risked their lives at Marathon'. Where is the difference? It lies, we are told, in 'the where and the when, the occasion and the purpose'. Eupolis used the oath when there was no need for comfort, and he weakened his effect by swearing by the inanimate object 'battle' instead of by the persons who risked their lives, thus missing the chance of 'deifying' the combatants as Demosthenes contrived to do. Demosthenes on the other hand used the figure to make his dispirited audience forget that Chaeronea was a defeat, and he did this without ostentatiously pointing the contrast with the victors of the Persian Wars. 'Longinus' evidently accepts the scholars' statement that Demosthenes actually had the comic passage in mind.

It seems to me that one may profitably think here of a famous place in Latin poetry where a line is taken from a somewhat trivial context and given a new setting in a much more solemn one. Catullus (66.39) made the lock of Berenice's hair exclaim *Inuita, o regina, tuo de uertice cessi*. Virgil (*Aeneid* 6.460) makes Aeneas say, in his sad and embarrassed apologia to Dido in the Underworld, *Inuitus, regina, tuo de litore cessi*. This tends to puzzle the reader. Are we to think that the borrowing is made *hoc animo ut uellet agnosci*, but yet not so as to bring back to our minds the context of Catullus' line? Or that the difference in tone and seriousness between the *Coma Berenices*, a court elegy, and the erotic episode in the epic is less than we would instinctively feel? Are they, in other words, on much the same stylistic level? I should prefer to suggest that Virgil is playing the *mimēsis* game in the way 'Longinus' supposes Demosthenes to have 'imitated' Eupolis. Catullus wasted a splendid line; Virgil shows how it can be put to better use.[25]

414463

D. A. Russell

Let us consider next a case where 'Longinus'' judgement is less clear. It is his thesis that Euripides lacked natural ability for the sort of grand fantasy that came easily to Aeschylus. He tries hard, however, especially in the portrayal of love and of insanity, and in this he is extremely successful. Thus (15.5) he makes efforts – presumably in the *Phoenissae* – to equal the heroics of *The Seven against Thebes*, and modifies the line of Aeschylus' *Lycurgeia* ἐνθουσιᾷ δὴ δῶμα, βακχεύει στέγη ('The house is possessed, the roof is rioting') into πᾶν δὲ συνεβάκχευ' ὄρος ('The whole mountain rioted with them'). Does 'Longinus' approve? He acknowledges that Euripides gave the line an additional flavour, perhaps a softening or sweetening one (ἐφηδύνας). He does not tell us what this is, so we note the obvious differences: 'mountain' for 'house', an increase in scale; the addition of συν – 'with', linking the feelings of the mountain with the feelings of the rioting bacchanals; the less vivid imperfect (συνεβάκχευε) for the historic presents (if that is what they are) of the original passage. It is not easy to strike the balance; but the implication of the argument is that Euripides' line, though a brave effort, is thought of as weaker than Aeschylus' unsophisticated grandeur.

Certainly sometimes the *mimēsis* ends in something undesirable. At 10.5–6, 'Longinus' explains how Aratus spoiled Homer. In a simile of the *Iliad* (15.628), the sailors 'tremble at heart for fear; for they are moving but a little way out of the reach of death':

τρομέουσι δέ τε φρένα ναῦται
δειδιότες· τυτθὸν γὰρ ὑπὲκ θανάτοιο φέρονται.

Aratus (*Phaenomena* 299) tries to appropriate this effect: ὀλίγον δὲ διὰ ξύλον ἄιδ' ἐρύκει ('A little plank keeps death away'). This, says Longinus, is trivial (μικρόν) and elegant (γλαφυρόν) rather than frightening. Moreover, he adds, the danger has been removed, because the plank *does* keep death away, and we are not left in suspense about the sailors' fate. The criticism is not unlike some of those Virgil–Homer comparisons that we noted in Probus and his school; but it does I think go a little deeper, perhaps because 'Longinus' is working with the principle that it is a proper function of 'the sublime' to let us feel frightened, and the stylistic and emotional lapses of Aratus can therefore be seen as elements making up his total failure.

Here, the model was worthy, but Aratus failed to live up to it. His ingenuity led him to destroy the essential feature. But there is another common cause of failure: the wrong choice of model. Xenophon

14

De imitatione

(*Respublica Lacedaemoniorum* 3.5) produced the strange conceit αἰδημονέστεροι αὐτῶν τῶν ἐν τοῖς ὀφθαλμοῖς παρθένων 'more modest than the very maidens in the eyes'. This turns on the double meaning of κόραι, 'maidens' and 'pupils'; in Xenophon's sentence κόραι in the second sense is replaced by a synonym of κόραι in the first sense, viz παρθένοι, 'virgins'. Not unnaturally, 'Longinus' (4.4) disapproves of this *jeu d'esprit* in a normally sober and virile writer. But what the historian Timaeus did with it, when he stole it, is far worse: he said of the tyrant Agathocles that he must have had 'harlots not maidens (κόραι) in his eyes'. Here, the pun on κόραι is conveyed in an even more oblique way, namely by setting in antithesis to κόραι ('pupils') a word which is the natural opposite of κόραι ('maidens'). This is real *cacozēlia*, the deliberate pursuit of corrupt taste.

Imitatio uitiorum is naturally often observed and condemned. It is the most obvious kind of bad imitation; and is very apt to occur in the mass of poor writers who try to emulate the successes of the great. Cicero saw it in orators (*De oratore* 2.90–1):[26]

> Multos imitatores saepe cognoui, qui aut ea quae facilia sunt aut etiam illa quae insignia ac paene uitiosa consectantur imitando. Nihil est facilius quam amictum imitari alicuius aut statum aut motum.

> *I have known many imitators who pursue in their imitation either things which are easy to copy or even conspicuous near-faults. Nothing is easier to imitate than a man's way of dressing or standing or moving.*

Horace saw it in his own imitators (*Epistles* 1.19.15ff.):

> decipit exemplar uitiis imitabile; quodsi
> pallerem casu, biberent exsangue cuminum.

> *A model whose faults can be copied takes people in; if I happened to be pale, they would take a dose of anaemic cummin . . .*

And Seneca, in a letter full of interesting comments on style, observed the infectious spread of this kind of imitation among the archaizers who crowded in after Sallust (*Epistles* 114.17):

> Haec uitia unus aliquis inducit, sub quo tunc eloquentia est, ceteri imitantur et alter alteri tradunt.

> *Some individual writer, the dominant force in literature at the time, introduces these faults, others imitate them and hand them on one to another.*

15

We may now attempt to summarize, largely on the basis of what we have seen in 'Longinus', the main criteria of successful *mimēsis*, as they were generally conceived. We can state, I think, five principles:

(i) The object must be worth imitating.
(ii) The spirit rather than the letter must be reproduced.
(iii) The imitation must be tacitly acknowledged, on the understanding that the informed reader will recognize and approve the borrowing.
(iv) The borrowing must be 'made one's own', by individual treatment and assimilation to its new place and purpose.
(v) The imitator must think of himself as competing with his model, even if he knows he cannot win.

Such a code of course does not go far towards explaining the practice of poets. Much of it is self-evident or vague. Our own study of the technique must go deeper than the evidence of ancient theory can take us, and examine many aspects which the rhetors either never saw or took for granted. Presumably, in antiquity as at any other period, any decent poet or orator knew more about his craft than the teachers from whom he learned the elements. None the less, the hints we can gather from the critics, and especially from 'Longinus', are not to be despised. We know from our observation of the literature how *mimēsis* pervaded it all; we see from the critics at least the general outlines of how it was judged. For them, as for us, the study of this process was an essential and important part of ἡ τῶν λόγων κρίσις 'the judgement of speech'.

2

David Bain

PLAVTVS VORTIT BARBARE
Plautus, *Bacchides* 526–61 and Menander, *Dis exapaton* 102–12

Latin literature began in 240 B.C. with the adaptation of a Greek play and for a long time drama was to be the predominant literary genre at Rome. For the most part this drama consisted of versions of Greek classics: in tragedy the fifth-century repertoire and particularly Euripides, in comedy the plays of the 'New Comedy', those of Menander and his contemporaries. It happens that much the best preserved part of early Latin literature is comedy, twenty plays of Plautus and six of Terence. This corpus has long been a subject of keen inquiry by historians of literature and literary critics, their purpose being to discover the method of composition of the Roman dramatists. The central problem has been to assess their degree of fidelity to their Greek models or, to put it another way, to determine their originality.

For long such an inquiry was gravely handicapped for lack of evidence. In the case of Terence there existed a modicum of useable material, some internal and external testimony as to his compositional activity. He himself made statements about the composition of his plays in his prologues. The commentary on his plays which goes under the name of Donatus occasionally notes where Terence diverges from his original and sometimes (but only with tantalizing infrequency) actually quotes what was in the Greek play.[1] For Terence's predecessor Plautus, however, evidence was much scarcer, a few fragments of Greek plays which were with varying degrees of probability supposed to correspond to passages in his plays and one passage in a prologue which apparently states that Plautus has made a cut in his original (Plautus, *Casina* 64ff.).

As is often the case when hard evidence is scarce, the views of scholars were widely divergent. Extreme attitudes were often to be found, scholars either regarding Plautus' plays as word for word translations (and as such valuable testimony for the technique and ethos of the lost Greek plays) or else supposing them to be extremely free adaptations. One attitude came into greater prominence in the late nineteenth

17

century largely as the outcome of the writings of the great Plautine scholar, Friedrich Leo. This was the view that Plautus when composing a play more often than not combined material from more than one Greek original. Such a procedure, which was indeed attested for Plautus and other early dramatists by Terence, came to be known as *contaminatio*.[2] The search for 'contaminated' plays became the dominant concern of Plautine scholarship. Those who pursued such inquiries tended to overstatement and to overconfidence in their findings, but they often revealed glaring inconsistencies in the course of the action of the plays they studied. Such inconsistencies were hard to attribute to the Greek authors and they made it difficult to take seriously those who regarded the plays as literal translations.

One vital piece of evidence for the methods of composition of Roman comic poets was available, but its implications were not always borne in mind. The second-century A.D. antiquarian and scholar Gellius in a chapter of his *Noctes Atticae* (2.23) provides us with what were until recent times the most extensive fragments of a Greek comedy which could be set against its Latin equivalent. Gellius begins by telling his readers that he frequently read and enjoyed Latin comedies, but that when he turned to the Greek originals the Latin plays seemed very poor by comparison. Fortunately for us he supports his opinion by quoting three passages of a Latin play alongside their Menandrean equivalents. The play is Caecilius' *Plocium* adapted from Menander's *Plokion*. Caecilius was a noted writer of comedy active in the period following Plautus' death and just prior to Terence's début.

The differences are startling.[3] The first pair of parallel passages shows Caecilius transforming a speech of 'simple' narrative[4] into a full-blown aria in various metres, full of figurative and rhetorical language that was absent from the original and containing an echo of Roman ritual terminology which again has no Greek counterpart. The second pair, rendering dialogue, shows Caecilius inserting a vulgar joke about bad breath and vomit, suppressing a reference which might have escaped a Roman audience and considerably revising the form of the conversation so as to make it resemble the routine of a stand-up comic and his straight man. The third pair is remarkable for the difference in length (four lines of Caecilius against nine of Menander) and also for the high-flown language of the Latin poet (Gellius speaks of his *uerba tragici tumoris*[5]).

The implications for the question of Plautus' methods of composition were there for all to see. It is clear that Caecilius was composing in the Plautine tradition:[6] all the phenomena found in the *Plocium* to be Caecilian (rather than Menandrean) can be paralleled in Plautus, lyric arias (*cantica mutatis modis*), Roman references, jokes about bad breath (cf. Plautus, *Asinaria* 894f. and *Mercator* 574f.) and the use of tragic language.[7] Even without further evidence regarding the form and character of Greek New Comedy one would be justified in arguing from the Caecilian passages that Plautus added a great deal of Roman colour to his originals and interfered considerably with their form. Fortunately we are now (as nineteenth-century scholars were not) in a position to obtain a clear, overall view of the form and technique of New Comedy.

For most of this century the discovery of papyri in Egypt has been advancing and illuminating our knowledge of the greatest exponent of the genre, Menander. The two most extensive finds have been the Cairo Codex which contains large parts of *Epitrepontes, Samia* and *Perikeiromene* and was published in 1907, and the more recently published Bodmer Codex which contains our only complete Menander play, *Dyskolos*, as well as large portions of *Samia* and *Aspis*.[8] It was the discovery of the Cairo Codex which led in 1922 to the publication of the epoch-making book on Plautus, Eduard Fraenkel's *Plautinisches im Plautus* (republished in an Italian translation with some additions and revisions as Fraenkel (1960)). Fraenkel was able to reveal the extent of Plautus' manipulation of his originals by using for comparison with Plautus the newly discovered Menander taken in conjunction with the plays of Terence. While Terence admittedly made structural changes to his originals, his technique was seen to be much closer to Menander than to Plautus; for example he rarely inserts purely Roman material.

Fraenkel found that many phenomena which recurred in Plautus were unattested or infrequent in Greek New Comedy and in Terence. His dialogue was often amplified and exaggerated, particularly when an actor first became aware of another's presence on stage. A stereotyped monologue opening was often to be found. In it the speaker claimed that what he had just done, seen or experienced exceeded some great achievement or marvel of the past. Plautus also provided many instances of riddling identification of the form '*x* is *y*' followed by explanation *in asyndeto*.[9] He showed a delight in puns which extended to those which would have been impossible in Greek. The formal language of Roman legal, governmental and religious institutions was exploited in a way that had no real analogy in Greek New Comedy: Menander does not seem to have availed himself of Athenian official language for effect. Also great use was made of military jargon, particularly in the mouth of slaves, and, as a corollary, of fantastically elaborate and grotesque descriptions of slave punishments.

These and other 'Plautine elements' isolated by Fraenkel provide invaluable tools for analysis. Although on any given occasion Plautus in writing thus may simply be giving his own colouring to the original there are many instances when Plautine elements accumulate. In such passages the dramatic action virtually comes to a stop and often there is to be found material which stands in contradiction to the surrounding context or which seems inappropriate to the characters involved. Fraenkel argued plausibly that such passages were independent compositions of Plautus, sometimes no doubt based upon ideas he had obtained from a reading of Greek plays, but not necessarily material lifted bodily from those plays and 'contaminated' with the play he was adapting. Thus Fraenkel undermined many of the arguments that had been adduced to prove that Plautus wrote *comoediae contaminatae*.[10]

Further discoveries of papyri have done little to shake Fraenkel's findings. Occasionally we come upon phenomena in Greek plays which look Plautine, but their occurrence lacks the regularity of the occurrence of Plautine elements and it was admitted, in any case, that some Plautine elements (obviously not the Roman puns and institutional language) had their starting point in Greek New Comedy.[11] Even so, however convincing a picture Fraenkel drew of Plautine creative activity, the discovery of an extensive portion of the original of one of Plautus' plays was still very much to be desired if only to remove nagging doubts.

Tyche, the patron goddess of New Comedy, answered scholars' prayers when she allowed just such evidence to come to light. In 1968 Professor Handley let it be known to the world that we had upwards of a hundred lines of what was obviously Menander's *Dis exapaton* ('The man who makes two deceptions'), the original of Plautus' *Bacchides*, and in an inaugural lecture presented a text of the more significant and legible part of it. Since then further parts have appeared in the OCT of Menander edited by Sandbach in 1972, but at the time of writing Handley's *editio princeps* is still eagerly awaited.[12]

The fragments of *Dis exapaton* come from the central part of the play and thus do not help solve the most interesting problem connected with the composition of *Bacchides*, the question whether Plautus has added a third deception to Menander's original two.[13] Nevertheless they have yielded a great deal of material to help further the study of Plautus' methods of composition and to assess his originality.

Before going on to a detailed examination of Plautus' *Bacchides*
526ff. and its Greek equivalent it is necessary to give a brief account of
what preceded this portion of the play. There is no good reason for
thinking that Plautus has radically altered the opening acts of the Greek
play, so that the summary which follows will cover the plots of both
plays. Plautus has, however, as elsewhere altered the names of some of
the characters.[14] The two young men, Mnesilochus and Pistoclerus
were in the original Sostratos and Moschos. The Menandrean slave
Syros became the Plautine Chrysalus (note the pun in *Bacchides* 704
and the allusion to the original in l. 649). Lydos the paedagogus
retains his name (note the pun, impossible in Greek, in l. 129). We are
in the dark about the names of the other characters in Menander. When
referring to them I shall use the name of the Plautine equivalent with
inverted commas round it.

Sostratos/Mnesilochus was sent to Ephesos from Athens by his
father 'Nicobulus' there to collect a debt owed his father. He was
accompanied by his slave Syros/Chrysalus. While abroad he met a
Samian courtesan named 'Bacchis' and fell in love with her. She had
hired herself out to a soldier 'Cleomachus' who took her with him to
Athens. Sostratos/Mnesilochus wrote from Ephesos to his friend at
Athens Moschos/Pistoclerus asking him to find where 'Bacchis' was
lodging. Moschos/Pistoclerus succeeded in discovering that she
had just arrived and was going to stay with her homonymous sister
who was an exponent of the same profession. (It is around this point
that the play began, the arrival of 'Bacchis' and the pursuit of her by
Moschos/Pistoclerus. The Plautine manuscripts lack the opening of the
play which is well under way when they resume. There are a number
of quoted fragments of the *Bacchides* which may be assigned to the lost
opening and we now possess the opening line of the Greek play, but
any attempt at reconstruction of the opening scenes must remain
highly speculative.)[15]

'Bacchis' from Samos asks her sister to find someone to help her
get away from the soldier and help her return to Samos. She fears the
soldier may continue to regard her as his property after her term of
employment has expired unless she gets money to buy herself out of it.
Her sister sees just such a protector in Moschos/Pistoclerus and
applies her charms to the task of winning him over. After she has
forced him to accept a dinner invitation, he departs to return a little
later with provisions for the meal and accompanied by his old tutor
Lydos who is already disturbed by what he sees. While they are inside
the courtesan's house, Syros/Chrysalus appears having come from the

harbour where he and his young master have just arrived from Ephesos. The slave has been sent ahead to find Moschos/Pistoclerus and this he does almost immediately. He learns that 'Bacchis' has been located and that there is need of money to get her away from the soldier. The resourceful slave promises that he will obtain the money. The money of course is already in the hands of Sostratos/Mnesilochus, the sum he collected for his father in Ephesos. Syros/Chrysalus has to find a way of holding on to this sum. He does this by telling 'Nicobulus' a lying story which accounts for his son not bringing the money back. When they left the harbour at Ephesos they were pursued by another boat and they thought it best to return to harbour and deposit the money in the safekeeping of an important Ephesian named Theotimos. 'Nicobulus' will have to go and collect it. The old man swallows the story whole and sets off to find his son. They do not meet. Lydos rushes out of 'Bacchis'' house to summon Moschos/Pistoclerus' father so that he may rescue his son from that den of iniquity. Sostratos/ Mnesilochus now arrives, having missed his father but having met Syros/Chrysalus. He arrives at quite the wrong moment because he encounters Lydos returning with 'Philoxenus'. The story told by Lydos leads Sostratos/Mnesilochus into a misunderstanding. Knowing of only one 'Bacchis' he believes that Lydos is describing the embraces of his loved one and Moschos/Pistoclerus and imagines that he has been betrayed. Without divulging his feelings he agrees to 'Philoxenus'' suggestion that he should rescue his friend from this dangerous situation.[16] It is in the course of this dialogue that the Menander papyrus begins. After the exit of Lydos and 'Philoxenus', Sostratos reflects on his position and resolves to give back the money to his father. A little later (the papyrus is very fragmentary here) we find him conversing with his father and telling him to pay no attention to Syros' 'vain story'.[17] He has the gold and he will give it back if his father accompanies him. In the next scene (again very fragmentary) the two have returned from the place where the money was kept and are apparently talking about Syros.[18] The father announces his intention of going to the market and once more Sostratos is left alone to reflect on 'Bacchis'' perfidy. During his monologue, Moschos emerges from 'Bacchis'' house.

It will be apparent to the reader who has Plautus' text before him that this encounter between Sostratos/Mnesilochus and 'Nicobulus' is absent from it. Plautus has cut out the two scenes between father and son and instead made Mnesilochus meet his father and pay over the money off stage. He does this because he is unable to reproduce the structure of the Menandrean play on the Roman stage without incongruity. Menander and the other poets of New Comedy had available to them act breaks during which some sort of choral performance took place and during which the audience might assume that a sufficient period of time had passed for any given off stage action to be completed.[19] In the papyrus of *Dis exapaton* the conversations between father and son are so divided and χοροῦ ('of the chorus') at the point of division indicates the interval between them. If Plautus had followed his original here, he would have had father and son depart somewhere off stage only to return immediately since on the Roman stage there were no such act breaks and there was no chorus (the act breaks to be found in our texts of Plautus do not go back any further than the Renaissance).[20] Plautus tries to get round the problem by having father and son meet off stage. In recasting the scene he flouts several of the conventions of the Greek comic theatre and before the discovery of the papyrus it was already suspected that Plautus had interfered with his original here.[21]

This brings us to the passages to be discussed, Plautus, *Bacchides* 526–61 ~ Menander, *Dis exapaton* 102–12:

> PI. rebus aliis anteuortar, Bacchis, quae mandas mihi:
> Mnesilochum ut requiram atque ut eum mecum ad te adducam
> simul.
> nam illud animus meus miratur, si a me tetigit nuntius,
> quid remoretur. ibo ut uisam huc ad eum, si forte est domi.
> MN. reddidi patri omne aurum. nunc ego illam me uelim 530
> conuenire, postquam inanis sum, contemptricem meam.
> sed ueniam mi quam grauate pater dedit de Chrysalo!
> uerum postremo impetraui ut ne quid ei suscenseat.
> PI. estne hic meus sodalis? MN. estne hic hostis quem aspicio
> meus?
> PI. certe is est. MN. is est. PI. adibo contra. MN.[22] contollam
> gradum.   535
> PI. saluos sis, Mnesiloche. MN. salue. PI. saluos quom peregre
> aduenis,
> cena detur. MN. non placet mi cena quae bilem mouet.
> PI. numquae aduenienti aegritudo obiecta est? MN. atque
> acerruma.
> PI. unde? MN. ab homine quem mi amicum esse arbitratus sum
> antidhac.   539
> PI. inprobum istunc esse oportet hominem. MN. ego ita esse
> arbitror.[23]   552

23

PI. opsecro hercle loquere, quis is est. MN. beneuolens uiuit
tibi.
nam ni ita esset, tecum orarem ut ei quod posses mali
facere, faceres. PI. dic modo hominem qui sit: si non
fecero   555
ei male aliquo pacto, me esse dicito ignauissimum.
MN. nequam homost, uerum hercle amicus est tibi. PI. tanto
magis
dic quis est; nequam hominis parui pendo gratiam.
MN. uideo non potesse quin tibi eius nomen eloquar.
Pistoclere, perdidisti me sodalem funditus.   560
PI. quid istuc est?

         Μο. εἶτ᾽ ἀκούσας ἐνθάδε
εἶναί με, ποῦ γῆς ἐστι; χαῖρε, Σώστρατε.
Σω.   καὶ σύ. ⟨Μο.⟩ τί κατηφὴς καὶ σκυθρωπός, εἰπέ μοι,
καὶ βλέμμα τοῦθ᾽ ὑπόδακρυ; μὴ νεώτερον   105
κακὸν κατείληφάς τι τῶν ἐνταῦθα; ⟨Σω.⟩ ναί.
(Μο.) εἶτ᾽ οὐ [λέ]γεις; ⟨Σω.⟩ ἔνδον γὰρ ἀμέλει, Μόσχε.
                            (Μο.) πῶς;
(Σω.)   ]φιλοῦντα τὸν πρὸ τοῦ χρόνον
                 ]α· τοῦτο πρῶτον ὢν ἐμὲ
                 ]ἠδίκηκας. (Μο.) ἠδίκηκα δὲ   110
ἐγώ σε; μὴ γένοιτο τοῦτο, Σώστρατε.
(Σω.) οὐκ ἠξίουν γοῦν οὐδ᾽ ἐγώ. (Μο.) λέγεις δὲ τί;

MOSCHOS: *So he's heard I'm here – where on earth is he?*
Greetings, Sostratos. SOSTRATOS: *The same to you.* MOSCHOS:
Tell me, why so downcast and gloomy and your glance half
tearful? You haven't come upon some new trouble here?
SOSTRATOS: *I have.* MOSCHOS: *Aren't you telling me, then?*
SOSTRATOS: *Yes, it's inside of course, Moschos.*[24] MOSCHOS:
What do you mean? SOSTRATOS: *. . . a friend till lately . . . this*
is the first of the wrongs you have done me(?). MOSCHOS: *I've*
wronged you? May that never be the case. SOSTRATOS: *I*
didn't expect it myself either. MOSCHOS: *But what are you*
talking about?

One may note at the outset that Plautus has changed the metre of the
scene. Here and in the scene which ended at l. 499, Plautus does not
render Menander's iambic trimeters with their Latin equivalent, iambic
senarii, but prefers to use longer lines with a different rhythm, trochaic

septenarii, the Latin equivalent of trochaic tetrameters. This is a characteristic procedure of Roman dramatists (compare Caecilius' transformation of a Menandrean trimeter speech mentioned above). Plautus has proportionately many more long lines than senarii while the bulk of Menander is written in trimeters and his use of other metres is sparing, the trochaic tetrameter being his second most common metre. In Plautus it is possible to observe some distinctions of tone between the language of his senarii and of his long lines (classified by the ancients as *cantica*) and lyric. Long lines and lyric are generally more dignified and apt to include tragic diction and figurative language more often than senarii.[25] Differentiation between trimeters and tetrameters is by no means so clear-cut in Menander.[26] Plautus by altering the metre has already determined that the tone will be more elevated and pathetic than that of the original.[27]

526–9: The sequence of entrances has been altered as a consequence of Plautus' deletion of the two scenes between father and son. In Menander the young man is on stage directly after the departure of his father and it is his friend who appears second. Here, however, Plautus needs something to fill the gap during which the money is supposed to be handed over off stage. Accordingly he brings on the friend first and Pistoclerus' words on entering (unlike Moschos') are delivered on an empty stage. Some but not all of the content of his entrance-speech is derived from Menander. Plautus has invented a motive for Pistoclerus' arrival on stage. In Menander no motive is expressed for Moschos' entry, which is characteristic of his art.[28] The audience are left to assume that he has come out to look for Sostratos. Plautus by dotting all the i's here is (as often elsewhere) much less natural and much more 'stagey'. He employs a form of entrance that was conventional on the comic stage. This consists of a character leaving the stage building and speaking back into it as if concluding a conversation begun off stage, his addressee remaining out of sight. Such entrances are extremely common in New Comedy (cf. e.g. Menander, *Dyskolos* 206). One wonders whether Plautus is here relying on his knowledge of the conventions of New Comedy or is simply bringing his character on in the manner Moschos was brought on in the original. It is not absolutely clear whether Moschos' words on entering in *Dis exapaton* are addressed to someone off stage or to the world in general, Moschos thinking aloud.[29] Perhaps Plautus adopted the former interpretation and perhaps he was right. At any rate it is characteristic of his stage technique that he makes it quite clear to the reader and spectator alike by adding the vocative *Bacchis* to Pistoclerus' utterance. In Menander such orientation is often left to the actor and the reader may have difficulty producing the scene in his imagination.[30]

When we set beside each other the parts where there is a correspondence ('nam illud ... remoretur' ∼ εἶτα ... γῆς), we meet a significant contrast in style. 'My *animus* wonders what is delaying him if a message from me has touched him' is very different from Menander's clipped and colloquial 'so he's heard I'm here – where on earth is he?' (Handley's translation which cannot be improved on). Plautus surely is some way removed from the everyday speech of young men here. Note the alliteration of *ani*mus *m*eus *m*iratur. *tetigit nuntius* is a high-flown expression although somewhat less so than the tragic fragment that can be quoted as a parallel, *tetigit aures nuntius* (*Tragica incerta* 23 Ribbeck[31]) where the presence of *aures* elevates the tone.[32]

530–3: The entry of Mnesilochus. Again we have a mixture of Plautine material and portions taken from the original. *reddidi patri omne aurum* is an addition. The last time the audience saw Mnesilochus he was on his way to hand over the gold to his father. On his return he immediately informs them that he has done what he intended to do. Such dramatic technique might seem naive and rudimentary, but in fact it is standard practice in New Comedy. Characters often return to the stage continuing (as it were) a conversation with the audience (cf. Menander, *Dyskolos* 259).[33] Plautus is here availing himself of a stock technique of the Greek poets.

ll. 530b–31 make use of Menandrean material. In the monologue Sostratos delivered after his second scene with his father, he looked forward to a meeting with 'Bacchis' now that he had divested himself of the gold (Menander, *Dis exapaton* 91ff.):

κὰι μὴν δοκῶ μοι καλήν τε κἀγαθὴν
ἰδεῖν ἐρωμένην ἂν ἠδ[έ]ως κενὸς
πιθανευομένην καὶ προδοκῶσαν ...

Now that I'm empty handed, I do believe I'd be glad to see my fine girl-friend trying on persuasion and expecting ...

This is the only part of that $11\frac{1}{2}$-line monologue which Plautus has touched. Perhaps much of the rest of it defeated him as it still defeats us.[34] By his omission, however, Plautus has deprived Mnesilochus of a statement of his feelings towards Pistoclerus. In *Dis exapaton* 98ff., Sostratos says that Moschos was foolish (ἀβέλτερον) and he may be

26

saying that he pities him. He announces at any rate that his feelings are mixed; although angry he does not really believe his friend to be the wrong-doer – the responsibility is the girl's. This curtailment of the character's statement about his feelings on the part of Plautus is relevant to the discussion that will arise over the psychological effectiveness of Plautus' remodelling of the confrontation between the young men.

ll. 532–3 have no equivalent in the Greek play but look back to Mnesilochus' monologue which ended at l. 525. There, after resolving to hand over the gold, he emphatically (notice the triple *caussa mea*) proclaims his determination to win pardon for Chrysalus:

> eadem exorabo Chrysalo caussa mea
> pater ne noceat neu quid ei suscenseat
> mea caussa de auro quod eum ludificatus est;
> nam illi aequomst me consulere, qui caussa mea
> mendacium ei dixit. uos me sequimini.   525

This passage had no analogue in Menander since Sostratos' equivalent monologue seems to end at l.30 when Sostratos notices his father arriving. Perhaps the Plautine passage serves as a reminder to us of how much more important the slave role is in Plautus than in Menander. Plautus directs his audience's attention away from the complicated feelings of the young lover towards the likely fate of the slave. It is clear, however, that pardon for Syros did play an important part in the second scene between Sostratos and his father (see n. 16).[35] Plautus having omitted that scene needs to make it clear to the audience that pardon was not immediately forthcoming and that Nicobulus' attitude towards Chrysalus is hostile; it is an important theme of the play that the slave deceives a master who is already deeply suspicious of him.[36]

534–8: the two young men become aware of one another's presence, approach each other and exchange greetings. Here the contrast between Plautus and Menander could not be greater. In Menander the meeting is effected without the least hint of the conventional or theatrical (the different order of entrances does not make any difference to the point I am making here). Moschos enters. If he is speaking back into the house, he will have his back turned towards Sostratos. When he turns round, he sees him and *immediately* addresses him. Likewise Sostratos does not, as he might have done, herald Moschos' entrance with a comment like 'Someone is opening the door' (cf. e.g. Menander, *Dyskolos* 188) nor when Moschos appears does he exclaim 'It's

Moschos!' All he does is return his friend's greeting, albeit somewhat curtly (see Sandbach (1973) ad loc.). Neither party announces his intention of approaching the other.

Scenes of meeting are the very stuff of New Comedy and the Greek poet had available to him a collection of formulae to cope with them. One might say that he would have had in mind something like the following schema:

Situation	Phrase
1 First meeting	'I hear a voice'/'I see someone'/ 'Who is this?'
2 Closer inspection	'Is it so and so?' 'It is.'
3 Taking the plunge	'I shall approach.'
4 Greeting	'Greetings.'

It is striking that although each individual situation occurs and each formula can be paralleled,[37] in Greek New Comedy the schema as a whole or anything like a whole is never to be found. On the other hand, in Plautus it is easy to find passages like this one where the schema is reproduced virtually intact and the formulae accumulate. Only the first stage is absent here, 'Is it so and so?' serving to mark first contact. It is striking too that the encounter is more long drawn out and artificial because of the duplication of formulae: both parties in the encounter go through the sequence.[38] What we have here is an elaborately symmetrical duet (the symmetry is carried on from the two entrance speeches which are both made up of four lines) of a kind much loved by Plautus (cf. particularly *Aulularia* 811ff. and *Rudens* 332ff.) and fully illustrated by Fraenkel (1960) in his chapter entitled 'Ampiamenti del dialogo'. There could in fact be no neater proof than this passage of the correctness of Fraenkel's thesis that Plautus expanded for comic purposes conventional situations of the Greek plays by accumulating formulae and prolonging unrealistically the length of time characters take to make contact on stage. Menander in this instance has no conventional formulae at all. Elsewhere in his plays we do meet what might be called 'stage-directional' phrases, but their occurrence is nowhere near as frequent in Menander as it is in Plautus.[39] Menander here as elsewhere seems to be trying to avoid giving his audience any hint of theatricality. He wants an action which looks lifelike. Plautus here as elsewhere shows a positive delight in the theatrical and drags in conventional elements at the expense of characterization. The meeting duet contains something else that is characteristically Plautine, the exploitation of military language and imagery.

'Is this my enemy?' says Mnesilochus and he sustains the image with *contollam gradum*.[40] The continuation is also at some remove from the original. In Menander, Moschos draws attention to his friend's appearance and asks him what is wrong (a common motif, cf. Menander, *Heros* 1ff.). Pistoclerus, however, in Plautus invites his friend to dinner and obtains an enigmatic refusal. Mnesilochus might be taken to be saying that he has a liver complaint. In fact he means the thought of such a dinner makes him angry. The ambiguity is pursued in the line that follows, *aegritudo* and *acerruma* applying both to illness and to emotional distress.

Dinner on return from abroad or from a long journey was no doubt a part of Greek life and such dinners seem to be integral to the plot of some of the plays that Plautus adapted (as with the dinner for Bacchis in this play and the dinner for the returned husbands in *Stichus*). It would be wrong, then, to regard invitations to such dinners, frequent as they are in Plautus, as exclusively Plautine. Nevertheless the invitations are tendered as here in formulaic language[41] and we might guess that the invitation to a newly returned friend was perhaps more institutionalized at Rome than it was in Greece. Significantly there are in Latin no less than three words to describe such a *cena*, *aduenticia* (cf. *Bacchides* 536 *saluos quom peregre a duenis*), *aduentoria* and *uiatica*.[42] Also of interest is the fact that Plutarch when he describes how he was entertained at a banquet after he returned from Alexandria speaks of 'a reception dinner (δεῖπνον ὑποδεκτικόν) as the Romans call it' (Plutarch, *Table-talk* 8.7.1 (*Moralia* 727B)). Perhaps, then, there is an explanation for Plautus recurring to this theme and justification for speaking of Roman colouring in this connection.

539–61: Mnesilochus accuses Pistoclerus. Up to this point the information gleaned from Menander's original about Plautus' activity would not have surprised the intelligent guesser familiar with Plautus and with New Comedy. There is nothing really unexpected in Plautus changing names, cutting scenes to eliminate the act break, omitting parts of a soliloquy, changing the metre and tone of trimeter passages, adding Roman colouring and guying conventions. What follows, however, is at least at first glance surprising since it shows Plautus making a change which does not quite fit into one of the expected categories of Plautine activity and reveals as Plautine a passage which no one had thought of denying Menander. In Menander once the two friends have exchanged greetings and Moschos, on observing Sostratos' gloomy appearance, has asked him to tell him what is the matter,

29

Sostratos almost immediately accuses his friend. Having explained that the trouble is 'inside' (if that is the correct interpretation of l. 107) he takes only two lines further before coming out with the direct accusation ἠδίκηκας 'you have wronged me'. In Plautus, however, Mnesilochus after his riddling remark about his health continues to mystify Pistoclerus when asked the source of his illness. 'The cause is a man I had thought my friend.' 'Such a man must be a scoundrel' replies the unsuspecting Pistoclerus. Mnesilochus agrees and when asked who the man is answers 'He is a friend of yours, otherwise I should have begged you to do him whatever harm you could.' 'Tell me who he is; if I do not harm him someway or other, you can call me the greatest of cowards.' 'He is a rogue, but he is still your friend.' 'All the more reason for telling me. I've no time for rogues.' Finally after nine lines of enigma and in response to Pistoclerus' third request to know the man's identity, Mnesilochus comes out with a direct accusation: *Pistoclere, perdidisti me sodalem funditus.*

The technique employed here – Mnesilochus speaking about the man directly involved in the action as if he were a third party – has many analogues in European drama and Pöschl (1973) has assembled a large collection of such phenomena which extends from Greek drama to Goldoni.[43] Pöschl argues that the change Plautus has been shown to have made here should lead to a reassessment of his originality. He believes that the new discovery confutes Fraenkel's view that Plautine additions were inorganic and failed to advance the action. According to him, Plautus has here seized upon an idea familiar to him from elsewhere in New Comedy and composed a scene which not only advances the action, but is actually *superior* to that of the original.

Before discussing this last claim, which I should say at the outset seems to me astonishing, not to say preposterous, I would point out that we cannot be absolutely certain that the inspiration for the use of the 'third man' motif did not come from *Dis exapaton*. It is in itself a perfectly plausible assumption that Plautus might have obtained the idea from another Greek comedy. Elsewhere in his plays we can often make a good case for the assumption that he has incorporated motifs he had come to know from plays other than the one he might happen to be adapting at the time.[44] However, in this case it is possible that the equivalent passage of the Greek play itself contained the germ of an idea which Plautus has expanded. ll. 108–9 are unfortunately fragmentary,[45] but they do at least contain one clear correspondence with *Bacchides* 539, φιλοῦντα τὸν πρὸ τοῦ χρόνον ('being a friend in previous times') ∼ *quem mi amicum esse arbitratus antidhac.* It may be that in ll. 108–9 Sostratos said something like 'I have found you, my friend till now, to be an enemy. This (treachery) I think the greatest of the wrongs you have done me.' This notion might have been expressed in an oblique form: 'I have found a man I thought my friend to be my enemy.' Only then would Sostratos turn to direct accusation. In that case Plautus would be less daring than Pöschl supposes, merely expanding on something he found in his original, not composing freely.[46]

However that may be, Pöschl's case deserves attention since whatever the starting point, Plautus has here deviated considerably from his original. It is implicit in Pöschl's view that Plautus was dissatisfied with what Menander had made of the meeting of the two young men.[47] For Pöschl the meeting is an anticlimax. The audience having been put into a state of keen anticipation are let down because Sostratos is too quick in coming out with his 'you have wronged me'. What Plautus has produced, says Pöschl, is at once more exciting, more comic and more interesting psychologically. To attribute greater psychological interest to Plautus than to Menander is near to heresy and although it would be wrong to dismiss such a view out of hand, one is at least entitled to expect a little more evidence to back up the suggestion than is forthcoming. The mental attitudes of Sostratos are not easy to uncover, in no small part because of the difficulty and incompleteness of his monologues and the fragmentary nature of ll. 108ff. Any discussion of his psychology is bound to be somewhat speculative.[48] Nevertheless despite these difficulties it is possible to believe that we are dealing with a character whose actions and words reflect a consistent psychological plan on the part of his creator. We possess the relevant part of Plautus' play complete, but I think it harder to say the same of his creation, Mnesilochus. His monologue in ll. 500–25 ~ *Dis exapaton* 18–30 which ought, given the dramatic situation, to reveal something of his state of mind begins with a series of jokes of a type greatly favoured by Plautus, the ἀπροσδόκητόν ('unexpected') or παρὰ προσδοκίαν ('contrary to expectation') statement where the sting is in the tail:

ne illa illud hercle cum malo fecit – meo	503
ni ego illam exemplis plurumis planeque – amo	505
nam iam domum ibo atque – aliquid surripiam patri	507
adeo ego illam cogam usque ut mendicet – meus pater	508

It seems questionable whether such jokey material is really appropriate either to the matter in hand or to the character.[49] Pöschl himself finds this passage '*etwas buffoneske*' and rightly comments that analogies are to be found in Aristophanes rather than in New Comedy. After these pleasantries, Mnesilochus calls himself to order and moves on to the theme of revenge against Bacchis, revenge to be implemented by handing over the gold to his father. The monologue ends as we saw earlier with attention being drawn to the possible punishment of Chrysalus.

It is hard to see in the monologue just described any improvement on Menander either in clarity or in psychological probability. As Maurach points out,[50] Plautus by laying such stress on the revenge element (512ff.) has altered the motivation of his character. In Menander the young man as well as being angry is afraid. Conscious of his own weakness when faced by the girl he loves, he knows too well the risk of confronting her while he still possesses the gold. He returns the gold not for vengeance, but for safety. He knows he is likely to lose it to her. His second monologue (*Dis exapaton* 91ff.), delivered when he has handed over the gold, contains, as Maurach suggests, probably just a hint of bluster (it is significant surely that when confronted by Moschos his confidence goes and his appearance reveals his true feelings (ll. 104f.)). He is trying to convince himself that he can cope with 'Bacchis'. Perhaps too his feelings are less mixed than he makes out and we are to see in his words about Moschos (ll. 98ff.) a reflection of his obsession with 'Bacchis'. One doubts whether Pöschl is correct in seeing a great build-up to the meeting of the young men. Plautus has scarcely done any more than Menander to heighten the tension. After ll. 489ff. we have very little indication of Mnesilochus' attitude towards Pistoclerus – a brief mention at the beginning of his monologue (ll. 500–1) and then the word *hostis* when Mnesilochus first sees him. This reflects Menander's treatment of Sostratos and Moschos. Sostratos' main concern throughout is with 'Bacchis' and her betrayal of him. His first monologue is about her, Moschos only getting a mention briefly at the beginning.[51] His second monologue is on the same topic Only at the end does he begin to think about his friend and this leads nicely into their meeting. All this seems consistent, probable and admirably worked out. The same can be said of the confrontation that follows. The Plautus scene, however, moves us on to a more rhetorical and less well motivated level. After the exaggerated by-play of ll. 534ff. – where is the subtle psychology there? – it presents us with a supposedly desolate young lover who thinks himself betrayed by his friend yet at the same time enjoys long drawn out teasing and riddles. Mnesilochus begins with an equivocation on the word *bilis*. One might argue that his counterpart Sostratos is initially mysterious with his mention of 'inside' (l. 107), but this is surely apt since inside is the person who absorbs all his attention. Mnesilochus' continuation introduces a repetitive[52] story of the false friend and a long drawn out refusal to answer Pistoclerus' questions.[53] Plautus here as elsewhere is more occupied with paradoxes, word-play and declamation than with psychological veracity.[54] Pöschl's belief that he is here more Menandrean than Menander arises from a misconception of Menander's art, an art expressed not so much in the words used by his actors as in what lies behind the words. Menander does not need large-scale effects or elaborate language to bring his characters to life and to produce exciting stage action.[55]

All this, the preceding discussion and the comparison in general of the two plays, might be thought to have led us back to a view-point that Pöschl deplores at the beginning of his monograph, epitomized by a statement of Leo (1966) 87: 'These comedies were finer and better before Plautus laid his hands on them.'[56] This was not the intention, but I suppose, if pressed, I would say that Leo's view seems to me essentially correct, indeed unassailable. I am reluctant to make such a value judgement not because I disapprove *tout court* of making value judgements about ancient literature – an excessively austere position to which some acquaintances of mine steadfastly adhere – but because in this instance value judgements have often been harmful to scholarship. They have done little to advance the study of Plautus and may be said to have bedevilled it. Latinists keen to defend the Italian writer against strictures such as Leo's have tried to do so by denigrating Menander and his contemporaries. This leads to a reaction, with angry defenders of Menander looking down their noses at Plautus, allowing him to have no merit at all and writing about him in such a way that they might almost be taken to hold him personally responsible for the failure of his originals to survive.

Unfavourable comparison of Plautus to Menander and the other Greek poets indeed goes back to antiquity. We have already mentioned Gellius' disparagement of the Roman poets compared to their originals. Quintilian while acknowledging the particular qualities of Plautus, Caecilius and Terence claims that, deprived of the advantage of writing in Attic Greek, they were able only to aspire to achieving a pale shadow of their originals.[57] Judged by such standards Plautus is on a hiding to nothing, but is this a fair or helpful way of judging him? One may doubt whether it is appropriate to regard Plautus as in any sense competing with Menander. Plautus was not part of a literary coterie. He was writing not to please critics or scholars but to win over and keep the attention of a 'live' audience in a theatre. He was writing too for an audience that was not Menander's audience, writing at a different time in a different place from Menander and employing a different theatrical form.[58] His achievement should be assessed accordingly. Comparison with Menander should not entail Menander being used as a touchstone, rather as a means to reveal Plautus' methods of composition, to characterize his work, not to discredit it.

The new Menandrean discoveries help highlight the vitality and exuberance of Plautus, aspects of his talent so memorably described in the final chapter of Fraenkel's great book. The encounter between Mnesilochus and Pistoclerus stands out in its own right, a different kind of scene from the one in the original, but certainly suspenseful and animated. No matter that it is unrealistic and that it unbalances the carefully worked-out psychology of the original. It belongs to a different category of theatrical writing in which the scene and the moment count for more than the overall effect. There are plenty of great plays that belong to such a tradition, those of Aristophanes for one, and, some would say, most of Greek tragedy. Plautus' theatricality too should not be mistaken for a crude lack of sophistication. His conscious delight in theatrical convention and his knowing attitude towards his characters indicates both a sophisticated playwright and a sophisticated audience.[59]

Anyone who studies New Comedy will soon, unless he is deliberately perverse or possessed of an acute blind spot, come to have a tremendous admiration for Menander. He will be unbalanced in his outlook, however, if he allows this admiration to obscure for him the very real merits of Plautus, just as an equally inevitable respect for Shakespeare's comedies should not prevent one from admiring the treatments of him by Rogers and Hart and Cole Porter. To liken Plautus' plays to such enjoyable travesties may, like Quintilian's view of Roman comedy as a pale shadow of the original, be somewhat of an exaggeration. I cannot help suspecting, however, that such a comparison brings us somewhere nearer the truth than does Quintilian's.

3

Ian M. Le M. Du Quesnay

FROM POLYPHEMUS TO CORYDON
Virgil, *Eclogue* 2 and the *Idylls* of Theocritus

THE POEM AND ITS PATRON: 'POLLIO AMAT NOSTRAM
QVAMVIS EST RVSTICA MVSAM'

The second *Eclogue* is an example of *imitatio* in Latin poetry at its
most skilful and its most successful.[1] But before turning to consider
the text in detail, it will be helpful to recall the cultural context in
which it was composed and designed to be read. The *Eclogues* were
written in the turbulent years which followed the assassination of
Julius Caesar (42–39 B.C.).[2] They were commissioned by Virgil's
patron, C. Asinius Pollio, a former friend and supporter of the dictator
and currently the friend and supporter of M. Antonius and the tri-
umvirs.[3] At this time he was reaching the summit of his meteoric career:
a consul designate and in command of the key province of Gallia
Cisalpina in 41; consul in 40; proconsul and destined to become a
uir triumphalis in 39. It is perhaps not immediately obvious why such a
man should be interested in promoting poems written in imitation of
the Hellenistic poet Theocritus. Personal taste doubtless played its
part. Pollio was himself a literary man whose tragedies had won some
fame. He was a friend of the leading 'Neoteric' C. Helvius Cinna and
the patron of the inventor of Latin love elegy, the *cantor Euphorionis*,
C. Cornelius Gallus. In his youth he had known Catullus who had
paid him a gracious compliment (12.8f.): *est enim leporum | differtus
puer ac facetiarum.* It is noteworthy that the poems he commissioned
were later complimented by Horace in very similar terms (*Satires*
1.10.44f.): *molle atque facetum | Vergilio adnuerunt gaudentes rure
Camenae.*[4]

It is, however, striking that the dominant characteristic of the literature of the last half of the first century B.C. is a systematic and self-
conscious attempt to create a literature worthy to stand beside that
of Greece. Gallus and Euphorion have been mentioned, but the work
of both poets has been lost and affords no insights. But the movement
does seem to have started during the dictatorship of Caesar. As

Cicero looked back on his career as an orator he felt that he had created a body of Roman oratory that was worthy of comparison with anything written by the Greeks. He then decided to set about the creation of a body of philosophical writing in Latin to match the writings of the Greek philosophers. The prefaces, especially that of the *De finibus*, set out his thinking clearly and explicitly. The Romans were now the rulers of the world and proud of their military and political success. But they felt inferior to the Greeks in the matter of culture: *doctrina Graecia nos et omni litterarum genere superabat, in quo erat facile uincere non repugnantes* (*Tusculan disputations* 1.3). They now felt that Latin was not inferior to Greek as a language; the Romans were not inferior to the Greeks in character or intelligence. It was time to fight back: *hortor omnes, qui facere id possunt, ut huius quoque generis laudem iam languenti Graeciae eripiant et transferant in hanc urbem, sicut reliquias omnes, quae quidem erant expetendae, studio atque industria sua maiores nostri transtulerunt* (*Tusculan disputations* 2.5). Cicero is of course talking primarily of philosophy. But the attitudes which he expresses correspond exactly to those which may be inferred from the practice of other writers. Virgil was among the first to take up his challenge.

These developments in attitudes to literature were of a piece with other trends.[5] The Roman aristocracy was quite consciously trying, as the Ptolemies had done for Alexandria before,[6] to make Rome the cultural centre of the world and a city worthy of her position as the *caput rerum*. This period saw the building of new public amenities: temples, roads, aqueducts, theatres, libraries.[7] Works of art were acquired to beautify the city. All this was financed by the aristocrats, usually from the spoils of war. These men also patronized the poets and the creation of a new Latin literature and it is surely no accident that the dates of publication so often coincide with the return of the patron from some lucrative campaign.[8] Against this wider background, the very fact that the *Eclogues* are imitations of Theocritus takes on a new significance and importance. Hellenistic literature was fashionable and very much admired by the cultured Romans of the forties and fifties. Theocritus was a major Hellenistic poet. To create in Latin an equivalent for his poetry was consequently to do something worthwhile. Imitation, then, is not a secondary or purely technical aspect of the poems: it is of central importance. It was probably as imitations of Theocritus that they were commissioned and merited patronage: it was as such that they demanded respect and recognition as a Roman achievement and, even, as a service to the state.[9]

A THEOCRITEAN POEM: 'SYRACOSIO . . .
LVDERE VERSV'

intentio poetae haec est, ut imitetur Theocritum Syracusanum (Servius).
In accepting this no doubt traditional Roman view of Virgil's purpose
in writing the *Eclogues* one point should be made clear at the outset.
To call these poems imitations is not to deny Virgil originality: to a
Roman, to be the first to match one of the great achievements of the
Greek writers was a claim to originality.[10] All our post-Romantic
notions and ways of thinking about the relationship between a Roman
writer and his model must be discarded. If in what follows the traditional vocabulary of echoing, borrowing, taking over, following,
adapting is used it should be considered as descriptive and functional,
but stripped of all pejorative and prejudicial overtones. My intention is
not to imply that Virgil was trapped and crushed by the inert weight of
an ineluctable literary tradition; nor that he was some mindless,
brutish oaf who could do no more than copy out random bits
that sprang from some greater mind than his and patch them together
round some equally unoriginal theme. Perhaps the most useful analogy
is with language. Any speaker of a language moves naturally from one
register to another. When he speaks to his child, a respected uncle, his
wife, his friend after sport, to a group of students, to an academic
conference, to a political meeting his language changes noticeably.
He uses different vocabulary, style, syntax and pronunciation. Certain
contexts even make certain subjects taboo; many severely limit the
appropriate way of speaking about many topics. Literature is a most
self-conscious and highly artificial use of language: not surprisingly it
is highly conventional. Literature is what literature is agreed to be at
any time in any culture and if we wish to read any literature but our
own we must learn the appropriate conventions as we try to learn the
idioms and social registers of a new language.[11] In short this essay is
not an attempt to emphasize or to maximize the indebtedness of one
poet to another. It is rather an attempt to show how thoroughly Virgil
has absorbed the techniques and detail of his avowed model to the
point where he can generate a wholly new poem 'in the language of
bucolic'.[12] It is not pastiche but creative writing within a tradition:
he preserves what he feels to be best and most distinctive and whatever
serves his purpose. He can extend and expand the tradition by making
new selections and combinations of material, by intelligent variation
and adaptation of the detail which the tradition provides, by the
introduction of new material analogous to the old. The techniques and
style of the model are as important as the details of content and

37

vocabulary; so too are less definable aspects such as the spirit and logical implications of the work. But it should not be forgotten that the imitator always strove to outdo his model and felt that he should be able to build upon and improve on the work of his predecessors.[13]

The early history of the text of Theocritus and the other *bucolici graeci* is clouded in obscurity.[14] Artemidorus of Tarsus collected the βουκολικαὶ Μοῖσαι into a single fold in the first century B.C.; his son Theon was responsible for an edition with commentary on Theocritus.[15] But the *Idylls* must have had fame and currency in the intervening two centuries. If they had not, there would not have been such a spate of imitators. The relationship of the collection or collections known to Virgil to those thirty *Idylls* still extant under his name is a matter for scholarly speculation.[16] It is reasonable to suppose that Virgil knew Theocritean poems which have not survived.[17] It is as certain as can be that he knew the work of the imitators of Theocritus far better than we can from the pitiful scraps which survive.[18] Certain points are reasonably clear. It may be inferred from the epigram of Artemidorus and from the anonymous *Lament for Bion* that in Virgil's day the fame of Theocritus rested primarily on his bucolic *Idylls*.[19] It may be inferred from Virgil's practice that his main concern was to match the achievement of Theocritus precisely in this area.[20] It is, however, far from clear ezactly which *Idylls* he found under the title of *Bucolica* and which therefore defined his notion of the genre. The evidence suggests that all the *Idylls* numbered 1–18 in modern editions were included, all of which Virgil knew.[21] The majority of his verbal imitations are, however, drawn from *Idylls* 1, 3, 4, 5, 7 together with the frame of 6 and two poems which modern critics tend to view as spurious, 8 and 9.[22] If this is correct, then Virgil would seem to have tried to 'improve' upon his model by purifying the genre and excluding material that had nothing to do with herdsmen. In a sense, he redefined the genre.[23] Such a view finds confirmation in the adaptation of *Idyll* 2, an urban poem, to the countryside in *Eclogue* 8. The transformation of *Idyll* 11 into *Eclogue* 2 achieves something similar by replacing the mythical Cyclops Polyphemus and his beloved, the sea nymph Galatea, with *pastor* Corydon and his beloved Alexis. The result is a poem more bucolic than its Theocritean model!

Once Virgil had decided upon which *Idylls* best suited his view of bucolic poetry he no doubt set about the task of learning to compose bucolic song (βουκολιάζεσθαι). Imitation was a regular aspect of any Roman's rhetorical education and it may be assumed that he used the standard techniques:[24] memorizing the poems; translation; paraphrase;

free compositions on set themes (such as the *locus amoenus*); and special stylistic effects (such as rustic dialogue) in which the aim was to match if not surpass the 'virtues' of the model;[25] intense analysis of the model poems, as like as not in discussion with Parthenius.[26] Imitation was not of course confined to the schoolroom. The preface to Cicero's *De finibus* (published perhaps two or three years before *Eclogue* 2, in 45 B.C.) reveals what a contemporary might have expected from a mature literary production which was also an imitation. It should be sufficiently faithful to the original to act as a substitute;[27] independent of the model in basic conception and in the ordering of material;[28] equal to the model in style[29] and interlarded with direct translation wherever possible and appropriate.[30] The second *Eclogue* fulfils such expectations perfectly.

On taking up this poem, the reader who is familiar with the *Idylls* finds himself in a thoroughly familiar world. The scene is set in Sicily (21),[31] not far from the sea (25).[32] As Corydon walks through the mountains and the woods (5),[33] he can see and smell the everyday life of the farm going on (11 *olentis herbas*; 66 *aspice*). It is midday in late summer.[34] Pan (31ff.) and the Nymphs, even Nais herself (46), are familiar deities.[35] All the characters in this rustic world bear Theocritean names with the significant and striking exceptions of the city-folk, Alexis and his master Iollas.[36] The fauna is mainly Theocritean: not just the cattle, sheep and goats, or the cicadas, lizards and stags but also the lioness, the wolf and the wild boar to which the rustic alludes freely.[37] Significantly again, the only animals which become a real focus of attention are the *capreoli*, and their introduction is a Virgilian innovation. They are an appropriate addition to fauna which already includes both goats and deer and are easy enough for the Roman reader to accept since they were a familiar sight in Roman country parks.[38] But part of their charm and attractiveness as a gift lies in their novelty. Similar innovation without violation of the *lex generis* is apparent with the flora. The majority are found in the *Idylls*.[39] But the variations are interesting. The *narcissus* finds a traditional but non-Theocritean role in the catalogue of flowers (48);[40] so too the *laurus* (54), which is joined by its traditional partner, the *myrtus*;[41] *casia* and *caltha* (49f.) are more exotic but perhaps equally traditional additions.[42] Theocritus mentions the diet of his rustics[43] but does not refer to the peasants' astonishing capacity for the garlic-based *moretum* (10f.).[44] He also refers to *cytisus* (cf. 64) as a favourite food of goats and adds the obscure αἴγιλος with an eye to wordplay and etymology;[45] Virgil adds *hibiscum*: *haedorum* and *hibiscum* frame the line (30) perhaps hinting at an etymological explanation of *hibiscum* as derived from *haedus* and *esca*.[46] Etymology certainly plays its part in the case of two other additions. The oak tree is a familiar feature of the Theocritean landscape under its generic name δρῦς and twice the tree is specified as φαγός.[47] Virgil, probably for reasons of etymology rather than botany, introduced the *fagus*, apparently with its Greek meaning of oak tree rather than its Latin meaning of beech tree.[48] Similarly, *uaccinium* (18) is used to translate ὑάκινθος and retains its Greek sense (as the epithet *nigra* shows).[49] Finally, the fruits offered to Alexis as love gifts: the *mala* (quinces) perform the same function in Theocritus but here they are described in terms which suggest their special suitability as gifts for a beloved boy like Alexis with down upon his cheeks (*malae*).[50] The adjective *cerea* implies that *pruna* are chosen because of their similarity to the skin of such a beloved.[51] The *castaneae nuces* (52) must therefore have been chosen because of their similarity to the male genitals as a suitably erotic rustic gift.[52]

The focus of interest in the second *Eclogue* is, however, Corydon rather than the countryside. He is in most respects a typical Theocritean herdsman in the sense that all the individual features of his character find a precedent in the *Idylls*. The most striking features of Corydon are that he is a herdsman and a lover who attaches as much importance to his musical abilities as to his flocks. The blend of characteristics is typical of, but peculiar to, the bucolic tradition. In general the ancient attitude to the rustic was highly ambiguous. From one point of view, the rustic was a vulgar buffoon, coarse both in intellect and in emotion. He was capable of lust and crude ditties but not of the sentimental love and exquisite poetry characteristic of lyric, elegy, epigram and the poetry of the *Neoteroi*, genres in which love is especially associated with the sophisticated, urban aristocrat.[53] This rustic buffoon would have been familiar to Virgil's contemporaries as the butt of much humour in comedy and, especially, in the *fabula togata* and the *fabula Atellana*. From the other point of view, the life of the city was seen as degenerate and corrupt and personal poetry and the life-style which it portrayed were seen as symptomatic of its decadence. On this view the rustic was a noble figure, the repository of pristine virtues: *et uirum bonum quom laudabant, ita laudabant, bonum agricolam bonumque colonum. amplissime laudari existimabatur qui ita laudabatur* (Cato, *De agricultura, praefatio* 2). This noble peasant would be familiar to Virgil's contemporaries from the rhetorical and oratorical tradition.[54] But love, especially homosexual or pederastic love, and learned poetry were as alien to him as to the rustic buffoon.

It is important, therefore, not to allow the modern familiarity with the herdsman of bucolic poetry to dull our sensitivity to the humorous effect of this delightful blend of incongruities. Corydon and his rustic world appeal to the urbane and urban reader because of their naturalness and their simplicity.[55] Yet the pretensions to urbane learning and sentimentality will strike him as comic. And he is not allowed to forget his disdain for the rustic world: the smell of garlic and of goats, the *sordida rura* and *humiles casae* (28f.).

A third source of humour lies in the constantly implied contrast between these latter-day rustics and the noble herdsmen of myth who were also singers and lovers: Paris, Daphnis, Amphion, Adonis and Apollo Nomios. The technique of substituting ordinary people, even low-class people, in the roles traditionally played by the figures of myth is standard in mime and in elegy.[56] Its effect is always humorous. They act out their roles in the shadow of their mythical counterparts. So Corydon's comparison of himself with Amphion (24) and Daphnis (26) evokes a smile: the discrepancy is more apparent than the similarity. A gentle humour which pervades the whole poem derives from the reader's constant awareness that Corydon is acting out the role of Theocritus' Polyphemus. But the humorous side of the poem should not be overemphasized. It is characteristic of Hellenistic poetry in general and of the *Idylls* in particular to treat characters from myth and from the lowest social classes as members of the same social class as that to which the poet and his readers belong and to exploit the resulting incongruities for humorous effect. But equally characteristic are the insatiable interest in the psychology and emotional life of the individual and a serious concern for the common humanity of man. As a study of a rejected lover the second *Eclogue* is as serious and searching as any Roman elegy. Humour and seriousness are not mutually exclusive.

In detail as much as in the basic conception of his character Corydon is a typical Theocritean herdsman. He is in love and neglects his work.[57] His love is homosexual[58] and his beloved comes from outside the rustic world.[59] He is appreciative of the music of the cicadas (*raucis*, 12).[60] He is self-conscious about the contrast between the sunburned rustic (*niger*, 16) and the fair-skinned townsman (*candidus*, 16) but he warns Alexis that, as a rustic himself, he has no preference (17f.).[61] This motif is combined with another, the hint that the beauty of the beloved is short-lived.[62] He talks of his beloved in metaphorical language drawn from nature (18, 63ff.).[63] He counts his wealth in pastoral produce.[64] He envisages himself and Alexis hunting together,[65] herding goats, and playing the pan-pipes (*fistula*) in imitation of Pan.[66] He sets great value on his pan-pipes which he describes in loving detail and which he has received as a gift from the dying Damoetas.[67] As tokens of his love he offers as gifts the *fistula*, animals, flowers and fruit.[68] His standard way of enhancing the value of what he offers is to refer to some other person who desires it: Amyntas (39); Thestylis (43); Amaryllis (52).[69] A more interesting adaptation of a Theocritean motif, or rather conflation of a number of motifs, occurs at *Eclogue* 2.45ff. Corydon here invokes Alexis like a deity: *huc ades . . . tibi . . . tibi . . .* (45f.).[70] His status is further enhanced when it is revealed that the Nymphs, themselves minor deities, will attend him and that *candida Nais* will gather for the *candidus Alexis* (16) the flowers which will miraculously bloom at his coming as at the coming of a god.[71] His presence in the country will be an *honos* (53).[72] The most important Theocritean precedent is at *Idyll* 8.41ff., to which the name Nais may be intended to allude.[73] There Menalcas and Daphnis praise their beloveds by saying that the countryside flourishes when they are present but withers in their absence, implicitly attributing to them the power of a deity. In *Eclogue* 2 this idea is combined with the motif of the lover's gifts of flowers and fruit.[74] He thus transforms his model, lending to the borrowed motifs a new complexity and significance.

The rustic setting and the main character are thus clearly contrived in such a way that the reader will be constantly reminded of the *Idylls*. But it should be emphasized that neither has been simply lifted from Theocritus. Rather they have been generated anew out of the mass of detail which goes to make up a bucolic *Idyll*: this precise selection and combination of material is found nowhere in Theocritus. The poem is at once familiar and Theocritean and at the same time new and Virgilian. In style too the same procedures operate. The subject of the poem, a rustic in love with an urban slave-boy, could be appropriately treated in a mime or *fabula Atellana*.[75] Yet here Virgil follows Theocritean precedent and treats it in hexameters, the metre earmarked for the deeds of gods, heroes, kings and warriors. The result is to enhance the sense of incongruity and to infuse the whole poem with a gentle humour.[76] Virgil also constantly evokes that verbal repetition and careful balancing of phrases, lines and sentences which is the most distinctive feature of Theocritus' style.[77] Corydon's habits of speech are also familiar. He talks of his love in metaphors and analogies drawn from the natural world; he uses extravagant mythological *exempla*; he is given to using proverbs or, rather, phrases which have the ring of proverbs such as *nimium ne crede colori* (17); *si numquam fallit imago*

(27); *trahit sua quemque uoluptas* (63).[78] Finally, the whole poem is interlarded with translations of tags, half-lines and phrases culled from the *Idylls*.[79] These do not appear to be used as allusions in the sense that the reader is supposed to recall the original and its context. Rather their sole function seems to be to make the poem sound Theocritean.

VARIATION ON A THEME: 'TV DEINDE SEQVERE'

The second *Eclogue* has so far been considered simply as a poem written in imitation of Theocritus with the intention of showing that the form and the style of the poem, the character of Corydon and his rustic world are typically Theocritean in the sense that they are composites generated out of the material which Theocritus himself had established as proper to this type of poem. Often the loss of so much ancient poetry allows us to go no further.[80] But in the case of *Eclogue* 2 it is possible to sharpen the focus. In this poem, as has long been recognized, Virgil combines imitation of two Theocritean poems in particular, *Idylls* 3 and 11. The models are clearly signalled and the reader is expected to recall them. At *Eclogue* 2.6f. *o crudelis Alexi . . . mori me denique coges*, at the very opening of Corydon's song, there is a quite unmistakable 'quotation' of the opening words of the goatherd's song, *Idyll* 3.6–9 ὦ χαρίεσσ᾽ Ἀμαρυλλί, . . . ἀπάγξασθαί με ποησεῖς ('o graceful Amaryllis . . . you will make me hang myself'). This is reinforced at *Eclogue* 2.14f. by the reference to *tristes Amaryllidis iras atque superba . . . fastidia*.[81] Corydon's former beloved is characterized in terms deliberately reminiscent of her namesake in *Idyll* 3 and the reader is thus invited to see Corydon as the literary descendant or counterpart to the goatherd of that poem. The allusion to *Idyll* 11 is similarly established by the equally prominent 'quotation' of Polyphemus' final words at the very end of Corydon's song (see below). Again, this is reinforced by the explicit allusion to the setting of *Idyll* 11 (*Siculis . . . in montibus*, 21) inserted into an extended and striking 'quotation' from this poem (see below).[82] The *contaminatio* of the two models is clearly exemplified in the combined imitation of *Idylls* 3.34–6 and 11.40–1 at *Eclogue* 2.41–4 (see below). By the time the reader has reached the end of the poem he will realize that *Idyll* 11 is in fact the primary model and *Idyll* 3 is secondary: the initial identification of the model has proved to be partially misleading. First and foremost Corydon is to be seen as an ordinary rustic counterpart to the Cyclops. In retrospect the reader will note the similarities between the narrative introductions of *Eclogue* 2 and *Idyll* 11 (see below). He will also recognize an allusion to the opening words of Polyphemus' song at *Eclogue* 2.6f. The most striking feature of Polyphemus' initial address is the etymological word play in (19f.) ὦ λευκὰ Γαλάτεια . . . λευκοτέρα πακτᾶς ('o white Galatea . . . whiter than cream cheese'), which is intended to point to the connection of the name Galatea and γάλα (milk).[83] Virgil uses the etymological principle according to which a thing is named from its opposite (*lucus a non lucendo*)[84] to suggest a derivation of the name Alexis from ἀλέξειν (to protect, defend) or from ἀλέγειν (to care). The effect is to produce a sort of oxymoron: 'o cruel saviour . . . will you compel me to die?' 'o caring one . . . do you not care for my songs?' In Virgil the etymology is not used as part of a pretty compliment but plays a full part in the argument: Alexis is implicitly being urged to live up to his name and not to belie his character.[85]

It is of course a standard technique of *imitatio* to combine two models (*contaminatio*).[86] Since the resulting poem can not be a carbon copy of either, it is an obvious way of achieving originality. Nor is it difficult to see why Virgil has chosen these two poems to combine. They are clearly linked by numerous verbal and thematic parallels.[87] And it may well be that Virgil had before him the precedent of *Idyll* 20 which also combines imitation of *Idylls* 3 and 11.[88] It is, however, difficult to define the nature of the relationship between the three poems and to explain the principles on which other allusions are introduced. This whole problem is greatly eased if the various elements of the poem are separated out: the speaker, the addressee and the relationship between them; the setting and its function; and the traditional category or type of literature to which the poem belongs, its genre.[89]

In *Idyll* 3 the speaker is a goatherd, an ordinary human rustic. The addressee is Amaryllis, apparently a rustic wench who lives in a cave. The relationship is erotic and heterosexual, of a type most familiar to readers of ancient erotic poetry: the rejected suitor is eager to win over the girl, whom he tends to place on a pedestal and treat as his superior. She is called νύμφα (9). The word denotes a (prospective) bride. This is a valuable clue to the goatherd's intention, reinforced by the reference to marriage in the first of the mythological exempla (γᾶμαι, 40). But the word also means Nymph in the modern sense and this together with the fact that she lives in a cave covered with ivy and fern (14) and is implicitly compared with both Aphrodite (46) and Demeter (49) suggests that he sees her as his goddess, his *diuina puella*.[90] The setting is the countryside and it serves to emphasize the incongruity which derives from these rustics aping the ways of sophisticated urban lovers.[91]

The genre to which the poem belongs is revealed in the very first word: κωμάσδω ('I go on a komos'). It is the genre komos, one of the commonest of the erotic genres (also called the paraclausithyron or song of the locked-out lover).[92] In this genre the lover attempts through a conventional series of pleas, promises, boasts and threats to win over his beloved for a kiss, a night of passion or even a more permanent union in marriage.[93] The poem opens with the goatherd abandoning his work to go on his komos.[94] He is next found outside the cave of his beloved Amaryllis. He establishes himself as the rejected lover, refers to his rustic appearance[95] and threatens to hang himself.[96] He offers gifts of apples,[97] refers to his wretchedness and wishes he were a bee so that he could get into his beloved's cave.[98] He describes his wretchedness again and complains of the cruelty of Love.[99] He contrasts the beauty of Amaryllis with her cruelty and asks her to embrace him. He threatens to tear up the garland he wears for her.[100] She still pays no attention and he again describes his wretchedness, threatening to commit suicide and telling how he has learned that she did not love him.[101] He offers another gift, this time a goat, and threatens to give it to another. He thinks that she is at last responding,[102] steps under a tree and sings, confident that she will not resist that![103] His song comprises a catalogue of recondite mythological *exempla* relevant to his situation. He complains of a headache, stops singing, and lies down to sleep or die on the threshold.[104] In this poem Theocritus has simply transferred the urban komos to the country and worked out what would happen if a goatherd went a-courting. The beloved's house is made into a cave. The incident takes place in the daytime and not at night. The gifts and manners of the suitor are adapted to suit the rustic character of the lover. Little attempt is made further to adapt the komos to its rustic setting: that would blur the desired incongruous effect.

Idyll 11 begins with a complimentary dedication to Theocritus' friend Nicias, a doctor and fellow poet. First, the moral of the poem is set out quite explicitly: the only cure for love is song. This vital clue to the meaning of the poem is picked up in the last lines (80–1). Next (7–18), Theocritus provides a narrative introduction to the story of Polyphemus and Galatea. At line 19, the song of Polyphemus begins. The speaker is a superhuman creature of myth, the man-eating monster of *Odyssey* 9. He is also a sentimental lover and a rustic. The incongruity is apparent, although its sources are different from those in *Idyll* 3. The addressee is his beloved Galatea, a beautiful sea-nymph and a denizen of a different world. Typically, little is made of her divinity: it is rather her human characteristics which are played up. The relationship between the two is exactly the same as in *Idyll* 3. The setting is again the countryside and more specifically, the sea-shore. The former serves to reinforce Polyphemus' rusticity; the latter acts as a witty substitute for the threshold of the beloved's house in the conventional urban komos. For the song of the Cyclops belongs to the same genre as *Idyll* 3: it too is a komos.[105] Or at least that is how it begins.

Polyphemus is a passionate but rejected lover who neglects his work for love (11) and goes on a diurnal komos (15) to the 'threshold' of his beloved. His komos begins with a series of rustic comparisons, a parody of the traditional lover's compliments.[106] He establishes himself as a cruelly neglected lover who is naively incapable of distinguishing the dream visions of the absent beloved from reality. He tells of his first meeting with Galatea and the origins of his passion. He refers to his grotesque appearance which he offsets with a catalogue of his pastoral wealth, boasts of his musical abilities and offers gifts (fawns and bear cubs). As the nocturnal, urban komast wanders the streets also in the daytime, restless with yearning of unrequited love, so the diurnal komast, Polyphemus, sings of Galatea at the dead of night (40).[107] Unable to enter her 'house', he asks her to come to him, a standard alternative (42ff.),[108] and catalogues the delights of life on the land and the beauties of the countryside in order to persuade her. He is willing to have his eye burned out to demonstrate his love (remember *Odyssey* 9) and complains that he was not born with gills so that he could take her a garland of flowers and receive a kiss. At least he will learn to swim if a stranger comes (Odysseus). Again he summons Galatea to come to him and he now envisages her as his future wife, sharing his life as a shepherd (63–5).[109] At first, the komast Polyphemus reacts to the total lack of response by abandoning his komos.[110] It was conventional for the lover to accuse his beloved of ἀδικία (injustice) when the love he offered was rejected.[111] It was equally conventional to threaten her with the consequences of her (his) unjust actions and to prophesy future suffering.[112] Pointedly this motif is here transferred to the Cyclops' mother (67): ἁ μάτηρ ἀδικεῖ με μόνα ('My mother alone does me wrong'). It is she, not (as in *Idyll* 3) the beloved, who will suffer when she sees how thin he has become and finds that he not only has a headache but that both his feet ache!

Then, at line 72, Polyphemus reacts even more strongly and renounces his love for Galatea: song has cured his passion.[113] Renunciation of love or of the beloved, the *renuntiatio amoris*, is another of the common erotic genres.[114] That the end of *Idyll* 11 should be seen as belonging to this genre and not to the komos is suggested by the verbal and thematic similarities to *Idyll* 30, a known example of the genre.[115] That it was so considered in antiquity is confirmed by the fact that another *renuntiatio*, the epigram of Macedonius the consul (*Anthologia Palatina* 5.245), pointedly alludes to these lines.[116] In short, when Polyphemus reacts to Galatea's unresponsiveness his intentions are completely reversed: his song modulates from komos and genuine attempts to win her into *renuntiatio amoris* and a genuine and successful attempt to give her up. The reaction is marked by a double self-address; he then accuses himself of folly and urges himself to be sensible and get back to his work. He bolsters his decision by citing proverbial wisdom at himself. He closes with an assurance to himself that he will find another girl as beautiful if not more beautiful among the girls who keep asking him to spend the night with them! In the end he has regained his self-respect.[117] The poem closes with two lines which pick up the moral of the introduction allowing the reader no room to doubt that the Cyclops has been successfully cured.[118]

Like *Idyll* 11, *Eclogue* 2 begins with the poet, *in propria persona*, providing a narrative introduction to his story. But here there is no explicit dedication and no statement of the moral. The first line provides the names and brief description of the two main characters. The name Corydon belongs exclusively to Theocritean herdsmen:[119] the implication is reinforced by *pastor*. The name Alexis is non-Theocritean but has equally traditional associations derived from erotic epigram: it is the name of a *puer delicatus*.[120] Again the implication is brought out by *formosum* and *delicias domini* (1f.).[121] The reader will naturally assume that Alexis is, like the conventional *puer delicatus*, a city-dweller (*urbanus*). This initial assumption is proved correct by *candidus* (17);[122] by the fact that he considers the *rura sordida* and the *casae humiles* (28f.); and, finally, by the fact that he is urged to leave the city to Pallas (60–2). The contrast between the lover and beloved is striking but conventional:[123] such an unsuitable pair could not be happy together. The incongruity of the rustic's passion is only highlighted by the word *ardebat* (1) which is a cliché for the aristocratic and urbane passions of elegy and lyric.[124] Corydon's feelings are further described in (2): *nec quid speraret habebat* ('and he knew he was not to hope for anything').[125] He was as certain as the reader that he would be rejected so he did not go to Alexis' house: he only (*tantum*, 3) went, time and again, to the woods and he went alone (*solus*, 4). Corydon had a purpose for doing what he did (*studio*, 5) but what it was that he was trying so hard to achieve the reader has to work out for himself.[126] He obviously is not trying to win over Alexis, as has been supposed. That would make no sense given that he deliberately went to a place where Alexis could not possibly hear him. In fact, Corydon has reacted to his wretched situation in a perfectly typical way by going in search of solitude in the countryside: he is behaving just like the Acontius of Callimachus' *Aetia*, like Gallus in *Eclogue* 10 or Propertius in 1.18 in similar circumstances.[127] He is doing precisely what Ovid advised the unhappy lover to do. His purpose may therefore be assumed to be the conventional one: he is seeking a cure for his love.[128] But Virgil leaves no doubt that his endeavours were in vain: *inani* (5) is emphatically the last word of the introduction. Ovid could have told him why (*Remedia* 579ff.): *quisquis amas, loca sola nocent, loca sola caueto.*

The majority of the parallels for Corydon as he is portrayed in these first lines are figures of mythology. The story-telling technique employed to introduce him emphasizes this. It was a standard procedure for the narrator of erotic tales to state simply the names together with a brief description and brief characterization of their relationship. The formula was commonplace in the rhetorical exercise of *narratio*[129] and well known from such prose paraphrases as the *Erotica pathemata* of Parthenius.[130] So Aristaenetus begins *Epistle* 1.10: Ἀκόντιος τὴν Κυδίππην καλὸς νεανίας καλὴν ἔγημε κόρην ('Acontius, a beautiful youth, married Cydippe, a beautiful maid'). This may be contrasted with the more sophisticated technique of his model, Callimachus (*Aetia* fr. 67.1–4 Pfeiffer):

Αὐτὸς Ἔρως ἐδίδαξεν Ἀκόντιον, ὁππότε καλῇ
  ἤθετο Κυδίππῃ παῖς ἐπὶ παρθενικῇ,
τέχνην – οὐ γὰρ ὅγ' ἔσκε πολύκροτος – ὄφρα λεγο..[
  τοῦτο διὰ ʒωῆς οὔνομα κουρίδιον.

Love himself taught Acontius, *when as* a boy he burned for the beautiful maiden Cydippe, *the art (for he was not cunning) so that he might win for all his life the name of lawfully wedded husband.*[131]

A third example of this same formula provides an even more exact parallel to *Eclogue* 2.1–5, except that the story is mythological. It comes from the Hellenistic poet Phanocles (fr. 1.1–6 Powell Ἔρωτες ἢ Καλοί – *Loves or Pretty boys*):

Ἢ ὡς Οἰάγροιο πάϊς Θρηΐκιος Ὀρφεὺς
  ἐκ θυμοῦ Κάλαϊν στέρξε Βορηϊάδην.

48

πολλάκι δέ σκιεροῖσιν ἐν ἄλσεσιν ἔζετ' ἀείδων
ὂν πόθον, οὐδ' ἦν οἱ θυμὸς ἐν ἡσυχίῃ,
ἀλλ' αἰεί μιν ἄγρυπνοι ὑπὸ ψυχῇ μελεδῶναι
ἔτρυχον, θαλερὸν δερκομένου Κάλαϊν.

Or as the son of Oiagros, Thracian Orpheus, loved Calaïs, the daughter of Boreas, with all his heart, and would often sit in shady groves singing of his yearning desire and his spirit was not at rest, but always sleepless cares gnawed away at his heart when he saw the youthful Calaïs.[132]

Virgil apparently expects his audience to relate his narrative introduction to this conventional formula[133] and to realize that he has substituted for the mythical characters the two ordinary human beings, Corydon and Alexis. The omission of the standard reference to the parents,[134] underlined by the substitute description of Alexis as *delicias domini* (2), emphasizes the low social status of these *terrae filii*. This type of substitution was familiar from mime[135] and so appropriate for a poem written in imitation of the hexameter mimes of Theocritus. This may have been a standard technique of the imitators of Theocritus. The anonymous *Idyll* 23 is sufficiently similar to Ovid, *Metamorphoses* 14.698–764 (the komos of Iphis to Anaxarete) to suggest that it is a transformation of a mythological tale from a common source into a low life, urban, homosexual komos.[136] The opening of that poem too is yet another version of the same formula.[137]

Idyll 11.7–18 is of course a further variation on the formula:

οὕτω γοῦν ῥάιστα διᾶγ' ὁ Κύκλωψ ὁ παρ' ἀμῖν,
ὡρχαῖος Πολύφαμος, ὅκ' ἤρατο τᾶς Γαλατείας,
ἄρτι γενειάσδων περὶ τὸ στόμα τὼς κροτάφως τε.
ἤρατο δ' οὐ μάλοις οὐδὲ ῥόδῳ οὐδὲ κικίννοις,   10
ἀλλ' ὀρθαῖς μανίαις, ἁγεῖτο δὲ πάντα πάρεργα.
πολλάκι ταὶ ὄιες ποτὶ τωὔλιον αὐταὶ ἀπῆνθον
χλωρᾶς ἐκ βοτάνας· ὁ δὲ τὰν Γαλάτειαν ἀείδων
αὐτὸς ἐπ' ἀιόνος κατετάκετο φυκιοέσσας
ἐξ ἀοῦς, ἔχθιστον ἔχων ὑποκάρδιον ἕλκος,   15
Κύπριδος ἐκ μεγάλας τό οἱ ἥπατι πᾶξε βέλεμνον.
ἀλλὰ τὸ φάρμακον εὗρε, καθεζόμενος δ' ἐπὶ πέτρας
ὑψηλᾶς ἐς πόντον ὁρῶν ἄειδε τοιαῦτα.

The Cyclops, for example, my fellow countryman, did very well on it, that legendary Polyphemus, when he was in love with Galatea, just as he was starting to have a beard around his mouth and

49

temples. He did not love with apples nor with roses nor with ringlets but with utter madness, and he regarded all else as secondary. Often the ewes came back to their fold on their own from the green pasture; while he sang of Galatea on his own and wasted away from dawn on the seaweed-covered shore with a most cruel wound beneath his heart, which a dart from the mighty Cyprian had implanted in his liver. But he found the cure, and (this he did while,) sitting on a high rock looking out to sea, he was singing this song . . .[138]

Here is the now familiar *A* loved *B* (8); further characterization of the lover (since such a role is unusual for a Cyclops) (9); and description of the nature of his passion (10–16) and of how Polyphemus reacted to his situation by going on a komos to his beloved. The reader is also told the result of his actions: he did not win Galatea but he did cure himself of his passion.

The passages of Callimachus, Phanocles, *Idyll* 23 as well as *Idyll* 11 have been claimed to be Virgil's direct model for the opening lines of the second *Eclogue*. But the words *pastor Corydon* allude unmistakably to Theocritus and the status of *Idyll* 11 as a model for this poem is clear enough. Virgil's technique of imitation here seems to be that he recognized the generic affinities of *Idyll* 11.7ff. to the conventional formula and so composed a variation on that formula to suit his own requirements. Apart from the generic similarities there are a number of verbal echoes. In Theocritus (12): 'Often the sheep came back from the green pastures'; in Virgil this action has been transferred to the shepherd: *adsidue ueniebat* (4) and the direction of the movement has been reversed: *inter densas . . . fagos*. The transfer was made easier by the fact that the sheep and the shepherd Polyphemus are linked by the use of the same adjective: αὐταί (on their own = of their own accord) and αὐτός (on his own = alone). It is translated by Virgil in the second sense as *solus* and placed in an emphatic position at the end of the line as it has been placed in an emphatic position at the beginning of the line in *Idyll* 11 (14). A second repeated word in Theocritus acts as the focus for the combination of this description of the Cyclops 'and he sang of Galatea alone . . .' (13–14) with the account in the last line (18) 'he was singing these words' (ἀείδων αὐτός . . . ἄειδε τοιαῦτα), which produces: *haec . . . solus . . . iactabat*. None of these echoes is, however, striking enough to signal the model for the reader and the only reason for not thinking them to be merely subliminal is the unmistakable allusion to *Idyll* 11 in what follows.

It is important to recognize that verbal imitation is not necessarily the most important level of imitation: the deliberate contrivance of thematic parallels achieved through variation on a common generic pattern is a fundamental technique.[139]

Once the reader has recognized the relationship between the two poems he will naturally respond to the implicit invitation to compare the two introductions and will realize that Virgil has inverted the moral of *Idyll* 11. Like Polyphemus, Corydon was passionately in love; unlike him, he had no hope and, instead of going on a komos, he went alone to the woods to find a cure. Polyphemus did not succeed in his attempt to win Galatea but he did succeed in finding a cure; Corydon did not even make a genuine attempt to win Alexis and he also failed to find a cure. Virgil's reversal of his model throws some light on the word *incondita* (4).[140] In part the word denotes the rough and rustic nature of his song, and acts as a stage direction for what follows. But it also suggests impromptu and unpremeditated song: it is rough and and rustic precisely because it was unpremeditated. Theocritus' friend Nicias had replied to *Idyll* 11 with a poem quoted in the scholia and perhaps known to Virgil, in which he adapted some famous words of Euripides: οἱ γὰρ Ἔρωτες | ποιητὰς πολλοὺς ἐδίδαξαν τοὺς πρὶν ἀμούσους ('For the Loves taught many men to be poets who had previously had no muse'). At any rate, Virgil is apparently making the same point: song did not cure Corydon; but love made this rustic into a poet.[141] The point is reinforced by the reference to Pan (32f.) as the inventor of the syrinx: Love made him a singer too! In part Virgil is simply seeking originality *vis-à-vis* his model by a form of *oppositio in imitando*. But it should not be forgotten that the ancients took love as seriously as the moderns take 'relationships'. Not only Ovid in the *Remedia* but Cicero and Lucretius discussed possible cures for love and it is noteworthy that Philodemus, one of Virgil's philosophy teachers, had refuted the claim that music could cure love, a view which had been upheld by the Stoic Diogenes with appeals to the dithyramb of Philoxenus of Cythera: according to the ancient scholia Philoxenus' dithyramb (*Polyphemus or Galatea*) had been the model of *Idyll* 11.[142] The views of the poets were clearly taken seriously and there is no reason to suppose that Virgil was not making a basically serious contribution to this debate.

It should now be clear that Virgil's technique of imitation is not purely verbal but operates also on the deeper levels of theme, genre and meaning. With this in mind, the relationship of the song of Corydon to *Idylls* 3 and 11 may be more fully appreciated. The speaker is

Corydon who has already been shown to be a thoroughly typical Theocritean rustic. As such he is an exact equivalent for the goatherd of *Idyll* 3 and quite unlike the mythical monster, Polyphemus. It is a consequence of this choice of speaker that Virgil was precluded from imitating and exploiting those parts of *Idyll* 11 relevant solely to Theocritus' characterization of the mythical Cyclops. Imitation of that poem is confined to those parts relevant to Polyphemus as a lover and a rustic. Corydon is not, however, a mere carbon copy of the goatherd in *Idyll* 3: the precise selection, combination and ordering of the detailed material are different. But one important technique has been taken over from that poem. The reader can place Polyphemus and Galatea in a familiar world of myth: he can not be expected to know the world of the lowly rustics. So in *Idyll* 3 the casual references to Olpis the tunny fisherman, Agroeo the sieve diviner and Mermnon's serving girl hint at the existence of a busy populated world and provide a context and a necessary background to the main action. Although the names and the details of the scenes and occupations are different, Virgil uses the same technique and for the same reasons in the second *Eclogue*. The effect of this change in speaker is thoroughly to 'bucolicize' the main model (*Idyll* 11) and this may have been intended as a deliberate and pointed 'improvement'.

The addressees and the beloveds in both *Idylls* 3 and 11 are girls, Amaryllis and Galatea respectively. Here Virgil has introduced a major modification: Corydon's beloved is Alexis, a *puer delicatus*. The effect of this is to underline the incongruity and the foolishness of his passion: rustics may take wives but they do not have fashionable passions for such boys. The fact that he is *urbanus* adds further point: Virgil has to make Corydon present himself and his world in such a way as will appeal to the presumed tastes of his addressee. The goatherd had obviously made no special appeal to the rustic Amaryllis to share with him the delights of living on the land. Polyphemus had emphasized naturally the advantages of the land as against the sea – the solid security of a cave, trees and cold fresh water – and had invited her to share with him activities which should have appealed to a girl – shepherding, milking and cheese-making. Corydon presents himself and his rustic world in a way that is deliberately reminiscent of the rhetorical praises of the countryside and thus calculated to present an idyllic image to his urbane and urban beloved. He also substitutes activities designed to be attractive to a *puer*. In particular, the reference to hunting is brought in immediately after the apparently damaging admission (28f. *sordida rura* and *humiles casas*) which it is clearly intended to offset.[143] The choice of a different type of addressee introduces a new perspective and is a major modification of both model poems. However, it is probably to be seen as a simple variation in selection and combination from the traditional material. Theocritus, *Idyll* 7.96ff. is a homosexual komos with an urban setting; *Idyll* 23 is also an urban homosexual komos; the unhappy wooing of the city girl Eunica by a rustic is the subject of *Idyll* 20.[144] Especially interesting is a poem of Bion (Fragment 11 Gow) which is a komos addressed to a shepherd boy. If the speaker was a rustic, then this was a homosexual variation on *Idyll* 3. But the komast describes himself simply as a lover and, in marked contrast to both *Idylls* 3 and 11, the komos takes place at night: he may therefore have been an urban lover. If so, Virgil has inverted the situation of that poem in making Corydon a rustic lover and Alexis an urban beloved.

Since Corydon has gone in search of solitude and relief from his passion, the reader naturally expects that his song will belong to the genre *renuntiatio amoris*. By the end of the song that expectation will prove to have been fully justified since Corydon does renounce his love for Alexis albeit unsuccessfully (*studio inani*, 5). But that is not how it begins. Although alone in the mountains, Corydon addresses Alexis directly (6–55), as though he could hear the mixture of boasts, pleas and promises directed at him. The apparent illogicality is softened by the fact that it was a commonplace that lovers imagine their beloved to be present when he is not[145] and lovers frequently address their beloved directly even when he cannot be expected to hear.[146] Moreover, it was a topos of the *renuntiatio amoris* for the lover to describe his previous feelings for his beloved[147] and the opening lines of Corydon's song (6–55) serve this purpose even though they are clearly not part of the *renuntiatio* proper. The clue to the generic identity of this section is provided in the very first words, no doubt just because it is such a paradox. Lines 6f. allude unmistakably to *Idyll* 3, the most obvious example of a Theocritean komos, and thus establish that the genre to which *Eclogue* 2.6–55 belongs is the komos. The fact that Corydon is not at the door of his beloved is emphasized by the omission of any reference to his house such as that found in the model. This simply confirms that Corydon's komos is actually a pseudo-komos and subordinated to the *renuntiatio* (56–72), as the introduction would lead one to expect. But it makes little difference to the lover whether his beloved cannot or just will not hear him and Corydon's song exploits fully the topoi of the genre komos.

Lines 6f. are an allusion-cum-variation to *Idyll* 3.6–9.[148] But

Corydon makes no reference to the beauty of his beloved (but note *o formose puer*, 17, etc.); nor to his house; nor to his own appearance (but see 25ff.). However, he retains the form of the original, a series of questions which have much the same import as the goatherd's 'Do you hate me?' (7) and the hint at suicide. He substitutes for the omitted komastic topoi others equally commonplace: Alexis is cruel; he does not care for his songs; he has no pity.[149] The first two accusations occur in *Idyll* 3 (18, 24, 39, 52ff.) and the third in another Theocritean komos (*Idyll* 7.119). The next lines (8–13), though thoroughly Theocritean in technique and detail, have no exact counterpart in either *Idyll* 3 or 11. But it has been noted that Theocritus had established the day-time as the proper time for a rustic komos. The conventional nocturnal komast regularly contrasts his wakeful vigil with the sleep enjoyed by others,[150] describes himself as suffering from the wind, rain and cold,[151] refers to the moon and stars[152] and is accompanied by musical instruments, flute-girls or singing.[153] Virgil is here again imitating the technique rather than the content of his models and so demonstrates his mastery of the nature of Theocritean komos. Corydon contrasts his wakefulness with the tiredness of the reapers retiring for their siesta; he further emphasizes his sleeplessness (a standard symptom of love) by reference to the cicadas whose song conventionally induced sleep;[154] he describes himself as suffering in the noonday heat; he refers to the sun; and he is accompanied by the singing of the cicadas. The ostensible purpose of these lines is the same as that of the topoi in their more conventional form: to arouse the pity of the beloved.[155]

Having failed to arouse pity, the komast may turn to threats and prophesy that the beloved will soon lose his beauty, that he will be sorry when their roles are reversed and the lover has found happiness with a new beloved and that he will die alone and unloved.[156] Lines 14–18 are variations on these topoi. The command *nimium ne crede colori* (17) hints at the 'swift decline of beauty' in combination with the contrast of fair city complexion and a sunburned rustic one. The motif is adapted to its rustic speaker by the use of the rustic analogy borrowed from *Idyll* 10.27–9. The word *cadunt* (18) hints allusively that Alexis will die alone and unloved. Lines 14f. are a more radical and significant variation on the traditional themes. Corydon refers not to some future beloved who will return his love but to two past love affairs in which his love was unrequited. The significance of this will become apparent later. The whole of this first paragraph, which begins and ends with strong verbal echoes of Theocritus, is largely imitation of the technique rather than the content of the model and independently adapts the traditional komastic topoi to their rustic setting. By contrast the next paragraph is based very closely on *Idyll* 11 (see below). But the lover's boasts about his abilities as a singer and his beauty are conventionally used by the komast, together with offers of faithful devotion and reminders of his youthfulness, to offset his poverty:[157] by contrast, Corydon, like Polyphemus, boasts of his wealth. The point of the modification is humorous: a *pastor* must have *pecua* (*pecora*, *pecudes*) and so have wealth (*pecunia*)! The conventionally venal and greedy beloved would hardly be impressed.[158]

The next section (28ff.) again adapts traditional komastic material to its rustic setting without close verbal imitation of *Idylls* 3 and 11. It was noted above how Corydon has adapted the komast's conventional invitation to his beloved to share his life to the character of Alexis. This topos does not occur in any other homosexual komos, which is hardly surprising given the naturally ephemeral or, rather, changing character of such pederastic relationships. At line 31, Alexis is challenged to imitate Pan and this leads into praise of Pan both as the inventor of the syrinx and as a god who cares, unlike Alexis, for herdsmen and their sheep. It is implied that Alexis should follow his example not only as a singer and a piper but also in caring for Corydon and his world. The triple repetition of the god's name has a hymnic effect[159] and so in form as well as function these lines are a modification of the standard appeal of the komast to a divinity for help.[160] Like the komast in *Idyll* 7, Corydon makes his appeal to Pan, rather than Venus or Amor, as is appropriate to his rustic character. This brief catalogue of the delights of country life blends into a catalogue of gifts. To the urbane and urban reader these are charming and attractive[161] but clearly not valuable enough to entice the beloved into the *sordida rura*. It was again conventional for the komast to offer gifts of little real value such as poems, apples and garlands and this the goatherd and the Cyclops had done. The elaboration, the ordering and the selection are, however, Virgil's own. The three gifts which balance the three activities of hunting, herding and piping are lovingly described and efforts are made to enhance the value of each: Amyntas envied the pipes which were an inheritance from a master of the art; Thestylis desired the roebucks which Corydon had captured at some personal risk; goddesses will gather the flowers and Amaryllis had loved the fruits which Corydon will gather himself. Again the technique is borrowed from *Idyll* 3. Each gift is described at greater length than the last – *fistula* (36–9) in four lines; *capreoli* (40–4) in five; flowers (45–55) in eleven – and the last description is subdivided into three items with each successive description shorter than the last – flowers (45–50) in six lines; fruits (51–3) in three; garland (51f.) in two – and this reverses the movement and brings the entire komos section to an end. However, the combination of the gifts theme with the invocation of Alexis as a *diuinus puer* underlines the hopelessness of Corydon's desires and it also emphasizes his loss of respect for himself and his world.[162] Similarly in *Idyll* 11, the garland motif is combined with the humiliating offer to let Galatea put out the Cyclops' eye.

The conventional komast reacts to the failure of his suit by lying down to sleep on the threshold, by going away as dawn arrives, by taking his life or by breaking in: his love remains as strong as ever. Corydon, however, reacts by renouncing his love for Alexis: the parallel with *Idyll* 11 is striking and apparently unique. What leads him to react in this way is not at once clear. The dedication of the garland is a fitting last act for a komast;[163] the sun is setting and as the nocturnal komast often ends as dawn rises, the time is right for the diurnal, rustic komast to end his song.[164] But this does not explain the nature of his reaction. Nor does Corydon change his mind for the same reason as Polyphemus: he knew from the outset that Alexis could not hear his pleas and so he cannot be influenced solely by the failure of his suit. One possibility remains. Virgil has integrated the rustic setting much more fully into the argument of his poem than Theocritus had done: in the introduction it served one conventional function in providing the wretched lover with solitude in his search for relief; in the komos section it was presented as an idyllic retreat for the *urbanus* and an ideal setting for happy love. There was a third conventional function for the countryside in erotic poetry: its peaceful and pleasant scenes delighted the unhappy lover and actually cured him of his passion.[165] Apparently then, as Corydon had been describing the delights of his rustic world in his effort to win over Alexis, those scenes had worked their calming effect on him until he reached the point where he could turn to formal renunciation of his beloved and so fulfil his original purpose. In this way Virgil has contrived to match exactly the generic pattern of his model (introduction, komos, reaction, *renuntiatio amoris*) while giving each element a novel twist and a new place in a new argument.

Corydon's formal renunciation of his beloved (56–73) is linked with that of Polyphemus (*Idyll* 11.72–9) both by genre and by a series of detailed verbal echoes. Both the model and the imitation exploit the same commonplaces of the genre.[166] So, Corydon addresses himself by name at 56 and again at 69, where *a, Corydon, Corydon* is an exact equivalent for ὦ Κύκλωψ, Κύκλωψ.[167] He recognizes his love as madness (69): *quae te dementia cepit!*[168] The word *dementia* (69) with its implicit notion of wandering of the mind is also an exact rendering of πᾷ τὰς φρένας ἐκπεπότασαι ('where have your senses flown?'), reinforced by the purely aural echo of πᾷ τὰς in *quae te*.[169] He resolves to find another beloved[170] and *inuenies alium . . . Alexin* (73) corresponds exactly to εὑρησεῖς Γαλάτειαν . . . ἄλλαν (76) ('you will find another Galatea'), although the noun and the adjective have been reversed so that the last line ends like the first with the name Alexis. But even when Virgil uses the same topoi as his model he tends to vary the expression. So it was conventional for the lover to urge himself to resume a more sensible and normal life.[171] Polyphemus says (73f.) αἴ κ' ἐνθὼν ταλάρως τε πλέκοις καὶ θαλλὸν ἀμάσας | ταῖς ἄρνεσσι φέροις, τάχα κα πολὺ μᾶλλον ἔχοις νῶν ('If you would go and weave baskets and cut green boughs and take them to the lambs, perhaps you would be much more sensible'). He refers fleetingly to basket-weaving; this becomes Corydon's main task and is described in more detail (72): *uiminibus mollique paras detexere iunco*. If Servius is correct, Corydon's reference to his unpruned vines and elms (70) is intended as a proverb,[172] like lines 58f.[173] and Polyphemus' τὰν παρεοῖσαν ἄμελγε· τί τὸν φεύγοντα διώκεις; (75) ('milk the one to hand; why pursue the one who flees?').[174] All these proverbs are used, as is conventional in the genre, to bolster the resolve of the lover.[175] Even so, pruning is another neglected chore for Corydon and as such it may be intended as a clever variation on *Idyll* 11.73f., since the prunings would be fed to the livestock, especially at harvest time when green pasture would be in short supply.[176]

Virgil has, however, also expanded his model and has done so by including topoi of the *renuntiatio* either not included at all or only implicit in *Idyll* 11. Corydon begins by reminding himself that he is a *rusticus* (56); but the word is also an accusation of stupidity which leads to his upbraiding himself for getting into such a predicament. Such self-reproach is conventional in the genre.[177] So too is the explicit statement of why the lover is giving up his beloved.[178] Corydon's reason is not, like Polyphemus', simply the unwillingness of the beloved, but his greed and, presumably, his unfaithfulness with the rich rival, Iollas. Both reasons are conventional.[179] Ovid urged the unhappy lover *saepe refer tecum sceleratae facta puellae* (*Remedia* 299) in order to foster hatred of the beloved, and specifically recommends that the lover should think of her greed and infidelity.[180] The rustic proverb at 58f. again acts as a reminder of work to be done and again

Ovid provides the explanation (*Remedia* 143f.): *qui finem quaeris amoris,* | *(cedit amor rebus) res age, tutus eris.* He even makes a specific recommendation (194f.): *ipse potes riguis plantam deponere in hortis;* | *ipse potes riuos ducere lenis aquae.*[181] Nonetheless, Corydon's first attempt fails, as such attempts often do,[182] and at 60–5 he makes a renewed attempt to win Alexis. He opens with the lover's cliché: *quem fugis, a demens?*[183] His use of *fugere* in the sense of 'to reject a lover's advances'[184] echoes Polyphemus' τὸν φεύγοντα. In *Idyll* 11 this word serves to recall the opening lines τί τὸν φιλέοντ' ἀποβάλλῃ ('why do you reject one who loves you?') and φεύγεις ('you flee', 24). This same device is employed by Virgil: *nec munera curat Alexis* recalls *Alexi, nihil mea carmina curas?* (6). But the commonplace description of the beloved as one who flees is put to novel use in the question *quem fugis?* This is coupled with an appeal to Alexis to follow the example of his namesake Paris–Alexander and desert the town for the country. The appeal is supported yet again by a variation on an erotic proverb, which is a virtual translation of *Idyll* 10.30f.[185] Once more Corydon finds his resolve and commands himself to behold the returning oxen (*aspice,* 66). So, Ovid urges the unhappy lover to contemplate the delightful scenes of country life with a thrice repeated *aspice* (*Remedia* 175ff.). Again Corydon reproaches himself for his burning passion and asks (68): *quis enim modus adsit amori?*[186] Almost the same question occurs in the other Theocritean *renuntiatio* (*Idyll* 30.12): ἀλοσύνας τί ἔσχατον ἔσσεται ('what will be the end of this folly?'). As already noted, Corydon urges himself to concentrate on his daily problems, again as Ovid recommends (*Remedia* 559f. *ad mala quisque animum referat sua, ponet amorem*),[187] and resolves to find another beloved, yet another standard cure.[188] It is apparently a textbook case: the cure should be complete. But, just as in *Idyll* 11, the song must be reconciled with the introduction where it is explicitly stated that Corydon failed in his endeavours. A vital clue is provided by Virgil's modification of his model. Polyphemus (76) had resolved to find another and perhaps even more beautiful Galatea. His chances of success are made credible by his reference to the other girls who have responded favourably to his advances and by the fact that there is no reason to think that it would be impossible to find someone as beautiful, even if not more beautiful, than Galatea. Corydon, however, seeks another Alexis *qui rusticos non fastidit.* But all that he has revealed about Alexis in his song, reinforced by the traditional associations of his name, underline that any Alexis would be a *puer delicatus et urbanus* and as such would reject the advances of a *pastor rusticus.* It is striking and significant that Corydon is unable to refer to any possible alternative lovers. On the contrary, the word *fastidit* (73) picks up *fastidia* (15) and reminds the reader that with the only lovers whom Corydon has mentioned he experienced exactly the same reaction he has had from Alexis. The fact that lines 14f. are an inversion of the 'other and better beloveds' topos employed by Polyphemus only underlines the point. Corydon is doomed to go on suffering unrequited love: whether with this or another Alexis makes little difference. He cannot be said to be cured.

From consideration of speaker, addressee, setting and genre as the major component parts of each poem the relationship of *Eclogue* 2 to its models has emerged clearly. Basically, the speaker and the setting of *Idyll* 3 have been integrated into the generic pattern of *Idyll* 11 and the similarities between the two poems have been exploited to harmonize the combination. A major innovation is introduced by substituting a different kind of addressee and by simply inverting the moral of the model. Within this framework the entire corpus of Theocritean poetry is exploited for appropriate details of content, style or technique which can contribute to an imitation of Theocritus which at one and the same time is sufficiently close to the original to act as a substitute and sufficiently novel and original to be of interest to the learned reader who knew Theocritus.[189] Equally important, this approach enables us to see how Virgil has worked in material derived from non-Theocritean sources without incongruity. At lines 45ff. Virgil has taken the embryonic descriptions of garlands and apples from Theocritus and elaborated them by drawing on the entire tradition of such descriptions from archaic lyric through Hellenistic poetry. The primary influence may have been the garland ecphraseis in the epigrammatic tradition.[190] At all events the famous Alexis epigram of Meleager (*Anthologia Palatina* 12.127 = 79 Gow–Page) has contributed a number of details: not only the name of the beloved but the noonday setting at harvest time; the conceit that the lover is burned by twin fires (*ardebat Alexin*, 1; *sole sub ardenti*, 13) and the contrast between the sun's fires which are extinguished at nightfall and the fires of love which continue to burn strongly (67f.); and the idea that the lover sees his beloved even when he is absent. By drawing in such material from these extraneous traditions as is appropriate to his subject Virgil is able to enrich and enlarge his imitations without violating the laws of the genre.

The fact that Virgil's main model survives perhaps almost intact should not lead us to neglect the possibility that his poems may also contain elaborate allusions to lost poetry. Particularly intriguing is a series of parallels with the pastoral romance of Longus, *Daphnis and Chloe* 2.32–7.[191] There the old *praeceptor amoris* Philetas, at celebrations in honour of Pan, claims that he has been second only to Pan at piping. He has at home a syrinx which 'one would believe to have been that very one which Pan first made' (ἣν ὁ Πὰν πρῶτον [MSS: πρώτην Villoison, Dalmayda] ἐπήξατο, 2.35.2).[192] While his son goes to fetch it, a friend tells the tale of Pan and Syrinx and the invention of the pan-pipes:[193] Syrinx used to herd goats, play together with the Nymphs and sing (αἶγας ἔνεμεν, Νύμφαις συνέπαιζεν, ᾖδεν, 2.34.1).[194] After losing her among the reeds Pan made the first pipe, binding together the unequal reeds with wax (τοὺς καλάμους κηρῷ συνδήσας ἀνίσους 2.34.3)[195] as a symbol of their unequal love. When the pipe arrives Philetas plays and Daphnis dances an imitation of Pan (ὁ Δάφνις Πᾶνα ἐμιμεῖτο, 2.37.1)[196] and as he does so he plays upon Philetas' pipes so effectively that Philetas willingly gives him the pipe and prays that Daphnis also should leave it to a worthy successor (τὴν σύριγγα χαρίζεται ... εὔχεται καὶ Δάφνιν καταλιπεῖν αὐτὴν ὁμοίῳ διαδόχῳ, 2.37.3).[197] The correspondences with *Eclogue* 2.31–9, both verbal and thematic, are so exact and so numerous that it is hard to believe that they are coincidental. Since there there is no good reason to suppose that Longus is imitating the *Eclogues*,[198] both writers must be assumed to be drawing, either directly or indirectly, on some lost Hellenistic poem.[199] It is hardly audacious to suggest that it was written by the namesake of the character in Longus, Philitas of Cos.[200]

There is also considerable circumstantial evidence to support a hypothesis that the second *Eclogue* was directly influenced by Gallus, Virgil's friend and a fellow protégé of Asinius Pollio, the inventor of Roman love elegy.[201] His elegies must have explored in detail the situation of the unhappy and rejected lover; he may have treated homosexual love, like Catullus and Tibullus, as well as his love for Lycoris. It is impossible to believe that his poetry did not contain one example of a komos or of a *renuntiatio amoris*, easy to believe that it contained more. From any or all of these aspects of his poetry Virgil could have drawn material, ideas, techniques or vocabulary and combined it with purely Theocritean material. Moreover, there are a number of considerations which suggest that this is precisely what he did. Corydon has a rival for Alexis, the *diues amator*, Iollas (2; 57). The rival is a stock figure in the komos and in the *renuntiatio* but he is completely absent from both *Idylls* 3 and 11.[202] By contrast he is an ever present threat in the elegies of Propertius, Tibullus and Ovid. It is as certain as it can be that he figured in the elegies of Gallus: compare *Eclogue* 10.22–3: *tua cura Lycoris | perque niues alium perque horrida castra secuta est*, and Propertius 1.8, a poem generally agreed to be influenced by Gallus. His introduction at the very beginning of the poem (2) is then probably a pointed allusion to Gallus: it is worth noting that, although it can hardly be doubted that Iollas is the *dominus* of Alexis in the strict legal sense, the phrase *delicias domini* inevitably suggests the meaning of the word *dominus* in erotic language where it denotes a lover.[203]

Other features of the poem lead to the same conclusion. The expansion of epigrams into major poems was a notable feature of Hellenistic poetic technique, both Greek and Roman. Several poems of Propertius' *Monobiblos* stand in a relationship to extant epigrams similar to that of *Eclogue* 2 to *Anthologia Palatina* 12.127 (Meleager). It may be assumed that Gallus used this technique.[204] In addition, there are some other more specific clues. First, two of Horace's *Epodes* (11 and 15) are so strikingly similar to Roman elegy in both theme and vocabulary that they must be assumed to reflect the influence of Gallus.[205] Both are *renuntiationes amoris*.[206] In particular, *Epode* 11, which shows no sign of being directly influenced by *Eclogue* 2, shares with it a number of themes. The lover in that poem claims that his passion has distracted him from his work; his former beloved was a girl (compare Amaryllis, 14) while his present beloved is a *puer delicatus* like Alexis; he is poor and had no success with his greedy mistress; the remedies provided by his friends will be of no more avail this time than they were before and the only cure will be yet another beloved. Here, as in *Eclogue* 2, the ability of the lover to free himself from individual *amours* is contrasted with his inability to cure himself of love; here also is a lover who admits his past lack of success with an earlier beloved.[207] That Virgil and Horace reflect the poetry of Gallus is supported by the fact that in *Eclogue* 10 Gallus is presented as bisexual (37–41) and in search of *medicina furoris* (i.e. *remedia amoris*) the efficacy of which he later denies (50–61).[208] It should be noted that in that poem he specifically rejects both song and the countryside as cures for love (*Eclogue* 10.62ff.) before concluding that (69): *omnia uincit Amor et nos cedamus Amori*.[209]

Secondly, as was noted above, the opening lines of *Eclogue* 2 find a parallel in Phanocles' story of Orpheus and Calais. Phanocles goes on to tell of the death of Orpheus at the hands of the Thracian women. In *Georgics* 4.524 Virgil places this incident beside Oeagrian Hebrus and the words of Gallus at *Eclogue* 10.65 (*Hebrumque bibamus*) have been taken to indicate that Gallus had treated the Orpheus story.[210] Thirdly, it was also noted above that the Acontius of Callimachus provides another parallel for Corydon and again the close verbal similarities between *Eclogue* 10 and Propertius 1.18 have been taken to indicate that Gallus had anticipated Propertius in imitating the *Acontius and Cydippe*.[211] Fourthly, the learned and heavily grecizing allusion to Amphion and Aracynthus (*Eclogue* 2.24) finds its only parallel at Propertius 3.15.41f. Propertius may be echoing Virgil; but that seems less likely than that both reflect a common source, probably Gallus.[212] Fifthly, *Eclogue* 2.3 *inter densas, umbrosa cacumina, fagos* is an example of the so-called *schema Cornelianum*, a highly artificial interlacing of words in which a noun (and adjective) are enclosed within another noun and adjective to which they are in apposition.[213] Finally, the line beginning *nec te paeniteat* (34) finds an exact parallel at Tibullus 1.4.47f. (*nec te paeniteat . . . atteruisse*) where Priapus is giving advice on how to succeed with *pueri*;[214] and another at *Eclogue* 10.17 in a context where it is reasonable to suppose quotation of Gallus' own words: Adonis is held up as an example for Gallus to follow and the fact that Propertius incorporates an allusion to Euphorion's account of the death of Adonis into his description of Gallus is a virtual guarantee that Gallus had himself imitated that poem in some way.[215] None of these points is conclusive evidence for Gallan influence on its own. But the accumulative weight supports the hypothesis, which is in general terms probable anyway.[216]

If these speculations have any force, then the relationship of *Eclogue* 2 to Theocritus was complicated by the fact that it was simultaneously a sustained allusion to the poetry of Gallus.[217] Corydon is not only a human counterpart to the monstrous Cyclops but also a rustic counterpart to Gallus. Much of the humour and the precise significance of the allusion is of course largely lost to us. But it is possible to see that the implicit allusion to Gallus would match very nicely the explicit dedication of *Idyll* 11 to Nicias. If his elegies still survived they may have thrown into relief Virgil's handling of the theme of *remedia amoris*. One final observation may be made. Both in the fact that it is written in imitation of a leading Hellenistic poet and in the fact that it treats the subject of love, the second *Eclogue* caters for the same literary tastes as the elegies of Gallus. The parallelism may go further. The most obvious difference between Hellenistic elegy and Roman elegy is that the former treats the love-life of humanized mythical characters while the latter handles the love-life of an ordinary human being, the poet. So Propertius in 1.18 himself plays out the role of Callimachus' mythical Acontius;[218] and in *Eclogue* 10 Virgil has cast Gallus in the role of the dying Daphnis of *Idyll* 1. The same shift of emphasis is apparent also in *Eclogue* 2 where Virgil has cast the very ordinary human Corydon in the role of the mythical Cyclops. Virgil's use of this standard technique may be one more aspect of his debt to Gallus. Although the modern reader of the *Eclogues* must resign himself to such fleeting and insecure glimpses of the dim shadows cast by the poetry of contemporary poets, he ought not to forget either that he has been robbed of a whole dimension of these highly allusive and esoteric poems.

CHALLENGE AT CLOSE QUARTERS: 'CONTENDERE VERSIBVS AMBO'

This essay will conclude with an examination of two passages of the second *Eclogue* which are particularly close verbal imitations of Theocritus. At this level imitation stands close to translation and is most easily analysed.

γινώσκω, χαρίεσσα κόρα, τίνος οὕνεκα φεύγεις·
οὕνεκά μοι λασία μὲν ὀφρὺς ἐπὶ παντὶ μετώπῳ
ἐξ ὠτὸς τέταται ποτὶ θώτερον ὣς μία μακρά,
εἷς δ᾽ ὀφθαλμὸς ὕπεστι, πλατεῖα δὲ ῥὶς ἐπὶ χείλει.
ἀλλ᾽ οὗτος τοιοῦτος ἐὼν βοτὰ χίλια βόσκω,
κἠκ τούτων τὸ κράτιστον ἀμελγόμενος γάλα πίνω·
τυρὸς δ᾽ οὐ λείπει μ᾽ οὔτ᾽ ἐν θέρει οὔτ᾽ ἐν ὀπώρᾳ,
οὐ χειμῶνος ἄκρω· ταρσοὶ δ᾽ ὑπεραχθέες αἰεί.
συρίσδεν δ᾽ ὡς οὔτις ἐπίσταμαι ὧδε Κυκλώπων,
τίν, τὸ φίλον γλυκύμαλον, ἁμᾷ κἠμαυτὸν ἀείδων
πολλάκι νυκτὸς ἀωρί. τράφω δέ τοι ἕνδεκα νεβρώς,
πάσας μαννοφόρως, καὶ σκύμνως τέσσαρας ἄρκτων.

(*Idyll* 11.30–41)

I know, graceful maiden, on account of what you flee: it is because a shaggy eyebrow stretches over my whole forehead from one ear to the other making a single brow and under it is a single eye and a broad nose above my lip. But although this is what I am like, I pasture a thousand head and from them I draw and drink the best milk: and cheese does not run out on me, neither in summer nor at harvest time nor at the end of winter; but my cheese racks are always more than well laden. And I can play the pipe like no other of the Cyclopes here as I sing of you, my dear sweet-apple, and of myself too, often in the dead of night. And I am rearing for you eleven fawns, all of them collared, and four bears' cubs.

63

despectus tibi sum, nec qui sim quaeris, Alexi,
quam diues pecoris, niuei quam lactis abundans.
mille meae Siculis errant in montibus agnae;
lac mihi non aestate nouum, non frigore defit.
canto quae solitus, si quando armenta uocabat,
Amphion Dircaeus in Actaeo Aracyntho.
nec sum adeo informis: nuper me in litore uidi,
cum placidum uentis staret mare. non ego Daphnin
iudice te metuam, si numquam fallit imago.   (19–27)

The Cyclops first acknowledges his ugliness (A) which he sees as the reason for his rejection by Galatea. As counter-attractions he mentions his wealth in flocks (B), his skill as a musician (C) and his gifts (D). Corydon presents his case differently. He begins simply by saying that Alexis has rejected him without knowing him: he can apparently see no reason why he should be rejected. He tells Alexis of his wealth in flocks (B), his skill as a singer (C) and then, explicitly rejecting the idea that he is ugly (A), he boasts of his beauty. The gifts motif (D) is omitted, at least for the moment. Virgil has reduced the number of points from four to three and reordered them so that humorous emphasis is thrown on the boast of beauty, which is an inversion of the Cyclops' admitted ugliness. The two passages are closest in the accounts of pastoral wealth. Polyphemus claims (34) βοτὰ χίλια βόσκω ('I graze a thousand grazing beasts'). The language is elevated by the alliteration and by the *figura etymologica*. Virgil's translation retains the alliteration (21): *mille meae Siculis errant in montibus agnae* but there is no trace of an etymology. However, the phrase *diues pecoris* (20) compensates for this omission, as it inevitably reminds the reader of the standard etymology *pecunia a pecu: a pastoribus enim horum uocabulorum origo*.[219] Although *mille* corresponds exactly to χίλια, *agnae* are not quite the same as βοτά. The point of the alteration is acutely observed by Servius: *ait agnas et a sexu et ab aetate laudauit (nam ex femineo sexu in pecudibus copiosior possessio prouenit)*. Corydon thus outboasts the Cyclops, for he has a thousand female lambs alone, not to mention rams, ewes or male lambs, and the flock will grow even bigger! That is surely wealth indeed! The other modifications are also significant, though slight. The substitution of the word *errant* for βόσκω removes even the slightest hint at the work of shepherding and produces instead an idyllic picture calculated to appeal to the sentimental townsman.[220] While no one doubts that Polyphemus' sheep are his own, Virgil makes Corydon explicitly claim the lambs as his own (*meae*, 21). The adjective reflects his pride of ownership and incidentally establishes his social status as a peasant farmer. The word, which would have added nothing to our knowledge of the Cyclops, adds significantly to the characterization of Corydon.[221] Finally, the phrase *Siculis in montibus*. This again makes explicit something implicit in the original. On one level it contributes to the praise of Corydon's flocks: 'the mountainous interior of Sicily is well suited to animal husbandry, particularly the raising of sheep'.[222] On another level it signals Virgil's debt to Theocritus in general, reinforces the allusion to *Idyll* 11 in particular, and underlines the fact that Corydon is the literary descendant of the Cyclops and is playing out his role.[223]

While l. 21 is an elaboration of a simple statement made by Polyphemus, the next line reverses the procedure and simplifies the model. Polyphemus boasted of having the best milk to drink and an unfailing supply of cheese. He is thus humorously characterized as a thrifty and provident farmer. Virgil makes a different point more suited to the character of his speaker: Corydon claims only an unfailing supply of fresh milk (22): *lac mihi non aestate nouum, non frigore defit*. Servius rightly explains: *caseus seruari potest, nec mirum est si quouis tempore quis habeat caseum: hoc uero laudabile est si quis habeat lac nouum*.[224] The picturesque details of the Cyclopean cheese store and the threefold division of the seasons have been replaced by the simple antithesis of winter and summer. Corydon has fresh milk even when drought causes a fall in yield and in winter when the lambs take all the milk.[225] The claim is designed to appeal to the townsman: milk was probably at all times a luxury of the countryman, the townsman having to make do with cheese which was easier to market.[226]

Corydon next turns to his skill as a singer. The boast is parallel to that of Polyphemus who claims to be better at piping than the other Cyclopes (38). But the human Corydon's comparison of himself with the mythical Amphion naturally has a very different effect. The technique is of course familiar from *Idyll* 3, but Amphion is nowhere mentioned in the Theocritean corpus. The *exemplum* has every appearance of being culled from some Hellenistic poem, either directly or indirectly through Gallus as suggested above. This prodigious display of learning is humorously incongruous on the lips of the rustic Corydon.[227] Its allusiveness adds to the effect: *Dircaeus* suggests both the role of Amphion as the founder of Thebes and that of his step-mother Dirce in keeping him from his kingdom; the archaic *Actaeo* enhances the geographical learning.[228]

Corydon turns finally to the matter of his looks. Again Virgil

Ian M. Le M. Du Quesnay

produces a variation on his model by introducing material from a different source. This time he goes to *Idyll* 6, the other Polyphemus poem which is closely related in genre and style to *Idyll* 11. There Theocritus had handled the appearance of the Cyclops in a different way (34–8):

καὶ γάρ θην οὐδ' εἶδος ἔχω κακὸν ὥς με λέγοντι.
ἦ γὰρ πρᾶν ἐς πόντον ἐσέβλεπον, ἦς δὲ γαλάνα,
καὶ καλὰ μὲν τὰ γένεια, καλὰ δέ μευ ἁ μία κώρα,
ὡς παρ' ἐμὶν κέκριται, κατεφαίνετο, τῶν δέ τ' ὀδόντων
λευκοτέραν αὐγὰν Παρίας ὑπέφαινε λίθοιο.

For indeed I am not bad looking as they say that I am. I know this, for recently I looked into the sea, while it was calm, and my beard was shown to be beautiful and beautiful my single eye, as judged by me, and it reflected a gleam from my teeth whiter than Parian marble.

Similarity of content is reinforced by verbal similarity in order to establish the allusion. The protest οὐδ' εἶδος ἔχω κακὸν is mirrored in *nec sum adeo informis* (25) and the vivid incidental detail πρᾶν in *nuper*. The close similarity only serves to highlight the change of ἐς πόντον ἐσέβλεπον to *me in litore uidi* (25). The contrast makes a point. While the monster Cyclops could conceivably have seen his reflection in a calm sea, the human Corydon could not. He could only have seen himself in a rock pool or in a smooth wet rock. Since the Mediterranean is not a tidal sea, it must be supposed that Corydon was on the shore just after a storm which has produced these conditions. This view is confirmed by the phrase (26): *cum placidum uentis staret mare*, which is thus a pointed variation on ἦς δὲ γαλάνα. The passage was rightly understood by Seneca, for whom such natural mirrors characterized *aetas illa simplicior* which *et fortuitis contenta nondum in uitium beneficia detorquebat nec inuenta naturae in libidinem luxumque rapiebat.*[229] It is thus appropriate for Corydon's attempt to portray his rustic world in terms intended to appeal to the urbane and urban Alexis.

There is one other pointed modification of the model. Polyphemus had claimed that he was beautiful in his own judgement. The ancient scholiasts duly explain the humour: a Cyclops may be ugly to humans but he is beautiful to a Cyclops! For παρ' ἐμὶν κέκριται Virgil has substituted *iudice te*. Corydon is confident enough of his beauty that he will enter a contest with Daphnis.[230] The obvious humour of the boast conceals an irony: Daphnis is an exemplary rustic beauty, but

66

the sun-burned beauty of the rustic is wholly alien to the fair townsman.[231] Virgil has thus given a clever twist to his model. Alexis
rejects Corydon precisely because he is *rusticus*: yet Corydon, in his
attempts to impress, boasts of having the rustic wealth of a Polyphemus, the rustic song of an Amphion and the rustic beauty of a
Daphnis. For all his efforts, his boasts emerge not only as absurdly
exaggerated (a lover's licence) but miscalculated.

Virgil's imitation of Polyphemus' description of his gifts (40f.)
is delayed until 40–4:

> praeterea duo nec tuta mihi ualle reperti
> capreoli, sparsis etiam nunc pellibus albo,
> bina die siccant ouis ubera; quos tibi seruo.
> iam pridem a me illos abducere Thestylis orat;
> et faciet, quoniam sordent tibi munera nostra.

It is here combined with imitation of a similar passage from *Idyll* 3
(34–6), a striking example of *contaminatio* which signals that the second
Eclogue is in general terms a *contaminatio* of these two *Idylls*.

> ἦ μάν τοι λευκὰν διδυματόκον αἶγα φυλάσσω,
> τάν με καὶ ἁ Μέρμνωνος ἐριθακὶς ἁ μελανόχρως
> αἰτεῖ· καὶ δωσῶ οἱ, ἐπεὶ τύ μοι ἐνδιαθρύπτῃ.

*Indeed I am keeping for you a white she-goat that has born
twins and which Mermnon's dark-skinned hired help also begs me
for; and I shall give it to her since you are so haughty with me.*

On the formal level the debt to *Idyll* 3 is in fact more obvious.
The nanny-goat has given birth to two kids and is white in colour: so
there are two roebucks with white markings who twice a day suck
dry the ewe's udders; φυλάσσω corresponds exactly to *seruo*, αἰτεῖ to
orat and καὶ δωσῶ οἱ ἐπεί to *et faciet quoniam*. Corydon also uses the
same device to enhance the value of his gift and it may be assumed that
Thestylis, like the reapers whose meal she is preparing (1of.) and
Mermnon's girl, is sunburned and a hired-help.[232] In one detail there is
a significant change. The goatherd says he will give the gift to another
since Amaryllis is disdainful of him; Corydon, however, remains
blind to the fact that it is he himself whom Alexis finds unattractive and
sees only a rejection of his rustic gifts. Such is the self-deception of the
unhappy lover.

The relationship of the passage to *Idyll* 11.40f. is more subtle. The
combination of the two passages is facilitated by the choice of roebucks

67

(*capreoli*) as a gift. These were wild animals which the Romans used to encourage on their lands for the elegance and pleasure which they added: in short, they are calculated to appeal to the urbane and urban Alexis.[233] The creatures offered to Galatea are also wild, suitable in ferocity and in quantity (eleven fawns and four bear-cubs) to the monstrous Cyclops, to the donor rather than the recipient. Polyphemus further enhances the value of his gifts by describing them as μαννοφόρως. The exact meaning of this word is obscure. The scholia take an alternative reading as their lemma: ἀμνοφόρως (lamb-bearing). Perhaps prompted by his knowledge of this reading, Virgil gives the *capreoli* a ewe to suckle. If so, he probably intends to signal his rejection of this reading: roebucks may have a sheep as a foster mother but they cannot possibly give birth to lambs! The scholia also say that μαννοφόρως means 'wearing golden neck-ornaments'. This is obviously nonsense, since the primitive and rustic Cyclops knows nothing of such luxury. The word may mean 'wearing a halter'; then the point would be that Polyphemus had trained these wild creatures so that they would make good pets for Galatea. But Virgil seems to imply that he understood the word to mean that they had markings on their coats which resembled some kind of harness, for he describes the *capreoli* as *sparsis pellibus albo*. He is probably correct. Imitation is here used to comment on and interpret the model, a fundamental technique of Hellenistic poetry.[234] A different kind of learning is reflected in the precision of Theocritus' biological knowledge. Aristotle had asserted that she-bears normally had five cubs. By contrast, Theocritus quite rightly attributes the four cubs to a plurality of parents and so unobtrusively reveals that he knew that the normal number was in fact one or two.[235] Virgil matches this aspect of his model's *doctrina* with the simple addition of *etiam nunc*. For he thus reveals that he knew that the dappled markings of the young roebuck disappeared once it had been weaned.

For the reader who is prepared to acquire the taste, the constant interplay between model and imitation becomes a source of intellectual and aesthetic pleasure. Paradoxically, the imitator strives to be as different from his model as possible while at the same time he contrives to be always reminiscent of his model. This analysis of *Eclogue* 2 has explored the various techniques of imitation used by Virgil. He has absorbed the mass of detail that goes to make a Theocritean bucolic so thoroughly that he can transform it to generate a new poem which is recognizably in the 'language of bucolic' but is not a simple reproduction of anything actually written by Theocritus. He has exploited the literary traditions independently of his immediate model in such a way that he is able to combine imitation of two *Idylls* (11 and 3) and also draw in material from other sources. Yet the relationship with *Idyll* 11 in particular is always there to highlight his individual handling of the tradition. When he imitates a particular passage closely, every opportunity is taken to vary the original in subtle ways. The result is a poem at once like and unlike the model: neither aspect of the poem should be emphasized at the expense of the other. The imitation of Theocritus adds an intellectual dimension to a poem concerned to portray the emotions of a man in love, hopelessly and helplessly. Throughout this poem intellectualism and learning balance emotion and sentimentality; humour balances seriousness and pathos. This combination of qualities, characteristic of much Roman elegy, makes a poem that is always elusive and fascinating and which richly rewards each new reading.

4

David West

TWO PLAGUES

Virgil, *Georgics* 3.478–566 and Lucretius
6.1090–1286

Virgil's account of a cattle plague at the end of the third book of the
Georgics draws heavily upon Lucretius' account of the plague at
Athens which ends the sixth and last book of the *De rerum natura*.
The purpose of this essay is to throw light upon the Virgilian passage
by comparing it with the Lucretian.

I THE AETIOLOGY

Hic quondam morbo caeli miseranda coorta est
tempestas totoque autumni incanduit aestu
et genus omne neci pecudum dedit, omne ferarum,
corrupitque lacus, infecit pabula tabo.

(Virgil, Georgics 3.478–81)

*Here once, through a disease of the sky, there arose a pitiable
season which burned with heat for a whole autumn, giving over to
death all manner of livestock and all manner of wild beasts,
polluting their drinking water and poisoning their food with
decomposing flesh.*

As a clinical history this is not satisfactory. What is the *tempestas*
which arose? Season? Time? Commotion? Calamity? And how *coorta*?
Arisen from the ground? or gathered somehow in the air? And how is
it helpful to say that a cattle plague arose because of a disease of the
sky? This is little more than a metaphor and it is followed by another,
when Virgil says that the season *burned* throughout the heat of a whole
autumn. And what is the *tabum* which infected the food and water?
It could perhaps refer to the plague with which the season infected the
drink and food of animals. But the usual meaning of *tabum* is 'decaying
gore or tissue', and on that explanation a more satisfactory chronology
is given: in l. 480 the season kills the animals and then (through their
corpses) infects their food and drink. This second explanation is

slightly strengthened by the lush grasses of 494, not infected but *laetis*. On either explanation, the ambiguity confirms our suspicions: Virgil is not interested primarily in clinical history. This passage has two metaphors. It has an editorial comment *miseranda*. It is subtly rhetorical: with *omne ferarum* we need to repeat *genus neci dedit* and with *corrupit lacus* we supply *tabo*. These ellipses and the quasi-anaphora of *omne . . . omne* lend rhythmic variety to what could have been four monotonous clauses. *Quondam*, 'once upon a time', gives the game away long before we come to the mythical names of the consultants in 550, 'Phillyrides Chiron Amythaoniusque Melampus'. This is legend, pathos, writing for effect. It is not science, or history.

   This passage is modelled on Lucretius' account of the plague in Athens, but in Lucretius we are in a different world.

> Nunc ratio quae sit morbis aut unde repente   1090
> mortiferam possit cladem conflare coorta
> morbida uis hominum generi pecudumque cateruis,
> expediam. primum multarum semina rerum
> esse supra docui quae sint uitalia nobis,
> et contra quae sint morbo mortique necessest   1095
> multa uolare. ea cum casu sunt forte coorta
> et perturbarunt caelum, fit morbidus aer.
> atque ea uis omnis morborum pestilitasque
> aut extrinsecus ut nubes nebulaeque superne
> per caelum ueniunt, aut ipsa saepe coortae   1100
> de terra surgunt, ubi putorem umida nactast
> intempestiuis pluuiisque et solibus icta.
> nonne uides etiam caeli nouitate et aquarum
> temptari procul a patria quicumque domoque
> adueniunt ideo quia longe discrepitant res?   1105
> nam quid Brittannis caelum differre putamus,
> et quod in Aegypto est qua mundi claudicat axis,
> quidue quod in Ponto est differre, et Gadibus atque
> usque ad nigra uirum percocto saecla colore?
> quae cum quattuor inter se diuersa uidemus   1110
> quattuor a uentis et caeli partibus esse,
> tum color et facies hominum distare uidentur
> largiter et morbi generatim saecla tenere.
> est elephas morbus qui propter flumina Nili
> gignitur Aegypto in media neque praeterea usquam.   1115
> Atthide temptantur gressus oculique in Achaeis

finibus. inde aliis alius locus est inimicus
partibus ac membris: uarius concinnat id aer.
proinde ubi se caelum, quod nobis forte alienum,
conimouet atque aer inimicus serpere coepit,   1120
ut nebula ac nubes paulatim repit et omne
qua graditur conturbat et immutare coactat,
fit quoque ut, in nostrum cum uenit denique caelum,
corrumpat reddatque sui simile atque alienum.
haec igitur subito clades noua pestilitasque   1125
aut in aquas cadit aut fruges persidit in ipsas
aut alios hominum pastus pecudumque cibatus,
aut etiam suspensa manet uis aere in ipso
et, cum spirantes mixtas hinc ducimus auras,
illa quoque in corpus pariter sorbere necessest.   1130
consimili ratione uenit bubus quoque saepe
pestilitas et iam pigris balantibus aegror.
nec refert utrum nos in loca deueniamus
nobis aduersa et caeli mutemus amictum,
an caelum nobis ultro natura coruptum   1135
deferat aut aliquid quo non consueuimus uti,
quod nos aduentu possit temptare recenti.
 Haec ratio quondam morborum et mortifer aestus
finibus in Cecropis funestos reddidit agros
uastauitque uias, exhausit ciuibus urbem.   1140
nam penitus ueniens Aegypti finibus ortus,
aera permensus multum camposque natantis,
incubuit tandem populo Pandionis omni.
inde cateruatim morbo mortique dabantur.

*Now I shall explain what is the cause of diseases and from where
the force of disease can suddenly come together and breathe a
death-dealing calamity upon the race of men and the tribes of
animals. First, I have explained above that there are atoms of
many things which give us life. There must be, correspondingly,
many atoms flying around bringing disease and death. When
these chance to come together and throw the sky into a disturbance,
the air becomes diseased and all that force of disease and pestilence either comes through the sky from other places, like clouds
and mists, or else, as often happens, it comes together on the
earth itself and rises when the wet earth begins to decay being
subjected to excessive rain, and heat from the sun. Do you not also*

see that those who leave their own home and native land are affected by the new sky and climate and water for the reason that these things are very different for them. For do we not think there is some difference between the sky in Britain and the sky in Egypt where the axis of the world is on the slant. And is there not a difference between the sky at Pontus and Cadiz and right to the tribes of men baked black by the sun?[1] Just as we see the differences between these four areas at the four different winds and quarters of the sky, so the colour and features of the inhabitants seem to differ widely, and diseases seem to affect them according to their nationalities. Elephantiasis occurs in the middle of Egypt, near the river Nile, and nowhere else. In Attica the feet are affected. In Achaea the eyes. So different localities are dangerous to different parts of the body, and this is caused by differences in the air. Similarly when a sky that is alien to us happens to move and a dangerous air begins to creep, it gradually seeps along like clouds and mist, and causes a disturbance wherever it goes and forces everything to change; and it comes to pass also that when it eventually arrives in our sky, it corrupts that and makes it hostile to us like itself. Suddenly, therefore, this new and malignant pestilence either falls into the drinking water, or settles deep into the very crops or the other foods of men or fodder of animals, or else its force remains suspended in the actual air, and when we breathe and take in air mixed with this, we must at the same time breathe this malignant pestilence into our bodies. This is often how pestilence comes to cattle also, and disease to slow-moving loud-bleating sheep as well. Nor does it make any difference whether we go to places which are healthy for us, and change the covering of sky about us, or whether it is nature which imposes upon us either a corrupted sky, or some other change of condition that can affect us by its new arrival.

This was long ago the cause of the disease, this was the death-dealing tide which once poisoned the fields of Cecropian Attica, made desolate its roads, and stripped its city of inhabitants. For it arose in the heart of Egypt, traversed the vast tract of air and expanse of sea, and fell at last upon the entire people of Pandion. It was this that gave them over in tribes to disease and death.

In Lucretius we are in a different world. A brief explanation of the cause of diseases is followed by an account of where they come from (*ratio . . . aut unde* 1090). They are caused by the gathering of atoms which disturb the sky (and hence the climate: the ambivalence of the word *caelum* operates throughout this passage), and make the air diseased. So much for the *ratio*. Now the source, *unde*. They come either from the earth or from abroad.[2] This is a very clear logical exposition, and its clarity is due partly to repetitions which help us to pick out the logical structure of the argument. This is sound pedagogic practice and it is characteristic of Lucretius.[3] For example, disease and death are mentioned together in this demonstrandum 1090–1, in the proof 1095, and twice in the description of the plague at Athens which is the *exemplum* 1138, 1144, (see also in 1221–2, 1232, 1250–1, 1255). Other important elements in this exposition are the gathering of the malignant atoms (*coorta* 1091, 1096, 1100 and 1141), their movement through the sky (*per . . . caelum* 1097, 1100 and *caelum* repeatedly 1103, 1106, 1111, 1119, 1123, 1134, 1135), and the infection of the air. This last appears not only at 1097, 1118, 1120, 1128, 1142, but also in *uentis* at 1111 and *auras* at 1129.

What is the logical function of 1103–37? It is an analogical argument to support Lucretius' idea that diseases are caused by the movement of the weather.

> Do you not see also that when a *man* moves from one country to another, he is affected by the change of weather and water. For (*nam* 1106) different countries have different weathers, and different diseases. Similarly (*proinde* 1119) when the *weather* moves from one country to another, it becomes dangerous to us. It makes no difference (1133) whether the man moves or the weather.

This is then all one argument and all supports by analogy the process invoked by Lucretius in 1099–1100. The concept of 'difference' is important at the beginning of this argument and *discrepitant*, *differre* twice, *diuersa* and *distare* occurring between 1105 and 1112 represent it forcibly to the reader. Similarly in 1119–25, *forte, aer, ut nebula ac nubes, conturbat, in nostrum uenit caelum, haec clades . . . pestilitasque* all serve to bind this reprise to the original enunciation of the argument (*cum casu . . . forte, aer, ut nubes nebulaeque, perturbarunt, per caelum ueniunt, ea uis . . . pestilitasque*, 1096–1100 and add *subito* 1125, cf. *repente* 1090).

The plague at Athens (1138–1285), which provides a spectacular, non-technical conclusion to the *De rerum natura*, fits the argument as an example of a disease which is caused in the way described in 1090–

1137. This is made clear by the connection *haec ratio quondam morborum et mortifer aestus* 1138, picking up *Nunc ratio quae sit morbis aut unde repente | mortiferam . . .* 1090–1.

This analysis helps us to apprehend the logic and also to understand the poetry. In 1091 the force of disease gathers and *breathes* a death-dealing disaster upon men and animals. *Conflare* is not an inert metaphor, 'to produce', or 'to gather', but locked functionally into the argument. This is poetry in the hands of a philosopher. The ornament, variety, and imagery subserve the argument.

So much for the logic of the Lucretian passage. Now let us examine further the resemblances between it and Virgil, *Georgics* 3.478–81. There, *quondam* refers to an obscure event in the unknown past in Noricum, between the Danube and the Alps; in Lucretius 1138 it refers to the plague at Athens in 430 B.C. *Morbo caeli* we found a bold metaphor, clinically not meaningful; in Lucretius 1097, 1119–24, 1135 we see the unhealthy atoms in the sky. *Coorta est tempestas* was also uninformative but in Lucretius we are clearly told what is gathering and where from. The third line of Lucretius (1092) refers to the family of man and the tribes of animals; Virgil in the third book of the *Georgics* is concerned with livestock, not mankind, but he still finds a division to correspond in *genus omne . . . pecudum . . ., omne ferarum*, every family of livestock, and of wild beasts. In Virgil 480–1 the pollution of food and water we found ambiguous, and expressed in subtly modulated rhetoric. In Lucretius 1126–7 there is perfectly plain science. The disease in the sky either falls into water, or settles deep into crops or the other food of men and fodder of animals. The value of this is not in any rhetorical modulation, but in its truth. How acute of Lucretius to see that it would settle deep into the very grain (*fruges persidit in ipsas*), and how sad when translators (not the great Munro) miss it ('settles on the corn itself', 'even on the crops').

These four Virgilian lines are full of Lucretian echoes. Even the rhythm of the fourth reproduces the rhythm of Lucretius' third, even to the unusual omission of the second coordinating conjunction:

> corrupitque lacus, infecit pabula tabo (481)

> uastauitque uias, exhausit ciuibus urbem (1140)

In Virgil 481 there is a strange switch, where, since *inficere* is the *mot propre* for dipping, dyeing, staining in liquids, we might expect *infecitque lacus, corrupit pabula tabo*. This inversion (see Eden (1975) on *Aeneid* 8.3) is very like what we find in a line where Lucretius is discussing the same phenomenon, *aut alios hominum pastus, pecudumque cibatus*, 1127, since *pastus* is the *mot propre* for animal fodder. The two Virgilian elements for which we have not yet found Lucretian analogues are *neci dedit*, for which we can compare *mortique dabantur*, Lucretius 1144; and the metaphor *incanduit*. This soon appears in Lucretius, in a literal use:

> octauoque fere candenti lumine solis
> aut etiam nono reddebant lampade uitam (1197–8)

> *Usually on the eighth day of blazing sunlight or sometimes the ninth appearance of the sun's torch, they gave up their lives.*

This work of Virgil's is not a mechanical cento like Ausonius' cento of Virgil. Virgil is not just sitting before a scroll open at Lucretius 6, culling a phrase here and a half-line there. He is saturated with the poetry of Lucretius, and its words, phrases, thought and rhythms have merged in his mind, and become transmuted into an original work of poetic art with a tone and intention and poetic thrust which are entirely his own.

2 THE SYMPTOMOLOGY

> nec uia mortis erat simplex; sed ubi ignea uenis
> omnibus acta sitis miseros adduxerat artus,
> rursus abundabat fluidus liquor omniaque in se
> ossa minutatim morbo conlapsa trahebat.
>
> (Virgil, *Georgics* 3.482–5)

> *Nor was the path to death simple, but when the fiery thirst driven through all the veins had shrunk the wretched limbs, there was again an abundance of fluid into which all the bones collapsed disintegrating with disease particle by particle.*

A clear account. The disease has two phases, shortage of moisture, followed by excess of moisture. This is effective rhetoric with its paradox and pathos, but it is not clinically credible. For one thing it is too simple to be true. For another, we might well wonder how Virgil, or his sources, came to observe the progressive solution of bone tissue in fluid.

This suspicion that we are dealing with a rhetorical creation rather than an attempt at description is confirmed by comparison with Lucretius. The progress of the symptoms is charted in great detail in 1145–98; first of all, a hot head and red eyes; then black blood in the throat, blocking the voice passage, and a bleeding, heavy and painful tongue; then the disease flows into the heart, and the barriers of life (*uitai claustra*, 1153) begin to break. Whether or not this is clinically credible, it is detailed, vivid and understandable. The affliction involves a descending liquefaction. For Lucretius death takes place with the separation of body and soul, and the departure of the soul is marked by the end of breathing (e.g. 3.580–614). So Lucretius now turns reasonably to second-phase symptoms: the disorders of the breathing. In 1154–5 the breath developed a smell like the smell of a corpse, and body and soul languished on the very threshold of death. Lucretius seems to have here some poetic and not quite rational interplay between the bolts of life (*uitai claustra*), the breath rolling a foul stench out of doors (*foras*), and the lingering of body and soul on the very threshold of death (*leti iam limine in ipso*). From the breath it is another reasonable transition to the groans and complaints and sighs of the dying and thence to their suffering from ulcers and from the burning of the internal parts to the bone (*intima pars hominum uero flagrabat ad ossa*, 1168). Sufferers tore off their clothes and leapt into water. There was no remedy. They were exhausted, fevered, sleepless. The doctors muttered inaudibly and were afraid (*mussabat tacito medicina timore*, 1179). At this point, the symptoms of the third phase, the signs of approaching death, were many (*multaque praeterea mortis tum signa dabantur*; 1182); and Lucretius notes them (1183–98) in the mind, the eyebrows, the face, the ears, the breath, the sweat, the painful yellow spit, the hands, the lips, the feet, the nostrils, the eyes, the temples, the skin, the jaws, the forehead. The patient died, as we have seen, on the eighth or ninth day.

In the Virgilian symptomology we thought we saw rhetoric; in Lucretius, realistic clinical detail in abundance. But not only that, we have also encountered in the Lucretius most of the elements which Virgil has built into his much smaller structure.

'Nor was the path of death simple'; *nec uia mortis erat simplex* (482) would suggest in Virgil that there were many different forms of death; or that the process of dying was complex. It is a surprise to read on and learn that the path of death is not single, but double, thirst followed by dropsy. So this preamble, although effective, provides a slightly deceptive introduction to Virgil's symptomology; nor is that symptomology relevant to Virgil's case descriptions in 480–547. In Lucretius, however, 'and many other signs of death were then presented', *multaque praeterea mortis tum signa dabantur* (1182), forms an entirely just preamble to the sixteen terminal symptoms which follow; and his symptomology is an integrated part of his account of the plague.

Virgil's first phase, the fiery thirst, *ignea sitis*, is mentioned in a dozen terms in Lucretius 1163–75 (including *ignis* 1167 and *sitis arida* 1175). Virgil's second phase, the dropsy, we have seen in 1152 (*morbida uis in cor maestum confluxerat*), and it appears also throughout the symptoms of a fourth phase in Lucretius where he describes the fate of those who survive the disease (1199–1214), with a black efflux from the bowels and infected blood pouring from bloated nostrils. All the strength of the man, his whole body flowed into this (*huc hominis totae uires corpusque fluebat*, 1204). Those who did not have this efflux of acrid blood found it flowing into the nerves and limbs and even into their private parts. Some lost their feet, their hands or their eyes, some even their memories. All of these details are clinically credible, but not, as we argued, what Virgil made of them, that the bones should gradually dissolve into the fluid. Now, however, the Virgilian idea of dissolving bones becomes explicable. It is a bold and general picture inspired by the loss of foot and hand in Lucretius. It is as though Virgil is supposing that the loss of the extremities means that their bones are dissolved in noxious fluid.

Finally, at a verbal level, the Virgilian 'ossa *minutatim* morbo conlapsa *trahebant*' (485) owes something to Lucretius' description of two different symptoms in 1190–1: 'in manibus nerui *trahere* et tremere artus | a pedibusque *minutatim* succedere frigus'. This is the only occurrence of *minutatim* in Virgil; Lucretius has it seven times. In general then Virgil has eschewed the clinical detail of Lucretius, but has put together words and concepts culled from Lucretius' richly detailed and coherent symptomology to produce a simplified picture of a disease in two phases which is emotionally effective, rhetorically arresting by means of paradox and pathos, and has no regard for historical or scientific truth. Attempts (e.g. Richter (1957), 319–20) to diagnose the disorder with the help of modern veterinary medicine are doomed to failure.

3. THE EPIDEMIOLOGY

In Lucretius' human epidemic the aetiology took 55 lines (1090–1144), the symptomology 70 (1145–1214) and his remarks about animals are confined to 10 lines (1215–24), out of the total of 161. In the 89 lines of Virgil's animal epidemic the aetiology and the symptoms take 4 lines each, and the bulk of his account (62 out of 89 lines) is devoted to the animals affected by the disease. In this passage then (486–547), Virgil is apparently working without a Lucretian model. Here therefore we may hope to be able to isolate the Virgilian in Virgil.

The *sacrificial animals* (486–93) are a logical cross-division, since they would include the calves, swine and bulls later to be treated. Virgil's object in starting a list of specific animals with this mixed class must be to involve religion and in particular to excite the emotions by the horror and the mind by the paradox of death at the altar. The horror is intensified by the failure of the infected entrails to burn on the altar or to provide usable evidence from which the haruspex could take the omens – a calculated inversion of the actual order of events (for *hysteron proteron* as an archaism or Homerism see Norden (1927) on *Aeneid* 6, Anhang 2.2). The paradox is intensified by the lack of blood in the plague victim. There was hardly enough to stain the knife whereas normally the jugular of a healthy ox would spurt about a couple of gallons of blood.

Paradox and antithesis are the mainsprings of the four short examples which follow (494–7). This shows most clearly in the sweet temper of the dogs and the madness which came upon them (hinc canibus *blandis rabies* uenit), but it appears also to be important to the calves, who die in the rich grasses and give up their sweet breath at full mangers:

> hinc laetis uituli uolgi moriuntur in herbis
> et dulcis animas plena ad praesepia reddunt.

To the obvious polar tension between *moriuntur* on the one hand and *laetis* and *plena* on the other, Virgil has added an evocation of the sweetness of the breath of calves. No doubt *reddebant uitam*, Lucretius 1198, somehow lies behind this (Virgil nowhere else uses *reddere* with any object meaning 'to die'), but this is an affectionate and sympathetic observation of animal life which is entirely Virgil's own.

Polar tension is a common pattern of thought in Roman poetry.[4] After these examples of it with the calves and the dogs, it will come as no surprise to find that it operates also with the swine in 497, where breathless coughing shakes them and chokes their fat throats, *faucibus angit obesis*. Swine do tend to have difficulties with their breathing but we should note also the paradox that a fat throat should be constricted, *angit obesis*.[5] The horse also starts with a polar tension. It was victorious in racing: now it falls to the ground and loses its energy and appetite, and Virgil's language is heavy with anthropomorphic suggestion.

> labitur infelix studiorum atque immemor herbae
> uictor equus.   498–9

There follow four symptoms – stamping of the hooves, drooping of the ears, cold sweat by the ears, and hard, dry skin. These are symptoms of equine disorder and therefore are not to be found in Lucretius, although the terminal symptoms of Lucretius' human disorders include sweat (1187) and hard skin (1195).[6] Next, Virgil explains that these are symptoms which occur in the early days before death (*haec ante exitium primis dant signa diebus*, 503) and this classification itself owes something to Lucretius 1182 (*multaque praeterea mortis tum signa dabantur*). Virgil then mentions four symptoms which occur if the disease develops. These four further symptoms are all Lucretian, but derived from different phases of the Lucretian analysis. The blazing eyes (*ardentes oculi*, 505) go back to Lucretius' first phase (*duplices oculos suffusa luce rubentes*, 1146): the *spiritus*, *gemitus* and *singultus* are mentioned in that order in Lucretius' second phase (1154, 1159, 1160): the black blood from the nose is a blend of two survivors' symptoms from Lucretius' fourth phase (1200 and 1203); the blocking of the throat and roughness of the tongue go back to Lucretius' earliest symptoms in 1148–50. Virgil's anthologizing and re-ordering of Lucretian symptoms confirms our earlier suspicions that it would be foolish to take his descriptions as a serious contribution to the history of veterinary medicine. Virgil has drawn upon Lucretius' symptomology for an account which has no coherence and makes no clinical sense, but which does produce a vivid and affecting picture of a sick horse. This is in line with his insertion of the wine cure for horses (509–14), a standard trick in ancient veterinary medicine (see Columella, e.g. 6.6.3, 6.7.2, 6.30.9). This enables Virgil to end with a pious moralization and spectacular climax as the horses in a resounding golden line rend their own bodies with their teeth in 512–13. And yet even here where Virgil is far from Lucretius he uses Lucretian words (*mox erat hoc ipsum exitio*, 511, cf. *hoc aliis erat exitio*, 1229).[7]

The last of the farm animals is the ox, and in treating its death Virgil achieves effects quite unlike anything in Lucretius' account of the plague:

> ecce autem duro fumans sub uomere taurus   515
> concidit et mixtum spumis uomit ore cruorem
> extremosque ciet gemitus. it tristis arator
> maerentem abiungens fraterna morte iuuencum,
> atque opere in medio defixa reliquit aratra.
> non umbrae altorum nemorum, non mollia possunt   520
> prata mouere animum, non qui per saxa uolutus
> purior electro campum petit amnis; at ima

soluuntur latera, atque oculos stupor urget inertis
ad terramque fluit deuexo pondere ceruix.
quid labor aut benefacta iuuant? quid uomere terras   525
inuertisse grauis?   (Virgil, *Georgics* 3.515–26)

Look, there falls a bullock while steaming at the hard plough,
vomiting blood and foam as it utters its last moanings. The
ploughman looses its yoke-mate grieving at his brother's death,
and walks sadly away leaving the plough stuck in the ground in
the middle of the furrow. The deep shade of the forest means
nothing to him now, nor do the soft meadows nor the river
rolling clearer than electrum over its stones and down to the
plain. His whole flank slumps, dullness presses on his eyes and
takes the life out of them, and his neck flows down to the ground
under its own weight. What pleasure does he have from his hard
work and faithful service, from all the heavy earth he has turned
with the plough?

This owes something to Lucretius but not to his description of the
plague at Athens. In his second book he has reason to argue that a
cow can recognize its own calf, and search for it when it is lost:

... completque querelis
frondiferum nemus adsistens et crebra reuisit
ad stabulum desiderio perfixa iuuenci,   360
nec tenerae salices atque herbae rore uigentes
fluminaque illa queunt summis labentia ripis
oblectare animum subitamque auertere curam
                          (Lucretius 2.358–63)

She stands in the leafy forest filling it with her lamentations and
keeps coming back to the stall, pierced with longing for her calf.
Nor do the tender willows, not the living dewy grass, nor those
rivers that glide past their full banks delight her mind nor
relieve her of the sadness she has suffered.

The resemblances between Lucretius and Virgil 520–2 are obvious, but
less illuminating than the differences. In Virgil 515 *ecce* is a direct call
from the poet to the reader, another subjective element like the
moralization in 513, and foreign to Lucretius. The sudden fall of the
bullock at the beginning of 516, while it is steaming with sweat from
pulling the plough, is the usual rhetorical contrast here with powerful
pathetic effect. The next detail, the vomiting of blood and foam, is
there to shock and move our pity. It is also a polar tension, the familiar

clash of red and white noted by Norden (1927) on *Aeneid* 6.9–10. The groaning, *gemitus*, also moves our pity. The next sentence has the polarities we have come to look for, *tristis arator* unyoking the *maerentem iuuencum*, and the plough stuck in the middle of the work. But more distinctively Virgilian are the sadness of the ploughman and the sadness of the yoke-mate grieving for his brother. The moralizations that follow reflect upon the futility of hard work, sobriety and simple living in moving terms which are human rather than bovine. All of the anthropomorphic elements, emotional and moral, the pathos frequently heightened by the contrasts we can draw between the sickly horse and cow and the healthy condition of the same animals earlier in the poem (1.118, 325, 3.160), these are distinctively Virgilian, a profound and intense feeling for animal life, which views the animal not truly, not in its own terms, but anthropomorphically, in terms of analogous sufferings of men. This is not always said. Klepl (1967), 73, for example, concludes that Virgil's plague demonstrates his pantheistic view of the world whereby man is governed by divine law and the animals participate in that association. The laws of Nature, she argues, and the spirituality of man are all part of the true pattern of the Universe. There can be nothing contrary to man which is not also contrary to the divine and contrary to Nature. In this sense the plague in Virgil is truly a condition of the Universe. This noble philosophy seems to me to be absent from Virgil's text, and false to Virgil's essential anthropocentricity.

In Lucretius, on the other hand, we have a cow's eye view of the landscape: the willow is mentioned as a favourite fodder, of goats, admittedly, not cows, in *Eclogues* 1.78 and 3.8; the grass is in growth, and therefore succulent; it has dew on it, it will therefore be cool and fresh to the taste; those rivers (the demonstrative pronoun conveys familiarity and affection) glide along level with their banks, they are therefore full and fresh and easily accessible to a cow's mouth. All these details would be appreciated by any cow of normal appetites. Virgil abandons the particular attraction of the willow leaves and accepts instead the more general pleasure of shade which human beings also might enjoy. He abandons the growth in the grass, and the dew, and cites what is rather a human comfort, its softness. He loses the abundance and accessibility of the river and again produces characteristics more likely to interest a man than a cow, that it is going over rocks, that it is making for the plain, that it is clearer than electrum. The cow would indeed be interested in its clarity but not in the Callimachean comparison (*Hymn to Demeter* 29).

In Lucretius' account of the plague, the passage about animal life is brief and closely relevant to the human scene. He explains that birds and wild beasts did not eat the unburied human corpses, or died if they did. They did not even emerge from the woods but stayed there, dying themselves. The only example Lucretius gives is the suffering of dogs and that is relevant to a plague in a city because they could have been seen dying in agony in the streets (1223). On the other hand Virgil's passage describing the suffering of wild animals (537–47) develops an impetus of its own and is irrelevant to the cattle plague at Noricum. It even includes fish and Noricum – like Illyria – has no coastline. Characteristic too is the order of the examples. The narrative of the plague has no bearing on it. Virgil simply runs through the standard categories, land animals, sea animals, underground animals, birds. Characteristic too that the descriptions are built on pathos and paradox.

> non lupus insidias explorat ouilia circum
> nec gregibus nocturnus obambulat: acrior illum
> cura domat; timidi dammae ceruique fugaces
> nunc interque canes et circum tecta uagantur.   540
> iam maris immensi prolem et genus omne natantum
> litore in extremo ceu naufraga corpora fluctus
> proluit; insolitae fugiunt in flumina phocae.
> interit et curuis frustra defensa latebris
> uipera et attoniti squamis astantibus hydri.   545
> ipsis est aer auibus non aequus, et illae
> praecipites alta uitam sub nube relinquunt.
>
> (Virgil, *Georgics* 3.537–47)

The wolf does not prowl around sheepfolds or make night raids upon flocks; a more desperate concern subdues him. Timorous does and swift-fleeing stags now wander about amongst the dogs and round the houses. The offspring of the measureless sea and every kind of swimming creature are washed ashore like the bodies of drowned men. Seals leave their usual habitat and take flight up rivers. The viper dies, fortified in vain in its curved lair. So does the watersnake, its scales standing up in horror. The air is fatal even to the birds who fall headlong leaving their lives beneath the high clouds.

This is a tissue of paradoxes and contrasts, of pathos and anthropo-morphism. *The wolf*, the arch-predator, is no longer a predator. A sharper need than hunger subdues him. *The deer*, proverbially nervous, are now fearless because dogs and human beings are too sick to bother about them. This proposition seems to be built partly on the sound observation that deer do come close to houses in snowy weather, but the search for paradox and contrast has led Virgil into a slight absurdity. The animal out of its natural habitat is a frequent and effective paradox in Latin poetry[8] but in propounding a world of sick wolves and dogs, Virgil seems to have supposed for no good reason that deer would be immune. Virgil's wolves are surely nearer the truth here. So is Lucretius in stating that wild animals did not come out of the forests during the plague at Athens, because they were sick and dying. Line 541 is a great roller of a line suggesting the vastness of the *fish* population and their expertise in swimming; 542–3 shows them washed ashore like drowned men. Pathos and paradox again. *Seals* in rivers, like deer near houses, is an observation of natural phenomenon, and Virgil has built motivation into the observation, suggesting that they have come into rivers to escape the pollution of their normal habitat, forgetting again that there is no reason to suppose that the rivers would be less infectious than the sea, or that seals would be less affected than fish. *Vipers* die. The contrast here is between their death and the elaboration of their fortifications. *Watersnakes* die too. Watersnakes have bristling scales. The paradox and the anthropomorphism here are in Virgil's suggestion that the scales are bristling with shock at the plague like the hair of an epic hero (*arrectaeque horrore comae, Aeneid* 4.280). Just as the sea was fatal to fish, so by a similar process the air is fatal to *birds*, but now at the end of this section, having toured earth, sea, under the earth, and the air, Virgil leaves his paradoxes and contrasts and produces an image of sheer poetry. According to familiar Pythagorean doctrine, when we die our bodies are returned to earth and our soul rises eventually to rejoin the divine soul, the aether, which envelops the universe. So the birds fall headlong, but they leave their share of breath in the air to go direct to reunion with God. Virgil in a later work makes the concept more explicit when a dove falls, *uitamque reliquit in astris* | *aetheriis* (*Aeneid* 5.517–18). This daring eschatological conceit is entirely Virgilian, but it includes Lucretian elements. *Aer . . . non aequus* owes something to phrases like *aer inimicus* which occur in Lucretius 1117–24 and to the description at 6.738–45 of the air above Avernus which is hostile to birds (*auibus contraria*) and makes them fall dead in mid flight (*praecipitesque cadunt molli ceruice profusae*). But there we find keen visualization of the physical implications of such a fall, as the necks lose their aerodynamic tautness, and the bodies fall forward along the line of flight with the curve of their fall like the curve of a liquid being poured.

This is an example of the important phenomenon we have already noted. The cattle plague in Virgil is based primarily upon the plague at Athens in Lucretius, but Virgil intersperses into his cattle plague reminiscences of other parts of Lucretius.

Another Virgilian pattern of thought, less commonly observed, is his tendency to carry his paradoxes towards the point of absurdity. In the lines which follow (531–3) the use of unmatched, wild oxen to draw the chariots of Juno is such an arresting proof of the dearth of domesticated beasts that we may not pause to wonder how these *uri* were immune when all around them were affected. But scrabbling with the nails to plant seeds (534–6) is surely a nonsense. The plague does not infect agricultural implements.

In our search for the Virgilian in Virgil we have found pathos and paradox, vivid observation, a keen sympathy with animals, the attribution of human feelings to them, and a tendency to absurd extremities of fancy. But even here, in Virgil's animal symptomology, where he had to take leave of his Lucretian model, he draws heavily upon the human symptomology of Lucretius, and also on completely different passages in Lucretius, without worrying about the coherence of the symptoms or their clinical verisimilitude.

4 VIRGIL'S CONCLUSION

praeterea iam nec mutari pabula refert,
quaesitaeque nocent artes; cessere magistri,
Phillyrides Chiron Amythaoniusque Melampus.   550
saeuit et in lucem Stygiis emissa tenebris
pallida Tisiphone Morbos agit ante Metumque,
inque dies auidum surgens caput altius effert.
balatu pecorum et crebris mugitibus amnes
arentesque sonant ripae collesque supini.   555
iamque cateruatim dat stragem atque aggerat ipsis
in stabulis turpi dilapsa cadauera tabo,
donec humo tegere ac foueis abscondere discunt.
nam neque erat coriis usus, nec uiscera quisquam
aut undis abolere potest aut uincere flamma;   560
ne tondere quidem morbo inluuieque peresa
uellera nec telas possunt attingere putris;
uerum etiam inuisos si quis temptarat amictus,

ardentes papulae atque immundus olentia sudor
membra sequebatur, nec longo deinde moranti   565
tempore contactos artus sacer ignis edebat.

                    (Virgil, *Georgics* 3.548–66)

*And then there was no advantage in changing diet. All the arts
men applied made things worse. The master physicians gave up,
Chiron son of Phillyra, and Melampus son of Amythaon. The
pale Fury Tisiphone emerged from the darkness of Styx and
raved in the light, driving pestilence and panic before her,
and raising her greedy head higher every day. The rivers and their
parched banks and the slopes of the hills resounded with the
ceaseless bleating of flocks and lowing of cattle. And now she was
dealing death in troops and heaping decomposing carcases in the
very stalls, until men learned to bury them in trenches in the
ground. For the hides were not usable and they could not be
sterilized in water or cauterized with flame. The fleeces could
not even be sheared because they were eaten away with disease
and filth and men could not put a hand to the rotten cloth hanging
on their looms. If anybody tried to put on these loathsome
clothes, his body would begin to smell and be afflicted by burning
pustules and filthy sweat, and in no time the sacred fire would be
feeding upon his infected body.*

Lucretius' account of the plague at Athens continues, after the
symptomology, with an account of the corpses (wild animals did not
eat them, or died if they did). This is followed by an account of the
social effects of the plague (1230–51) and then by a description
of the scenes in the country and the city (1252–86). None of this is
directly helpful to Virgil in his account of a cattle plague. Once again,
therefore, the ending is to a large extent independent composition.
But independent as it is, once again many of its elements can be found
in Lucretius' assertion that one man's remedy was fatal to others (1227–
9). Virgil's failure of the medical arts is like *mussabat tacito medicina
timore* (Lucretius 1179) but without the fear and the muttering in
pregnant juxtaposition with the silence. Instead Virgil has a line of
four rolling Greek mythological names, referring to the archetypal
herbalist and the archetypal healer by spells. Melampus adds, in effect, a
characteristic religious element to Virgil's account. And Tisiphone is
another religious addition entirely in consonance with Virgil's use of
mythology in didactic epic, and entirely foreign to Lucretius' practice.
Yet even here Tisiphone raises her greedy head ('*auidum* caput') and

87

Lucretius has written in 1236 about the greedy disease (*'auidi* contagia morbi'). The metaphorical head appears in the assault on religion in his preface, *caput a caeli regionibus ostendebat*, 1.83. *Cateruatim* is used in Virgil only here, in l. 556, but we have seen the dialectical importance of the word at Lucretius 1144 (cf. 1092). The climax and conclusion of this episode in the *Georgics* is the spread of the cattle plague to human beings and there almost every word is traceable to something in Lucretius. For *ardentes* compare 1172 and 1180. For *papulae* compare the *ulcera* mentioned at 1166. For sweat see 1187. For stench (of breath in Lucretius) see 1155. For *contactos* see 1236 (just quoted). For *artus sacer ignis edebat* compare Lucretius 1167 *ut est per membra sacer cum diditur ignis*. There is also a typical distinction. Lucretius is comparing the ulceration to erysipelas, the holy fire or accursed fire, *sacer ignis*, and this is clinically a useful comparison. In Virgil the pustules are not compared to erysipelas, they are said to *be* the *sacer ignis*. Virgil suggests that the disease was erysipelas, or included it, or else perhaps he is using the technical term loosely and emotively, 'the accursed fire'. Lucretius is more cautious.

So much for an examination of the plague in *Georgics* 3 in the light of the plague in Lucretius 6. We have isolated many Virgilian traits – rhetorical elaboration (mainly antithesis, polar tension, paradox, absurd extremes); emotional tone (the emotion being often a pity for animal life), anthropomorphism, religion, moralization and a tendency to write for effect, and lose sight of truth. In Lucretius we found a greater concern with the accurate description of observable phenomena.

It is salutary to remember that the Lucretius is as closely modelled upon Thucydides as Virgil is on Lucretius and that scholars who have compared the two find in Lucretius a straining for effect, rhetorical elaboration, emotionalism and moralization.[9] This surprise ending may suggest that these comparative analyses are extremely illuminating, and dangerous. Virgil is rhetorical by comparison with Lucretius. This does not mean that it is helpful to say that Virgil is rhetorical, or Lucretius not rhetorical. Lucretius is emotional by comparison with Thucydides. But it would be misleading to say, *tout court*, that Lucretius is emotional or that Thucydides is dispassionate. A comparison with Greek medical writings shows that Thucydides' account of the plague is dramatic and compassionate and poetic, artistically patterned to demonstrate Thucydides' view of history.[10] The characteristics elicited by comparison are valid as comparisons, not by themselves.

5

C. W. Macleod

HORATIAN *IMITATIO* AND *ODES* 2.5

I HORATIAN 'IMITATIO'

Horace's ambition in the *Odes* as he states it at the end of the first poem is to have himself ranked with the lyric writers of ancient Greece. To join them, he had to imitate them. Imitation can have many levels; and the relation Horace indicates to the reader between his own work and the Greek lyrists' covers a wide variety of connections. Most obvious of these is the reproduction of lyric metres, above all the Sapphic and Alcaic stanzas. Likewise obvious are verbal echoes, especially those which begin a poem: thus in *Odes* 1.18 or 1.37 the first words translate the first words of poems of Alcaeus; or the description of winter and the invitation to drink which begin *Odes* 1.9 contain elements taken from another Alcaean opening. We can count on it that *Odes* which start in this way develop very differently from the Greek poem they allude to; but it is not only in such divergences that Horace shows himself original. For imitation itself can be conceived as a form of originality. This is in Horace's case partly because to imitate Sappho and Alcaeus is a novel thing to do:

> ... hunc fidibus nouis,
> hunc Lesbio sacrare plectro
>   teque tuasque decet sorores (*Odes* 1.26.10–12)

> princeps Aeolium carmen ad Italos
> deduxisse modos (*Odes* 3.30.13–14)

> hunc [*sc.* Alcaeum] ego, non alio dictum prius ore, Latinus
> uolgaui fidicen (*Epistles* 1.19.32f.)

But these same passages also tell us something more: that for Horace acknowledging his debt to his predecessors is also a way of characterizing completely, if summarily, his own achievement as a lyric poet.[1]

Horace's own words suggest, then, that what he imitates is not merely metres or lines or poems of Alcaeus, but a whole poet. So his work naturally embodies a concept of Alcaeus, one which corresponds to the Latin poet's own character and purposes. Indeed the model is not only imitated: it is itself modelled by the mind of the imitator, who is both creative and critical: creative in regenerating his exemplar, critical in distinguishing what is worthy of imitation in it.[2] Horace had already done this with Lucilius. In the programmatic *Satires* (1.4, 1.10, 2.1) different qualities of Lucilius are taken as exemplary (and distinguished from those which are not); and each of them corresponds to an aspect of Horace's own work, which is also, as a whole, a renewal of the genre of Lucilian satire.

So it is worth considering Horace's portrayal of Alcaeus in the *Odes* for what it reveals about the Latin poet's conception of himself and his aims. In *Odes* 1.32 Horace addresses his 'lyre':

> Poscimus, si quid uacui sub umbra
> lusimus tecum, quod et hunc in annum
> uiuat et pluris, age dic Latinum,
>   barbite, carmen,
>
> Lesbio primum modulate ciui,
> qui ferox bello, tamen inter arma
> sive iactatam religarat udo
>   litore nauim,
>
> Liberum et Musas Veneremque et illi
> semper haerentem puerum canebat
> et Lycum nigris oculis nigroque
>   crine decorum.
>
> o decus Phoebi et dapibus supremi
> grata testudo Iouis, o laborum
> dulce lenimen medicumque,[3] salue
>   rite uocanti. (*Odes* 1.32.1–15)

I pray, if ever at ease in the shade I played with you something that might live through this and later years, come, strike up a Latin song, lyre first tuned by the citizen of Lesbos, that fierce fighter who still in the midst of war, or when he had moored on the watery shore his storm-tossed ship, sang of Bacchus and the Muses and Venus, and of the boy [Cupid] who forever clings to her, and of Lycus with his beautiful black eyes and black hair. Pride of Phoebus, joy of the banquets of Jupiter the king, pleasant and soothing antidote to suffering, hail as I duly call upon you.

The lyre is invoked like the Muse, a solemn and Pindaric motif;[4] its songs are to last for years; it is the pride and pleasure of gods. The lyre, then, represents the inspiration and grandeur of lyric. At the same time, for Alcaeus – who, like Horace, dealt with both politics and wine or love in his poetry – it was a pleasant antidote to his labours. This too is part of the dignity of lyric (cf. *Ars poetica* 405–7). Likewise for Horace, to be a poet is to be one who knows how to make the most of life's sensuous enjoyments amidst its cares (e.g. *Odes* 1.26, 2.3); and thus in both the Greek and the Latin poet long-lasting inspiration and everyday humanity combine to produce work that both pleases and elevates.

Odes 2.13 begins with a curse on the tree which nearly crushed Horace to death on his Sabine estate; the poem then reflects that whatever our precautions, sudden death can always carry us off. It goes on (21–40):

> quam paene furuae regna Proserpinae
> et iudicantem uidimus Aeacum
>   sedesque discretas piorum et
>   Aeoliis fidibus querentem
>
> Sappho puellis de popularibus,
> et te sonantem plenius aureo,
>   Alcaee, plectro dura nauis,
>   dura fugae mala, dura belli!
>
> utrumque sacro digna silentio
> mirantur umbrae dicere; sed magis
>   pugnas et exactos tyrannos
>   densum umeris bibit aure uulgus.
>
> quid mirum, ubi illis carminibus stupens
> demittit atras belua centiceps
>   auris et intorti capillis
>   Eumenidum recreantur angues?
>
> quin et Promethus et Pelopis parens
> dulci laborem decipitur sono,
>   nec curat Orion leones
>   aut timidos agitare lyncas.

How nearly I saw the realm of dusky Persephone, and Aeacus giving judgement, and the separate dwelling-place of the just, and Sappho complaining on Aeolian strings of the girls of her homeland, and you, Alcaeus, making grander music with your

C. W. Macleod

*golden plectrum from the hardships of the sea, the hardships of
exile, the hardships of war. The astonished shades hear both of
them in the reverent silence they deserve, but the packed crowd
drinks in more eagerly the tale of battles and tyrants driven out.
No wonder, when those songs cause the hundred-headed beast
[Cerberus] to lower his black ears in amazement, and refresh the
snakes twined in the Furies' hair. At the pleasant sound, even
Prometheus' and Tantalus' sufferings are beguiled and Orion
loses the will to chase lions and fleeting lynxes.*

Here love-poetry is ascribed to Sappho, while Alcaeus represents only
political poetry. The grandeur of his songs charms the shades as
Orpheus, the archetype of poetic inspiration, did. Horace claims a
kind of divine inspiration for himself in the *Odes*, especially as a political poet (cf. 3.4, 3.25); here, as elsewhere, he links such proud claims
with the recognition that he is also an ordinary man.[5] Like everyone, he
is subject to death at any moment; but his art outlasts it, even in some
sense raises him above common mortality.[6] And yet Alcaeus' art,
which elevates and refreshes its audience, is also the record of hard-
ship and struggle.[7] So too some of Horace's grandest *Odes* are those
which express gloom or anxiety about his country (e.g. 1.2, 2.1, 3.3,
3.6). Just as in 1.32 the poet's inspiration was bound up with the
man's pleasures, so in 2.13 with his own or his city's troubles.

Finally, *Epistles* 1.19.21–33 where Horace looks back over his
achievement in the *Epodes* and *Odes*:

> Libera per uacuum posui uestigia princeps,
> non aliena meo pressi pede. qui sibi fidet
> dux reget examen. Parios ego primus iambos
> ostendi Latio, numeros animosque secutus
> Archilochi, non res et agentia uerba Lycamben.
> ac ne me foliis ideo breuioribus ornes
> quod timui mutare modos et carminis artem:
> temperat Archilochi Musam pede mascula Sappho,
> temperat Alcaeus, sed rebus et ordine dispar,
> nec socerum quaerit quem uersibus oblinat atris,
> nec sponsae laqueum famoso carmine nectit;
> hunc ego, non alio dictum prius ore, Latinus
> uulgaui fidicen.

*I trod like a free man, a pioneer, over unoccupied territory; I did
not follow in others' footsteps. The man who is sure of himself*

92

will lead the swarm. I was the first to bring the Parian iambus into Latium: I followed the metre and the spirit of Archilochus, but not his matter and his words that hound Lycambes. And in case you should reduce my laurels because I was afraid to change his metre and technique: Archilochus' muse was controlled by manly Sappho and controlled by Alcaeus, though he differs in matter and economy; he does not look for a father-in-law to smear with poisoned verses nor plait in lampoons a noose for his bride; and it was he, unsung by previous lips, that I diffused in Latin lyrics.[8]

This account of the *Odes* reflects, needless to say, the concerns of the *Epistles*: in a book entirely devoted to Horace's search for wisdom, in which the practice of poetry is seen in its relation to right living, Alcaeus becomes above all an ethical exemplar. He is not afraid to be original, 'free', as Horace himself was already to some degree in the *Epodes*; and he restrains the malice and violence of his predecessor. However, the contrast of Alcaeus and Archilochus also suggests something true about the spirit of the *Odes* as opposed to the *Epodes*. For vituperation plays a much smaller part in the latter book than in the earlier one; one of the *Odes*, 1.16, is in fact a farewell to such poetry. Further, the *Odes* are more concerned with stating an ideal of life, one in which friendship, as opposed to the hostility associated with the *Epodes*, figures prominently.[9]

What counts, then, about Alcaeus as portrayed in Horace's writing is less his techniques or products than the poetic inspiration and the human being that his work contains. He becomes not merely a model, but a matrix, one from which Horace can produce different images of his own work. Thus he is to the Latin author not only a unique individual but also the lyrist, even the poet, *par excellence*; and in imitating him, Horace imitates as much as anything his originality or independence.

Now all this, if true, has consequences for the understanding of particular *Odes* in their relation to particular Greek poems. First, we may expect the presence of Greek lyric (both Alcaeus and others) to be pervasive, but thoroughly transmuted; and less than obvious analogies may be more revealing than close verbal ones.[10] And indeed in Horace, or any poet worth the name, influences are absorbed, not merely displayed. Second, imitation of Alcaeus, or of any single lyric poet, in no way excludes imitation of anyone else in the same place. 'Anyone else' means in the first instance other lyric poets; but it may also be extended to cover, for example, Hellenistic epigrams. That should not be seen as a contrast to imitation of the archaic lyrists, but rather, since the tradition of Greek personal poetry flows down from lyric into epigram, as its natural accompaniment.[11]

So in dealing with *Odes* 2.5 I have quoted a wide variety of passages and poems, not from a firm conviction that all of them were in Horace's mind as he wrote, but rather in order to sketch the tradition he worked in and illustrate his relation to it through precise analogies and contrasts. I shall not be concerned to prove that Horace had in mind this or that Greek poem; for such proofs can rarely be given. But if we examined the influence of earlier poetry on Horace only through quite obvious echoes, that would be unfaithful to the poet's aims and methods. The study of *imitatio*, then, should not be sharply distinct from the study of poems in their literary tradition through critical comparison and analysis. And this principle is not a merely theoretical postulate; the very nature of the object, poetic creation, demands it.

2   ODES 2.5

Nondum subacta ferre iugum ualet
ceruice, nondum munia comparis
   aequare nec tauri ruentis
     in uenerem tolerare pondus.

circa uirentis est animus tuae
campos iuuencae, nunc fluuiis grauem
   solantis aestum, nunc in udo
     ludere cum uitulis salicto

praegestientis. tolle cupidinem
immitis uuae: iam tibi liuidos
   distinguet autumnus racemos
     purpureo uarius colore.

iam te sequetur: currit enim ferox
aetas et illi quos tibi dempserit
   apponet annos; iam proterua
     fronte petet Lalage maritum,

dilecta quantum non Pholoe fugax,
non Chloris albo sic umero nitens
   ut pura nocturno renidet
     luna mari, Cnidiusue Gyges,

quem si puellarum insereres choro,
mire sagaces falleret hospites
discrimen obscurum solutis
crinibus ambiguoque uultu.

Not yet is she strong enough to bear the yoke on her neck, broken in, not yet to do equal duty with a mate or take the weight of the bull charging into sex. Your heifer's mind is on green fields: now she soothes in rivers the burdensome heat, now she plays with calves in a watery clump of osiers, eager and frisky. Put away desire for the unripe grape; soon autumn will pick out for you the darkening clusters with its diverse shades of purple. Soon she will come after you; for fierce time runs on and will add to her account the years it has deducted from yours: soon Lalage will level her wanton forehead at a husband, she whom you love more than the elusive Pholoe, more than Chloris, whose white shoulder shines like the moon shimmering on the sea by night, or Cnidian Gyges, who, set in a troupe of girls, would take in the most perceptive of strangers, blurring the distinction with his flowing hair and ambiguous face.

Horace's opening image, with its playful eroticism, is related to a poem of Anacreon; both poets compare the girl to an animal which is still 'frisking about' in the meadows and has yet to be 'mounted':

πῶλε Θρηικίη, τί δή με
λοξὸν ὄμμασι βλέπουσα
νηλέως φεύγεις, δοκεῖς δέ
μ' οὐδὲν εἰδέναι σοφόν;
ἴσθι τοι, καλῶς μὲν ἄν τοι
τὸν χαλινὸν ἐμβάλοιμι,
ἡνίας δ' ἔχων στρέφοιμί
σ' ἀμφὶ τέρματα δρόμου·
νῦν δὲ λειμῶνάς τε βόσκεαι
κοῦφά τε σκιρτῶσα παίζεις,
δεξιὸν γὰρ ἱπποπείρην
οὐκ ἔχεις ἐπεμβάτην.

(Anacreon 72 Page)

Thracian filly, why do you, throwing sidelong glances, avoid me relentlessly? Do you think I am so simple? Make no mistake, I will put the bit on you properly, and with the reins in my hands will guide you round the corners of the race-course. But now you pasture on the meadows and frisk about nimbly; for you do not have a skilled rider to mount you.[12]

But whereas Anacreon speaks to the girl, Horace speaks to her wooer· Who is the man? In theory he could simply be someone anonymous· But elsewhere in the *Odes* the addressee, if not named, is otherwise clearly distinct from the poet (1.16, 2.18, cf. *Epodes* 4, 6, 8, 12). Here this is not so; and the list of past loves would make the poet unusually well informed if they were not his own. Conversely, Horace sometimes recalls by name, in his character as an aging or retired lover, former amours of his (*Odes* 1.5, 1.33, 4.13); and an epigram by Meleager (quoted below) is a version of that motif to which *Odes* 2.5.17–24 is quite close. Moreover, if Horace is the lover here, that produces a pleasingly ironic contrast to the end of *Odes* 2.4, where he had declared himself past it; and in general, the two poems seem to make a balancing pair: in 2.4 Horace imagines a friend 'marrying' a slave-girl, in 2.5 himself 'mating' with someone better. But if it is not made entirely clear that Horace is speaking to himself, that has its point. Explicit self-address on the part of a lover goes easily with self-pity or self-dramatization:[13] thus for example Catullus (8.1f.)

> miser Catulle, desinas ineptire
> et quod uides perisse perditum ducas

> *Catullus, you poor wretch, stop being a fool and treat what you can see is gone as lost*

or Propertius (2.8.17f.)

> sic igitur prima moriere aetate, Properti?
> sed morere; interitu gaudeat illa tuo!

> *So you will die in your youth then, Propertius? Go on, die! Let her rejoice in your death!*

Such a note would jar in this poem, and indeed is foreign to Horace in general. Sappho too avoids it: in her poem 1 it is Aphrodite who with the smiling superiority of a goddess calls her by name, and who with a faintly mocking repetition utters the 'again' (δηὖτε) that the Greek lyrists so often use of themselves in love:[14]

> σὺ δ', ὦ μάκαιρα,
> μειδιαίσαισ' ἀθανάτῳ προσώπῳ
> ἤρε' ὄττι δηὖτε πέπονθα κὤττι
> δηὖτε κάλημμι

κὤττι μοι μάλιστα θέλω γένεσθαι
μαινόλαι θύμῳ· τίνα δηὖτε πείθω
.].σάγην ἐς σὰν φιλότατα; τίς σ᾽, ὦ
Ψάπφ᾽, ἀδικήει;

καὶ γὰρ αἰ φεύγει, ταχέως διώξει,
αἰ δὲ δῶρα μὴ δέκετ᾽, ἀλλὰ δώσει,
αἰ δὲ μὴ φίλει, ταχέως φιλήσει
κωὐκ ἐθέλοισα

(Sappho ll. 13–24 Lobel–Page)

. . . . *And you, blessed goddess, with a smile on your immortal
face, asked what was the matter with me again, why I was
calling again, what was my maddened heart's desire. 'Whom
shall I coax again . . . into loving you? Who, Sappho, is doing
you wrong? For if she avoids you, she will soon come after you;
if she does not take gifts, she will give them; if she does not love,
she will soon love, whether she like it or not.'*

Horace's admonitory tone, which distinguishes *Odes* 2.5 from Anacreon 72, and his image of the grapes owe something to a piece by
Alcaeus which seems to tell an aging person to give up love:

Τίς τ᾽ ὦ πον[
εἴπη[. . . .] . [
παρέσκεθ᾽ ᾧ[
    δαίμον᾽ ἀναίτιο[

δεύοντος οὐδέν· καὶ [γὰ]ρ ἀνοιΐ[ας
τὰς σᾶς ἐ.[.]υ.[᾽]σ᾽ ἀλλ᾽ ἔμ[ε]θεν συ[
παυσαι, κάκων δε[. . . . .]όντω[ν
    αἴ τι δύναι κατεχ[. . . . .]ο·

σοὶ μὲν γ]ὰρ ἤ[δ]η περβέβα[τ]αι χρό[νος
κ]αὶ κάρπος ὄσσ[ο]ς ἦς συνα[γ]άγρετ[αι
τὸ κλᾶμμα δ᾽ ἐλπώρα, κάλον γά[ρ,
    ο]ὐκ ὀλ[ί]γαις σταφύλαις ἐνείκη[ν

. . .]ψ[.], τοιαύτας γὰρ ἀπ᾽ ἀμπέ[λω
. . . .]υς γ . . . . . .ι σκοπιάμ[
τά]ρβημι μὴ δρόπ[ω]σιν αὖταις
    ὄμφ]ακας ὠμοτέραις ἐοίσαις.

..]τοι γὰρ οἰ τὰ πρόσθε πονήμ[ενοι
..]εσκ[ο]ν· οὐδέπ[..].τ[....].[
...]ηκε·καρτε.[........] .. [
...]ασίαν παρεχε̣[

(Alcaeus 119 Lobel–Page)

... the god who is not to blame ... when there is no need (?); for he stopped (?) your folly. But listen to me and stop; with troubles ... if you can ... For the time has come round for you now, and all the fruit that there was is gathered; but as for the shoot, there is hope that, being so fine, it will bear a good crop of grapes ... for from such a vine ... I fear they may pluck the still unripe grapes ... for those who worked (?) before ...[15]

But whereas in Alcaeus both the older and the younger person are vines, Horace is the one who will pluck the grapes (as Anacreon will mount the filly). So while Horace tempers the gay arrogance of Anacreon with the sterner mood of Alcaeus, he is still, like Anacreon, looking forward to sensual enjoyment for himself. This kind of expectation, summed up in the initial 'Not yet', is also found in two Hellenistic epigrams which begin in the same way:

οὔπω σοι καλύκων γυμνὸν θέρος οὐδὲ μελαίνει
βότρυς ὁ παρθενίους πρωτοβολῶν χάριτας,
ἀλλ᾽ ἤδη θοὰ τόξα νέοι θήγουσιν Ἔρωτες,
Λυσιδίκη, καὶ πῦρ τύφεται ἐγκρύφιον.
φεύγωμεν, δυσέρωτες, ἕως βέλος οὐκ ἐπὶ νευρῇ·
μάντις ἐγὼ μεγάλης αὐτίκα πυρκαϊῆς.

(Philodemus, *Anthologia Palatina* 5.124)

Not yet is your summer flower stripped of the bud, nor is the grape that puts out its first virgin charms yet darkening; but already the young Cupids are sharpening their swift arrows, Lysidice, and a hidden fire is smouldering. Let us run, we unlucky lovers, before the dart is on the string. I foretell soon enough a great fire.

Οὔπω τοξοφορῶν οὐδ᾽ ἄγριος ἀλλὰ νεογνός
οὑμὸς Ἔρως παρὰ τὴν Κύπριν ὑποστρέφεται
δέλτον ἔχων χρυσέην, τὰ Φιλοκράτεος δὲ Διαύλου
τραυλίζει ψυχῇ φίλτρα κατ᾽ Ἀντιγένους.

(Asclepiades, ibid. 12.162)

Not yet is my love armed with a bow or dangerous; he comes home, a tiny boy, to Venus with a golden writing-tablet in his hands; and he lisps to the soul of Diaulus the words Philocrates used to win Antigenes.[16]

Horace shares with Philodemus also the image of the grapes and the loving sensuousness with which it is expressed; but in this Greek epigram the coming grapes turn out to be, not a presage of enjoyment, but a danger-signal, and consequently that image gives way to the image of fire. This, it would seem, makes the force of Horace's opening 'Not yet' more like Asclepiades' than Philodemus': both Horace and Asclepiades are, on the face of it, simply waiting for time to do what it must do, begin their courtship and lead it to success. And just as in Asclepiades the boy's reading a love-poet is a preparation for love, so in Horace the 'heat' (*aestum*) that the heifer cools in the stream, and the frisky eagerness (*praegestientis*) which she shows in playing (*ludere*) with the calves, are the forerunners of her full readiness for sex.

But this confidence is qualified in a way that accords once more with Alcaeus, who sets together as 'vines' the two persons in his poem in order to contrast them in respect of their age. The years that time adds to Lalage, it takes from Horace: as she approaches maturity, he approaches old age. This gives an undertone of doubt and sadness to the threefold 'soon' (*iam*), which seems at first to express a calm certainty like the 'soon she will come after you' (ταχέως διώξει = *iam te sequetur*) of the goddess in Sappho 1. A similar irony attaches, in fact, to Sappho's threefold 'again': if Aphrodite has come to help her yet once more, that shows how firm the divine favour is and suggests that Sappho's prayer will be granted; but by the same token it means that because she is forever in need of such help, she is forever an unhappy lover. So it is that Horace exploits the full meaning of Alcaeus' image: what pictures sexual pleasure also pictures the passage of time. The autumnal grape of ll. 10–12 does both these things; likewise the echo of ll. 3–4 in 13–14: the bull 'charges into sex' but 'fierce time runs on'.[17] The detail here is reminiscent of the epigrammatist Alkaios:

Πρώταρχος καλός ἐστι, καὶ οὐ θέλει· ἀλλὰ θελήσει
ὕστερον· ἡ δ' ὥρη λαμπάδ' ἔχουσα τρέχει.
(Alkaios of Messene, *Anthologia Palatina* 12.29)

Protarchus is beautiful and unwilling. He will be willing in time; but beauty runs with a torch in its hand.

Both he and Horace speak of time 'running'. Alkaios in his homosexual love-poem uses the image of the torch-light relay-race, because that

99

was a sport practised by boys; Horace too finds an image appropriate
to his context – that of the bull he used in ll. 3–4. But in Horace it is
the poet himself from whom time is taking something away. So at
this point we may wonder whether the husband of l. 16 will be Horace
and even whether, if the heifer were in her own time to make for the
bull, the bull would by then be unable to run at her.[18]

In the last two stanzas Horace looks back instead of forward, as he
had done up till now, and remembers past loves. Similar is an epigram
by Meleager:

> Ναὶ μὰ τὸν εὐπλόκαμον Τιμοῦς φιλέρωτα κίκιννον,
>   ναὶ μυρόπνουν Δημοῦς χρῶτα τὸν ὑπναπάτην,
> ναὶ πάλιν Ἰλιάδος φίλα παίγνια, ναὶ φιλάγρυπνον
>   λύχνον, ἐμῶν κώμων πολλ᾽ ἐπιδόντα τέλη,
> βαιὸν ἔχω τό γε λειφθέν, Ἔρως, ἐπὶ χείλεσι πνεῦμα.
>   εἰ δ᾽ ἐθέλεις καὶ τοῦτ᾽, εἰπέ, καὶ ἐκπτύσομαι.
>
> (Anthologia Palatina 5.197 (cf. 198))

> *I swear by Timo's beautiful sportive curls, by Demo's perfumed
> sleep-beguiling skin, and by the love-play of Ilias, by the wakeful
> lamp that has witnessed the mysteries of my many revels – I
> have little breath left, Cupid, on my lips. But if you want that
> too, speak the word and I will give it out.*

The accumulation of names, as in the Meleager poem, carries a hint of
self-mockery: it characterizes the poet as the incorrigible lover. But
the epithets that go with them do not simply, like Meleager's, recall the
lover's pleasures; for what Horace had in the past was less than what
he envisages in the future. Pholoe was what Lalage is at the moment,
hard to get (*fugax*). The pure white moon over the black sea contrasts
with the various shades of purple in the grape-clusters on the vine.
The image recalls Sappho:

> νῦν δὲ Λύδαισιν ἐμπρέπεται γυναί-
> κεσσιν ὡς ποτ᾽ ἀελίω
> δύντος ἀ βροδοδάκτυλος †μήνα
> πάντα περ(ρ)έχοισ᾽ ἄστρα· φάος δ᾽ ἐπί-
> σχει θάλασσαν ἐπ᾽ ἀλμύραν
> ἴσως καὶ πολυανθέμοις ἀρούραις·
> ἀ δ᾽ ⟨ἐ⟩έρσα κάλα κέχυται τεθά-
> λαισι δὲ βρόδα κἄπαλ᾽ ἄν-
> θρυσκα καὶ μελίλωτος ἀνθεμώδης·
>
> (Sappho 96.6–14 Lobel–Page)

> ... *Now she shines out among the Lydian women like the rosy-fingered moon after sunset, surpassing all the stars; light spreads over the salt sea and the fields of flowers alike, dew falls lovely and roses bloom, and soft chervil and flowery melilot.*[19]

In both contexts the moon is a paradigm of beauty; but in Horace its beauty is colourless and remote. Moreover, in Sappho it shines on land as well as sea; and it is the source of dew which causes flowers to spring up. But Horace's moon shines only on the sea: it merely rejoices the eye. Finally, Gyges. Again a contrast: autumn decorates and points up (*distinguet*) the grapes with purple, while he, the epicene, would be indistinguishable (*discrimen obscurum*) in a chorus of girls. The ambiguous charms of the boy are thus contrasted with the ripening beauty of the woman. Lalage, then, will bring completeness of enjoyment; but will she come in time for Horace? The abundant imagery of the poem, which at first expresses sensuous feeling, turns out to contain also sterner reflections; and its near-crudity represents appropriately and coolly the urgency of masculine lust. So by portraying together mounting desire and declining age, *Odes* 2.5 makes a sobering statement about life.

3   CONCLUSION

In his love-poetry, Horace regularly appears as an older, even aging man. This goes with a tendency to distance passionate feelings: he is too aware that love is common to all men to be utterly absorbed in his own. Now it is natural to contrast the lover with the philosopher, the slave of passion with the master of it; and yet there is a genuinely ethical strain in Horace's love-poetry. For the experience of love is set in an understanding of life and an art of living. This could be said in some degree of all poets worth the name, but it seems particularly true of Horace because of his quality of humane detachment, which is also the essence of what rhetoricians call *ethos*.[20] It is, moreover, connected with the element of imitation in his art. For as an imitator he related himself to a whole tradition, and one in which poets present their lives and their selves to the reader. So the discrimination the imitator must exercise concerns not only the technique but the character of his models; and indeed critiques of style, which unites both these things, inevitably carry ethical implications: this truth is expressed with particular plainness in ancient criticism,[21] not least in Horace's literary *Epistles*.[22] In other words, Horace's methods as an artist would naturally complement his life as a man, in enlarging his comprehension and refining his judgement of how men respond to experience and express their responses.[23]

So the poet who in the *Epistles* turned his skills entirely to the question of how to live is present already in the *Odes*, as he was in the *Satires*; and he is revealed not merely in overt moral teaching, but more subtly and pervasively in the character that lives in the poems. This is not a solemn or superior person. He can slyly exploit his advancing years and his blameless life to further his cause as a lover (1.17; cf. 1.13); and he can wittily and ruefully recognize that he cannot escape his passions (1.19; 3.26). But it is a man who has learned what ancient admonition and consolation taught from Homer onwards: that to live with themselves and each other men must know that their desires and their frustrations or sufferings are not unique, that their humanity and their mortality are shared.[24] As elsewhere in Horace, so in *Odes* 2.5 – and all the more because it is addressed to the writer – this detachment from self, which does not mean denial of it, finds true expression.[25]

6

E. J. Kenney

IVDICIVM TRANSFERENDI

Virgil, *Aeneid* 2.469–505 and its antecedents

I

Vestibulum ante ipsum primoque in limine Pyrrhus
exsultat telis et luce coruscus aena.   470
qualis ubi in lucem coluber mala gramina pastus,
frigida sub terra tumidum quem bruma tegebat,
nunc positis nouus exuuiis nitidusque iuuenta
lubrica conuoluit sublato pectore terga
arduus ad solem et linguis micat ore trisulcis.   475
una ingens Periphas et equorum agitator Achillis,
armiger Automedon, una omnis Scyria pubes
succedunt tecto et flammas ad culmina iactant.
ipse inter primos correpta dura bipenni
limina perrumpit postisque a cardine uellit   480
aeratos, iamque excisa trabe firma cauauit
robora et ingentem lato dedit ore fenestram.
apparet domus intus et atria longa patescunt,
apparent Priami et ueterum penetralia regum,
armatosque uident stantis in limine primo.   485
at domus interior gemitu miseroque tumultu
miscetur, penitusque cauae plangoribus aedes
femineis ululant; ferit aurea sidera clamor.
tum pauidae tectis matres ingentibus errant
amplexaeque tenent postis atque oscula figunt.   490
instat ui patria Pyrrhus, nec claustra nec ipsi
custodes sufferre ualent; labat ariete crebro
ianua et emoti procumbunt cardine postes.
fit uia ui; rumpunt aditus primosque trucidant
immissi Danai et late loca milite complent.   495
non sic, aggeribus ruptis cum spumeus amnis
exiit oppositasque euicit gurgite moles,
fertur in arua furens cumulo camposque per omnis

cum stabulis armenta trahit. uidi ipse furentem
caede Neoptolemum geminosque in limine Atridas,   500
uidi Hecubam centumque nurus Priamumque per aras
sanguine foedantem quos ipse sacrauerat ignis.
quinquaginta illi thalami, spes tanta nepotum,
barbarico postes auro spoliisque superbi
procubuere; tenent Danai qua deficit ignis.   505

II

For his narrative of the Fall of Troy Virgil had no Homeric model, but the later literary tradition was both copious and diverse. This abundant material he selected and shaped as it suited his grand design, applying to it that process of discipline which was what the ancients meant by 'art'.[1] The passage chosen for discussion here is one that brilliantly illuminates the quality of Virgil's poetical craftsmanship as seen in the painstaking adaptation of themes taken from earlier poetry. Its specifically Virgilian character results from the transfiguring spell cast by his sombre but splendid imagination on what he chose to appropriate to his own uses. The spell works, in part at all events, in virtue of the shape imparted to the episode. As will be seen, it has a highly-organized and self-contained structure, carefully devised so as to manipulate the reader's sympathies by throwing into relief a central dominating idea of great power.

We may briefly remind ourselves of the situation and the story so far. The last hours of Troy are narrated as seen through the eyes of Aeneas. This was no doubt, given the plot of the *Aeneid* as Virgil decided it, a necessity; and though Virgil turned it brilliantly to account, it did pose certain technical problems, of which this passage offers an example. Aeneas quits the general mêlée when he sees the Greeks massing to assault the royal palace (434–52); he enters by a back way and mounts to the roof, where he helps to overturn a turret on to the attackers, with great execution (453–67). The check is only momentary;

ast alii subeunt, nec saxa nec ullum
telorum interea cessat genus.[2]

The assault is instantly renewed under the demoniac leadership of Neoptolemus; the Greeks burst into the palace; and Polites and Priam are ruthlessly slaughtered. All this, we are to imagine, Aeneas witnesses aghast from his coign of vantage, until (559–66) the fate of Priam suddenly puts him in mind of his own father and, looking round, he finds himself alone. *How* he sees everything that he is supposed to see it is idle to discuss. It is unnecessary to suppose, with Heinze, that Virgil meant his readers to visualize Priam's palace as a Roman house with an *atrium*, into which Aeneas would have been able to see from the roof.[3] Nor, if this was his intention, would it have at all facilitated the suspension of disbelief required of the reader at vv. 483–5, where we suddenly and without warning find ourselves seeing with the eyes of the Greeks and Neoptolemus rather than with those of Aeneas. Virgil, as Heinze acknowledges, here relies on the sheer power of imaginative projection to carry off this fine effect.[4] One would, however, suppose that the success of this technique depends on not drawing attention to it, on the poet's not going out of his way to remind the reader of Aeneas' role as narrator at precisely those points where a moment's pause for reflection might break the spell and set him on worrying about practicalities. It is therefore the more striking that Virgil appears to do just that at vv. 499–505, with a much more drastic impairment of the illusion than at vv. 483–5. That most readers (or so I should guess) notice nothing amiss there too until directed to take notice by analytically-minded scholars is a tribute to the pathetic power of Virgil's rhetoric; and perhaps the risk of their realizing that Aeneas was 'in fact' little better placed to see most of these things than Sam Weller to bear testimony to what passed between Mr Pickwick and Mrs Bardell was a small one. In at all events the second of these two (structurally connected, as will be seen) passages the risk, such as it was, was taken deliberately in order to embody an effect that Virgil had found and admired in Ennius. The breaking of the 'realistic illusion' (so to call it) must there be interpreted in the context of Virgil's indebtedness to his predecessors; and that in turn entails consideration of the structure into which his borrowings were assimilated.

III

The attack on the palace is framed by two magnificent similes.[5]

(i) *471–5*. The final assault is headed by Pyrrhus, a glittering and sinister apparition (469–70). The name by which he is identified on this, his first active appearance in the poem,[6] illustrates the symbolic role for which he is cast:[7] Pyrrhus (Πύρρος), 'the flame-coloured'. Here is the fire in which all Troy is to be consumed (624–5), personified in the slayer of her king.[8] The name is thrown into relief by its position at the end of the verse after the self-enclosing phrase 'uestibulum . . . limine' and by the following enjambment.[9] Pregnant also is the emphasis in the collocations

$$\overline{\text{uestibulum ante ipsum primo}\underline{\text{que in}} \text{ limine}}$$

'on the very threshold of the antechamber itself':[10] the 'tragic significance of the *limen*'[11] will become clear as the action develops. Another suggestive touch is the word 'exsultat'; peculiarly appropriate to Pyrrhus through complex mythological and aetiological associations.[12] But it is above all the following simile which colours Virgil's presentation of Pyrrhus–Neoptolemus.

For this comparison he drew on more than one source. First, Homer:

> ὡς δὲ δράκων ἐπὶ χειῇ ὀρέστερος ἄνδρα μένῃσι,
> βεβρωκὼς κακὰ φάρμακ᾽, ἔδυ δέ τέ μιν χόλος αἰνός,
> σμερδαλέον δὲ δέδορκεν ἑλισσόμενος περὶ χειῇ·
> ὣς Ἕκτωρ ἄσβεστον ἔχων μένος οὐχ ὑπεχώρει.
>
> *(Iliad* 22.93–6)

> *As a mountain snake confronts a man before its lair, gorged with poisons and possessed with a deadly anger, and glares terribly as it lies coiled about the lair, so did Hector hold his ground with inextinguishable courage.*

In Homer Hector awaits the onslaught of Achilles; the comparison with the snake illustrates his refusal to retreat in the face of the threat to his homeland. In Virgil the emphasis is reversed: the snake is now a symbol of aggression and it is the son of Achilles who is the aggressor, the father of Hector who is presently to be attacked. The irony of this reversal is clearly deliberate and forms part of the intended effect of the simile in its Virgilian context.[13]

Secondly, for the colouring of his description and for the aggressive characterization of the snake Virgil, in the manner of the *doctus poeta*, has drawn on a very different writer, the dry and difficult Nicander. Here three passages[14] of the *Theriaca*, Nicander's didactic poem on poisonous creatures, are laid under contribution:

> ....τῆμος ὅτ᾽ ἀζαλέων φολίδων ἀπεδύσατο γῆρας
> μῶλυς ἐπιστείβων, ὅτε φωλεὸν εἴαρι φεύγων
> ὄμμασιν ἀμβλώσσει, μαράθου δέ ἑ νήχυτος ὄρπηξ
> βοσκηθεὶς ὠκύν τε καὶ αὐγήεντα τίθησι. (31–4)

> *. . . at the time when the snake sloughs the withered scales of age, moving feebly forward, when in spring he leaves his den, and his*

sight is dim; but a meal of the fennel's sappy shoots makes him swift and bright of eye.[15]

μηδ' ὅτε ῥικνῆεν φολίδων περὶ γῆρας ἀμέρσας
ἂψ ἀναφοιτήσῃ νεαρῇ κεχαρημένος ἥβῃ. . . (137–8)

Beware too when the Viper, having doffed the wrinkled scales of age, comes abroad again exulting in his new-found youth.

οὐδ' ἄρ', ὅταν χαράδρεια λίπῃ καὶ ῥωγάδα κοίλην
ἦρος ἀεξομένου ὁπόθ' ἑρπετὰ γαῖα φαείνῃ,
ἀκρεμόνος μαράθοιο χυτὸν περιβόσκεται ἔρνος,
εὖτ' ἂν ὑπ' ἠελίοιο περὶ φλόον ἄψεα[16] βάλλῃ. . . (389–92)

Nor at spring's oncoming, after it has quitted gully and hollow cleft in the season when earth brings reptiles to light, does it browse upon the waving shoots on the fennel's branch, when it clothes its limbs with their new skin beneath the sun . . .

It is from these passages of Nicander that Virgil has culled and combined the ideas of light, hibernation and rejuvenation that play an essential part in his picture of Pyrrhus–Neoptolemus as Achilles *rediuiuus*. But he has added a further trait present in neither of his originals. For Nicander's harmless fennel he has substituted a very slightly more precise Latin version of Homer's somewhat mysterious κακὰ φάρμακα: *mala gramina*, 'evil herbs'. This may reflect yet another learned source, or learned interpretation of Homer, for Aelian records (as fact, not legend) that snakes intending to ambush a man or an animal eat poisonous roots and herbs;[17] and what is especially striking in the context of the present discussion is his ascription to them of malice aforethought. The effect of this combinatory technique is that in Virgil the period of hibernation, treated by Nicander as a time of torpor and feebleness, is transformed into an image of brooding malignity.[18]

Thirdly, Virgil has drawn on himself, borrowing vv. 473–5 almost entire from different parts of his extended description of the *chersydrus* in the third book of the *Georgics:*

> squamea conuoluens sublato pectore terga (426)
> cum positis nouus exuuiis nitidusque iuuenta (437)
> arduus ad solem et linguis micat ore trisulcis (439).

The passage in the *Georgics* is in its turn based on *Theriaca* 359–72; but for the descriptive touches borrowed for the Pyrrhus simile

Virgil may have been indebted to yet another of Nicander's snakes, his asp:[19]

ἀλλ' ὅταν ἢ δοῦπον νέον οὔασιν ἠέ τιν' αὐγήν
ἀθρήσῃ, νωθῆ μὲν ἀπὸ ῥέθεος βάλεν ὕπνον,
ὁλκῷ δὲ τροχόεσσαν ἄλων εἰλίξατο γαίῃ,
λευγαλέον δ' ἀνὰ μέσσα κάρη πεφρικὸς ἀείρει.   (164–7)

Yet when it hears some strange noise or sees a bright light, it throws off from its body dull sleep and wreathes its coil in a circular ring upon the ground, and in the midst it rears its head, bristling in deadly fashion.

Comparison with Virgil's prime source, Homer, throws light on the intentions and methods of both poets. Homer's simile is simple but extremely effective; it illuminates a single moment and a single trait of character and behaviour. The descriptive detail is confined to a single verse, so as to focus attention on the essential points of the illustration. It can be readily understood and appreciated without reference to anything outside the immediate context; and it is none the worse for that. Virgil's dazzling picture is much more elaborately, indeed ambitiously, conceived and executed. Its central intention, however, like that of Homer's, is essentially simple: it is designed to illuminate (here the *mot juste*) a single fact, that Pyrrhus is the son of Achilles, whose heroic force lives again in him.[20] Where it differs profoundly from its original is in the aura of symbolic association which Virgil's elaborate descriptive techniques diffuse around it – part of the complex network of symbolism that pervades and indeed informs the *Aeneid*. Scepticism on this point is misplaced.[21] Rather the critic ought to expect to encounter symbolism in the poem and to be surprised at its absence. Schlunk's suggestive monograph has shown that Virgil was well acquainted with the general tendencies of Alexandrian Homeric criticism. These included awareness of the role played in poetry by symbol and image, so that it is probable *à priori* that Virgil was consciously alive to the implications of his imagery.[22] The snake-imagery which, as Knox has argued in a now classic article, dominates Book 2 of the *Aeneid*, is especially and specifically appropriate to Pyrrhus–Neoptolemus as not merely the son but the reincarnation of his father Achilles.[23] These ideas were already current in the literary tradition long before Virgil.[24] Richmond has suggested that 'it is merely a coincidence that the snake has a new skin, and that the name of Neoptolemus contains the Greek word for "new" '.[25] If that were all, the argument might pass muster; but it does not exhaust the contribution made by coincidence to what Richmond regards as the misinterpretation of the simile. If Virgil did not intend his readers to make the suggested connections with the literary-mythological tradition associating the Aeacidae in general and Neoptolemus in particular with snakes,[26] it is surely a remarkable accident that led him to illustrate Neoptolemus' first active appearance in the narrative with a snake-simile, and that an especially elaborate one? The choice in itself of a snake to illustrate a warrior *attacking*, rather than the conventional lion or wolf, is unexpected, in fact unique in the *Aeneid*.[27] The fact that Homer had used the snake-simile – also, be it noted, uniquely[28] – of a hero in a posture of *defence* would hardly have sufficed in itself to recommend the idea for adaptation here. It can only have been the existence of a tradition associating snakes with the Aeacidae that suggested to Virgil his brilliant stroke of reversing the application of the simile and using it of the son of the hero who in the original context was the aggressor and the occasion, not the subject, of the comparison.

(ii) *496–9*. Pyrrhus is 'young, strong, flashing, evil';[29] in the simile of the snake with its associations, actual and mythological, Virgil conveys a sense of all that is malevolent in animal nature. This evocation of Pyrrhus' character as the *individual* incarnation of heroic *uis* divorced from all the other heroic virtues is complemented by an image of *collective* force – again presented in isolation from any other heroic or military quality – embodied in the second simile, which illustrates the irruption of the Greeks into the palace. Here too Virgil has drawn on more than one predecessor. First, again, Homer:

θῦνε γὰρ ἂμ πεδίον ποταμῷ πλήθοντι ἐοικὼς
χειμάρρῳ, ὅς τ' ὦκα ῥέων ἐκέδασσε γεφύρας·
τὸν δ' οὔτ' ἄρ τε γέφυραι ἐεργμέναι ἰσχανόωσιν,
οὔτ' ἄρα ἕρκεα ἴσχει ἀλωάων ἐριθηλέων
ἐλθόντ' ἐξαπίνης, ὅτ' ἐπιβρίσῃ Διὸς ὄμβρος.
πολλὰ δ' ὑπ' αὐτοῦ ἔργα κατήριπε κάλ' αἰζηῶν·
ὣς ὑπὸ Τυδεΐδῃ πυκιναὶ κλονέοντο φάλαγγες
Τρώων, οὐδ' ἄρα μιν μίμνον πολέες περ ἐόντες.

(*Iliad* 5.87–94)

For Diomede raged across the plain like a winter torrent in full flood, as it sweeps away the dikes in its headlong course. They cannot hold it, nor can the fences round the fertile orchards check its sudden coming, when Zeus' rain falls heavily. Many are the fair works of men that it destroys. So did Diomede drive the massed battalions of the Trojans before him, and many though they were they could not withstand him.

This passage clearly provided Virgil with the general idea and some of the details of his own simile.[30] In Homer, however, the treatment (in interesting contrast with the simile previously discussed) is relatively discursive; the emphasis moves, *via* the transition from dikes to orchard-fences, from the destructive power of the water in its course to a more generalized evocation of its eventual effects on the man-made landscape. Virgil concentrates on a single, sharply-focused image of irresistible force in action. In doing so he obviously had present to his mind a passage in the most forceful of all Latin writers, Lucretius:

> nec ratione fluunt alia stragemque propagant   280
> et cum mollis aquae fertur natura repente
> flumine abundanti, quam largis imbribus auget
> montibus ex altis magnus decursus aquai,
> fragmina coniciens siluarum arbustaque tota,
> nec ualidi possunt pontes uenientis aquai   285
> uim subitam tolerare: ita magno turbidus imbri
> molibus incurrit ualidis cum uiribus amnis.
> dat sonitu magno stragem uoluitque sub undis
> grandia saxa, ruit qua quidquid fluctibus obstat.

(*De rerum natura* 1.280–9)

This too is clearly modelled on the simile in the *Iliad*;[31] Lucretius has considerably enlarged the scale of the original, but he has at the same time contracted its scope. The description, ample as it is, concentrates on the single idea that he is seeking to convey, that of the force exerted by wind, the invisible explained on the analogy of the visible. The comparison with Virgil is instructive, showing, in Austin's excellent formulation, 'Lucretius' immense power and (by contrast) Virgil's tautness'.[32] The word 'taut' is well chosen. By Augustan standards Lucretius' treatment is diffuse; the composition is monumental and the effects broad, depending less on the artful placing of this or that element than on a swelling accumulation of quite simple but weighty words and phrases. The writing is almost formulaic, in the poet's 'linear' style, with the argument – for he writes to convince by impressing, not merely to impress – strongly articulated by the verse.[33] Virgil has condensed and distilled both his originals in a single tightly-constructed sentence which deserves detailed analysis:

non sic, aggeribus ruptis cum spumeus amnis
exiit oppositasque euicit gurgite moles,
fertur in arua furens cumulo camposque per omnis
cum stabulis armenta trahit.

non sic: 'not so (irresistibly)'; the brief adverbial phrase formally carries the entire weight of the following comparison. Cf. *qualis* at v. 471. Neither here nor in the previous simile is there any resumptive/ correlative phrase in the manner of Homer or of Lucretius' 'sic igitur debent . . .' (290).

aggeribus ... moles: the first half of the simile consists of a subordinate clause framed by two words of almost but not completely identical sense (cf. 493 'ianua . . . postes'), which might at first glance seem to stand for the two banks which are powerless to confine the river. However, the word *agger* has the specific notion of a dike or levée designed to confine the stream, whereas *moles* suggests the more general idea of any barrier that may be opposed to the floodwaters in their course.[34] The clause thus exemplifies Virgilian 'theme and variation'; the idea in 'aggeribus ruptis' is taken up and expanded in the words that follow the graphic 'exiit', the description so to say growing and developing with the thing described.

exiit ... euicit: the verbs complement and reinforce each other. The enjambment in 'amnis | exiit', with diaeresis[35] following, expresses the sudden collapse of the containing bank and the subsequent surge, and the strong molossus $(- - -)$ 'euicit' suggests the sustained and irresistible power of the released water. To this effect the treatment of the caesura, obscured by the elided *-que*, also contributes. Virgil no doubt chose *euinco* partly for the sake of its military connotations, here obviously appropriate, partly for the sound of *ui* in 'euīcit' (cf. 494 'fit uia ui'), partly for the sake of the reiterated prefix *e-*, a device characteristic of Lucretius; he is in fact the first Latin poet, so far as we know, to use this compound.

fertur ... trahit: just as the subordinate clause was framed by two nouns embodying the idea of obstruction, so the main clause is framed by two verbs, one passive and one active, suggesting the uncontrollable course of the waters once the barriers are broken. The impression of force is assisted by the alliteration: '*f*ertur . . . *f*urens *c*umulo *c*ampos'.

camposque ... trahit: repeated, with 'trahit' for 'tulit', from *Georgics* 1.482–3, a description of the Po in flood which forms part of a list of portents. Virgil has combined ideas from the beginning of the Homeric (θῦνε γὰρ ἄμ πεδίον) and the end of the Lucretian passages ('ruit qua quidquid ... obstat'). As in Lucretius, the image of indiscriminate destruction provides the simile with a summarizing climax. Here, however, it has an additional dramatic function, to prepare for the abrupt transition in mid-verse back to the horrors of the Sack, and to this end Virgil is specific where Lucretius generalizes. 'Cum stabulis armenta', things animate and inanimate alike, brings us back to the palace and its inhabitants.

This sentence containing the simile moves rapidly, with strong enjambment between vv. 495–6 and 497–8, and it ends, as has just been noted, abruptly. This effect reproduces the speed with which events move after Pyrrhus has smashed down the doors. At one moment the Greeks are still outside; at the next the barriers are down and the palace fills to its uttermost extent with the human tide:

late loca milite complent.

The collective singular 'milite', suggesting an undifferentiated mass of soldiery flooding into every corner, and the phrase 'late loca', suggesting a wide expanse of countryside, prepare the way for the following simile as neatly as the end of the simile in its turn prepares for the transition back to the narrative. This is a *tour de force* of densely effective writing: every word, almost every syllable, contributing to the whole.

IV

Two other passages call for discussion in the light of their literary antecedents, certain or probable.

(i) *486–95.* On v. 486 Servius comments: 'AT DOMVS INTERIOR de Albano excidio translatus est locus.' Scholiasts who tell us that a whole passage is 'taken' from somewhere else are not always as precise as might be wished.[36] Here, however, collateral evidence is available. The destruction of Alba Longa by Tullus Hostilius is narrated by Livy in a highly-coloured passage which offers certain obvious, though it must also be added superficial, similarities with Virgil:

> Quae [*sc.* legiones] ubi intrauere portas, non quidem fuit *tumultus* ille nec *pauor* qualis captarum esse urbium solet, cum *effractis portis* stratisue *ariete* muris aut arce *ui* capta *clamor* hostilis et cursus per urbem *armatorum* omnia ferro flammaque *miscet*, sed silentium triste ... ut ... nunc *in liminibus* starent, nunc *errabundi* domos suas ultimum illud uisuri peruagarentur

... *uocesque* etiam *miserabiles* exaudiebantur *mulierum*. (Livy 2.29.2–3, 5)

It is generally accepted that both Livy and Virgil were indebted here to Ennius' *Annales*; Ennius in his turn must have drawn for his poetical colouring on a Greek source now lost such as Arctinus' *Iliupersis*.[37] How far the 'locus' referred to by Servius is to be taken as extending is uncertain; Norden detected Ennian coloration in 'fit uia ui' and 'late loca',[38] and the ambiguous 'ariete' – to be read literally meaning 'battering-ram' or figuratively meaning 'battering'? – may have been transferred from an originally more appropriate context such as that in which it is found in Livy.[39]

However, speculation about the precise extent and character of Virgil's debt to Ennius is unprofitable. What can be said with assurance is that his treatment of the well-worn commonplace 'pauor qualis captarum esse urbium solet' is condensed and selective. He concentrates on what were clearly, as the passage of Livy shows, conventional motifs: confusion, the noise of wailing women,[40] and the last farewells to the doomed home. But these evidently standard elements are carefully adapted to the requirements of their new context. The grammatical subject of the first part of the sentence, 'at domus ... ululant', is the palace itself, which is thus made to cry out under Pyrrhus' brutal assault as a woman screams when she is violated.[41] The implication that the sack of the palace is a kind of rape is allied to the symbolic role of the *limen* already mentioned. Relevant here also (though the detail itself is traditional: Apollonius, *Argonautica* 4.26–7) is the emphasis on doorways in 4.490.[42]

(ii) *499–505*. Suddenly, with the urgent 'uidi ipse ... uidi', the person of the narrator re-emerges with a vengeance. In Virgil's account of the Sack of Troy it is the death of Priam that forms the climax;[43] it is this that brings home his own situation to Aeneas:

at me *tum primum* saeuus circumstetit horror (559).[44]

The narrative (506–58) of the murder of the king is managed in an 'objective' epic style which allows Aeneas to function unobtrusively as 'a mere reporter'.[45] With the passage which precedes it and completes the account of the sacking of the palace it is far otherwise: Aeneas is made to stress his own role in the drama, as anguished witness of the profanation of the inmost secret chambers of the royal family. Neoptolemus, now quite wild with the general blood-lust,[46] and the Atridae confront Hecuba and Priam: dynasty against dynasty, youth against age, force against feebleness, the future against the past, the long external threat of the ten years' siege now present and realized in the violation and destruction of the royal bridal chambers.

In writing these lines Virgil had in mind a famous passage of Ennius' *Andromacha*:

> o pater, o patria, o Priami domus,
> saeptum altisono cardine templum.
> uidi ego te adstante ope barbarica,
> tectis caelatis laqueatis,
> auro ebore instructam regifice.
> haec omnia uidi inflammari,
> Priamo ui uitam euitari,
> Iouis aram sanguine turpari.
>
> (*Scaenica* 92–9 Vahlen² = 87–93 Jocelyn)[47]

This was the passage which provoked Cicero to his well-known outburst 'o poetam egregium . . . praeclarum carmen!' (*Tusculanae disputationes* 3.45–6); he quotes or alludes to it more than once, and Plautus appears to parody it at *Bacchides* 933 'o Troia, o patria, o Pergamum, o Priame periisti senex'. Evidently it was tolerably familiar to Roman readers. It is noteworthy that Ennius makes Andromache describe Priam's palace as a 'temple enclosed by high-sounding hinges';[48] Virgil's own emphasis on ideas of violation and profanation, together with the recurrent image of the *limen*, suggests that his debt to Ennius here goes beyond purely verbal borrowings. In transferring Andromache's vision of the culminating desecration of the Sack to Aeneas, he represents the ultimate bitterness of the Trojan defeat as mirrored in the humiliation of the royal house – here identified with the secret courts and chambers of the palace, the innermost source of Trojan power, the birthplace of her past and future kings. With consummate dramatic irony this desolating vision is witnessed by the heir to Troy's renewed greatness – the hero who in the fulness of time will be revealed as the first founder of Troy resurgent – and narrated by him to the Carthaginian queen who is herself to be numbered among the victims of Rome's destiny.

v

There is general agreement among critics as to the excellent construction of *Aeneid* 2: Austin sums up succinctly in speaking of 'a noble simplicity of design'.[49] Structure and treatment alike are dramatic:

within the overall tripartite framework of the book the main emphasis falls on the long central section;[50] and within this section again the emphasis is central, on the royal palace and the fate of King Priam.[51] Our passage in turn lies at the very centre of these encircling structures and embodies a very striking example of ring-composition,[52] of a type more commonly associated with Catullus than with Virgil:[53]

469–70 (2 verses): Pyrrhus *exsultans*
  471–5 (5): Simile characterizing Pyrrhus
    476–8 (3): The Greeks attack
      479–82 (4): Pyrrhus breaches the door

        483–90 (8): THE SCENE INSIDE THE PALACE

      491–3 (3): Pyrrhus breaks down the door
    494–5 (2): The Greeks rush in
  496–9 (3 +): Simile characterizing the Greeks
499–500 (1): Neoptolemus *furens*

    500–5 (4 +): THE DESECRATION OF THE PALACE

The symmetry, though undeniable, is not obsessively arithmetical; and the transition from the figure of Neoptolemus to the concluding epitome of profanation and murder is managed with great subtlety. Two features of this final passage call for particular comment. Down to v. 499 all the periods are end-stopped; the second simile, in contrast, terminates abruptly at the fourth-foot caesura with the short word 'trahit'. This, coupled with the strong enjambment of vv. 499–500 that follows, has the effect of, so to speak, sweeping the reader into the palace on the tidal wave of the invading Greeks and bringing him abruptly face to face with the highly condensed *tableau vivant* of vv. 500–2. This itself, it may be noted, is an example of ring-composition on a small scale:

499b–500a: Neoptolemus (murderer)
  500b–501: The Atridae confront the Trojan royal family
501b–502: Priam (victim).

In assigning double duty, as it were, to Priam, as this analysis suggests, Virgil employs a kind of sleight-of-hand that is characteristic of him. Something analogous can be seen at work in the ambiguity of the words 'limine' (500) and 'postes' (504). 'Limine' would appear to refer to the outer door which Neoptolemus has been attacking; but what are the 'postes'? According to Wistrand they cannot be the doors of the *thalami*, for the reference in 'auro spoliisque superbi' must be to tro-phies of war, which are appropriate only to the main entrance.[54] Furthermore the wording of 'postes . . . procubuere' seems intended to recall 'procumbunt . . . postes' at v. 493; and the concluding phrase 'tenent Danai qua deficit ignis', picking up v. 495 and resuming the main narrative, would seem to follow naturally on a reference to the breaking down of the *outer* door. On the other hand, 'auro spoliisque' can be read as a hendiadys meaning 'plundered gold', and the syntax, with 'thalami' and 'postes' in asyndeton sharing the same verb, seems to point to the *postes* as being those of the bridal chambers. In that case the descriptive phrase in v. 504 would refer, as in the Ennian original, to the magnificent decorations of the palace interior rather than to trophies; compare 2.448 'auratas . . . trabes, ueterum decora alta parentum'. Is Virgil being deliberately ambiguous? If he is, the critic must ask why; for ambiguity in poetry is not a good *per se*. Why, at the end of a passage in which every visual detail is sharply observed and focused in his most accomplished manner, should Virgil have left the reader in this particular perplexity? At this point it may be helpful to recur to the structure of the passage.

The centrepiece of the enclosing and thematically corresponding pairs, emphasized by its length (eight verses) as well as by its centrality, has as its subject the scene within the palace. The last word of v. 482, 'fenestram', opens the door, so to say, to a fine stroke of the poet's imagination: the frenetic course of the action is miraculously suspended for a few heartbeats while the reader sees, through the eyes of the attacking Greeks,[55] Aeneas' status as narrator being momentarily forgotten, the scene revealed by the gaping hole in the door. The artistry of these verses almost defies praise. On v. 483 Austin's note can scarcely be bettered: 'The line has no strong caesura either in the third or the fourth foot, and no caesura at all in the fourth: the effect is a metrical picture of a vista, stretching far into the distance.'[56] At the end of this vista the next verse reveals the heart of the palace, the *penetralia*; v. 484 is so worded as to lift the reader on to a new plane of emotional and moral response. Pyrrhus' breach of the door is made to appear the first stage of a process of profanation of a holy place:[57] not only because mention of the *penetralia* implies the women's quart-ers (cf. 486–8) but because to a Roman all houses were holy, being the abode of gods, the Penates, with whom the word *penetralia* is etymo-logically connected – a fact of which Virgil's readers were aware.[58] Finally at v. 485 attention is directed back again to the *limen* from which the vision ('apparet . . . apparent') is taking place; and we share with the Greeks, in this eerie moment of stillness, the shock with which their gaze is suddenly recalled from the long receding vistas opening before them to the grim motionless figures awaiting their assault just the other side of the door. Again there is a cyclic movement within the sentence, as at vv. 500–2, from the door to the *penetralia* and back again.

The description that follows (486–90) has already been discussed in the light of its possible literary antecedents. Here the 'objective' narrator takes over again; the word 'at' diverts the reader's attention with some abruptness from 'the situation *in limine primo*, where all is grim defence'[59] to the confusion deep within the palace.[60] No overt transition back to the main action is provided; the self-contained spondaic word 'instat', with its smashing rhythm, suffices to set things in motion once more. However, it may be suggested that the reference to doors in v. 490 unobtrusively provides a secondary transitional impulse. These doors are deep within the palace, but they too carry with them the implication of the *limen* and its symbolical associations, particularly powerful, as already remarked, in this book. Here indeed 'the tragic action moves from *limen* to *limen*'.[61]

VI

This last observation may perhaps assist with the problem of the ambiguity apparently attending the identification of the *limen* and the *postes* in vv. 500–5. The schematic analysis of our passage has shown that its structure is not purely concentric. There is a clear thematic correspondence between vv. 483–90, which stand at the centre of the concentric arrangement, and vv. 500–5, which stand outside it.[62] The question was asked above: what is the point of the ambiguity about *limen* and *postes*, if it exists and is deliberate? With this question must now be coupled a second, of some general importance: what is the point of the elaborate structure of the whole passage and, in particular, of the correspondence between the central and the final sections? Structural analysis of Greek and Latin poetry is an entertaining pastime; is it critically rewarding? It can produce wildly divergent results, in terms both of the structures purporting to be detected and of the conclusions to be drawn as to their function, if any.[63] In this case, however, it seems that the effect intended, and triumphantly achieved, by Virgil is not difficult to grasp. The centrepiece of his narrative of the Sack of Troy and hence of Book 2 of the *Aeneid* is the destruction of the royal palace, the symbol of Trojan empire. At the end of his description that inner centrepiece is brought out and displayed, almost (since all interpreters agree on the dramatic character of Book 2) with the effect of the *eccyclema*[64] in a great theatre; violated and profaned it lies open to view. Whatever further slaughter and destruction may still be in store, at this point the ruin of Troy is consummated:

urbs antiqua ruit multos dominata per annos (363);

with the fall of her royal house the fall of the city is accomplished.

The recurrent image of the *limen* that pervades, if it does not actually dominate, our passage makes its culminating appearance in an apparently ambiguous guise. As to this, Wistrand makes a point that deserves more attention than it seems to have received: 'The lines 503 and 504 are connected not through association by contact but through association by contrast. The innermost court and the children represent the future of Priam's house: The façade adorned with gold and war trophies the glorious past. Neither escapes annihilation.'[65] This is well observed and expressed, but I should wish slightly to qualify Wistrand's acute insight. It is, I think, misconceived to try to distinguish as precisely as Wistrand does two ideas which Virgil himself has gone out of his way to fuse and combine. It is not as if this sort of thing were uncharacteristic of him: throughout the *Aeneid* visions of the past and the future are constantly superimposed.[66] What is possibly the most striking instance of this in the entire poem occurs not many verses later in the picture of Priam's headless corpse on the seashore.[67] The repeated transitions in our passage between inner and outer doors and the ambiguity of 'postes' at v. 504 are part of this pattern of symbolic coexistence, which is spatial as well as temporal. The door smashed down by Pyrrhus and the doors of the *thalami* are merged in Virgil's vision of events into a comprehensive symbol of the profanation of the palace. This was his way, designed to puzzle the literal-minded; but, as James Henry has said: 'It is easier for flesh and blood to inherit the kingdom of God, than for a matter-of-fact expositor to enter into the meaning of Virgil.'[68]

Nowhere is the gulf between Latin poetry of the first rank and the rest more clearly evident than in respect of the adaptation of earlier literature.[69] Ovid, we are expressly told, borrowed in the hope that his borrowings would be recognized and admired; the same must have been true of Virgil and of all *docti poetae*. What a poet makes of what he takes from others is individual and unpredictable. In this passage Virgil's theme or *leitmotiv* and the emphasis laid upon it are, so far as our knowledge of the tradition allows such claims, original to him. He chose, however, to place it in a setting of two similes based closely, in terms of superficial similarity, on Homer, Nicander and Lucretius. The effect of these similes, in themselves and in view of their function in the episode, is worlds away from their originals. The other poet laid under contribution is Ennius – until Virgil arose to claim the title himself, the Roman Homer. Here the debt is more in the article of stylistic and emotional coloration. What is distinctively Virgilian about the resultant whole is due not only to his personal qualities of temperament and imagination but also to the intensely thoughtful shaping that his borrowed material has undergone. The essential principle of any sound structure is subordination: each member has a strictly defined function to perform, and its existence is justified only in virtue of the necessity of that function.[70] It is the process of re-creative craftsmanship that these *disiecta membra* of poetry or near-poetry have experienced that is responsible for the final effect. Unexpectedly perhaps, at all events for those who take a romantic view of literary creation, that effect is one of profound emotional intensity.

The capacity to surprise is one of the hallmarks of genius. As regards Virgil, Macrobius clearly grasped the point, though he puts it crudely:

> denique et iudicio transferendi et modo imitandi consecutus est ut quod apud illum legerimus alienum aut illius esse malimus aut melius hic quam ubi natum est sonare miremur.
>
> (*Saturnalia* 6.1.6)

These are the sentiments of a Maronolatry that disparages unjustly by contrast, just as a certain type of Homeric critic still gratuitously denigrates Virgil. What concerns us here is what Virgil achieves with his borrowed material in its new setting. The pathetic effect of this passage is conveyed in images of malignant renewal, violence, destruction and profanation suggested to him by earlier poetry. The emphasis which he gives them is purely his own. It has recently become fashionable to suggest that the poets of the Augustan 'Establishment', so called, even Virgil and Horace, were not so whole-heartedly committed to the regime as the conventional accounts would have us believe.[71] However, the *Aeneid* can by no stretch of the interpreter's imagination be seen as a document of protest. Broadly speaking it seems clear that Virgil acquiesced in the Augustan settlement and that his poem is a testament of hope, if not of unquestioning faith, in the future of Rome and in her mission. On the other hand there is too much feeling emphasis in the poem on death, misery and destruction to make it possible to read it as an unqualified expression of optimism. The promised land was hardly attained after many years in the wilderness of suffering; for the words

> tantae molis erat Romanam condere gentem

cannot be read as referring only to the tribulations of Aeneas and his followers. This note of qualification hangs over the entire poem. The destruction of Troy, like the death of Turnus at the end of the poem, is a symbol of what had to be suffered in order that the divine plan for Rome might be fulfilled. Did Virgil think the price too high? We cannot tell; perhaps Virgil himself could not have given a straight answer to the question. Too much in the *Aeneid* is equivocal, too much is ambivalent; it does not state, it suggests. Much of its suggestive power resides in echoes and adaptations of earlier literature such as those discussed here. However functionally perfect the assimilation into their new context, these borrowed images still retain something of their original vitality:

> dissimili uiuunt specie retinentque parentum
> naturam.

Virgil surely intended it to be so.

7

Francis Cairns

SELF-IMITATION WITHIN A GENERIC FRAMEWORK

Ovid, *Amores* 2.9 and 3.11 and the *renuntiatio amoris*

Imitation is one of the most difficult concepts in literary criticism. It is hard to establish in any literature criteria for determining with certainty when one passage is a conscious imitation of another.[1] But in ancient literature there are additional obstacles: particular forms like epic or elegy have their own special and relatively limited subject matter and vocabulary; and important works in every form have been lost. The influence of generic 'formulae' and of recurrent topoi must also be taken into account.[2] To some extent these factors cancel each other out. For example, a poet is more likely to imitate his own and other poets' earlier work when it is both in the same genre and in the same form. But nevertheless it is all too easy to suppose that imitation is present where it is not, or, where it is present, to make incorrect identifications of sources. Even when imitation is fairly certain and the principal source is known, problems remain. A work influenced by a specific literary predecessor may also be indebted to the stock material of a genre and to standard commonplaces. Again, when a predecessor is himself imitating an earlier work, imitation of the predecessor may involve a simultaneous reference to the earlier work.[3] Finally, the poet may in addition to his principal source be adding material from one or more secondary sources. This is the so called *contaminatio* which seems to be a hallmark of much Hellenistic and post-Hellenistic literature.[4] All these processes can be involved at once in a single work.

In this essay a complex Ovidian case of imitation within the influential confines of a single genre will be examined. Ovid's main literary source for *Amores* 3.11 is his own *Amores* 2.9 and his self-imitation and self-variation is conditioned throughout by the fact that both elegies draw also on the generic formula of the *renuntiatio amoris* and that both, and *Amores* 3.11 in particular, make use of members of that genre by other poets.

Amores 3.11

Multa diuque tuli: uitiis patientia uicta est.   1
    cede fatigato pectore, turpis Amor.
scilicet adserui iam me fugique catenas,
    et, quae non puduit ferre, tulisse pudet.
uicimus et domitum pedibus calcamus Amorem;   5
    uenerunt capiti cornua sera meo.
perfer et obdura! dolor hic tibi proderit olim;
    saepe tulit lassis sucus amarus opem.
ergo ego sustinui, foribus tam saepe repulsus,
    ingenuum dura ponere corpus humo?   10
ergo ego nesciocui, quem tu conplexa tenebas,
    excubui clausam seruus ut ante domum?
uidi, cum foribus lassus prodiret amator
    inualidum referens emeritumque latus;
hoc tamen est leuius quam quod sum uisus ab illo;   15
    eueniat nostris hostibus ille pudor!
quando ego non fixus lateri patienter adhaesi,
    ipse tuus custos, ipse uir, ipse comes?
scilicet et populo per me comitata placebas:
    causa fuit multis noster amoris amor.   20
turpia quid referam uanae mendacia linguae
    et periuratos in mea damna deos?
quid iuuenum tacitos inter conuiuia nutus
    uerbaque compositis dissimulata notis?
dicta erat aegra mihi; praeceps amensque cucurri;   25
    ueni, et riuali non erat aegra meo.
his et quae taceo duraui saepe ferendis;
    quaere alium pro me qui uelit ista pati.
iam mea uotiua puppis redimita corona
    laeta tumescentes aequoris audit aquas.   30
desine blanditias et uerba, potentia quondam,
    perdere; non ego sum stultus, ut ante fui.
luctantur pectusque leue in contraria tendunt
    hac amor, hac odium; sed, puto, uincit amor.
odero, si potero; si non, inuitus amabo: 35
    nec iuga taurus amat; quae tamen odit, habet.
nequitiam fugio, fugientem forma reducit;
    auersor morum crimina, corpus amo.
sic ego nec sine te nec tecum uiuere possum
    et uideor uoti nescius esse mei.   40

aut formosa fores minus aut minus improba uellem:
 non facit ad mores tam bona forma malos.
facta merent odium, facies exorat amorem:
 me miserum, uitiis plus ualet illa suis.
parce per o lecti socialia iura, per omnes   45
 qui dant fallendos se tibi saepe deos,
perque tuam faciem, magni mihi numinis instar,
 perque tuos oculos, qui rapuere meos.
quicquid eris, mea semper eris; tu selige tantum,
 me quoque uelle uelis anne coactus amem.   50
lintea dem potius uentisque ferentibus utar
 et quam, si nolim, cogor amare, uelim.

Amores 2.9

O numquam pro me satis indignate Cupido,   1
 o in corde meo desidiose puer!
quid me, qui miles numquam tua signa reliqui,
 laedis, et in castris uulneror ipse meis?
cur tua fax urit, figit tuus arcus amicos?   5
 gloria pugnantes uincere maior erat.
quid? non Haemonius, quem cuspide perculit, heros
 confossum medica postmodo iuuit ope?
uenator sequitur fugientia, capta relinquit,
 semper et inuentis ulteriora petit.   10
nos tua sentimus, populus tibi deditus, arma;
 pigra reluctanti cessat in hoste manus.
quid iuuat in nudis hamata retundere tela
 ossibus? ossa mihi nuda relinquit Amor.
tot sine amore uiri, tot sunt sine amore puellae;   15
 hinc tibi cum magna laude triumphus eat.
Roma, nisi inmensum uires promosset in orbem,
 stramineis esset nunc quoque tecta casis.
fessus in acceptos miles deducitur agros,
 mittitur in saltus carcere liber equus,   20
longaque subductam celant naualia pinum
 tutaque deposito poscitur ense rudis;
me quoque, qui totiens merui sub amore puellae,
 defunctum placide uiuere tempus erat.
'uiue deus posito' si quis mihi dicat 'amore',[5]   25
 deprecer; usque adeo dulce puella malum est.

cum bene pertaesum est, animoque relanguit ardor,
    nescio quo miserae turbine mentis agor.
ut rapit in praeceps dominum spumantia frustra
    frena retentantem durior oris equus,   30
ut subitus prope iam prensa tellure carinam
    tangentem portus uentus in alta rapit,
sic me saepe refert incerta Cupidinis aura
    notaque purpureus tela resumit Amor.
fige, puer; positis nudus tibi praebeor armis;   35
    hic tibi sunt uires, hic tua dextra facit.
huc tamquam iussae ueniunt iam sponte sagittae;
    uix illis prae me nota pharetra sua est.
infelix, tota quicumque quiescere nocte
    sustinet et somnos praemia magna uocat;   40
stulte, quid est somnus gelidae nisi mortis imago?
    longa quiescendi tempora fata dabunt.
me modo decipiant uoces fallacis amicae:
    sperando certe gaudia magna feram;
et modo blanditias dicat, modo iurgia nectat;   45
    saepe fruar domina, saepe repulsus eam.
quod dubius Mars est, per te, priuigne Cupido, est,
    et mouet exemplo uitricus arma tuo;
tu leuis es multoque tuis uentosior alis,
    gaudiaque ambigua dasque negasque fide.   50
si tamen exaudis, pulchra cum matre, rogantem,
    indeserta meo pectore regna gere.
accedant regno, nimium uaga turba, puellae;
    ambobus populis sic uenerandus eris.

The element of self-imitation found in *Amores* 3.11 is characteristic
of much ancient poetry and it is always found accompanied by
variation. For Hellenistic Greek poets and their late Republican and
Augustan successors it was a practice as important as the imitation
of other literary sources. It was of course encouraged by the tendency
of anthologies of epigrams, including the *Garland* of Meleager, to
juxtapose or place in near proximity poems on the same theme. A
number of Hellenistic and Roman cases of self-imitation are currently
becoming better understood.[6] Self-imitation is conspicuous for example
in the Theocritean komoi;[7] and it can be seen in the late Republic in
Catullus' reworkings of the same theme in his three *basia* poems.[8] In
the early Empire there are instances like Tibullus' three komoi (1.2,

1.5 and 2.6),[9] his three versions of erotodidaxis (1.4, 1.6 and 1.8)[10] and his re-use of the framework of 1.7 in 2.1,[11] Propertius' self-imitation of 1.3 in 2.29[12] and of 1.8 in 2.26[13] and Horace's series of 'symptoms of love' odes,[14] anathematika,[15] and palinodes,[16] where the later poems look back to the earlier. The tendency must have been encouraged by poets' need, in large collections of short poems, to use the same genre more than once without being repetitious and their enjoyment of the challenge this need posed.

Ovid's refashioning of *Amores* 2.9 in 3.11 belongs then to an established tradition of self-imitation and self-variation, often as here within the boundaries of the same genre. In such cases the two poems can be seen simultaneously from two viewpoints; first the similarities between them, both verbal and conceptual, can be examined; and second they can be regarded as variations on a single generic formula, with the latter written in the consciousness that certain ways of handling the material have been pre-empted by the author's earlier treatment of the same genre.[17] Ovid, *Amores* 2.9 is fairly easily recognizable as a member of the genre *renuntiatio amoris* despite Ovid's sophisticated use of many of the generic commonplaces. The following list of primary and secondary elements of the genre will assist its identification.[18]

Primary elements

A   1. The speaker (a lover).

    2. The addressee (the beloved).

    3. An act of renunciation of the addressee by the speaker.

Secondary elements (topoi)

B   1. The lover's previous sentiments for the beloved.

    2. The lover's formal renunciation of his beloved/love.

    3. The lover's reasons for rejecting love/the beloved

      (i) The lover's coming to the age of discretion/retirement from love.

      (ii) The beloved's infidelity (and perjury).

      (iii) Unwillingness of beloved.

    4. The lover's rivals/successors.

    5. The future miseries of the lover's rivals/successors, mainly ill-treatment and infidelity by the beloved.

    6. The future miseries of the beloved, mainly loss of this/all lover(s).

    7. The lover's present state of mind always implicitly, sometimes explicitly described as one of

      Conflict   or   Contentment.

8. The beloved's attempts to win back the lover.
9. The lover's resolve to find a better beloved.

In *Amores* 2.9 the primary elements A1 and A3 appear in their standard form: the speaker Ovid is a lover (A1) and his renunciation of Love (A3) is made explicit in 23f. A2 appears in a sophisticated form in l. 1, where Ovid substitutes the love-god, Cupido, for the normal addressee, the beloved. Such substitutions are common in generic composition[19] and this particular one – the replacement of a human addressee with a god – is paralleled several times in the *renuntiatio* itself (see below, p. 128).

Amores 2.9 also contains many of the secondary elements of the genre. ll. 1–18 are a series of accusations levelled at Cupido by Ovid. The god is idle and does not take sufficiently vigorous action on behalf of Ovid (1f.); Ovid is his faithful soldier, but Cupido repays him by wounding him (3f.), whereas he ought to be burning and shooting his enemies, non-lovers (5f.). Even Achilles healed the enemy whom he had wounded (7f.); and the huntsman loses interest in his prey once it is captured (9f.). But Cupido harms those who accept his rule, and leaves his enemies in peace, although there are vast numbers of men and girls unconquered by him (11–16). If Rome had taken the same attitude she would never have conquered the world (17f.). Since *Roma* and *Amor* are palindromes, Ovid may be making the witty point that their opposite behaviour is natural. These complaints combine[20] two topoi of the genre; the lover's previous sentiments, usually for the beloved, but here, since the addressee is Love, for Love (B1); and the lover's reasons for rejecting Love or the beloved (B3). Ovid claims that he has always been loyal and devoted to Love and that he is rejecting Love because of the god's sloth, cruelty and ingratitude. Two metaphors – the *miles* of 3ff. and the *populus* of 11f. – expand these topoi. A soldier enrolling under the banner of a commander in antiquity entered into a relationship of mutual loyalty and support, as did one nation entering into a bond of dependency upon another. Ovid has fulfilled his part of the bargain but Love has not. The metaphors thus allude to the topoi of infidelity (B3 (ii)) and unwillingness (B3 (iii)) which normally apply to the beloved but are transferred here to the substitute addressee, Love.

Four *exempla*, which begin at l. 19, carry the elegy forward towards Ovid's formal renunciation of Love in 23f. (B2). These *exempla* express another of Ovid's reasons for rejecting Love, namely that in his weariness he feels he has come to the age of retirement (B3 (i)).

The soldier retires from the army and gets his allotment of lands; the race horse and warship[21] eventually become too old for service; and the gladiator retires from the arena (19–22). Ovid, who has fought so many campaigns under the standard of Love, now feels it is time for him also to live in peace (23f.).[22]

At this point Ovid's thought takes a new turn. Some editors have therefore divided the poem and begun a new elegy at 25. However, there is no manuscript or other justification for this division; and the unity of *Amores* 2.9 has been amply demonstrated by the work of a number of scholars. The connections between its two parts have been most recently discussed by K. Jäger and G. Lörcher,[23] who regard it correctly as a dramatic soliloquy, unfolding and changing over the period of time in which it is imagined as spoken. Because the work of these scholars may be less familiar to readers than texts which divide the elegy, it may be useful to list here briefly those internal correspondences which guarantee its unity:[24]

(1) 2 (*o in corde meo*) = 52 (*meo pectore*).

(2) 5: cur tua fax urit, FIGIT tuus *arcus* amicos?
  and
  13f.: quid iuuat in **nudis** *hamata* retundere *tela*
        ossibus? ossa mihi **nuda** relinquit Amor
  =
  34–8: notaque purpureus *tela* resumit Amor.
        FIGE, puer; positis **nudus** tibi praebeor armis;
          hic tibi sunt uires, hic tua dextra facit.
        huc tamquam iussae ueniunt iam sponte *sagittae*;
          uix illis prae me nota *pharetra* sua est.

(3) 15f. = 53f. with *puellae* in same *sedes* in 15 and 53.

(4) 20 = 29f. (horse image) – note especially *equus* (20 and 30) in same *sedes*.

(5) 21 = 31ff. (ship image) – note especially *pinum* (21) and *carinam* (31) both at end of line.

(6) 22 (*deposito* ense) = 25 (*posito*) – note especially *posito* in the same metrical position in pentameter and hexameter respectively, and see below, p. 130.

(7) 23f. = 41f. (on the basis that *defunctum . . . uiuere* (24) in one of its two senses means 'to live a life of death').[25]

(8) 23f. (esp. *uiuere* (24), | = | 25f. (esp. *uiue* (25), *amore*
    amore (23), *puellae* (23)) | | (25), *puella* (26))

Additional support for the unity of *Amores* 2.9 can be derived first from consideration of its thematic structure (see below, p. 132), and second from analysis of its use of the constructive principle of 'reaction'. In a number of genres the speaker or addressee can 'react' to the unfolding situation in ways which extend the scope of the genre.[26] Such 'reactions' commonly take the form of a change of mind by the speaker, and this is what happens in *Amores* 2.9: having in 1–24 renounced Love, Ovid changes his mind in 25ff. and returns to his former allegiance to Love. This type of 'reaction' would have been particularly easy for an ancient reader to understand because it is so common in the genre *renuntiatio amoris*. It is first found in a known *renuntiatio* in the Hellenistic period – Theocritus, *Idyll* 30. It surfaces in the epigrammatic tradition in *Anthologia Palatina* 5.184 (Meleager) and later in *AP* 12.201 (Strato). In the Augustan age it occurs in lyric (Horace, *Odes* 3.26) and in elegy (Propertius 2.5). Ovid, *Amores* 3.11 is another elegiac example (see below, pp. 132ff.). The frequency of the lover's change of mind in *renuntiationes* naturally reflects the well-known human reluctance to break off love-affairs.

In 25–54 further topoi of the genre present themselves. ll. 25–8 portray the conflict which can arise in the lover's mind when he attempts to renounce love (B7). Two similes expand on this situation in 29–34 until the conflict is resolved in Ovid's declaration of resumed allegiance to Love (35–8), which reverses the renunciation of 23f. The next section (39–46) contains material which in most *renuntiationes* would constitute topoi B3, B4 and B5: the lover's reasons for renouncing love; his rivals; and their sufferings. In particular Ovid emphasizes the deceitfulness and unwillingness of his beloved (B3 (ii), (iii)). However, he uses these topoi in a new and paradoxical way which will be explained below. Finally in 47ff. Ovid addresses Cupido, describing the god's powers, reiterating his fidelity to him and begging him to extend his kingdom to the *puellae*. This last request is a witty allusion to the normal resolve which the lover makes to find a better beloved (B9).

This summary of the topoi can now be enlarged upon. To begin with, in the majority of *renuntiationes* a lover renounces his beloved. But in *Amores* 2.9 Ovid renounces the Love-god himself. This, as was noted, is not unparalleled: in *Anthologia Palatina* 5.179 (Meleager) Eros is addressed and sent packing with a barrage of threats to destroy his bow and arrows, clip his wings and chain his feet; and in Horace, *Odes* 3.26 Venus is the addressee of a *renuntiatio*.[27] It is clear then that Ovid is exploiting a Hellenistic tradition of renouncing Love. This is of course one aspect of a broader Hellenistic tendency to make the Love-god the object of threats and reproaches of greater and lesser degrees of seriousness. By renouncing Love rather than a particular beloved, Ovid is able to introduce the generic topoi in novel forms. But he is also to some extent revealing the *persona* which he advanced in the programmatic *Amores* 1.1, 1.2 and 1.3, where first he was not in love at all, then he was in love but not with any one in particular, and only finally did he fall in love with a specific girl. This *persona* with its cooler and more detached attitude to Love contrasts with the established *personae* of Propertius, who is devoted to one mistress, and of Tibullus, who is faithful to one mistress at a time. Ovid sometimes approximates to the Propertian/Tibullan character, but the specifically Ovidian *persona*, which is the springboard for much of the wit and cynicism which marks off his poetry from that of his predecessors, keeps reappearing, as it does here.

As has been noted, *Amores* 2.9.1–18 is a detailed anticipation of Ovid's rejection of Love rather than a mistress, which finally comes in 23f.; and in 1–18 faults analogous to those normally leading the lover to reject his beloved are attributed to the Love-god. Ovid amusingly combines in these lines two areas of causation usually kept apart in the *renuntiatio*. Normally the lover gives up love because he has been ill-treated (B3 (ii), (iii)) or because he has reached the time for retirement from love, that is, the age of greater discretion (B3 (i)). However, Ovid first attacks Love for neglecting and harming him; and then he speaks of being ripe for retirement. In both the ill-treatment section (3) and the retirement section (19) he compares himself with a *miles*. The repetition of the word draws our attention to the novel combination of ideas and makes Ovid's point tellingly: he has suffered so much that he is tired of love (cf. also 27: *cum bene pertaesum est*) and so feels it time to retire. Naturally Ovid is not making a serious point when he combines these ideas. The wit of the first couplet warns that what follows is equally humorous. In 1f. Ovid's opening charge is that Cupido is *desidiosus*. This is a paradox: since Love was traditionally associated with *otium*,[28] Ovid should not have expected him to be anything else.

The central portion of the elegy relies for its interest mainly on the 'reaction' of 25ff. To make quite sure that his readers realize that the same poem is continuing in l. 25 Ovid forges word links between 23f. and 25f.: *uiuere* (24) is picked up by *uiue* (25), *amore* comes in 23 and 25, and *puella(e)* in 23 and 26. Such devices, which can be conceptual or verbal or both, commonly link different parts of the same work in Hellenistic poetry. They have been found between scenes in Menander[29] and between sections of other Hellenistic poems.[30] The *uiuere–uiue* link of ll. 24 and 25 is reinforced by another subtler touch. As was noted above (p. 127), l. 22 (*tutaque de*posito *poscitur ense rudis*) is echoed in l. 25 ('*uiue deus* posito' *si quis mihi dicat* '*amore*'); and the similar metrical position of (-)*posito* helps the echo. But there is more; both lines are imitations of Propertius 1.9.8, which is part of the couplet

> me dolor et lacrimae merito fecere peritum
> atque utinam posito dicar amore rudis. (7f.)

The occurrence of *posito* here in the same *sedes* as in *Amores* 2.9.22 is noteworthy; so is the witty borrowing by Ovid of the word *rudis* in the same *sedes* in *Amores* 2.9.22 but with a different meaning. *Amores* 2.9.25 imitates Propertius' *dicar amore* in *dicat* '*amore*' with *uariatio* in *sedes*, in the grammatical form of *dicat* and in the division between direct and indirect speech. It is worth also noting that *merito* in Propertius 1.9.7 is answered by *merui* in *Amores* 2.9.23: *me quoque, qui totiens merui sub amore puellae*, where *amore* recurs as second last word in the line, as it is in Propertius 1.9.8. The use of this couplet of Propertius in the four lines bridging the two parts of *Amores* 2.9 is a particularly effective demonstration of the elegy's unity; and it provides a valuable insight into the subtlety of Ovid's techniques of imitation.

By l. 35 Ovid has shown that his mental conflict has been resolved and that he is fully subject to Love again. Further wit now follows. In ll. 35 ff. Ovid first alludes to the charges of ill-treatment which lovers usually bring against their beloved as reasons for rejection (B3 (ii), (iii)) and then shows his desperation as a lover and the extent to which his allegiance to Love has been resumed by willingly accepting all these sufferings as part and parcel of his renewed attachment to Love. The paradox is patent: Ovid begins by offering himself voluntarily as a target for Love's arrows (35–8). Then he claims that the sleeplessness of the deprived lover is preferable to sleep, which is nothing more than a *mortis imago* (39–42). The deceitfulness of a mistress (43) is welcome also because, in hope at least, Ovid will win *gaudia magna* (44). Whether a mistress is loving or hostile, whether he enjoys her or goes off unsatisfied, Ovid will accept it (45f.). The concept which begins the next section (47ff.), that Love and War are both of uncertain outcome, sums all this up; and the reference to Mars (47f.) balances and elucidates the *miles* image of 3ff. and 19. In accepting these sufferings for himself Ovid is taking upon himself the future miseries which normally in a *renuntiatio amoris* are the lot of the lover's rivals and successors (B5). In addition, Ovid's mistress has no need to try to win back her lover (B8) since Love has already done this for her. The elegy ends (47–54) with Ovid praying to Cupido and his mother Venus to accept him back as a subject. He does not, as the lover often does in the *renuntiatio* (B9), resolve to find a better beloved; he simply prays that Cupido and Venus will conquer the *puellae* too. There may be an oblique hint here of B6 – the beloved's future miseries – since if she becomes subject to love, she will inevitably suffer. But Ovid is thinking more of his own advantage if Love answers his prayer. Everything after l. 26 thus illustrates the theme stated in it: that the *puella* is a *dulce malum* which Ovid accepts. In this way Ovid compensates for his concentration on Cupido as his addressee. The *puella* of l. 26, who reappears more specifically as the *amica* of 43 and the *domina* of 46, can only be Corinna. Ovid's grandiose attempted rejection of Cupido and its failure does not really affect his relationship with Corinna. He is still her neglected lover who hopes for better nights.

Thematically *Amores* 2.9 falls into the following ring-structure:[31]

A¹   1–2 Ovid protests to Cupido that the god is doing nothing for him (i.e. not winning over his mistress).

B¹   3–18 Ovid complains that Cupido torments his allies instead of conquering his enemies.

C¹ 19–24 *Exempla* (including horse and ship) preface Ovid's wish to retire from love.

D   25–8 In spite of his weariness of love, Ovid cannot give it up.

C² 29–34 Similes of horse and ship illustrate Ovid's return to love.

B² 35–46 Ovid accepts ill-treatment by his mistress.

A² 47–54 Ovid prays to Cupido (and Venus) to rule him and add the girls also to his kingdom.

Amores 3.11 can now be examined. Its unity too has been denied by some editors but again it has been demonstrated beyond doubt.[32] Most of the correspondences between its two parts may be set down briefly:[33]

(1) 1 (*uitiis*) = 44 (*uitiis*)

(2) 5 (*uicimus*) = 34 (*uincit*)

(3) 7 (*perfer et obdura* – cf. Catullus 8.11) = 33f. (*hac amor, hac odium* – cf. Catullus 85)

(4) 21f. (*periuratos . . . deos*, 22) = 45f. (*fallendos . . . deos*, 46 – with *deos* in same final *sedes*)

(5) 28 (*uelit*) = 50 (*uelle uelis*, cf. *uelim*, 52)
(6) 29 (*uotiua*) = 40 (*uoti*)
(7) 29f. (ship coming to harbour image) = 51 (ship leaving harbour image)

In thematic terms *Amores* 3.11 does not display the commoner ring-structure but the less common 'parallel' structure, which reveals a few further verbal links between the two parts:

A¹ 1–8 Internal conflict between *uitia* and *patientia*. (Note especially in 1f.: *uicta est, pectore, Amor.*) Ovid claims that he has escaped (note: *fugique*, 3) and defeated Love; he urges himself to endure his pain.

B¹ 9–20 Ovid was often excluded by his mistress (9–16) (note: *ergo ego*, 9) even though he escorted her constantly (17–20).

C¹ 21–6 His mistress's lying pledges, perjuries by the gods, and treacherous infidelities.

D¹ 27–32 Rejection of mistress: ship arriving in harbour image.

A² 33–8 Ovid's internal conflict. (Note especially in 33f.: *pectus, uincit, Amor.*) The victory of Love; Ovid cannot escape his mistress. (Note: *fugio, fugientem*, 37.)

B² 39–44 Ovid can neither live without his mistress or with her. (Note: *sic ego*, 39.)

C² 45–8 Ovid prays to his mistress, invoking her by their pledges, in the name of the gods who allow her to perjure herself by them, and by her divine beauty.

D² 49–52 Ovid accepts his love for his mistress: ship leaving harbour image.

The Roman reader of the *Amores* would have linked 3.11 with 2.9 primarily because they are both *renuntiationes*[34] and both involve a similar 'reaction'. The specific verbal and conceptual links between the two elegies which will be indicated would have confirmed that Ovid was imitating his earlier work and would also have underlined the differences between Ovid's two treatments of the commonplace generic material.[35] In this way Ovid combined the originality demanded of all genre pieces with self-imitation *cum variatione*. These links and the relations between the two elegies and their literary predecessors will be treated first; and then an attempt will be made to interpret them.

Both *Amores* 2.9 and 3.11 begin with apostrophe of the Love-god. This is clearly intended to reinforce the reader's recognition of a kinship between them. Another initial similarity between them also helps. At 2.9.2 Ovid addressed Cupido as *o in corde meo desidiose puer*. In 3.11.2 he addresses him in the words *cede fatigato pectore, turpis Amor*. The link is strengthened by 2.9.52: *indeserta meo pectore regna gere*. This line falls in A² of the ring-structure of 2.9, while line 2 falls in A¹. The third line of 3.11 continues with another concept also linked with 2.9: *scilicet adserui iam me fugique catenas*. The phrase *fugi catenas* suggests the word *fugitiuus*, 'runaway slave'. Now in the third line of 2.9 Ovid made the claim that he had never left the standard of love (3f.). At first sight the two notions – runaway slave and deserting soldier – might seem very far apart. But the same Latin word *erro* could cover both.[36] Tibullus had used *erro* of a deserting 'soldier' of love:

> ure, puer, quaeso tua qui ferus otia liquit,
> atque iterum erronem sub tua signa uoca.
>
> (Tibullus 2.6.5f.)[37]

So Ovid is contradicting at the beginning of 3.11 a posture of loyalty to love which he had adopted at the beginning of 2.9. The implications of this for the meaning of 3.11 will be explored below (pp. 138f.). Ovid goes even further: in 2.9 Cupido was throughout a conquering force, a triumphant general controlling Mars and ruling widely; in 3.11 this concept is inverted in lines 5ff. Here in a pointed verbal and conceptual contrast to 2.9.5f., where Cupido was spoken of in terms of *uincere*, Ovid claims that Amor has been conquered and is being trampled underfoot by Ovid (*uicimus et domitum pedibus calcamus Amorem*), who himself wears the horns of power.[38]

Having made his dependence on his own 2.9 evident in 3.11.1–6 Ovid then combines further allusions to 2.9 with reminiscences of his poetic predecessors, mainly looking in this area to examples of the same genre. To begin with, he refers to Catullus 8, another *renuntiatio amoris*:[39] *Amores* 3.11.7 derives almost directly from Catullus 8.11, *sed obstinata mente perfer obdura*. At a later point Ovid uses other poems of Catullus. Here, however, he may be thinking also, albeit much less obviously, of a Tibullan *renuntiatio* (1.9). *Amores* 3.11.7–28 draws ultimately on commonplace lists of lovers' sufferings at the hands of their beloved and of services performed by lovers for their beloved.[40] But the part dealing with services is possibly influenced on a non-verbal level by the similar list at Tibullus 1.9.41ff. and, more remotely, by another at Tibullus 1.4.39ff., which is not a *renuntiatio* but erotodidaxis. But within this section Ovid refers both verbally and conceptually in 3.11.9 (*ergo ego sustinui, foribus tam* saepe repulsus) to his own *Amores* 2.9.46 (*saepe fruar domina,* saepe repulsus *eam*). Then at *Amores* 3.11.19f. there seems to be some influence of a Propertian *renuntiatio,* 3.24 and 25: *Amores* 3.11.19f. echo Propertius 3.24.1ff. in a general way and there is the particular coincidence of *noster amor* (*Amores* 3.11.20 and Propertius 3.24.3). Then self-imitation is combined with another reflection of this same Propertian elegy. At *Amores* 2.9.21f. the retired warship resting in the dockyard was a symbol of Ovid's wish to retire from Love; and at 2.9.31f. Ovid compared his situation with a ship almost touching land and then carried out to sea by a sudden wind:

> ut subitus prope iam prensa tellure *carinam*
> *tangentem portus* uentus in alta rapit.

At 3.11.29f. the image recurs in an expanded and varied form: Ovid's ship coming home from the rough mid-seas symbolizes his rejection of love; and later in 3.11, at lines 51f., the ship which puts out to sea symbolizes Ovid's return to love. At 2.9.31f. Ovid is drawing on Propertius 3.24.15–18:

> ecce coronatae *portum tetigere carinae*
> traiectae Syrtes, ancora iacta mihi est.
> nunc demum uasto fessi resipiscimus aestu,
> uulneraque ad sanum nunc coiere mea;

and his use of the same symbol at two points in *Amores* 3.11 relies both on his own *Amores* 2.9 and on the same passage of Propertius.

Next, *Amores* 3.11.31f.:

> desine *blanditias* et uerba, potentia quondam,
> perdere; non ego sum STVLTVS, ut ante fui

recalls both *Amores* 2.9.41f.:

> STVLTE, quid est somnus gelidae nisi mortis imago?
> longa quiescendi tempora fata dabunt

and 2.9.45f.:

> et modo *blanditias* dicat, modo iurgia nectat:
> saepe fruar domina, saepe repulsus eam

with *blanditias* in the same *sedes.* The latter passage also contains the phrase *saepe repulsus* which, as was noted above, was echoed in 3.11.9.

In the second half of 3.11 there may be some general indirect influence of Propertius 2.5, with its antithesis between the beloved's beauty and character; and there seems to be further non-specific reminiscence of Tibullus 1.9, which makes great play of this distinction. But both Propertius and Tibullus were in these elegies simply taking over Catullan concepts; and in *Amores* 3.11 Ovid is predominantly looking back directly to Catullus. *Amores* 3.11.33f.:

> luctantur pectusque leue in contraria tendunt
> hac amor, hac odium; sed, puto, uincit amor

refer to:

> Odi et amo. quare id faciam, fortasse requiris;
> nescio, sed fieri sentio et excrucior

(Catullus 85)

and two other Catullan poems (72 and 75) make great play with one of the themes which recurs in the second half of *Amores* 3.11 – that the lover cannot love his mistress less because of her faults. But even here Ovid is combining with reminiscence of Catullus imitation of his own *Amores* 2.9. 3.11.33f. also looks back obliquely to 2.9.25–8:

> 'uiue deus posito' si quis mihi dicat 'amore',
> deprecer: usque adeo dulce puella malum est.
> cum bene pertaesum est, animoque relanguit ardor,
> nescio quo miserae turbine mentis agor.

In both elegies Ovid is portraying the conflict between love and the desire to reject love, with love possessing the superior power; and in both the train of thought is making a sudden change of direction. Indeed the most striking similarity between *Amores* 2.9 and 3.11 is this 'reaction' which occurs later in 3.11 than in 2.9, but in both cases is expressed quite clearly in the first couplet where Ovid confesses to a faltering in his resolve (2.9.25f., 3.11.33f.).

Catullan influence continues in 35–44 and surfaces in ll. 49 and 52. *anne coactus amem* (49) and *cogor amare, uelim* (52) may be compared with *cogit amare magis sed bene uelle minus* (Catullus 72.8). Reminiscences of *Amores* 2.9, however, again manifest themselves, not on the verbal, but on the conceptual and structural level, in 3.11.45–52. Like 2.9.47–54, 3.11.45–52 is an eight-line prayer parody. In 2.9 the parody began with four lines expressing the power of the god,[41] his control over Mars and his supreme ability to give and withhold joy.[42] Then Ovid humbly begged Cupido to rule him and the *puellae*,[43]

promising him worship as a reward.[44] In 3.11 the parody is signalled by
the *o* of 45,[45] the *per* etc. of 45–6,[46] the insertion of the *o* in formal
religious style after the *per*,[47] the *quicquid eris* of 49[48] and the explicit
magni mihi numinis instar of 47. The prayer in 2.9 was naturally
directed to Cupido, the addressee of the poem, along with his mother
Venus. In 3.11 it is directed, equally naturally, to the addressee of that
elegy, the mistress whom Ovid has attempted to reject.[49] In some
renuntiationes amoris, namely Horace, *Odes* 1.5 and 3.26, Tibullus
1.9 and Propertius 3.24, a dedication symbolizes the contented thank-
fulness of the lover who feels that he has managed to escape love.
In *Amores* 2.9 and 3.11 the prayers should probably be understood as a
substitute motif[50] appropriate to the lack of success of the *renuntiatio*.

There are several alternative or joint ways of approaching the
phenomenon of poetic self-imitation in general. To begin with it
can be regarded from a technical viewpoint. The poet, having created
or accepted from a generic tradition a particular conceptual structure
in one work, may re-use it in varied form because this is easier or more
interesting for him than inventing a new structure. He may feel that
he is improving on his earlier performance, or merely that composing
a variation on the same theme offers him more or different scope. This
aspect of self-imitation probably has more to do with the poet's
'private' craft than with the reader's response. On the other hand self-
imitation can concern the reader more closely. The poet may by self-
imitation be making a comment on his earlier work or indicating change
in his attitudes or in his poetic personality. Here the amount which the
reader ought to deduce from a particular case of self-imitation must
depend on its obtrusiveness. If it is obvious and easy to grasp, then
presumably he is intended to notice it and to speculate about it.

In ancient poetry, the clearest cases of meaningful self-imitation are
pairs of poems like Tibullus 1.8 and 1.9,[51] or 2.3 and 2.4,[52] which stand
side by side in a book and deal with the same basic situation. In such
cases it is certain that the reader was meant to take each as casting light
on the other. Where two poems stand separated by a single intervening
poem, as for example Catullus 5 and 7 (if their arrangement is original)
and Propertius 1.7 and 1.9, a similar conclusion must be drawn. But
when the two poems are in different books, as are *Amores* 2.9 and 3.11,
albeit in different books of the same collection, the identity in genre and
the large number of verbal and thematic coincidences, particularly
at the beginning of 3.11, are essential guides to the reader. The inter-
action in *Amores* 2.9 and 3.11 of repeated generic commonplaces with
specific pieces of self-imitation and imitation of other poets who had

worked within the same genre naturally makes it very difficult to know what, if any, conceptual conclusions Ovid wished his reader to draw. But some suggestions can be advanced.

One area of interpretation relates to literary history. Ovid seems to have been conscious that 2.9 was his first contribution to the genre *renuntiatio*, which had been employed by two of his elegiac predecessors, Tibullus and Propertius. He was always alive to literary canons, particularly to that of elegy, and *Amores* 2.9 may reflect his concern about his own place in it. In *Amores* 2.9 Ovid is in one sense underlining his status as an independent poetic force within the genre *renuntiatio*. The elegy contains a fair number of reminiscences of Propertius and Tibullus,[53] but it is sparing in its allusions to earlier elegiac *renuntiationes*. *Amores* 2.9.48f.: '*et mouet* exemplo *uitricus arma* tuo: | *tu* LEVIS *es* . . .' refers to Tibullus 1.9.40: '*sed precor* exemplo *sit* LEVIS *illa* tuo' and *Amores* 2.9.31f. to Propertius 3.24.15–18 (see above, p. 134) and these seem to be the only examples. *Amores* 3.11, however, is freer in its references to elegiac *renuntiationes* by Tibullus and Propertius (see above, pp. 133ff.) and it makes use also of a Catullan *renuntiatio* (8). This can be seen as an expression of Ovid's confidence in his own status as an elegist. Having established himself with 2.9 as the author of an elegiac *renuntiatio* not heavily dependent on earlier elegiac examples of the genre, Ovid could then in 3.11 combine imitation of it with free use of the *renuntiationes* of his predecessors. In this way he asserted his equality with Catullus, Propertius and Tibullus as an established author within the genre.

There seem to be significant differences in meaning between the two elegies which are underlined by their similar development and bipartite nature and by the element of self-imitation in 3.11. These are most clearly signalled by the change of addressee between them. *Amores* 2.9 is addressed to Cupido but 3.11, after an initial apostrophe of Amor, turns to Ovid's mistress, who must be Corinna, as its real addressee. This is linked with the fluctuation of Ovid's *persona* in the *Amores* noted above, from witty withdrawn observer to elegiac lover of the Propertian/Tibullan type. The first of these aspects is portrayed in 2.9, the second in 3.11. In 2.9 Ovid is somewhat detached and certainly over-hopeful throughout. He imagines that Love is the problem, and that Love can be rejected in an abstract way. He makes a smug, legalized complaint against Love and declares that he will retire from Love's service. Even after his change of mind Ovid is still too sanguine. He accepts as part of his resumed allegiance to Love sufferings which other poets renouncing love use as reasons for doing so. But Ovid is still looking on the bright side. He accepts frustration, sleeplessness and deception, but he hopes that there will be pleasures too: the girl is a *dulce malum* (26); and he ends with a prayer to Cupido and Venus to help him by making the *puellae* fall in love. But in 3.11 the situation has changed. Ovid's *puella* has not fallen in love with him; and Ovid has realized that Love cannot be dealt with in an abstract way. The problem is a particular mistress and if he is to escape from Love he has to reject that mistress. The verbal links between the two elegies underline the changed situation, which in effect amounts to the failure of Ovid's prayer at the end of 2.9. In 2.9.46 the line *saepe fruar domina, saepe repulsus eam* expressed both the joys and sorrows Ovid expects. But at 3.11.9 *tam saepe repulsus* emphasizes that only the sorrows have been forthcoming. This trend is reinforced by the more detailed exposition of the lover's miseries in 3.11. In 2.9.29ff. sleeplessness, deception, reproaches and rejection were spoken of in general terms. In 3.11 they are detailed precisely (9ff.): Ovid's lying sleepless on the ground, while his rival lies in his mistress's arms; Ovid's having to watch, and be seen by, his satisfied rival coming out of his mistress's house in the morning; his mistress's treacherous exchange of signals with lovers at dinner parties; false oaths and lies about illness (9ff., 21ff.). These details are much more realistic and painful than the generalities of 2.9, and they are set precisely in their komastic and symposiastic contexts. Again the reminiscences of *stultus* and *blanditiae* strengthen the impression of an Ovid who is now more seriously hurt by his experiences. In 2.9.41f. Ovid regarded the non-lover as *stultus*. But in 3.11.32 Ovid claims that he is no longer *stultus*, that is, no longer a lover. When he says *non ego sum stultus, ut ante fui*, the phrase *ut ante fui* is a specific allusion *per contrarium* to *Amores* 2.9. The mention of *blanditiae* in the two elegies is another part of the same complex. In 2.9.45 the mistress's *blanditiae* are part of the renewed love which Ovid longs for after his change of mind and they are a compensation for the sufferings he accepts along with them. In 3.11.31f., however, the mistress's *blanditiae* are part of a vain attempt by the mistress to persuade Ovid to maintain his attachment to the *stultitia* of love.

It is because Ovid thinks that he has seen the truth in 3.11 as opposed to his state of self-delusion in 2.9 that he is, paradoxically, even more confident at the beginning of 3.11 of his ability to reject his mistress than he was of his prospect of rejecting Love in 2.9. In 3.11.3 he says: *scilicet adserui iam me fugique catenas*. The phrase *adserui me*, strictly speaking, involves a legal impossibility. A slave could not take steps to claim free status on his own initiative. He was required to find a free citizen to act as his *uindex* and *adsertor in libertatem*.[54] Of course *adserere se* could sometimes be used in non-technical contexts just to mean 'free oneself'.[55] But the whole line shows that Ovid is aware of the legal impropriety of what he has done. He is saying in effect 'I have given myself my freedom – that is, I am a runaway'; *fugi* and *scilicet* draws the reader's attention to the irony of his claim. The line, therefore, depicts Ovid as a runaway slave who is illegally claiming to be free; and of course it must be remembered that under Roman law a runaway slave who, when caught, claimed to be free faced more serious consequences.[56] The legal irregularity demonstrates Ovid's hubristic self-confidence; and it is also an advance warning to the reader that Ovid will not succeed in his attempted escape from Love. Ovid's arrogance is again shown in his paradoxical claim in 3.11.5ff. that he has conquered and overthrown Love – the complete opposite of the situation in 2.9, where Love was an all-conquering force (see above, p. 133); and it is manifested also in the longer time he is able to hold out against the 'reaction' in 3.11 as opposed to 2.9 (thirty-two lines and twenty-four lines respectively).

The result of Ovid's attempted escape from Love in 3.11 is, as it was in 2.9, failure. The use in the two elegies of the two ruling metaphors of Hellenistic poetry dealing with the attempts of lovers to escape from love stresses that this result was even more inevitable in 3.11 than in 2.9. 2.9 involved the retirement topos applied to a faithful soldier who had never deserted the colours. 3.11 uses the runaway slave motif also given large-scale treatment by Propertius[57] and hints at the retirement topos of 2.9 only in the oblique *cede fatigato* (2). If Love would not allow his *miles*, Ovid, to retire after faithful service in 2.9, he is even less likely to let his slave Ovid run away in 3.11; and escape from Love by flight is according to the Hellenistic topos found in extended form in Propertius 2.30 A and B impossible.[58] But Ovid is at the end of 3.11 nearer to a true assessment of his situation than he was at the end of 2.9. There he was overwhelmed by Love but had no real understanding of his defeat, and could end with an optimistic fantasy. In 3.11, however, Ovid begins with a much more confident and determined stance against Love; and he realizes early in the elegy that the mistress, not Love, is the essential figure in his plight. He ends in a much more abject state, but with the further understanding that the real issue for him is not whether he can escape from Love – for he clearly cannot – or what his sufferings are to be – for these are not at his discretion – but whether his mistress wants him to love her willingly or unwillingly (49f.).

In this sense 2.9 was essentially a poem which offered no solution to the problem of the suffering lover except self-delusion. It consisted of two principal paradoxes. The latter of these, found in the second half of the elegy, has already been described. It consists of Ovid's optimistically regarding as acceptable conditions for yielding to love the factors normally urged as good cause for abandoning love. The first half of the elegy contained the complementary paradox that Ovid urged as his main reason for abandoning Love his loyalty to Love (an inversion of topos B3 (ii) transferred to the lover?) which had gone unrewarded. Ovid is therefore left half-hopeful but uncomprehending. But in 3.11 Ovid does perceive a glimmer of a solution. He sees the importance of the mistress and comes to understand that he has no free will in relation to love. He also learns why this is so. In the first half he sums up his good reasons for leaving his mistress; in the second half he confesses that they are insufficiently strong to allow him to succeed in leaving her. The cause of his weakness is that these good reasons involve his mistress's character and treatment of him; and they remain good and valid. But they do not at all affect her beauty, which is in fact the sole attractant force upon Ovid. Ovid can only pray to her to be kind to him: she has the full and final say. At the end of 2.9 Ovid prayed to the Love-god, even though he had earlier complained about that god's failure to help him. In 3.11 Ovid, however, turns to his mistress as a really effective divinity (47), to whom the other gods defer (45f.). Cupid controlled Mars in 2.9.47f.; in 3.11.45f. Corinna controls all the gods.

The different thematic structures of 2.9 (ring) and 3.11 (parallel) are to some extent related to the emotional complex portrayed in each. Naturally a poet with Ovid's Hellenistic literary background would have welcomed such variation for its own sake; and there is moreover a gradation in technical difficulty between the two structures, since the parallel, as well as being rarer in antiquity, involves problems of thematic handling which require greater poetic skill than the ring. However, there seems also to be some significance in Ovid's *variatio*. In 2.9 the ring showed us Ovid going back on his earlier position point by point. He returns to his starting-point, his emotions altered, his intellectual grasp not much improved. But the parallel structure of 3.11 reflects the sharper intellectual apprehension which Ovid has throughout the elegy and particularly in the second half. It is as though *Amores* 3.11 consisted of a pair of advocates' speeches – against and for love – with the second advocate winning the day by splitting and turning his opponent's arguments.

A¹ I have escaped from love.

A² You are trying to escape from your mistress's bad behaviour, but her beauty brings you back.

B¹ My mistress won't have me with her, even though I cling to her. She has treated me badly.

B² You can neither live with her or without her. She has indeed a bad character: but your love is caused by her beauty.

C¹ She perjured herself by the gods.

C² They allow it, so she is a more powerful divinity.

D¹ I shall give her up.

D² No chance: the only issue is whether you will love her willingly or unwillingly – and she will decide that (49). You can only hope that she will choose the former.

8

Tony Woodman

SELF-IMITATION AND THE
SUBSTANCE OF HISTORY

Tacitus, *Annals* 1.61–5 and *Histories* 2.70, 5.14–15

ANNALS 1.61–2

In the year A.D. 15 Germanicus, nephew and adopted son of the emperor Tiberius, led a Roman army into the heart of Germany. Finding himself near the Teutoburg Forest, where Quintilius Varus and three legions had been massacred by the native chieftain Arminius six years before, Germanicus decided to visit the site of the disaster and pay his last respects to his dead countrymen. We owe our knowledge of this episode to two main sources: Suetonius, who mentions it in one brief sentence,[1] and Tacitus, whose account is, by contrast, extremely long (*Annals* 1.61–2):

> Igitur cupido Caesarem inuadit soluendi suprema militibus ducique, permoto ad miserationem omni qui aderat exercitu ob propinquos, amicos, denique ob casus bellorum et sortem hominum. praemisso Caecina ut occulta saltuum scrutaretur pontesque et aggeres umido paludum et fallacibus campis imponeret, incedunt maestos locos uisuque ac memoria deformis. primo[2] Vari castra lato 2 ambitu et dimensis principiis trium legionum manus ostentabant; dein semiruto uallo, humili fossa accisae iam reliquiae consedisse intellegebantur. medio campi albentia ossa, ut fugerant, ut restiterant, disiecta uel aggerata. adiacebant fragmina telorum equorumque artus, simul 3 truncis arborum antefixa ora. lucis propinquis barbarae arae, apud quas tribunos ac primorum ordinum centuriones mactauerant. et cladis eius superstites, pugnam aut 4 uincula elapsi, referebant hic cecidisse legatos, illic raptas aquilas; primum ubi uulnus Varo adactum, ubi infelici dextera et suo ictu mortem inuenerit; quo tribunali contionatus Arminius, quot patibula captiuis, quae scrobes, utque signis et aquilis per superbiam inluserit.

62 igitur Romanus qui aderat exercitus sextum post cladis annum trium legionum ossa, nullo noscente alienas reliquias an suorum humo tegeret, omnes ut coniunctos, ut consanguineos aucta in hostem ira maesti simul et infensi condebant. primum exstruendo tumulo caespitem Caesar posuit, gratissimo munere in defunctos et praesentibus doloris socius. quod Tiberio haud probatum, seu cuncta 2 Germanici in deterius trahenti, siue exercitum imagine caesorum insepultorumque tardatum ad proelia et formidolosiorem hostium credebat; neque imperatorem auguratu et uetustissimis caerimoniis praeditum adtrectare feralia debuisse.

Germanicus was therefore overwhelmed by a desire to pay his last respects to the soldiers and their commander; and the army there present was moved to pity for their relatives and friends, for the fortunes of war and the fate of men. Caecina had been sent ahead to reconnoitre the unknown forests, to bridge the flooded marshes and to shore up any ground likely to prove treacherous. Then they entered the melancholy site, which was gruesome to set eyes upon and in the memories which it evoked. First there was Varus' camp, a wide area with its headquarters marked out, testifying to the strength of the three legions; next there was the rampart, half-destroyed, and the low ditch where the mortally wounded had evidently huddled together. In the middle of a plain there were whitening bones, lying scattered where soldiers had fled, and piled up where they had made their last stand. Broken pieces of weapons lay nearby, and horses' limbs, and skulls fixed to the trunks of trees. In the surrounding woods there were altars at which the barbarians had engaged in the ritual slaughter of tribunes and first-rank centurions. And survivors of the disaster, who had escaped from the battle or from captivity, recalled where the legates had fallen and where the standards had been captured, where Varus had received his first wound and where he had died by his own doomed hand. They pointed to the mound where Arminius had held his victory rally and arrogantly mocked the military standards, to the number of gibbets for the prisoners of war, and to the pits.

And so the Roman army there present, six years after the disaster, started to bury the bones of the three legions: since no one knew whether they were covering over the remains of relatives or

> *not, they treated everyone as if they were kith and kin, while their anger against the enemy mounted with their grief. It was Germanicus who, in sympathy with his men and as a welcome gesture towards the dead, laid the first turf for the burial mound. But Tiberius did not approve – either because he criticized everything Germanicus did, or because he believed that the sight of the unburied dead had deterred the army from fighting and increased their fear of the enemy; besides, a general empowered as an augur to celebrate the sacred rites ought not in his opinion to have come into contact with relics of the dead.*

It will be seen that Tacitus has taken great care over the structure of this account. The first sentence introduces two themes: (*a*) Germanicus' desire to bury the dead soldiers ('igitur cupido Caesarem inuadit ... militibus ducique'), (*b*) the reaction of the present army ('permoto ad miserationem omni *qui aderat exercitu* ob propinquos ... et sortem hominum'). There then follows a long central 'panel' (*c*) where Tacitus describes the scene of devastation which had brought about (*a*) and (*b*): 'praemisso Caecina ... per superbiam inluserit'. Finally Tacitus returns to the two themes with which he began, although in reverse order: (*b*) 'igitur Romanus *qui aderat exercitus* ... infensi condebant', (*a*) 'primum exstruendo tumulo caespitem Caesar posuit ... feralia debuisse'. The whole episode is thus an example of ring-composition (*abcba*),[3] which on one occasion is made explicit by the repetition of a key phrase (italicized, just above).[4] While it is clear that Tacitus regarded (*a*) as historically the most important element in the episode, as we shall see below (p. 148), there can be no doubt that his literary imagination was roused more by the remainder of the episode. My evidence for this last statement may be gathered by way of an enquiry into Tacitus' source for the event.

From where did Tacitus derive the information for his account? After all, the detailed nature of his description is remarkable, considering that the event took place a full century before he came to describe it. Since it is known that *Bella Germaniae* had been written by the earlier historians Aufidius Bassus and the elder Pliny, scholars have suggested one or other of these works (both of which have conveniently failed to survive) as a possible source.[5] But I would rather point to a quite different possibility. In A.D. 69 Vitellius had visited the site of the first Battle of Cremona; and Tacitus, a few years before he came to describe Germanicus' visit to the Teutoburg Forest in the *Annals*, had already described this more recent visit of Vitellius in *Histories* 2.70:

Tony Woodman

Inde *Vitellius* Cremonam flexit et spectato munere
Caecinae insistere Bedriacensibus campis ac uestigia recentis
uictoriae lustrare oculis *concupiuit*. foedum atque atrox
spectaculum: intra quadragensimum pugnae diem lacera
corpora, *trunci artus*, putres uirorum *equorumque* formae,
infecta tabo humus, protritis arboribus ac frugibus dira
uastitas. nec minus inhumana facies uiae, quam Cremon- 2
enses lauru rosaque constrauerant, *exstructis altaribus
caesisque uictimis* regium in morem; quae laeta in praesens
mox perniciem ipsis fecere. *aderant* Valens et Caecina 3
monstrabantque pugnae *locos: hinc* inrupisse legionum
agmen, *hinc* equites coortos, *inde* circumfusas auxiliorum
manus; iam tribuni praefectique, sua quisque facta extol-
lentes, falsa uera aut maiora uero miscebant. uolgus quoque
militum clamore et gaudio deflectere uia, spatia certa-
minum recognoscere, *aggerem* armorum, *strues corporum*
intueri mirari; *et erant quos uaria sors rerum lacrimaeque et
misericordia subiret.* at non Vitellius flexit oculos nec tot 4
milia insepultorum ciuium exhorruit: laetus ultro et tam
propinquae sortis ignarus instaurabat sacrum dis loci.

*From there Vitellius deviated to Cremona, and having seen
Caecina's gladiatorial exhibition, he desired to set foot on the
plain at Bedriacum and see with his own eyes the traces of the
recent victory. It was a macabre and horrifying sight: less than
forty days had elapsed since the battle, and there were mutilated
corpses, trunks, limbs, and the shapes of decomposed men and
horses; the ground was stained with gore, and the flattened
trees and crops presented a scene of terrible devastation. Equally
barbaric was the view of the road, where the people of Cremona
had strewn laurel and roses, and built altars for the victims
whom they slaughtered: such tyrannical behaviour, however
satisfying at the time, was soon to be the cause of their own
destruction. Valens and Caecina were present, and they pointed
out the various important areas of the battle-site: where the
legionary column had burst out, where the horsemen had massed,
and where the auxiliaries had completed their encirclement.
Already the tribunes and prefects were each boasting of their
own achievements, adding fabrications and exaggerating the
truth; and the ordinary soldiers too, shouting happily as they left
the road, re-traced the battle-field and proudly examined the*

> *pile of weapons and heaps of corpses. Some were affected by the variability of fate, by tears and by pity; but not Vitellius, who gazed impassively on the many thousands of unburied citizens. Unable to restrain his delight, and unaware of the fate that was so soon to befall him, he sacrificed to the gods of the place.*

As may be seen from the italicized words and phrases, there are numerous and noteworthy similarities between this passage and that from *Annals* 1 already quoted. How are they to be explained?[6] A *first* suggestion might be that the similarities are inevitable, given the comparable subject matter of each passage. One would expect to find corpses in any description of a battle-field, and the reflections on fate and pity are hardly unusual in such a context. Again, Tacitus' phrase *ut fugerant, ut restiterant, disiecta uel aggerata (ossa)* in *Annals* is paralleled quite closely by a passage of Livy in which Hannibal re-visits the site of the Battle of Cannae (22.51.6 'iacebant tot Romanorum milia, pedites *passim* equitesque *ut* quem cuique fors aut *pugna iunxerat* aut *fuga*');[7] and both *hic ... illic ... ubi* etc. in *Annals* and *hinc ... hinc ... inde* in *Histories* are paralleled by a passage of Virgil in which the Trojans wander over the deserted battle-field of the Troad (*Aeneid* 2.29–30 '*hic* Dolopum manus, *hic* saeuus tendebat Achilles; | classibus *hic* locus, *hic* acie certare solebant'). Alternatively, one might use these same correspondences with Livy and Virgil to put forward a *second* suggestion: perhaps there existed a literary prototype (for example, in a now lost passage of Ennius) which has exerted a common influence over Livy and Virgil on the one hand and the two Tacitean passages on the other?

Yet I do not think that either of these suggestions constitutes the true explanation of the similarity between the two passages of Tacitus. The most remarkable parallel between the two passages is the way in which, half-way through each, Tacitus introduces the men who had survived their respective disasters and who conveniently happened to be on hand to point out various important areas. This detail seems to me so unusual, and unparalleled elsewhere,[8] that it places the many other correspondences in a different light. In view of this detail I would contend that Tacitus in *Annals* 1.61–2 has imitated his earlier account in the *Histories*,[9] and that this contention is corroborated both by the number and variety of the other correspondences and also by the fact that he repeats the process in *Annals* 1.64–5, a few chapters later. I shall return to this last point in the next section (pp. 149–51); but first I should like to note how Tacitus in the present case has varied his earlier account in *Histories* 2.70.

When in the ancient world a writer imitated another writer, he would take care to weld the imitated material into its new context, to vary it, and if possible, to improve upon it. That this practice also held good for self-imitation is shown by Tacitus here. In *Histories* Tacitus refers to the vicissitudes of fortune at the end of his description ('et erant quos uaria sors rerum . . .'), whereas in *Annals* the corresponding sentiment ('permoto ad miserationem . . . ob casus bellorum et sortem hominum') is placed at the beginning of the episode: in *H.* the statement is thus emphatically and climactically placed because Tacitus wishes to draw from the episode the moral that Vitellius will himself be soon overtaken by the vagaries of fate ('laetus ultro et tam propinquae sortis ignarus');[10] whereas in *A.* he wishes nothing to conflict in importance or significance with the moral of chapters 61–2 as a whole, namely Tiberius' characteristically critical reaction to Germanicus' act of piety. Again, in *H.* Tacitus continually stresses the appearance presented by the battle-field of Cremona (cf. *lustrare oculis, spectaculum, monstrabant, non . . . flexit oculos*),[11] whereas in *A.* he dispenses with such mediating vocabulary and tells his story in a more immediate and vivid manner (cf. only *uisu . . . deformis*). On another occasion, however, the same word is used both times but its meaning has changed: *trunci* in *H.* is either an adjective = 'mutilated' (agreeing with *artus*, 'limbs') or a noun = 'trunks of bodies', whereas in *A.* it means 'trunks of trees'.

Instead of the prosaic *Vitellius . . . concupiuit* in the *Histories* we now have *cupido Caesarem inuadit* in the *Annals*, an echo of Sallust's phrase *potiundi Marium maxuma cupido inuaserat* (*Jugurtha* 89.6).[12] Instead of *exstructis altaribus* we now have *barbărae ārae*, which Soubiran well describes as 'cacophanie évidente . . . elle suggère concrètement la barbarie des rites d'immolation et la répulsion du narrateur romain'.[13] And while there is one clear echo of Virgil in *Histories* (*infecta tabo humus* ~ *Georgics* 3.481 *infecit pabula tabo*), there are several in *Annals*: *medio campi albentia ossa* ~ *Aeneid* 12.36 *campique ingentes ossibus albent*;[14] *truncis arborum antefixa ora* ~ *Aeneid* 8.196–7 *foribusque adfixa superbis* | *ora*;[15] and *uulnus . . . adactum* ~ *Aeneid* 10.850.[16]

It is interesting to note that none of these three Virgilian reminiscences belongs to the same category of imitation. The first is an example of what I shall later call 'substantive imitation' (for a definition see below, p. 152): it is highly unlikely that Tacitus had any historical evidence for whitening bones in the middle of the plain; more probably he has added an apparently factual detail which in reality is simply borrowed from Virgil. The second is a 'significant imitation': since the doorposts on which the skulls hang belong to Cacus, whom Virgil describes as *semihomo* (l. 194), this monster thus serves as a prototype for the semi-human barbarians who fastened Roman skulls to tree-trunks.[17] The third is merely a 'verbal echo', but even from this lowest form of imitation conclusions can be drawn: the very fact that Tacitus' phraseology may be traced back to Rome's most illustrious epic poet indicates the elevated style of the passage – an observation which remains true whether or not the echo was intentional and whether or not Tacitus' readers recognized it.

ANNALS 1.64–5

After Germanicus' visit to the site of the Varian disaster, his legate Caecina is compelled by harrying natives to pitch an uncomfortable camp amidst constant defensive fighting. On this occasion our knowledge of the incident derives from Tacitus alone (*Annals* 1.64.1–3, 65.1):

> Barbari, perfringere stationes seque inferre munitoribus nisi, lacessunt circumgrediuntur occursant: miscetur operantium bellantiumque clamor. et cuncta pariter 2 Romanis aduersa: locus uligine profunda, idem ad gradum instabilis, procedentibus lubricus; corpora grauia loricis; neque librare pila inter undas poterant. contra Cheruscis sueta apud paludes proelia, procera membra, hastae ingentes ad uulnera facienda quamuis procul. nox demum 3 inclinantis iam legiones aduersae pugnae exemit. Germani ob prospera indefessi . . .
> 65 nox per diuersa inquies, cum barbari festis epulis, laeto cantu aut truci sonore subiecta uallium ac resultantis saltus complerent, apud Romanos inualidi ignes interruptae uoces, atque ipsi passim adiacerent uallo, oberrarent tentoriis, insomnes magis quam peruigiles.

In their efforts to break through the guardposts and attack the workers, the barbarians engaged in harassment, encircling manoeuvres and charges. The shouts of the workers and fighters were confused, and everything was equally unfavourable to the Romans: the place, with its deep mud, provided unreliable footholds and was too slippery to allow any progress; their bodies

*were weighed down by armour, and in the waves they were unable
to throw their javelins. On the other hand, the Cherusci were long
accustomed to fighting in marshland: they had long limbs, and
their huge spears were effective at long-range wounding. Nightfall finally rescued the now sagging legions from their losing
battle; but the Germans, tireless in success . . .*

*It was a disturbed night, though for different reasons. The
barbarians at their celebration feasts filled the valleys and echoing
forests with their victory or war songs. On the Roman side the
fires were fitful, and voices hesitant: they lay against the rampart,
or wandered among the tents, unable either to sleep or keep watch.*

Again we must ask how Tacitus could possibly have acquired so
many details of a routine frontier engagement which had taken place a
century before he came to describe it. And again I would point to
another such battle between Romans and Germans which took place
in A.D. 70 and which Tacitus had already described in his *Histories*
(5.14.2–15.2):

Ea loci forma, incertis uadis subdola et *nobis aduersa*:
quippe miles Romanus *armis grauis* et nandi pauidus,
Germanos *fluminibus suetos* leuitas armorum et *proceritas*
15 *corporum* attollit. igitur *lacessentibus* Batauis ferocissimo
cuique nostrorum coeptum certamen; deinde orta trepi-
datio, cum *praealtis paludibus* arma equi haurirentur.
Germani notis uadibus persultabant, omissa plerumque
fronte latera ac terga *circumuenientes*. neque ut in pedestri
acie comminus certabatur, sed tamquam nauali pugna uagi
inter undas aut, si quid *stabile* occurrebat, totis illuc corp-
oribus *nitentes* . . . eius proelii euentus utrumque ducem   2
diuersis animi motibus ad maturandum summae rei discrimen erexit: Ciuilis instare fortunae, Cerialis abolere
ignominiam; *Germani prosperis feroces*, Romanos pudor
excitauerat. *nox apud barbaros cantu aut clamore, nostris* per
iram et minas acta.

*Such was the appearance of the place, treacherous with hidden
swamps and unfavourable to us: for the Roman soldiers were
weighed down by weapons and terrified of swimming, whereas the
Germans, long accustomed to the rivers, took advantage of their
light armour and tall bodies. While the Batavi therefore engaged
in harassment, our most intrepid men all began to fight; but*

*panic struck when weapons and horses started to be swallowed up
in the unusually deep marshes. But the Germans fairly ran
through their native swamps, and disregarding the opposing
front-line they encircled the flanks and rear. Contrary to what you
would expect in an infantry battle, there was no close fighting,
but the men wandered in the waves as if during a naval encounter;
or else, if a reliable patch of ground showed up, they strove
towards it with all their might. . . The result of that particular
battle encouraged each commander to bring the whole operation
to a decision, although for different reasons: Civilis wished to
press home his good fortune, Cerialis to redeem his disgrace.
Thus the Germans were fierce on account of their success, while
the Romans were spurred on by shame: night on the barbarian
side was spent in singing or shouting, on ours in anger and threats.*

As on the previous occasion, some of these correspondences are not
unexpected in such a context: harassing and encircling (*lacessunt* and
circumgrediuntur in *Annals* ∼ *lacessentibus* and *circumuenientes* in
Histories) take place in most battles, while the size of barbarians and
the uncongeniality of their haunts (*procera membra* ∼ *proceritas
corporum; uligine profunda* ∼ *praealtis paludibus*) were always remarked
upon by Romans and belong to the conventions of ethnographical
writing.[18] But there are also more specific and telling details (*Germani
ob prospera indefessi* ∼ *Germani prosperis feroces*); and most remarkable
of all are the strikingly close accounts of the night scenes (*diuersis*¹
animi motibus . . . *nox apud barbaros cantu aut clamore, nostris* ∼ *nox per*
diuersa . . . *barbari* . . . *laeto cantu aut truci sonore* . . . *apud Romanos*)[19]
and the coincidence in each passage of the phrase *inter undas*, a highly
idiosyncratic description of fighting in swamps.[20]

These last two details seem to me to belong to the same category as
the survivors in the previous pair of passages (see above, p. 147), and
they persuade me that in *Annals* 1.64–5 Tacitus is imitating his own
earlier description in *Histories* 5.14–15. On this occasion, however,
Tacitus does not seem to have been much concerned to vary his earlier
account. *nisi* in *Annals* is used of the successful efforts of the Germans,
whereas *nitentes* in *Histories* is used of the desperate efforts of the
Romans; and whereas in *H.* the phrase *apud barbaros* is used merely
for the sake of variation with *nostris*, in *A.* the phrase *apud Romanos*
is used to show that 'the Romans are passive and helpless in contrast
to the active and triumphant Germans' (cf. *Germani . . . complerent*).[21]

SUBSTANTIVE IMITATION

If this general hypothesis for *Annals* 1.61–2 and 64–5 is accepted, it is natural to enquire to what extent, if at all, Tacitus' accounts in these chapters are true.[22] Did Germanicus visit the Teutoburg Forest at all, for example, or has Tacitus simply invented the whole episode on the basis of *Histories* 2.70? It has already been noted that we also have Suetonius' statement attesting Germanicus' visit (above, p. 143), but this corroborates *Annals* 1.61–2 only if it can be demonstrated that Suetonius has not derived his information from Tacitus. Unfortunately, Suetonius' relationship to Tacitus is in general obscure;[23] but some clarification is perhaps possible in the present case. Most scholars would agree that Tiberius' criticism of Germanicus' burying the soldiers, which Tacitus reports at 1.62.2, derives from the *acta senatus*;[24] and we should note that it is the act of burial, without any hint of criticism, which Suetonius singles out in his brief reference. It thus seems likely that both Suetonius (who as a top civil servant had access to the imperial archives) and Tacitus are independently indebted to the official records on this matter, in which case we may be fairly certain, at the very least, that Germanicus' visit actually did take place. For Caecina's battle with the Germans at 1.64–5, on the other hand, we have no other evidence apart from Tacitus; but since he tells us a few chapters later that 'decreta eo anno [A.D. 15] triumphalia insignia A. Caecinae' (1.72.1), we may assume that Caecina would hardly have received this honour from Tiberius if his activities in Germany had not warranted it.

I would therefore conclude that the plain fact of Germanicus' visit or of Caecina's battle is undeniable, but that the details of Tacitus' elaborate descriptions of each event are entirely derived from the passages of the *Histories* which I have quoted.[25] The passages from the *Annals* are thus examples fo 'substantive imitation', by which I mean the technique of giving substance to a poorly documented incident by the imitating of one which is much better documented.[26] On this view, the question of Tacitus' sources for *Annals* 1.61–2 and 64–5, which I raised earlier (p. 145), must now be allowed to lapse: for the bulk of the narrative in these chapters Tacitus needed no source (in the generally accepted sense of that term) at all – whether Aufidius, Pliny or anyone else.

Tacitus' technique, as I have described it, may sound scandalous to the majority of his modern readers, who evidently still regard him as a faithful historian;[27] but that is because they fail to take account of the way in which ancient writers wrote history. In the first place, ancient historians were regularly far more concerned with probability than reality,[28] and very often the relative antiquity and geographical distance of an event are guides as to how an ancient historian might have treated it: century-old episodes in the heart of Germany, such as Tacitus relates in *Annals* 1.61–5, were presumably more susceptible of falsification or elaboration than contemporary events close to home (though even these were by no means immune). In the second place, ancient historians resorted to 'substantive imitation' far more regularly than is sometimes supposed. A few examples will illustrate this.[29]

Elsewhere in Book 1 of the *Annals* there is substantive imitation by Tacitus of Livy 1.41 at chapters 5–6,[30] of Livy 3.13 at chapter 23.2, and of Livy 8.32.12–13 at chapter 35.5.[31] Livy himself is recognized to have imitated Homer, Herodotus and Thucydides.[32] Thucydides was in fact a favourite source for imitative historians. The second-century A.D. literary critic Lucian, in his book *How to write history* (15), tells us of a contemporary historian who was so captivated by Thucydides that he inserted into his own history of the Parthian Wars a fictitious plague modelled entirely on the Athenian plague described so vividly by his eminent predecessor. 'He lifted it completely from Thucydides, except for the Pelasgicon and the Long Walls where those who had caught Thucydides' plague had settled; but as for the rest, it *began in Ethiopia* (as in Thucydides), then *descended into Egypt.*' We may at first sight find this hard to believe, but Procopius' description of the plague which is said to have hit Byzantium in A.D. 540 manifests exactly the same characteristics (2.22–3).

I doubt whether it ever occurred to ancient historians to question their use of this technique, but if a philosopher of history had pressed them to defend it, I suspect their answer would have been along the following lines. Thucydides believed that historical events will, at some point in the future and in more or less the same ways, recur, and that there are cycles of history.[33] This belief was taken up by numerous ancient writers,[34] among whom Tacitus himself is prominent (*Annals* 3.55.5 'nisi forte rebus cunctis inest quidam uelut orbis, ut, quemadmodum temporum uices, ita morum uertantur'), and can easily be applied to the two cases we have been discussing. For example, given that Vitellius in A.D. 69 was visiting a battle-site and that such a visit was doubtless not much different from Germanicus' to the Teutoburg Forest in A.D. 15, Tacitus would not, I believe, have regarded it as in any way unusual that he should describe the latter in terms of the former: this was an illustration of history repeating itself, with the qualification that Vitellius had been victorious whereas Germanicus' predecessor Varus had not.

DELECTATIO LECTORIS

We can only speculate why Tacitus in *Annals* 1.61–2 and 64–5 chose to spend so much time on episodes for which, on the present hypothesis, he had little or no source material. Sometimes, it is true, a writer will produce correspondences from which he wishes some particular significance to emerge: we have already noticed an occasion where Tacitus imitates *Aeneid* 8 for precisely this reason (above, p. 149), and some other examples of this phenomenon might be helpful. It has been shown that Tacitus has described Livia's role in the accession of Tiberius at *Annals* 1.5–6 in very similar terms to his account of Agrippina's role in the accession of Nero at *Annals* 12.66–13.1:[35] by means of close linguistic correspondences Tacitus wishes 'to invest the accession of Tiberius with the same air of questionable legitimacy that attended Nero's accession and to stress how Tiberius, in just the same way as Nero, owed his position to the machinations of the emperor's widow'.[36] Again, when Tacitus begins the fourth book of the *Annals* with a character sketch of Sejanus which is closely modelled on Sallust's description of Catiline, he wishes his readers to see in Sejanus a re-incarnation of the same criminal qualities which Catiline had displayed. I find it very hard to believe, however, that this happens in either of our two present cases: to see Germanicus as a forerunner of Vitellius, for example, would be absurd; and I do not see any evidence that Tacitus has presented Germanicus' behaviour as an ideal from which Vitellius has flagrantly departed.[37]

I think the reasons for Tacitus' 'substantive self-imitation' in *Annals* 1.61–2 and 64–5 are more straightforward and lie elsewhere – in entertainment. However foreign it may be to us today, historians in the ancient world were expected to provide their readers with entertainment, *delectatio lectoris*,[38] a responsibility of which Tacitus expresses himself only too well aware (cf. *Annals* 4.32.1, 33.2–3). Battle-scenes such as that at *Histories* 5.14–15 were a particularly common method of supplying this *delectatio*,[39] as Tacitus knew full well (*Annals* 4.33.3 'uarietates proeliorum . . . retinent ac redintegrant legentium animos', cf. *Histories* 1.2.1 'opus adgredior . . . atrox proeliis'); and if by some remote chance a writer of his calibre failed to realize the potential effect of an episode like *Histories* 2.70, there was always his friend the younger Pliny to supply him with 'feedback' (see *Letters* 7.33). Naturally this suggestion cannot be proved; but I think it is significant that, as is generally recognized,[40] Tacitus' account of events in Germany in *Annals* 1 is quite out of proportion to their historical importance: he seems to have 'written up' these sections because he enjoyed them and because he knew from experience that they would entertain his readers.

In 1935 the foreign correspondent of a certain English newspaper, finding himself without much material to report, despatched to England stories which supposedly dealt with the build-up to the Abyssinian war but which were in fact derived from an old colonel's military reminiscences, published several years previously in a book entitled *In the country of the Blue Nile*. The correspondent's newspaper was delighted with the reception given to these stories by its readers, and accordingly sent him a series of congratulatory telegrams – whereupon a colleague remarked to him: 'Well, now we know, it's entertainment they want!'[41] The colleague had only then come to realize what had been known long ago to Tacitus, to whom the foreign correspondent's technique would have seemed very familiar.

9

K. W. Gransden

LENTE CVRRITE, NOCTIS EQVI

Chaucer, *Troilus and Criseyde* 3.1422–70, Donne,
The Sun Rising and Ovid, *Amores* 1.13

OVID

IAM super oceanum uenit a seniore marito
    flaua pruinoso quae uehit axe diem.
quo properas, Aurora? mane: sic Memnonis umbris
    annua sollemni caede parentet auis.
nunc iuuat in teneris dominae iacuisse lacertis;   5
    si quando, lateri nunc bene iuncta meo est.
nunc etiam somni pingues et frigidus aer,
    et liquidum tenui gutture cantat auis.
quo properas ingrata uiris, ingrata puellis?
    roscida purpurea supprime lora manu.   10
ante tuos ortus melius sua sidera seruat
    nauita nec media nescius errat aqua;
te surgit quamuis lassus ueniente uiator
    et miles saeuas aptat ad arma manus;
prima bidente uides oneratos arua colentes,   15
    prima uocas tardos sub iuga panda boues;
tu pueros somno fraudas tradisque magistris,
    ut subeant tenerae uerbera saeua manus,
atque eadem sponsum †cultos† ante Atria mittis,
    unius ut uerbi grandia damna ferant;   20
nec tu consulto nec tu iucunda diserto;
    cogitur ad lites surgere uterque nouas;
tu, cum feminei possint cessare labores,
    lanificam reuocas ad sua pensa manum.
omnia perpeterer; sed surgere mane puellas   25
    quis, nisi cui non est ulla puella, ferat?
optaui quotiens ne nox tibi cedere uellet,
    ne fugerent uultus sidera mota tuos!
optaui quotiens aut uentus frangeret axem
    aut caderet spissa nube retentus equus!   30

inuida, quo properas? quod erat tibi filius ater,
    materni fuerat pectoris ille color.   32

Tithono uellem de te narrare liceret: 35
    femina non caelo turpior ulla foret.

illum dum refugis, longo quia grandior aeuo,
    surgis ad inuisas a sene mane rotas;

at si quem manibus Cephalum complexa teneres,
    clamares 'lente currite, noctis equi.'   40

cur ego plectar amans, si uir tibi marcet ab annis?
    num me nupsisti conciliante seni?

aspice quot somnos iuueni donarit amato
    Luna, neque illius forma secunda tuae.

ipse deum genitor, ne te tam saepe uideret,   45
    commisit noctes in sua uota duas.

iurgia finieram. scires audisse: rubebat,
    nec tamen adsueto tardius orta dies.

                        (Ovid, *Amores* 1.13)

Now on the sea from her old love comes shee,
That drawes the day from heavens cold axletree.
Aurora whither slidest thou? downe againe,
And birds for *Memnon* yearly shall be slaine.
Now in her tender armes I sweetly bide,
If ever, now well lies she by my side
The aire is colde, and sleepe is sweetest now,
And birdes send forth shrill notes from everie bow.
Whither runst thou, that men, and women, love not?
Hold in thy rosie horses that they move not.   10
Ere thou rise starres teach seamen where to saile,
But when thou comest they of their courses faile.
Poore travailers though tierd, rise at thy sight,
And souldiours make them ready to the fight,
The painfull Hinde by thee to field is sent,
Slow oxen early in the yoake are pent.
Thou coosnest boyes of sleepe, and dost betray them
To Pedants, that with cruell lashes pay them.
Thou makste the suretie to the lawyer runne,
That with one worde hath nigh himselfe undone,   20
The lawier and the client hate thy view,
Both whom thou raisest up to toyle anew.
By thy meanes women of their rest are bard,

Thou setst their labouring hands to spin and card.
All could I beare, but that the wench should rise,
Who can indure, save him with whom none lies?
How oft wisht I night would not give thee place,
Nor morning starres shunne thy uprising face.
How oft, that either wind would breake thy coche,
Or steeds might fal forcd with thick clouds approch.   30
Whither gost thou hateful nimph? *Memnon* the elfe
Received his cole-blacke from thy selfe.
Say that thy love with *Cæphalus* were not knowne,
Then thinkest thou thy loose life is not showne?
Would *Tithon* might but talke of thee a while,
Not one in heaven should be more base and vile.
Thou leav'st his bed, because hees faint through age,
And early mountest thy hatefull carriage:
But heldst thou in thine armes some *Cæphalus*,
Then wouldst thou cry, stay night and runne not thus.   40
Punish ye, because yeares make him waine?
I did not bid thee wed an aged swaine.
The Moone sleepes with *Endemion* everie day,
Thou art as faire as shee, then kisse and play.
Jove that thou shouldst not hast but wait his leasure,
Made two nights one to finish up his pleasure.
I chid no more, she blusht, and therefore heard me,
Yet lingered not the day, but morning scard me.

(Marlowe)

The lover's complaint that dawn has come too soon is an ancient motif which became popular in medieval and Renaissance poetry. It occurs frequently in the Greek Anthology, but its most influential treatment by a classical poet is Ovid, *Amores* 1.13.[1] This famous piece is not merely an amplification of epigram;[2] it is an extended conceit in which various rhetorical techniques and figures are exploited and parodied. The picture of Aurora leaving the bed of Tithonus, with which the poem starts, is used by Ovid again at *Heroides* 18.111–14 (Leander to Hero): although the context and manner are quite different, there is the same contrast between the enforced and reluctant parting of a pair of lovers and the alacrity with which Dawn leaves old Tithonus' bed. Were she sleeping with someone younger, she might be less disposed to early rising, and thus be in harmony rather than conflict with the desires of lovers. Ovid returns to this point in the present poem at 35–40 ('if you were in bed with someone like Cephalus, you'd cry for night's horses to slow down'). The allusion in the first line of *Amores* 1.13 to the unnamed Tithonus as *seniore marito* establishes the point on which the poet's conceit turns. Tithonus is contrasted with the poet-lover on two counts: he is old, and he is a husband – a stock figure of erotic elegy. The sophisticated Augustan reader would also appreciate the joke about Cephalus, the beautiful (and married) youth wooed by Aurora: 'nec tamen Aurorae male se praebebat amandum. | ibat ad hunc sapiens a sene diua uiro' (*Heroides* 4.95–6).

The whole of this poem except the first and last couplets is an address to Aurora by the poet-lover. In ancient literature, addressees are often more important than the speaker,[3] but here Ovid presents Aurora ambiguously by alluding to her private life and loves in ll. 33–4 and 37–8. An address to a deity is a prayer or a hymn, and it has been suggested that Ovid is parodying the form and content of the kletic hymn (ironically substituting 'don't come' for 'come'):[4] thus she is called 'ingrata uiris, ingrata puellis' (9), instead of the expected 'grata'. Ovid is wittily exploiting the tongue-in-cheek Hellenistic treatment of mythology, in which the deity's private life is played off against his or her public function. Dawn's public function or natural duty is to rise each day at the duly appointed hour, and she fulfils it in the poem's last couplet, where the pun on *rubebat* refers both to her public function and her private life. Her blushes stand for the sunrise, imperturbable and punctual, yet they also represent her confused response to the poet's *exposé* of her *amours*, which formed the last section of the poem.

We may also see the poem as a mock request to Dawn to perpetrate an *adynaton* (a reversal of nature). In ll. 41–4 Ovid cites two familiar precedents: the Moon and Endymion (cf. Leander's prayer to the Moon in *Heroides* 18.60–74) and Jupiter and Alcmena. The reference to Jupiter, with its mock epic periphrasis *ipse deum genitor*, forms the climax (or anti-climax) of Ovid's case, and emphasizes the poet's deflationary treatment of myth. Jupiter and Luna altered the course of nature for their own sexual gratification: Aurora (having lost her lover) has no such motive, but, on the contrary, a strong motive for keeping to the normal cosmic timetable.

Such citation of precedents to strengthen one's case was also a normal feature of the rhetorical *suasoria*, in which a parade of *exempla* was intended to ensure the success of the speaker's case. Structurally, this poem can be seen as a *suasoria*, or rather as a loose parody of one, containing the main elements as prescribed in the rhetorical hand-books.[5] Setting aside the introductory and final couplets, ll. 3–4 constitute the *exordium*, which is followed by the *narratio*, giving reasons why Dawn should delay. There is a parody of the panegyric (in which the god's powers are praised and his exploits recalled), and there is even a *refutatio*, in which a counter-argument (here that of Tithonus' senility) is comically disposed of: 'num me nupsisti conciliante seni?' has an ironically forensic tone. Thus, although the poet is ultimately unsuccessful in his *suasoria*, it will by now be clear that his true success lies in the skill with which he adapts and parodies the forms and techniques of rhetoric.

Suasoriae usually dealt with matters of general concern, and the charm of Ovid's parody lies in its wholly private preoccupation, most notably in the *narratio*, a typical piece of erotic elegy. 5–8 are elegant, carefully wrought lines: the assonances *nunc iuuat . . . nunc . . . iuncta* and *lacertis . . . lateri* yield an entwining effect ('we've never been so close together as we are now'), while the triple anaphora of *nunc* emphasizes the importance of the present moment ('surely you can't think of separating us *now?*'). The second of the two couplets, with its deep sleep, cold dawn breeze and bird-song, has a post-sexual pastoral calm. 9–10 repeat *quo properas*, which will occur (intensified) for the third time at 31.[6] We then move to the first of the poem's two principal sections, 11–24, a series of *exempla* in which the poet shows how his fellow creatures in the workaday world suffer from Dawn's coming. Ovid here effectively juxtaposes this topos – Dawn as the bringer of fresh tasks to the toiling masses – with the topos of the lover's complaint. The Dawn–work topos is common: cf. *Amores* 1.6.65–6 'iamque pruinosos molitur Lucifer axes, | inque suum miseros excitat ales opus', where the word *miseros* recalls Virgil, *Aeneid* 9.182–3 'Aurora interea miseris mortalibus almam | extulerat lucem referens opera atque labores'; it is characteristic of Virgil to contrast *miseris* with *almam* and then to intensify it again in *opera atque labores*. Another instance of the topos is A. E. Housman, *Last Poems* 11:

> Yonder see the morning blink:
> The sun is up and so must I,
> To wash and dress and eat and drink
> And look at things and talk and think
> And work, and God knows why.

The incompatibility of love and business is itself a common topos; the entire ethos of Virgilian pastoral turns on the antithesis *otium/negotium*, with pastoral itself as the perfect expression of *otium*. In erotic elegy, the contrast turns up in Donne's *Break of Day*:

> Must business thee from hence remove?
> O that's the worst disease of love.

The poet-lover traditionally lives wholly in the world of his own feelings, which his poetry variously dramatizes, and in l. 25 Ovid turns again to his own case. *Omnia perpeterer* parodies Propertius 2.26B.35, in which the earlier poet's serious indicative, *omnia perpetiar*, is modified into an ironically bathetic subjunctive.[7] I could bear all that, says Ovid (who abandoned the law and is neither sailor, traveller, soldier, farmer, apprentice or seamstress), in his best mock-heroic vein – so long as I don't have to bear girls getting up at dawn. Only a man who has no girl could bear *that*. *Quis, nisi cui non est ulla puella, ferat?* is couched in Ovid's neatest epigrammatic style, exploiting the possibilities of Latin word-order within the metrical limitations imposed by the pentameter, and pointed further by the repeated sound-echoes of *quis, nisi cui non est* and of *ulla puella*. The last word, *ferat*, repeating the sense of *perpeterer*, rounds off the couplet.

In the two balancing couplets 27–30, each beginning with *optaui quotiens*, the poet says he has often previously prayed for the *adynaton* he now desires, and has thought of ways it might be brought about: there is a witty blend of the mythological (a celestial traffic accident) and the Lucretian/scientific (Dawn delayed by wind and cloud, as if a sufficiently dark and dismal morning might actually simulate the *adynaton*). At 31, with the final *quo properas*, we revert to the traditional figure of envious Dawn which occurs also in Greek poetry[8] and is perhaps linked to the mythological enmity between Venus and the sun (the sun was the first to see Venus and Mars together).[9] This figure is a commonplace in Renaissance poetry:

> Look, love, what envious streaks
> Do lace the severing clouds in yonder east . . .[10]

In the poem's last section, Ovid, as has been noted above, parodies both the hymn and the *suasoria*: instead of a panegyric celebrating the god's great deeds, we are given a scandalous reminder of Aurora's erotic entanglements: has she, who has cheated her old husband, the right to refuse lovers extra time? Ovid's tone here becomes one of forensic mock indignation, mixed with conspiratorial complicity: if Aurora still had, as Ovid has, a lover . . .: *complexa teneres* in 37 corresponds to *nunc iuuat in teneris . . . iacuisse lacertis* in 5, but Ovid's pleasures are in the present indicative, Dawn's are in the 'absent' subjunctive. There is a further correspondence between the final couplet and the opening one; the first ends with *diem*, the last with *dies*, the final nominative constituting the mocking and anti-climactic triumph of nature over myth and giving a final gloss-finish of sophisticated realism to a poem whose theme might have lent itself to over-indulgence in fancy.

Like most erotic elegies from Propertius to Donne, this is a dramatic poem, but the drama is static, the rhetoric often forensic, and the poem works by a mixture of detachment and involvement, the one constantly correcting the other. The 'serious' element – the warm yet refreshing erotic confession, the strong passage about the workers – is set against the fanciful and embellishing mythology. Ovid has a unique capacity for humanizing the fantastic; his irony never goes so far as to alienate our interest, being at once deflationary and sentimental.[11]

Ovid's style is marked by an immense clarity. Even when metre dictates, or encourages, a dislocation of word-order, Ovid turns this to his advantage and uses it to point the meaning more sharply. Ovid's is a poetry of antithesis and paradox rather than ambivalence, of statement rather than suggestion, and this is reflected in the texture of the verse. There is a general avoidance of 'colourless' or 'indifferent' words, and also of elision – two features which are in marked contrast to the style of Virgil, where bold and frequent use of elision and a fondness for qualifying words are largely responsible for the strangely wavering surface and undercurrents of unresolved meanings which characterize his mature style.[12] In avoiding elision, and in writing hexameters in which dactyls largely predominate (as against the naturally spondaic character of Latin),[13] Ovid produced a rapid flow in which verbal and metrical units are precisely defined and do not blend or blur into each other. In this poem, apart from the aphaeresis in *meo est* (6),[14] there are only two weak elisions (of -*ĕ*, at 19 and 22); and there are only two hexameters in which spondees predominate: 13 (which expresses slow weariness) and 21 (a dragging resentment). The diction throughout is largely free from lexical affectation. *Pruinosus* (2) is not attested before Ovid (cf. also *Amores* 1.6.65); and *feminei labores* and *lanificam manum* (23–4) are both borrowed from Tibullus 2.1,[15] the latter adjective being of the compound type much favoured by the new poetry of the Augustans.

Ovid's most brilliant epigrammatic effects are found in his handling of the pentameter,[16] which imposed challenging formal restrictions on Roman poets, especially when the licence of polysyllabic endings became impermissible. Skilled *variatio* was needed to avoid monotony, but inevitably certain disyllabic words tended to recur at the end of the pentameter. Ovid uses a form of *manus* (a key word in the highly tactile *Amores*) four times at the end of pentameters in this poem, and in all but four of the other poems in *Amores* 1 the word occurs in this position at least once. Throughout Latin poetry, rhyme, assonance and homoeoteleuton occur:[17] the most interesting example here is that of *auis* at 4 and 8, juxtaposing Memnon's mythological birds and the real bird which sings to the poet and his mistress.

Ovid shows great skill in varying the limited range of symmetrical patterns possible in the pentameter. The commoner types, in which a noun and adjective in agreement balance each other before the caesura and at the end of the line (e.g. a/ - - A, A/ - - a) are mixed with the less common (e.g. - a/ A b B, - a/ - A B). Occasional lines dispense with a structure of returning symmetry and offer a straight syntactical progression, like the famous *clamares lente currite, noctis equi.*

One of the most striking features of Ovid's style is to be found in the rhetorical skill shown in starting lines – and poems – with strong words which capture the reader's attention and make an immediate declaration. This power to arouse and satisfy interest with dramatically arresting statements is an aspect of Ovid's art which, perhaps indirectly and without conscious awareness on his imitators' part, found its way into much Renaissance poetry. Donne, on whom the influence of Ovid is considerable, is particularly celebrated for his exploitation of this device.

In this poem the opening (and wholly dactylic) hexameter hurries us expectantly forward to the dramatic outcry *quo properas* of 3, itself repeated at 9 and intensified as *inuida, quo properas* at 31. Some of the other poems of the *Amores* have more brilliantly effective openings: e.g. the paradoxical and epigrammatic *militat omnis amans* of 1.9, or the solemn buttonholing of the reader in 1.8:

> est quaedam (quicumque uolet cognoscere lenam,
> audiat) est quaedam . . .

or the dramatic direct address of 1.6:

> ianitor (indignum) dura religate catena.[18]

Apart from Donne, no English poet has responded more successfully to the dramatic, epigrammatic and antithetical qualities of Ovid's style than the first and greatest English translator of the *Elegies*, Marlowe, whose own *Hero and Leander* contains his most Ovidian and often-quoted line ('Whoever loved, that loved not at first sight?')[19] and whose Dr Faustus, in his final speech, gives a new and terrible meaning to *lente currite, noctis equi*, as he cries despairingly for time to stand still and save him from damnation. In his version of the present poem, Marlowe is particularly successful in bringing out the sense of ll. 11–12, in which the poet starts his catalogue of workers to whom Dawn's coming is unwelcome with the sailor, who sails happily by starlight but is lost at dawn.[20]

The easy, relaxed movement of Marlowe's heroic couplets shows a mastery of the form sometimes mistakenly supposed not to have been attained by English poets until the late seventeenth century. This can perhaps best be appreciated by looking at the last eight lines. Here the couplets are treated as units in which the second line of each 'answers' the first and completes the point. In the penultimate line, Marlowe scrupulously preserves the metrical and dramatic breaks at *finieram* and *audisse*: the inversion of the sequence from Ovid's 'you could tell she heard me – she blushed' to 'she blushed and therefore heard me' is justified by the fact that in English prosody 'blushed' takes the most emphatic place in the line. It seems probable that the reading of Ovid was itself a principal cause of the early development in English verse of an antithetical, dramatic and epigrammatic style of couplet-writing.

OVID AND CHAUCER

Chaucer's indebtedness to Ovid is too great to permit, and too well known to require, any general documentation here.[21] The dawn complaint of Troilus in *Troilus and Criseyde* 3 differs in structure, tone and texture from Ovid's poem but rhetorical treatment of the topos is closer to Ovid than to any medieval model.[22] There are seven stanzas. The first five lines of the first stanza are addressed to Criseyde, but Troilus then addresses Night, who is apostrophized down to the end of the second stanza. After a stanza of authorial narrative, Troilus resumes his complaint with an apostrophe of three verses to Day and 'the sonne Titan' (a conflation of Tithonus and the sun). The Ovidian source is guaranteed by the allusion at 1428 to Almena (*sic*) and Jove, and in the address to the sun at 1465–9: 'What! hold your bed ther, thow, and eke thi Morwe!' ('keep your bed and your tomorrow morning too'). The impudent tone of this is clearly Ovidian and mediates between Ovid and Donne, who in *The Sun Rising* calls the sun 'busy old fool'.

In the first and fourth stanzas Troilus appears as full of grief, piteous distress, heart's tears and heaviness – a typical victim of medieval courtly love. Elsewhere, however, he adopts the wittily reductive persona of the Ovidian poet-lover. The Ovidian tone, as would be expected, is most evident in the address to the sun, with its attack on envious day (the conventional epithet appears at 1454) for 'pouring in' on lovers and not leaving them in peace, and the suggestion that others need daylight more urgently than lovers – both motives recur in Donne's poem. The dismissive wit of 'Go selle it hem that smale selys grave' (again the ironic use of 'Go' recurs in Donne) is very English, but the *reductio ad absurdum* is directly elicited by Chaucer from the Ovidian contrast between the workaday world and the self-indulgent world of lovers.

Troilus' address to night is a variation of Ovid's rhetorical scheme. In *Amores* 1.13 the poet-lover does not address night directly, but Aurora's famous hypothetical words are a request to night's horses to go more slowly. Troilus addresses 'rakle' (hasty) night with a dark and restless eloquence which mirrors his own inner turmoil and distress. The meaning of 1438–40 is 'may God for thy haste and unkind wickedness bind thee fast to our hemisphere' (so that night becomes perpetual). This *cri-de-coeur* for eternal darkness develops the concept of a blessed dispensation which is first expressed in 1429–32 and which has no counterpart in Ovid, but the intervening lines (1433–5) about animals and 'folk' complaining against night for letting day afflict them with toil strongly recall Ovid's lines about the workers for whom night's end signals a return to work.

The seven-line stanza used by Chaucer ('rime royal') is not at first sight adapted to the epigrammatic as fully as is the Latin elegiac (or the English 'heroic') couplet. It is the metre of extended narrative and of the lengthy, satirical complaints of medieval and early Renaissance poetry. However, each stanza ends with two pairs of rhymed couplets which help the poet to accommodate changes of tone from medieval seriousness to the more direct, ironic tone of the authorial commentator for whom Ovid constitutes an often-proclaimed authority. This is the couplet of the *Canterbury Tales*, with their frequently reductive, tongue-in-cheek humour.

Chaucer combines two personae in his Troilus: the Ovidian elegist who can mock the conventions of his own rhetoric, and the medieval courtly lover. Indeed, Troilus' despair gains its resonance from the poet's controlling sense of a doomed relationship and of the ultimately tragic ironies of courtly love, within which the Ovidian aubade functions as a kind of static rhetorical interlude before the main narrative is resumed. The wit lightens the texture while reinforcing the meaning of the surrounding narrative, that nothing can stay the inexorable course of fortune. This double tone emerges again in the more aggressive self-assertive stance of the poet-lover in Donne.

Chaucer retains the two allusions, Jove–Alcmena and old Tithonus, as by now part of the stock-in-trade of the topos, but mythological jokes play a subordinate part in his treatment. Nor does he parody any formal suasorial scheme. Troilus' address is a medieval complaint, in which satirical diatribe and strong feeling go hand in hand. Amplification, variation and repetition are characteristic features of complaint. Here, for instance, 1463 rounds off a point already made in the stanza. The mythological allusions offer embellishment by *exemplum* even though they are no longer structurally so important as in Ovid (where they are essential to the suasorial form since they apply specially to the addressee). Mediated through Ovid, Chaucer's allusions become a tribute by the vernacular poet to classical authority. A few stanzas beyond the point where our excerpt stops, Criseyde expresses the permanence of her love in a series of classical *adynata*:

> That first shal Phebus fallen fro his spere,
> And everich egle ben the dowves fere,
> And everi roche out of his place sterte
> Ere Troilus out of Criseydes herte. (1495–8)

The poet's irony must be fully felt here in the light of Criseyde's coming unfaithfulness. Chaucer uses his figures not only with the greatest economy and tact but also with a full sense of their effectiveness within a long narrative structure.

OVID AND DONNE

> Busy old fool, unruly sun,
>   Why dost thou thus,
> Through windows, and through curtains call on us?
> Must to thy motions lovers' seasons run?
>   Saucy pedantic wretch, go chide
>   Late school-boys, and sour prentices,
>   Go tell court-huntsmen, that the King will ride;
>   Call country ants to harvest offices;
> Love, all alike, no season knows, nor clime,
> Nor hours, days, months, which are the rags of time.   10
>
>   Thy beams, so reverend, and strong
>   Why shouldst thou think?
> I could eclipse and cloud them with a wink,

But that I would not lose her sight so long:
   If her eyes have not blinded thine,
   Look, and tomorrow late, tell me,
   Whether both th'Indias of spice and mine
   Be where thou left'st them, or lie here with me.
Ask for those kings whom thou saw'st yesterday,
And thou shalt hear, All here in one bed lay.   20

   She is all states, and all princes, I,
   Nothing else is.
Princes do but play us: compared to this,
All honour's mimic; all wealth alchemy.
   Thou sun art half as happy as we,
   In that the world's contracted thus;
   Thine age asks ease, and since thy duties be
   To warm the world, that's done in warming us.
Shine here to us, and thou art everywhere;
This bed thy centre is, these walls, thy sphere.   30
                (Donne, *The Sun Rising*)

The continuity and modification of the classical tradition is a process which can best be studied, not by generalization, but by setting imitations against models. In *The Sun Rising* Donne's wittily reductive tone clearly derives from *Amores* 1.13.[23] The addressee here is the sun himself: in the joke about his age in the last stanza we catch an echo of the Titan–Tithonus conflation. The poem ends not with a mock-defeat but with a triumphant and challenging paradox. This figure, itself brilliantly exploited by Ovid (*Amores* 2.19 is a good example), was popular in the Renaissance and was particularly favoured by Donne, who wrote a set of prose *Paradoxes and problems* as well as many poems which depend for their point and effect on the use of paradox. But the poem's most conspicuously 'Renaissance' quality is to be found, perhaps, in the vigour and conviction of its hypothesizing: thus the poet does not begin by asking for a stay of nature but by asking why things are as they are; the second lines of the first two stanzas are structurally correspondent:

Why dost thou thus . . .

Why shouldst thou think . . .

Having reproved the sun for interrupting his love, and having challenged his power to do this, Donne turns in the last stanza to a new

and startling proposition. If the sun cannot be dissuaded from awaken-
ening the lovers, let it then at least shine nowhere else except on the
lovers.

The Ovidian elements in the poem can readily be isolated. First,
there is the contrast between the world of lovers and the workaday
world. The sun is told to 'Go chide late schoolboys and sour prentices'
in direct recollection of Ovid's 'tu pueros somno fraudas tradisque
magistris' and the reference to farming in 'Call country ants to harvest
offices' is a variation of Ovid's 'prima bidente uides oneratos arua
colentes'. But the colloquial vigour and sardonic directness of the
imperative 'go', found also in Chaucer (1462), is more dramatic than
Ovid's present indicatives which apostrophize dawn in a series of
formal exemplary topoi.

In Donne, schoolboys, farmers and huntsmen are distinguished from
lovers primarily because they are all slaves to time, while lovers are,
or ought to be, free of it: in 9–10 the sense that lovers belong in a pre-
lapsarian world (whereas hours, days, months, the 'rags of time', are
the clothes Adam and Eve put on to face the fallen world of toil)
can, perhaps, just perceptibly be felt. In Donne's poem the lovers
proclaim their immunity from time, while the whole point of Ovid
and Chaucer is their awareness of a circumscribing and indifferent
reality: the classical *adynaton*, in which sunrise is delayed, is transformed into a splendid and hyperbolic conceit, in which the poet
proposes that the entire world as surveyed by the rising sun can be
subsumed in the lovers. This is itself a variation of a hyperbole common
in Renaissance love poetry, in which the mistress includes all the
world's treasure. Indeed, Donne's 'both the Indias' may be an echo
of a sonnet by an English Petrarchist, Spenser (*Amoretti* 15):

> Ye tradeful merchants, that with weary toil
> do seek most precious things to make your gain,
> and both the Indias of their treasure spoil,
> what needeth you to seek so far in vain?
> For lo, my love doth in herself contain
> all this world's riches . . .

But the idea of the sun's all-seeing eye goes further back, to Ovidian
sun-myth with its erotic connections. The sun in *Metamorphoses* 2.32
oculis . . . aspicit omnia, and cf. 4.172 *uidet hic deus omnia primus*. It is
in the story of the sun seeing Venus and Mars in bed, as told by Ovid
in *Metamorphoses* 4, that the tradition of his hostility to lovers is
established. Indeed, the whole passage is of interest in the present

context. Ovid tells how the sun told Vulcan of his wife's adultery; in revenge, Venus afflicted the sun with love for Leucothoe (ll. 195–7):

> quique omnia cernere debes
> Leucothoen spectas et uirgine figis in una
> quos mundo debes oculos.

The sun, says Ovid wittily, even perpetrates *adynata*, by rising too early and forgetting to set: in these lines a cosmic intensity adds power to the Hellenistic fancy (200–1):

> deficis interdum, uitiumque in lumina mentis
> transit, et obscurus mortalia pectora terres.

Donne invites the sun to behave as myth records he once did: 'Shine here to us and thou art everywhere.' But Donne neatly modifies the conceit by using the Tithonus–Titan conflation: 'thine age asks ease',[24] so by concentrating on their bed the sun can retire from his daily round; he can cease to be a toiler and become a self-indulgent ally of love. Nowhere in Donne's poem is the Ovidian element stronger than in these closing lines; yet 'Shine here to us and thou art every-where' is celebratory, universalizing the lover's experience with a passionate intensity which goes beyond the confines of erotic elegy. The final conceit turns on a stock medieval and Renaissance analogy between the microcosm (man) and the macrocosm; but the witty contrast between domestic and cosmic imagery in the last line (bed/walls//centre/sphere) is entirely appropriate to the Hellenistic manner of Ovidian erotic elegy. So too Ovid's Aurora is both a mistress and a cosmic phenomenon. Donne's conceit is itself a variation on a famous Christian paradox, 'infinite riches in a little room'.[25] But the emphasis throughout this last stanza is on the poet and his mistress rather than on the sun:

> . . . that's done in warming *us*.
> Shine here to *us*, . . .
> *This* bed thy centre is, *these* walls . . .

This emphasis is first stated unequivocally at

> She is all states, and all princes, I,

where the poet-lover is the dominant element in the poem. Already in Chaucer we have seen that the poet's dominant concern is with Troilus' feelings, within which the Ovidian wit is subsumed. Ovid's elegies are certainly not devoid of passionate feeling on the lover's part (*Amores* 3.11B.47–8):

> perque tuam faciem, magni mihi numinis instar,
> perque tuos oculos, qui rapuere meos.

But that is a poem about love's agonies not love's triumphs. Ovid tends to see love's triumphs as victories of Cupid over himself, a kind of servitude (*Amores* 1.2.28):

> haec tibi magnificus pompa triumphus erit

– or as pure erotic self-indulgence. In *The Sun Rising* the lovers themselves triumph over myth by creating their own alternative world. Donne links this to the world of cosmic reality by using a metaphysical conceit. Such conceits can easily be accommodated to Ovidian poetry, yet they depend upon systems and habits of thought unknown to the ancient world.[26]

IO

Niall Rudd

PYRAMUS AND THISBE IN SHAKESPEARE AND OVID

A Midsummer Night's Dream and *Metamorphoses* 4.1–166

THE OVIDIAN FRAMEWORK

The tale of Pyramus and Thisbe in Book 4 of the *Metamorphoses* comes within a group of stories set in Boeotia. The previous book begins with Cadmus and ends with Pentheus (the Theban king who was so horribly punished for resisting Dionysus). Book 4 itself begins with the daughters of Minyas, king of Orchomenus. These girls also offended Dionysus; for instead of joining in his worship they stayed at home telling stories. And they too were punished: as dusk fell, the scent of saffron and myrrh filled the air, wild music was heard, vines sprouted from their looms, and they were suddenly turned into bats.

Within this Boeotian setting we have three love-stories told by the daughters of Minyas. The first is that of Pyramus and Thisbe, the second (in three related parts) is about the Sun, and the third concerns the Carian water-nymph Salmacis. The girl who told of Pyramus and Thisbe[1] had other stories which she could have recounted. She thought first of the Babylonian goddess Derceto (44–6) who was changed into a fish;[2] then of Derceto's daughter (Semiramis) who became a bird; and then of an unnamed nymph who turned boys into fishes and eventually became a fish herself. But she settled finally on the story of how the white mulberry became red. Of these tales three, and possibly all four, are Babylonian.[3] The oriental setting is mentioned explicitly in v. 56: Pyramus was the most handsome young man and Thisbe the loveliest of the girls *quas Oriens habuit*. So at the very beginning we learn that Ovid has in mind an eastern story of youth and beauty.

To approach our next point we must return to Semiramis. In so far as she is a historical figure Semiramis is to be identified with the Assyrian queen Sammu-ramat, a woman of Aramaic descent who rose from the royal harem to become the wife of King Shamshi-Adad the fifth (824–810 B.C.) and the mother of King Adad-Nirari the third. After her death legend supplanted history, and by 400 B.C., when Ctesias was at the Persian court, Semiramis had become the daughter of

Derceto the Syrian goddess of love and war – the counterpart of the Babylonian Ishtar and the Phoenician Astarte. According to the account of Ctesias, as preserved in Diodorus Siculus 2, the baby girl was exposed at birth but was protected by doves and then brought up by the keeper of the royal herds who called her Semiramis – a name derived from the Syrian word for 'doves'. As a young woman she captivated the world conqueror Ninus (the mythical founder of Ninevah) and became his wife. When he died she built him a modest memorial in the form of a tomb one mile high and one mile wide. After gaining this constructional experience she went on to found the city of Babylon, and then embarked on a long series of travels and conquests. Eventually, after an unsuccessful expedition against India, she disappeared. Some say she turned into a dove. As she had the habit of murdering all her lovers a spider might have been a more suitable metamorphosis.

One more phase remained in the career of this remarkable woman. In a sentimental novel, which some scholars place as early as 100 B.C., she appears along with her cousin Ninus.[4] The three surviving fragments show that, although he is already an illustrious general, Ninus is still a lad of seventeen; Semiramis is only thirteen. The two are very much in love, and Ninus pleads with his aunt Derkeia for permission to marry her daughter (Derkeia being the goddess Derceto, who like the other two has dwindled into a cosy bourgeois figure). Puerile as it seems to have been, the novel must have travelled far beyond its place of origin. For, while the fragments came to light in Egypt, an illustration of the story has been found in a mosaic at Antioch dating from the second century A.D.[5]

However, the only Semiramis that we meet in Ovid is the *grande amoureuse* described by Ctesias.[6] And this has a bearing on our topic, for when Thisbe is called *Babylonia Thisbe* (99) and is described as living

> ubi dicitur altam
> coctilibus muris cinxisse Semiramis urbem (57–8)

she is thereby linked with a city of romance and adventure.

THE STORY

The girl chose the story, we are told, because it was not well known – 'quoniam uulgaris fabula non est' (53). *When* was the story not well known? The answer ought to be 'in the legendary period of Orchomenus' past', in which case the assertion could naturally claim no historical authority. Did Ovid, then (or his source), simply want to provide a plausible reason for the girl's choice? Perhaps. But there is no reason to think that the tale of Pyramus and Thisbe would have been any *less* familiar than the other stories which are passed over. The phrase, therefore, will not bear close examination. But in regard to the Roman readership one may perhaps conclude that Ovid would have avoided making the statement if the story had in fact been familiar in his own time. If so, it looks as if the situation altered after the appearance of the *Metamorphoses*; for in the fifty years following Ovid's death the suicide of Thisbe became a fairly common subject of Pompeian wall-painting.[7]

The structure is a simple threefold scheme of separation, decision, and union, the relative proportions being roughly 2, 1 and 6. At the outset we are told that the young couple's love has grown from a childhood acquaintance (59–70); it is reciprocal (62); and it aims at marriage (60). But in Lysander's famous words 'the course of true love never did run smooth' (*MND* 1.1.134). In all great love stories there must be some kind of barrier that keeps the lovers apart and tests their devotion, whether it is a family feud (as in *Romeo and Juliet*), religion (as with Eloise and Abelard), a stretch of water (as with Hero and Leander), or just a wall. The wall, of course, is the physical extension of the parents' veto. We are not given reasons for this opposition; Ovid simply says 'sed uetuere patres' (61). But the proximity of boy and girl makes their separation the more tantalizing. As Ovid points out, it is precisely the *communis paries* (66) that keeps them apart. Another consequence of the fathers' opposition is that the love of Pyramus and Thisbe must be kept secret; they can only communicate by signs (63). Yet this very secrecy makes their feelings more intense:

quoque magis tegitur tectus magis aestuat ignis. (64)

Passion heightens perception; for they alone spy a chink in the wall (68) and use it to exchange endearments.

Then comes the decision: they will meet outside the town at night. It is a dangerous plan, especially for the girl; but love gives her courage (96). After reaching the spot Thisbe is frightened by a lion, and as she runs away drops her shawl. When Pyramus sees it, he is overwhelmed with guilt: he ought never to have involved her in such danger, and having done so he should certainly not have been late (109ff.). He plunges his sword into his body, calling on the lions to tear his corpse to pieces. In the cave Thisbe is still afraid, but she is more afraid of letting Pyramus down. She emerges and finds him at the point of death; whereupon her reaction is exactly the same as his – she takes the blame (*causa* in v. 152) and resolves to follow him. Uttering a final prayer that they may be buried together she falls on his sword. And so the lovers achieve union at last, but only in death.

So we have a tale from the east of violent death in a forest by moonlight; a tale of two beautiful young people whose love is mutual and equal and aims at marriage, but is frustrated and forced into concealment; a love which involves all the faculties, overcomes fear, is full of tenderness and concern, and is faithful unto death. I have summarized the familiar story in these terms, because it has sometimes been stated by scholars who should have known better that romantic love was unknown in classical antiquity.[8] If true, this would be a fact of momentous importance, and it would greatly strengthen the case of those who regard the ancient world as desperately foreign. But it is not true, as the story of Pyramus and Thisbe amply demonstrates.

But now we must draw a distinction. If Pyramus and Thisbe are romantic lovers, it does not follow that Ovid can here be labelled as a romantic poet. For combined with the elements noted above are certain features of style which suggest that Ovid is not continuously involved with the lovers' feelings. Consider first such expressions as 'sed uetuere patres: quod non potuere uetare' (where *potuere* rhymes with *uetuere* while half echoing the sounds of *patres*), 'hinc Thisbe, Pyramus illinc' (where the separation implied in *hinc/illinc* is reinforced by the chiasmus), 'tutae . . . murmure blanditiae minimo transire solebant' (where a tiny whisper passes safely through a tiny chink), 'lux . . . praecipitatur aquis, et aquis nox exit ab isdem' (which elegantly conveys the alternating pattern of day and night), ' "una duos" inquit "nox perdet amantes" ' (where at such an extreme moment Pyramus still manages to shape a sequence of adjective adjective noun noun, in which the adjectives present a numerical antithesis). The marvellous neatness and dexterity of such phrases remind us we are still reading the author of the *Amores*. Or again, take those beautiful lines

> oraque buxo
> pallidiora gerens exhorruit aequoris instar,
> quod tremit, exigua cum summum stringitur aura. (134–6)
> *Her face paler than boxwood, she trembled like the sea which*
> *shivers when its surface is ruffled by a faint breeze.*

Beautiful; but at this critical moment does it not imply a slight distance between the poet and his subject?

The disconcerting lines which compare Pyramus' blood to water spurting from a burst pipe (121–4) seem to be a less successful instance of the same kind. If there *is* a fault on Ovid's side, it is surely better to assume a small lapse of stylistic judgement than to imagine that the poet is inviting us to laugh at the stricken Pyramus.[9] It is worth remembering, however, that not everyone appears to have found the simile absurd. Although Gower left it out, Chaucer took it in his stride:

> The blood out of the wounde as brode sterte
> As water, when the conduit broken is.[10]

And though Shakespeare could easily have turned it into something ludicrous in *A Midsummer Night's Dream* he did not take the chance. On the other hand, in *Titus Andronicus* after alluding to the death of Pyramus (2.3.231–2) he goes on to describe the blood coming from the mouth and nostrils of the unfortunate Lavinia (2.4.22ff.); and in doing so he uses a rather similar idea:

> notwithstanding all this loss of blood,
> As from a conduit with three issuing spouts.

So while Shakespeare disregards the Ovidian simile in his burlesque he does draw on it quite seriously in a tragic context.

Finally, there is the address to the wall:

> 'inuide' dicebant 'paries, quid amantibus obstas?...' (73)
> '*You mean old wall*', they would say, '*why do you stand in the way of people in love? It wouldn't have cost you much to let us embrace properly; or if that's too much you might at least have opened wide enough for us to kiss.*'

Then, anxious to be fair, they add: 'But we're not ungrateful; we admit it's through you that our words find their way to loving ears.' Or, to put it more briefly, thank you very much for being cracked. Surely this is deliberate. Like all lovers, Pyramus and Thisbe are a little absurd; they live in a private world. But it is precisely their remoteness from ordinary life – the drab world where unglamorous problems exist and are dealt with by common sense and calculation – that is their glory. Ovid knew this very well, and so did Shakespeare. *A Midsummer Night's Dream* bears ample testimony to the magic of love – and to its silliness. And if in that play Pyramus and Thisbe are used mainly to illustrate the silliness, we can at least say that Shakespeare was developing a hint provided by Ovid himself.

Before we leave the *Metamorphoses* three points deserve attention which, though very small, yet illustrate Ovid's subtlety as a narrative poet. In vv. 93–5 Thisbe cleverly opens the door in the darkness, slips out without the knowledge of her family, and covering her face makes her way to the tomb. The phrase 'adopertaque uultum' is a graphic touch, vividly realizing the idea of stealth. But it is more than that, for it makes us aware, however dimly, that she is wearing a shawl over her head. In v. 90 we read that the mulberry tree was close to a cool spring – 'gelido contermina fonti'. It is the kind of detail which one easily skims over as a piece of conventional scene-painting. But this is the spring which later attracts the lion and so precipitates the tragedy. Mention has already been made of blood. As there are over a dozen references one wonders how Ovid avoids monotony. He does so, it seems, not just by varying the grammatical form of each expression but by directing attention now to the movement (*emicat* in v. 121), now to the temperature (*tepebat* in v. 163), now to the different colours of blood, whether red (as implied by *recenti* in v. 96) or black – the darker colour of clotted blood being naturally assimilated to the shade of mourning (*atram* in v. 125 and v. 165, *pullos et luctibus aptos* in v. 160). He also varies the meaning of *caedes*, which signifies the blood of dead cattle in v. 97, the blood of Pyramus in vv. 125 and 163, and death in general at v. 160.

OVIDIAN INFLUENCE IN 'A MIDSUMMER NIGHT'S DREAM'

Before we come to Shakespeare's treatment of Pyramus and Thisbe it may be useful to notice some more general signs of Ovidian influence in *A Midsummer Night's Dream*. This can best be done by recalling the main structural elements of the play. The outer frame (*a*) is represented by the court of Theseus on the eve of his marriage to Hippolyta.[11] Within that we have (*b*) the love-intrigue of the two couples Hermia/Lysander and Helena/Demetrius, (*c*) the quarrel of Oberon and Titania, and (*d*) the amateur dramatics of Quince and company.

(*a*) When we first meet Theseus in 1.1 we are told that he is 'Duke Theseus' of Athens, that he has defeated the Amazons and their queen in battle but now intends to marry Hippolyta

> with pomp, with triumph, and with revelling.

All these details are found in Chaucer's poem *The Knight's Tale* (1–12) and either less clearly or not at all in Plutarch's *Life of Theseus*.[12] Yet Shakespeare had certainly read the biography too, for in 2.1.78–80 there is a reference to Theseus' affaires with Perigouna, Aegle, Ariadne and Antiopa – all of whom are mentioned by Plutarch and none by Chaucer; moreover, in 5.1.47 we hear of Theseus' kinship with Hercules, which is also recorded by Plutarch alone. In 4.1.109ff. Theseus and Hippolyta go hunting, as they do in *The Knight's Tale* 825ff. But Hippolyta's memories of her hunting with Cadmus in Crete and Theseus' description of his hounds are based on Ovid. The Shakespearian lines run as follows:

> HIPP. I was with Hercules and Cadmus once,
>   When in a wood of Crete they bay'd the bear
>   With hounds of Sparta: . . .
> THES. My hounds are bred out of the Spartan kind,
>   So flew'd, so sanded; . . .
>   a cry more tuneable
> Was never holla'd to, nor cheer'd with horn
> In Crete, in Sparta, nor in Thessaly.

First, what was Cadmus doing in Crete? To understand what has happened we have to look at the beginning of *Metamorphoses* 3, where the abducted Europa arrives in Crete (2) and her brother Cadmus is told to search for her (3–4). A hasty glance might easily miss the fact that Cadmus himself is *not* in Crete but back home in Sidon. Later in the book, after Cadmus has founded Thebes, his grandson Actaeon goes hunting. One of his dogs is Cretan and another Spartan:

> Gnosius Ichnobates, Spartana gente Melampus. (208)

Others are from a Cretan father and a Spartan mother:

> et patre Dictaeo sed matre Laconide nati
> Labros et Agriodus et acutae uocis Hylactor. (233–4)

Labros is the Greek for 'furious', but Golding mistakenly derived it from the Latin *labrosus* 'having large lips' and so translated 'large flewed hound'. This in turn accounts for Shakespeare's 'flew'd', which means 'having pendulous chaps'. Shakespeare's 'sanded' probably comes from Golding's 'Tawnie' (260), which does not correspond to anything in Ovid but may represent a guess at the meaning of Asbolus (218) – another Greek name, which means 'soot'.[13]

Towards the end of the play (5.1.43) Theseus is asked to choose what performance he would like to see from a list of shows available. First there is 'The battle with the Centaurs' – an event in which the Duke himself had taken part. This he turns down – understandably, since the story told how the wedding-reception of his friend Pirithous had been turned into a bloody shambles (*Met.* 12.210ff.). The reason which Theseus actually gives for his decision is that Hippolyta has already heard the story in a version which made Hercules the central figure:

> that have I told my love
> In glory of my kinsman Hercules.[14]

The next show offered is

> The riot of the tipsy Bacchanals,
> Tearing the Thracian singer in their rage.

That, of course, is the story of Orpheus' death as related at the beginning of *Met.* 11. The third show is a non-Ovidian satire. The fourth is Pyramus and Thisbe, and that is what Theseus selects.

(*b*) In the context of the love-intrigue there is only one Ovidian story which need be mentioned at present, viz that of Apollo and Daphne. In 1.1.168 Hermia declares her loyalty to Lysander, swearing

> by Cupid's strongest bow,
> By his best arrow with the golden head.

This is the arrow which Cupid shot at Apollo (*Met.* 1.469ff.). The actual phrase probably came from Marlowe's *Hero and Leander*, which Shakespeare had apparently seen in manuscript:

> Thence flew Love's arrow with the golden head. (1.161)[15]

Later, in 2.1.231, Helena sees herself taking part in a chase in which the Ovidian roles have been reversed and she, as Daphne, pursues the reluctant Demetrius/Apollo:

> Run when you will, the story shall be changed;
> Apollo flies, and Daphne holds the chase.

(*c*) The fairies have diverse origins. Puck, or Robin Goodfellow, is from Warwickshire folklore (though it seems that Shakespeare had also read of him in *The Discoveries of Witchcraft* by Reginald Scot, published in 1584); Oberon appeared in the romance *Huon of Bordeaux* and also in Green's *James IV*; Titania, in name at least, is from Ovid. But Shakespeare made some important changes, of which the most relevant here concerns the quasi-Olympian pattern of their relationships.[16] Thus Oberon and Titania, like Jupiter and Juno, preside over the fortunes of certain chosen mortals (2.1.74–6). Like Jupiter, Oberon has an eye for attractive girls (2.1.64ff.); Titania has a touch of Juno's jealousy, and (although the ownership has been switched) her pretty Indian page-boy may well be a reminiscence of Ganymede. When she and Oberon are at odds, the effect is felt in the world of nature (2.1.88ff.).[17] Finally, Puck is both a messenger and a prankster like Mercury. All these changes are, in a sense, Ovidian.

(*d*) In the performance of the mechanicals' play (5.1) 'Pyramus' compares his loyalty to that of Limander (200), that is, of course, Leander, who is the subject of *Heroides* 18 and 19.[18] And shortly afterwards (202–3) the two lovers compare themselves to Shafalus and Procrus, i.e. Cephalus and Procris, whose story is told in *Met.* 7.694ff.

Such allusions, then, occurring in all the major divisions of the play, help to create a general Ovidian ambience.

THE MECHANICALS' PRODUCTION

Shakespeare, as everyone knows, used Ovid in several ways – in allusions, in Latin quotations,[19] and in references to Ovid himself.[20] Much the most interesting cases, however, are those in which an Ovidian story has been woven into the fabric of a play. A good example would be the use of the Philomela myth in *Titus Andronicus* (and again in *Cymbeline*). But the most famous instance is undoubtedly the burlesque of Pyramus and Thisbe in *A Midsummer Night's Dream*.

We start with the casting scene in 1.2. Here, from the very beginning, Quince the producer is eclipsed by Bottom. No sooner has he shouted 'Is all our company here?' than Bottom butts in and advises him to call a roll 'generally, man by man, according to the scrip'. Quince is just about to comply when Bottom interrupts again: 'First, good Peter Quince, say what the play treats on; then read the names of the actors, and so grow to a point.' Quince gives the title: 'The most lamentable comedy, and most cruel death of Pyramus and Thisbe', at which Bottom remarks: 'A very good piece of work, I assure you.' This implies, quite falsely, that he knows what the play is about; for when given the part of Pyramus he has to ask 'What is Pyramus? a lover, or a tyrant?' On hearing that the main character kills himself most gallantly for love, Bottom at once has visions of his own histrionic powers: 'Let the audience look to their eyes! I will move storms, I will condole in some measure.' Had Pyramus been a tyrant that too would have been well within Bottom's scope: 'I could play Ercles rarely, or a part to tear a cat in, to make all split.' When the part of Thisbe is assigned to Flute, Bottom again intervenes: 'An [if] I may hide my face, let me play Thisbe too. I'll speak in a monstrous little voice "Thisne,

Thisne!"' The same happens again when the moronic Snug is given the lion's part, which is nothing but roaring: 'Let me play the lion too', pleads Bottom. Quince hastily points out that 'Pyramus is a sweet-faced man; a proper man, as one shall see in a summer's day; a most lovely, gentleman-like man', and therefore can be played by no one but Bottom. Thanks to this blatant appeal to Bottom's vanity, arrangements are allowed to proceed. In this section, then, Shakespeare not only gives us the cast of the play but also reveals the exuberant self-confidence of his main comic character.

The mechanicals next meet at rehearsal (3.1). Here it is worth looking a little more closely to see what has been taken from Ovid. Of the wall and the opportunities it afforded for comic business something will be said presently; but one detail may be mentioned here. According to Ovid, Pyramus and Thisbe used to address the wall when they had taken up their positions (*constiterant*)

> inque uices fuerat captatus *anhelitus oris*. (72)

What does this mean? One idea, adopted by the Loeb translator, is that the lovers heard each other breathing. That was also Chaucer's view:

> Upon that o syde of the wal stood he,
> And on that other syde stood Tisbe,
> The swote soun of other to receyve.
>> (*The Legend of Good Women* 750–3)

Golding, however, wrote:

> Now as at one side Pyramus and Thisbe on the tother
> Stood often drawing one of them the pleasant breath from
>> other. (89–90)

Here the combination of 'drawing' with 'pleasant' suggests the idea of scent rather than hearing; and that is almost certainly the right interpretation. For although *anhelitus* can mean 'panting', we are not told that the two youngsters arrived breathless after dashing down the garden; in fact *constiterant* points the other way. More positively, in the *Ars amatoria* (1.521) when Ovid is warning his readers against the hazards of bad breath he says:

> nec male odorati sit tristis *anhelitus oris*.

So Golding was right. Apart from being more poetically arresting this gave Shakespeare an opening for a joke:

> BOTTOM: Thisby, the flowers have odious savours sweet, –
> QUINCE: Odorous, odorous![21]
> BOTTOM: – odorous savours sweet:
>> So hath thy breath, my dearest Thisby dear.

Another joke, of comparable subtlety, is extracted from the name of King Ninus, who is mentioned just once in Ovid's narrative (*ad busta Nini* in v. 88). This time the speaker is Flute, taking the part of Thisbe:

> I'll meet thee, Pyramus, at Ninny's tomb. (102)
> QUINCE: 'Ninus' tomb', man.

But the correction is of no avail. At the performance (5.1.270) Flute enters, stares around him, and starts to speak:

> This is old Ninny's tomb. Where is my love?

The point was the same in Shakespeare's day as in ours: 'ninny' meant a nit-wit. And the joke implies, I think, that Shakespeare had the Latin (as well as a translation) in front of him. For 'Ninny's tomb' has rather more point for someone construing *ad busta Nini* than for one who is relying solely on 'Ninus tumb', which is Golding's rendering. Because it is so close to the Latin, the phrase may in fact preserve an Elizabethan schoolboy joke.

The last reference has taken us to the performance in Act 5, and that is where the comic possibilities of the wall are most fully exploited. Shakespeare's effects range from the mild facetiousness of 'walls are so wilful to hear without warning' (5.1.212–13) – a reference to the proverb 'walls have ears' – to verbal fooling like

> I see a voice: now will I to the chink,
> To spy an I can hear my Thisbe's face (195–6)

and

> Show me thy chink to blink through with mine eyne. (179)

These last words lead to the broad humour of the v-sign, as Wall holds up his fingers – a gesture politely acknowledged by 'Pyramus':

> Thanks, courteous wall:[22] Jove shield thee well for this!

Broader still are Thisbe's lines:

> My cherry lips have often kiss'd thy stones (193)[23]

and

> I kiss the wall's hole, not your lips at all. (205)

Again, when Pyramus exclaims

> Curs'd be thy stones for thus deceiving me!

Theseus remarks that the wall should return the curse. Bottom cannot resist setting him right, even though it involves stepping out of character:

> No, in truth, sir, he should not. 'Deceiving me' is Thisby's cue.

We saw above how Ovid's single reference to Ninus was elaborated by the playwright. Another feature mentioned only once in Ovid is the wood: the lion returns there after drinking ('dum redit in siluas' in v. 103). Shakespeare, too, says little about the wood; it is referred to very briefly in 1.2.105 ('meet me in the palace wood') and again in 3.1.3–4 ('this green plot shall be our stage, this hawthorn-brake our tiring house'). But we do not *need* anything more explicit, since that is where the rehearsal is taking place. The moonlight too is referred to only once by Ovid: Thisbe sees the lion *ad lunae radios* (99). For Shakespeare moonlight is so central that it is given the status of a character. As the producer says: 'one must come in with a bush of thorns and a lanthorn, and say he comes to disfigure, or to present, the person of Moonshine' (3.1.63ff.).

Night, which is mentioned several times by Ovid, is not brought on stage by Shakespeare, but in 5.1.172ff. it does receive from the hero a passionate apostrophe:

> O grim-look'd night! O night with hue so black!
> O night which ever art when day is not!
> O night! O night! alack, alack, alack!
> I fear my Thisbe's promise is forgot.

This is rather odd. In Ovid it is *morning* when the lovers plan their elopement (81ff.); there is no mention of any earlier promise of Thisbe's, nor is Pyramus in any way alarmed (why should he be?). It almost looks as if the hack script-writer who is supposed to have supplied the mechanicals' piece has confusedly imagined Pyramus in the wood at night awaiting Thisbe's arrival and has then transferred that scene to the garden, where it makes very little dramatic sense.

As for the blood, which recurs as a motif in Ovid's story, Shakespeare reserves it for the performance in Act 5, where it is given full weight in Quince's prologue:

Whereat, with blade, with bloody blameful blade,
He bravely broached his *boiling* bloody breast.

This is another passage which suggests that Shakespeare had read the original Latin; for Ovid writes:

demisit in ilia ferrum,
nec mora, *feruenti* moriens e uulnere traxit.
*He plunged the blade into his entrails, and immediately, as he
died, he drew it from the* boiling *wound.*

Golding merely says 'bleeding wound'.

Taking these points together we can see that the wall which separated the lovers, the moonlight which shone on their death, the royal tomb, the surrounding forest, and the shedding of blood – all features which helped to make Ovid's a romantic story – have been fastened on by Shakespeare and turned into farce. It is, of course, excellent fun. And yet, though it may have cast ridicule on some intermediate poems and sketches on the same theme,[24] it did not destroy the original. In fact non-classical readers would probably admit that in spite of all the fooling some sense of the pathos of Ovid's story still comes through.

RAMIFICATIONS

So far we have considered the tale of Pyramus and Thisbe only in relation to the mechanicals' production. But it also has wider and more subtle implications. First, as presented by the mechanicals, the story parodies the relationship of Lysander and Hermia. By providing, as it were, a distorted mirror-image of romantic love Shakespeare complicates and deepens an effect which on its own might be too sweet and sentimental. At the same time, for all its buffoonery, the production gently reminds us of the tragic possibilities of romantic love, especially when it defies parental opposition. (One thinks naturally of *Romeo and Juliet.*) The parodic function of Pyramus and Thisbe has been mentioned by various writers, but as far as I know the details of the correspondence have not been fully explored. Moreover, it appears that the influence of Ovid's story is not confined to Lysander and Hermia but makes itself felt (with varying degrees of strength) throughout the play.

In the opening scene Theseus is not only a powerful prince; he is a lover yearning for his marriage-day:

> but O! methinks how slow
> This old moon wanes; she lingers my desires. (1.1.3–4)

Hippolyta answers:

> (*a*) Four days (*b*) will quickly steep themselves in night;
> (*b*) Four nights will quickly dream away the time . . .

In Ovid, once the couple has decided to elope, the day seems to pass all too slowly – 'lux tarde discedere uisa' (91); then

> (*a*) lux . . .
> (*b*) praecipitatur aquis et (*b*) aquis nox exit ab isdem.

> *the day quickly steeps itself in the water and from the same water night emerges.*

The form and phrasing, though not identical, are similar enough to justify comment, especially when taken in conjunction with the other more general Ovidian features of love, yearning for marriage (cf. 5.1.33–7 and 39–41), and moonlight. Theseus and Hippolyta, however, do not enter the wood until dawn and so do not participate in the dream.

We now move on to Hermia and Lysander. At the very beginning we hear of a barrier to their marriage: Egeus has forbidden it ('sed uetuere patres'). But there is the further complication that Hermia is being pressed to marry someone else. She asks the penalty of disobedience – very courageously: 'I know not by what power I am made bold' (59). This sounds like an unconscious echo of Ovid's Thisbe: 'audacem faciebat amor' (96) – a phrase rendered by Golding as 'Love made her bold'. In answer Hermia is told that if she refuses to comply she must either die or else enter a nunnery. Faced with this impasse, Lysander says:

> If thou lov'st me then,
> *Steal* forth thy *father's house* to-morrow night,
> And in the wood, a league *without the town*, . . .
> There will I stay for thee. (1.1.163ff.)

Golding's translation says that Pyramus and Thisbe resolved

> To *steale* out of their *fathers house* and eke the Citie *gate* . . .
> They did agree at Ninus Tumb to *meete without the towne.*
> (106 and 108)

After gaining Hermia's consent Lysander discloses the plan to Helena:

To-morrow night, when Phoebe doth behold
Her silver visage in the wat'ry glass . . .
Through Athens' *gates* we have devis'd to *steal*.
HERM. And in the wood . . .
There my Lysander and myself shall *meet* (209ff.)

This plan will get Hermia and Lysander into the wood; Demetrius,
we are told, will follow (247).

In the next scene Quince decides that the actors must have secrecy
for their rehearsal: '*meet* me in the palace wood, a mile *without the town*,
by moonlight' (1.2.105ff.). The exact place is 'at the Duke's oak' – a
suitably sturdy substitute for Ovid's mulberry tree.[25] If at this point
we are inclined to question the relevance of Ovid's story, we need only
recall that Bottom and Flute are the stage Pyramus and Thisbe.

With the fairies in 2.1 the Ovidian echoes are naturally much
fainter; yet when Oberon and Titania meet in the wood, Oberon's
first words are 'Ill met by moonlight' (60). And when, later on, he
sends Puck to fetch 'love-in-idleness' he describes it as

a little western flower
Before milk-white, now purple with love's wound (166–7) –

an expression which must surely recall Ovid's mulberry

quae poma alba ferebat
ut nunc nigra ferat contactu sanguinis arbor (51–2)

*how the tree which used to bear white fruit now bears black because
it has been stained by blood.*[26]

Demetrius now enters, upbraiding Helena; and here the parallel
is applied to the other pair of lovers:

You do impeach your modesty too much,
To leave the city . . . ('urbis quoque tecta relinquant' in v. 86)
To trust the opportunity of night ('nocte uenires', in v. 111)
And the ill counsel of a desert place
(perhaps a reminiscence of
'neue sit errandum lato spatiantibus aruo' in v. 87
combined with 'in loca plena metus' in v. 111)
With the rich worth of your virginity ('dignissima' in v. 109?).

As Helena continues to follow him, Demetrius utters a threat which
represents a variation of the Ovidian theme:

> I'll run from thee and hide me in the brakes,[27]
> And leave thee to the mercy of wild beasts. (227–8)

In the next scene (2.2) Lysander tries to lie down beside Hermia, saying:

> One turf shall serve as pillow for us both;
> One heart, one bed, two bosoms, and one troth. (41–2)

This conceit, which is elaborated in the speech that follows, recalls the one/two combination found in Ovid:

> 'una duos' inquit 'nox perdet amantes' (108)
> nunc tegis unius, mox es tectura duorum (159)
> quodque rogis superest, una requiescit in urna. (166)

Shortly after, Helena finds Lysander:

> But who is here? Lysander! on the ground!
> Dead? or asleep? I see no blood, no wound.

How close this is to the Pyramus and Thisbe story can be seen by turning on to 5.1.332–4:

> THISBE: Asleep, my love?
> What, dead, my dove?
> O Pyramus, arise!

We have now followed the characters into the wood, but we have not yet mentioned the factor which precipitates the drama, namely error. In Ovid, ironically, Pyramus and Thisbe arrange to meet at Ninus' tomb in order to avoid one kind of error – that of losing their way:

> neue sit errandum lato spatiantibus aruo. (87)

But they do not succeed in avoiding the other kind of error – that of tragic misapprehension. The agent of error is, of course, the lion, which leaves blood-stains on Thisbe's shawl. But the idea is given a further, almost Sophoclean, twist in v. 128 where Thisbe nerves herself to leave the cave 'ne fallat amantem'. Alas, she has already 'deceived' him.[28] In Shakespeare's wood there are two agents of error – Oberon, who squeezes the magic juice onto Titania's eyes, and Puck, who first erroneously squeezes the juice onto Lysander and then, out of sheer mischief, turns Bottom's top into the head of an ass. These actions all lead to the misapprehensions or illusions of love. Such illusions may be said to have started before the beginning of the play: Lysander, according to Egeus, has 'bewitch'd the bosom' of Hermia (1.1.27). Demetrius, however, is still enthralled by Hermia's beauty: 'he *errs*, doting on Hermia's eyes' (230). Once the lovers enter the wood these illusions give rise to the most delicious complications, which reach their climax in 3.2; and by that time the fairy queen has become enamoured of an ass. The action, with all its intricacy, centres on romantic love – that mysterious phenomenon which gloriously transcends common sense, leading to ecstasy or misery, and sometimes lapses into utter absurdity. Such love can only be assessed by judgement: one asks whether it goes against reason, or has reason behind it to strengthen and endorse it. Both kinds of answers are given at various points in the play. But assessment is one thing and action another. In the play, as in life, the 'reasonable' man cannot always impose his will. In 1.1.57, for instance, Theseus tells Hermia that she must make her love conform to her father's view and happily marry Demetrius:

> Your eyes must with his judgement look.

But she is unable to obey. Moreover, we cannot be sure that when a character claims to have reason on his side he is necessarily right. When, for example, in 2.2.115–16, Lysander says to Helena

> The will of man is by his reason swayed,
> And reason says you are the worthier maid,

he is not using his reason at all; he is under a spell. The dramatist's irony is iridescent. Thus when Puck utters one of the most famous lines in the play: 'Lord, what fools these mortals be!' we feel like retorting 'Quite, and whose fault is that?' Finally, one must bear in mind that the conflict in the play is resolved in the end by redirecting the affections of Demetrius; and this is accomplished not by reason but by magic – the juice is never removed from his eyes. Reason, of course, applauds the result, but the vital agency is irrational.

Others better qualified, however, have studied the illusions of romantic love and their ramifications in *A Midsummer Night's Dream*; I would only remark that the germ of the idea was present in Ovid. The crucial difference is that whereas the error of Pyramus is tragic and leads to death, the lovers' errors are comic and lead to eventual reconciliation. In Ovid the concluding ritual is burial:

> quodque rogis superest una requiescit in urna (166)

and the heroine dies childless. In Shakespeare the ritual is the comic ritual of marriage, which promises children and celebrates the continuation of life:

> To the best bride-bed will we,
> Which by us shall blessed be;
> And the issue there create
> Ever shall be fortunate.
> So shall all the couples three
> Ever true in loving be. (5.2.33ff.)

The second kind of illusion is the illusion of the theatre. In general we enter this illusion simply by enjoying the work. But as we watch the casting, rehearsal, and performance of the interlude we surrender to an even more subtle wizardry. For here is the greatest of all dramatists apparently demonstrating in considerable detail how to wreck a play. We must assume, I take it, that Bottom and his friends are in earnest throughout and play the piece absolutely straight. Such an assumption raises a question which I have not seen answered,[29] but it does seem necessary to one's whole conception of the mechanicals, and without it the good-natured condescension of Theseus and the rather less good-natured condescension of Philostrate and the others no longer make sense. Peter Quince, therefore, and his friends, quite unconsciously, set about the self-stultifying task of presenting a drama *without* dramatic illusion. If the text calls for moonlight or a wall, it is not enough to convert these entities into stage props; the props themselves must be given voices to explain their functions. With regard to the death of Pyramus we have an even more exquisite absurdity; for not only are the players unaware of destroying illusion, they are actually afraid of creating too much.[30] So, for the ladies' sake, a prologue must be written to assure them that Pyramus is not really killed; and another prologue must make it clear that the lion is in fact Snug the joiner.

Another way of preventing the willing suspension of disbelief is to mangle the writer's sense. This is done by mispronunciation (Ninny's tomb), malapropisms (odious savours), misuse of words ('obscene' for 'unseen'), the disregard of sense-units (all for your delight we are not here), and most disastrously by speaking all one's part at once, cues and all. Finally, there are the almost limitless possibilities of bad verse: clichés, padding, monotonous rhythm, tortured rhyme, and above all pompous rhetoric. Research has brought to light many specimens of the faults which Shakespeare was mocking: Heywood's translation of Seneca, Golding in his feebler moments, Edwards' *Damon and Pythias*, the anonymous *Appius and Virginia*, parts of Kyd's *Spanish Tragedy*. These are just a few examples. But one does not have to be familiar with such texts (thank heaven) in order to understand why Philostrate's eyes watered when he heard

> But stay, O spite!
> But mark, poor knight,
> What dreadful dole is here!
> Eyes, do you see?
> How can it be?
> O dainty duck! O dear! (5.1.283–8)

All this, I have said, destroys illusion. But here we must salute the bard's matchless ingenuity; for by making it impossible to believe in Bottom as Pyramus the lover he has made it certain that we shall accept him as Nick Bottom the weaver. The same applies in a lesser degree to the other mechanicals. And as we watch the atrocious performance in Act 5, we suddenly realize that we are in the same audience as Theseus, Hippolyta, and the four lovers, straining to catch their whispers and joining in their superior giggles.

The mention of Shakespeare himself brings us to the greatest illusion of all, since it includes everything else: I mean the illusion of poetry. This is implicit in every line of the play whether verse or prose, and whether the speaker is a gossamer fairy or a gross clown. But it comes into the open in 5.1 when Theseus adds the poet to the lunatic and the lover (7):

> The lunatic, the lover, and the poet,
> Are of imagination all compact.

In understanding this speech, which has caused a great deal of comment, a number of different considerations must (one feels) be kept in mind. First, the tone is one of friendly but rather patronizing banter. The Duke is in a good humour and certainly does not mean to *censure* these forms of irrationality; at the same time he does not take them seriously. In modern terms one might almost imagine him declaring: 'These poets are odd chaps. What extraordinary things they dream up!' Having said that, one must immediately point out that the products of the poetic imagination are genially dismissed, not in the idiom of the officers' mess, but in the most vivid and energetic verse. Moreover, Theseus' opinion is not left unchallenged. Hippolyta observes that the lovers who have emerged from the wood tell an impressively coherent story, and that although their attitudes have changed, they have changed in such a way as to produce harmony; all of which adds up to something more solid than her fiancé admits:

> But all the story of the night told over,
> And all their minds transfigured so together,
> More witnesseth than fancy's images,
> And grows to something of great constancy. (23–6)

Although these lines refer to a specific group of lovers, they cast doubt on Theseus' generalization about lovers as a whole. Perhaps they also raise the question whether he has said the last word on poetry. Finally, one might well argue that Theseus' words cannot be confined to his character or to their immediate context. On their own they can be accepted quite seriously as a respectful account of what poets do. Such a favourable interpretation would not have been strange to anyone who had read Sidney's *Apology*.[31]

Had Shakespeare at this point put Ovid out of his mind? Perhaps not entirely. After speaking of 'the poet's eye in a fine frenzy rolling' Theseus goes on:

> And, as imagination bodies forth
> The forms of things unknown, the poet's pen
> Turns them to shapes, and gives to airy nothing
> A local habitation and a name. (14–17)

To elucidate the meaning of this no doubt one must go to the Platonic tradition – in particular to Plotinus, who maintained that the artist might by-pass the sensible world and have direct access to the Ideas; he would then convey these Ideas in the particular terms of his own medium – whether stone, paint, or words.[32] But for the *expression* of Theseus' lines Shakespeare perhaps owed something to a poetic rather than a philosophical source. The opening words of the *Metamorphoses* are:

> in noua fert animus mutatas dicere formas
> corpora.
> *My mind bids me tell of forms turned into new shapes.*

When the interlude is over and the court has left, Puck enters with a broom and says:

> Now the hungry lion roars,
>   And the wolf behowls the moon;
>
>   .   .   .

Now it is the time of night
    That the graves, all gaping wide,
Every one lets forth his sprite,
    In the church-way paths to glide:
And we fairies, that do run
    By the triple Hecate's team,
From the presence of the sun,
    Following darkness like a dream,
Now are frolic.

The verses are, of course, intelligible on their own; but when the eye moves down, lighting on *lion, moon, night, graves* (implying death), *fairies, Hecate* (or Titania), *darkness,* and *dream,* it is hard not to think that Puck is in some way glancing back over the play. If there is anything in this notion, it is clear that the story of Pyramus and Thisbe is included in his summary. When he has finished his sweeping, it only remains for Oberon and Titania to pronounce a final blessing and for Puck to close the play.

The thesis of this essay (which does not pretend to deal with more than one aspect of the work) might, therefore, be condensed by saying that the dramatist set out to show how love can transpose (1.1.233), how Bottom was translated (3.1.124–5), transformed (4.1.70) and transported (4.2.4), and how the minds of all the characters were transfigured (5.1.24). The result was Shakespeare's *Metamorphoses* – the most magical tribute that Ovid was ever paid.

II
EPILOGUE

'Imitation and self-imitation', writes Brink, 'are among the outstanding features of Latin poetry.'[1] But imitation also poses problems. In the first place, as several of our contributors have emphasized, cases where one author imitates another are difficult to establish. Similarities of word or thought or phrase can occur because writers are indebted to a common source, or because they are describing similar or conventional situations, or because their works belong to the same generic type of poem.[2] Only patient scholarship and a thorough familiarity with the relevant material can reveal whether the similarities cannot be explained by any of these three reasons. In such cases we may be fairly certain that direct imitation of one author by another is taking place.

As is demonstrated by the contributors to this book, there are many types of imitation in Latin literature. The simplest type, a straight imitation of one author by another, is illustrated by Bain and West in their respective discussions of Plautus–Menander and Virgil–Lucretius. A more complex type is treated by Du Quesnay, who shows that in *Eclogue* 2 Virgil has combined imitation of two *Idylls* of Theocritus (*contaminatio* is the name which has been given to this procedure). Du Quesnay, however, goes further, and argues that from similarities between *Eclogue* 2 and other later poetry we can deduce that both Virgil and these later poets were also borrowing from a common source – the poetry of Gallus, which is now almost entirely lost. A similar multiplicity of antecedents is discussed by Kenney and Macleod in their analyses of *Aeneid* 2.469–505 and *Odes* 2.5 respectively. Macleod develops the view that imitation for Horace involves not only the use of original texts but also a conception of the persona and the achievement of the poet imitated, and a direct personal reaction to that conception.[3] Comparative criticism has in this case led to an attempt to reconstruct one poet's view of another.

Cairns and Woodman both tackle self-imitation, and both are aware of the difficulties of that notion. A concerto by Vivaldi may closely resemble another. One landscape by Claude may be very like another. Such examples may be classed as self-imitation, or self-extension, or may be viewed as considered self-commentaries. But the relationship may be lesser still. They may rather be separate examples of a particular kind of work undertaken with no conscious thought of the earlier examples. Grieg greatly admired a waltz he heard one day and asked the pianist who had composed it. 'You did', was the reply, and by this consideration readers may argue that we have no guarantee that in one renunciation of love Ovid is making any conscious reference to another, or that Tacitus is remembering his first 'visit to a battle-field' as he writes his second. Resemblances detected by critics may all be merely the repetitions which we would expect to find when the same mind with the same basic artistic language revisits, after some extra experience of literature and of life, a scene which it has already worked over. But whatever the biographical truth, these comparative studies throw into light the qualities of both the earlier and the later writings, the artistic range of the language, the fruits of the extra experience, and the wealth of the resources of these writers. The miracle of two Bach fugues is more than twice the miracle of one of them.

There are also many types of literature, prose as well as poetry, in which imitation can occur: comedy, pastoral, didactic, lyric, epic, elegy and historiography are all represented in this book. Of these the most surprising to the modern reader is perhaps the last. From a modern work of narrative history we would expect to learn 'what actually happened'; but from Woodman's analysis we infer that Tacitus tells us some things which may never have happened at all. Tacitus is prepared on occasion to invent the substance of his history, a practice which has serious implications for classical historiography in general. In this respect Tacitus is much closer to ancient poetry than he is to modern historiography: he takes over existing material and uses it to create a new literary work.

When Latin poets took over such existing material, they were expected to vary it and, if possible, to improve upon it. 'imitatio per se ipsa non sufficit', said Quintilian (10.2.4). Hence imitative passages invite the kind of comparative analysis which will reveal the individual qualities of the authors concerned. West compares Virgil's cattle plague with Lucretius' human plague in order to detect the 'Virgilian in Virgil'. The collocation of Ovid, *Amores* 1.13 and Donne's *The Sun Rising* vividly shows the different tone and different intellectual procedures of the two poets as they each engage a heavenly body in a battle of wits.

Ovid the rhetorician asks Lady Dawn to perpetrate a reversal of nature (*adynaton*) by delaying her arrival (ll. 3, 10). He pours out a stream of separate *exempla* and separate mythological arguments to support his request (ll. 11–22 and 33–44 respectively), but he nowhere concentrates on what is evidently the real reason for his request, namely his mistress and his enjoyment of being in bed with her. On the contrary, he speaks only in general terms (e.g. 5 *iuuat*, 26 *cui non est ulla puella*) and only in one line (39) does he refer to himself as currently in love (*amans*). Having demanded an impossibility and given no convincing reason for its accomplishment, Ovid not surprisingly fails in his request. In Donne's poem, on the other hand, his mistress dominates the second half of the poem and is so familiar that Donne need only refer to her namelessly as 'she'. This practice would of course lead to confusion if Donne followed Ovid in addressing a female Dawn, so he chooses the male Sun, whose character he begins by assassinating: the Sun is an old busybody (l. 1), and an unwelcome visitor (3 'call on us'); even more to the point, he is a peeping tom because he peers through curtained windows (3, cf. 'sawcy', 5). More realistically than Ovid, Donne the metaphysician asks for no impossibility: he develops a series of linked conceits, scoffing at the impotence of a Sun that can be eclipsed by the blinking of the lover's eye, or dazzled by the brightness of his mistress's. Then from the conceit that his mistress comprises all the glories of all the world traversed by the Sun Donne moves on to claim that the lovers are the world, and then juggles triumphantly with the consequences of that proposition – that the Sun can see only half of the world and is therefore half as happy as the lovers who can enjoy it all, and that the bed is the centre of the Sun's rotation and the walls of the bedroom are the sphere within which it orbits. Donne concludes by actually inviting the Sun to 'Shine here to us', something which the poem began by complaining about! Thus the Sun gets his own way with Donne, as Aurora had with Ovid; but there can be little doubt that Donne, unlike Ovid, has the better of the verbal battle.

Donne has varied the material which he found in Ovid: comparable variation can be seen in almost any of the imitative Latin passages discussed by our contributors, for it was an accepted way of achieving originality in poetry. Thus Kenney points out that in Homer it is Hector, when confronted by Achilles, who is compared to a snake defending his ground; but in Virgil the emphasis is reversed: the snake symbolizes aggression, and it is the son of Achilles who is the aggressor, the father of Hector who is presently to be attacked. But we may ask whether poetic originality amounts to no more than this. Is there no such thing as absolute originality in Latin poetry?

If there is, it is perhaps most likely to occur, not in genres such as epic or drama where the material is traditional anyway, but in those where the writer purports to be relating actual experiences.[4] A typical example in Latin poetry would be the account which Horace gives of his journey to Brundisium in (probably) 37 B.C. in *Satires* 1.5. Yet this poem is at the same time an imitation of an earlier satire by Lucilius, who had described a journey which he had made to Sicily. The dual nature of Horace's poem is typical of much Latin poetry. How can such a poem, which is apparently 'actual' (and therefore original) but demonstrably 'literary' (because imitative), in fact be original?

Our answer to this question is likely to depend, at least in part, on how we believe the imitation came to be present in Horace's poem. Two possible explanations are discussed in a masterly fashion by Fraenkel:[5]

> It would be wholly inadequate to assume that Horace wrote the *Iter Brundisinum* primarily because his mind was full of lively pictures of the journey which he had undertaken in the spring of 37 B.C., that he wished to express this personal experience and that then, secondarily as it were, adorned his poem with certain features borrowed from Lucilius' *Iter Siculum*. But it would be equally inadequate to assume that Horace was primarily bent upon renewing in some way the satire written by Lucilius about his journey to Sicily and that the experience of his own journey, with which a lucky coincidence provided him, only served to colour and vary the fundamentally Lucilian pattern of his poem ... The 'primary' and the 'literary' type of experience blend with such perfect harmony that it would be idle to try to assign priority to the one or the other ... Only the joint impact of a personal experience and a literary tradition was capable of bringing forth a particular poem.

This 'joint impact' can be illustrated further with the help of more modern poets, whose processes of composition are more fully documented. Discussing the poetry of Shakespeare, Milton and Coleridge among others, John Press has remarked that

> almost every poet of merit has drawn upon his reading in order to enrich his experience of daily life, and to impose a coherent order upon the whirling images that clamour for

admission to the body of his verse. The facile distinction between life and literature is meaningless in this context, since both are raw material of equal value to the poet.[6]

An excellent illustration would be Keats, who, we are told,

> read with an intensity that can hardly be imagined . . . He went through every word of a book, annotating, underlining, and marking nearly every page from cover to cover, absorbing every phrase, cadence and intonation of the author. What might be a pastime with other men was a passion with him, not a passive exercise but an active pursuit.[7]

It is therefore not surprising that Keats' 'life, his letters, his words, thoughts, and his poems themselves take on the character of whatever book he is studying'.[8] It would seem that this kind of process more than adequately explains the character of such a poem as Horace, *Satires* 1.5, and hence of much of Latin poetry of this type. A poet's reading is not an alternative to his actual experiences but an intrinsic part of them; and the reflection of that reading in his poetry in no way diminishes the originality of that poetry.

There is no reason why Latin poetry should be any less original than that of Keats and the rest. And indeed Gransden and Rudd in this book demonstrate how Chaucer, Shakespeare and Donne relied on their Latin predecessors in much the same way, and to as great an extent, as the Latin poets relied on theirs. *A Midsummer Night's Dream*, for example, ends with a glorious travesty of Ovid's tale of Pyramus and Thisbe. Rudd shows how the affecting details of Ovid's story are grossly traduced by the mechanicals in their desire to be horrifying without being credible; but the correspondences he finds between Ovid's story and the love stories of *A Midsummer Night's Dream* show that Shakespeare's knowledge of the *Metamorphoses* has enriched the whole play and in particular has contributed to his reflections on the nature of illusion and of change, which gives such richness to this comedy. The travesty is also a tribute. Ovid is the starting point for thoughts which leave Ovid far behind.

Why then is Latin poetry so often thought to be less original than English poetry? In many ways the Latin poets themselves have been their own worst enemies, by continually insisting on their indebtedness to their Greek predecessors – Horace the Roman Alcaeus, Propertius the Roman Callimachus and so on. And modern scholars have not helped by adopting the phrase 'Latin literature and its Greek models' to express this relationship. The word 'model' is used by analogy with sculpture, yet the analogy is doubly unfortunate. In the first place, traditional sculptors have intentionally reproduced more or less exact likenesses of their models; and modern scholars often talk as if Latin poets began their poems with the intention of exactly reproducing a Greek poem but then 'deviated' from their model to 'include' (or 'introduce') some Roman material for the sake of 'originality'. On this view the ideal poem ought to be Catullus 51, where three quarters of the poem is a translation of Sappho but the final stanza (assuming it is in place) is Catullus' own composition. No wonder Latin poetry is accused of unoriginality if its originality is thought to amount to no more than this! In fact, of course, such a view is a total misrepresentation – it strongly resembles the second of the alternatives rejected so forcefully by Fraenkel above. Even granted that the literary and social atmosphere of the Augustan age (to take a classic case) was highly Hellenized,[9] how can scholars believe that (say) Horace would need to *include* Roman material in poetry which he, a Roman, was writing?

The second characteristic of sculpture is that the sculptor's artefact, no matter how brilliant, is undeniably less 'real' than the living model itself. Hence the analogy has persuaded people to think that an imitative Latin poem is somehow intrinsically inferior to the Greek poem which is being imitated – and Russell in his essay observes that this was a view which was held, rather paradoxically, even in antiquity itself. It may seem pedantic to highlight this terminology, but in our view it has considerably contributed to the low estimation which in some quarters Latin literature still enjoys. In our opinion the word 'model' should be avoided in favour of some word such as 'predecessor' or 'antecedent', denoting chronological anteriority and nothing more. Even the word 'imitation' is full of danger: it has been abandoned by modern students of English literature precisely because of its suggestions of the spurious or the second-hand;[10] yet in its Latin form it is firmly embedded in the writings of ancient literary critics and there is now no way of dispensing with it.

The general conclusions which may be drawn from this collection of essays are unsurprising: that writers, and in particular writers of Latin, are often imitators; that imitations are often original creations; that comparative studies of antecedent(s) and imitator can often shed valuable light on both; that the imitator moveth as he listeth and therefore that there is no set grammar of comparison for the critic to apply: he must simply be apt to see what is there. The only law is that when a creative artist imitates, his product may well have the immeasurable originality that is characteristic of great art.

NOTES

I | DE IMITATIONE

The most important modern treatments of this subject are Kroll (1924), 139–84; Stemplinger (1922); Bompaire (1958), 13–154. Of the ancient texts quoted most often in this chapter, Quintilian, *Institutio oratoria* 10.1–2 is translated in Russell–Winterbottom (1973), 380–404 (see also Peterson (1891) on Quintilian 10, and Steinmetz (1964)); 'Longinus' is translated in Russell–Winterbottom (1973), 462–503, and in many other modern versions, e.g. Dorsch (1969); the fragments of Dionysius' *De imitatione* and the Pseudo-Dionysian *Ars rhetorica* are in the Teubner edition (*Dionysii Halicarnassensis opera*, vol. 6 = *Opuscula*, vol. 2, ed. H. Usener–L. Radermacher), but there is no modern English translation, nor is one promised in the Loeb edition of Dionysius' *Critical essays* by Stephen Usher, of which the first volume has appeared.

1 *patrii sermonis egestas* is a phrase used by Lucretius (1.832 = 3.260, cf. 1.139) when admitting the difficulty of expressing philosophical or scientific matters in Latin.

2 At *Odes* 3.30.13 Horace boasts of having reproduced in Latin the *Aeolium carmen* of Sappho and Alcaeus, who wrote in the Aeolian metres. At *Georgics* 2.176 Virgil boasts that he is reproducing in Latin the *Ascraeum carmen* of Hesiod, the didactic poet who lived in Ascra in Boeotia.

3 See David Bain, above, pp. 17–34.

4 For this passage see Jensen (1923), p. vi.

5 *De ideis* 1, pp. 215ff. Rabe; Russell–Winterbottom (1973), 562.

6 Reading ἐκγόνων (Sylburg) for εἰκόνων in the last clause.

7 Quintilian 10.2.3 'necesse est aut similes aut dissimiles bonis simus. similem raro natura praestat, frequenter imitatio'.

8 *De antiquis oratoribus*, preface (Russell–Winterbottom (1973), 305ff.).

9 This passage of Seneca provides our only knowledge of Dorion (he need not be the same person as the authority on fish referred to by Athenaeus). *metaphrasis* is what we might today call paraphrase, saying the same thing in different words: it was a common educational exercise (see Bonner (1977), 255–6). The Homeric passage being 'metaphrased' is *Odyssey* 9.481. Similar material (though inconsistent with the treatment of the episode quoted here) is found in an example of 'frigidity' (τὸ ψυχρόν) in Demetrius περὶ ἑρμηνείας 115: ἐπὶ τοῦ

Κύκλωπος λιθοβολοῦντος τὴν ναῦν τοῦ Ὀδύσσεως ἔφη τις· Φερομένου τοῦ λίθου αἶγες ἐνέμοντο ἐν αὐτῷ ('someone said of the Cyclops' pelting Odysseus' ships with a stone: "goats grazed on the stone as it sped through the air"').

10 Aulus Gellius, *Noctes Atticae* 9.9.12–17, translated in Russell–Winterbottom (1973), 548ff. See Austin (1971) on *Aeneid* 1.498ff.

11 Horace's phrase to describe poetic originality (*Ars poetica* 131).

12 Aulus Gellius 17.10 (cf. Macrobius, *Saturnalia* 5.17): translation in Russell–Winterbottom (1973), 550ff. See Barigazzi (1966), test. 42, and Intro., p. 68.

13 Aulus Gellius 12.1.10; Barigazzi (1966), test. 38.

14 Macrobius 5.11.5–8.

15 Those who wish for more may consider, e.g., Macrobius 5.11.2–3 (the bee-similes in *Aeneid* 1.430 and *Iliad* 8.300); 5.11.8 (the helmsman in *Odyssey* 5.270ff. sees Pliades and Bootes at once, Palinurus in *Aeneid* 5.513ff. turns his head to look at the constellations in a natural order); 5.13.18 (in *Aeneid* 6.582, in contrast to the description of the Aloadae in *Odyssey* 11.308, Virgil 'mensurarum nomina non ausus attingere'); 5.13.31ff. (Fama of *Aeneid* 4.176ff. is not well modelled on Homer's Eris (*Iliad* 4.442ff.), because when Fama grows immense 'fama esse iam desinit et fit notio rei iam cognitae'.) The vast majority of the comparisons in Macrobius, however, are given without explanation of what the critic thought to be the decisive points.

16 We should perhaps read κινουμένης, so that the ψυχή, not the ἐνέργεια, is 'roused'.

17 *Ars poetica* 411.

18 Brink (1971) on Horace, *Ars poetica* 134.

19 See C. W. Macleod, above, pp. 89, 93. Horace's view of the relation of Alcaeus to Archilochus is important; he saw that he was more civilized and so better than his model.

20 Pseudo-Dionysius, *Ars rhetorica*, p. 305.

21 *Diatribes* 2.13.14ff.; *Encheiridion* 33.12.

22 Latin *furtum*. The term *plagiarius* ('kidnapper', 'slave-stealer') is applied to literary theft in an elaborate metaphor by Martial (1.53).

23 Ἀλλ' ὡς ἀπὸ καλῶν ἠθῶν ἢ πλασμάτων ἢ δημιουργημάτων ἀποτύπωσις. See Russell (1964) on 'Longinus' 13.4.

24 See in general Kroll (1924), 139–84, and Stemplinger (1912); also *OCD* s.v. 'plagiarism'.

25 On these lines of Catullus and Virgil see also Clausen (1970), 90–1.

26 Cicero's remarks are part of a longer discussion of *imitatio* in *De oratore* 2.87–97, on which see now Fantham (1978).

2

PLAVTVS VORTIT BARBARE

For bibliography on the literature arising from the publication of parts of *Dis exapaton* see *CGF* p. 131 and Questa (1975) (Questa provides the most up to date version of the Greek text). I have not been able to take account of any work that came to my notice after

October 1977. It should be obvious that I am greatly indebted to the works of Handley (1968), Jacques (1968), Questa (1969), Gaiser (1970), Sandbach (1973) and Pöschl (1973).

1 On Terence's compositional activity and originality see Haffter (1967) and Ludwig (1968).

2 *contaminatio* is the term used by modern scholars to describe the activity here discussed. The word is not so used in antiquity and there has been considerable debate on the question whether Terence in using the verb *contaminare* (Terence, *Andria* 16, *Hauton Timorumenus* 17) meant to suggest 'combination' rather than simply 'spoiling'. For references and discussion see Marti (1963), 23ff. See also below, p. 212 and n. 86, p. 229 and n. 4.

3 See Leo (1967), 221ff. and Williams (1968), 363ff.

4 The formal simplicity of the passage disguises a highly emotional utterance. See Bain (1977), 205. The monologue does contain one or two high-flown expressions for which see Questa (1975), 70 n. 61.

5 On this see Haffter (1934), 86.

6 See Wright (1974), 87ff. With the partial exception of Terence, Roman comedy presents very much of a stylistic unity. See Wright (1974) passim and Fraenkel (1935) 628ff.

7 Not that tragic language is not exploited in Greek New Comedy. Its use there, however, is much less widespread than in Plautus, and its effect generally more complex. See Sandbach (1969), 124ff.

8 For a brief account of the rediscovery of Menander see Sandbach (1973), 2ff. and for a fuller treatment which concentrates on the last twenty years, Arnott (1970). Outside the two discoveries mentioned in the text, the most considerable finds have been of portions of *Sikyonios* and *Misoumenos*.

9 'asyndeton' means 'unconnected', lacking a connective particle. Often in Latin and Greek two statements are juxtaposed without connection, the second being an explanation of the first. The classic example of this Plautine element is Plautus, *Mercator* 361 *muscast meus pater: nil potest clam haberi* ...

10 Fraenkel was still a firm believer in contamination, a chapter of his book being devoted to five 'contaminated' plays (Fraenkel (1960), 243ff.). Later he retracted a good deal of what he had written there (op. cit. 431ff.), but reaffirmed that Plautus did 'contaminate' his plays. It is doubtful whether, without new evidence from papyri about Greek originals, contamination can be proved in any given case. The *Miles* remains the strongest candidate. For recent research on Plautine *contaminatio* see Gaiser (1972), 1058–63.

11 See Bain (1977), 154ff.

12 It is announced as *Bulletin of the Institute of Classical Studies*, supplement number 22. At the time of writing there was no immediate prospect of its appearance.

13 Menander, *Dis exapaton* 47ff. does confirm that Chrysalus' lying story (Plautus, *Bacchides* 249–336) formed part of the original, but no one could seriously have questioned that. On the whole problem of the

third deception see Williams (1956), 450ff. and Questa (1975), 46ff. For a vigorous restatement of the view that Plautus has added a third, final deception see Thierfelder (1975), 97ff.

14 See Handley (1968), 19 n.4.

15 For attempts at such a reconstruction see Gaiser (1970), 65ff., Bader (1970) and Webster (1974), 130 and the remarks of Tränkle (1975) 117 n. 9. Discussion of fr. 8 will have to be reconsidered in the light of de Nonno's discovery (de Nonno (1977), 391ff.).

16 In the Greek play it is assumed by 'Philoxenus' that he will do this. He does not reply to the request of 'Philoxenus'. Plautus obscures a nice touch of the original in having him reply *factum uolo* (l. 495). See Del Corno (1975), 14f.

17 The reading of *Dis exapaton* 53 is]μῶν· μὴ πρόσεχε κενῶι λόγωι not ἐκείνωι λόγωι (OCT). See Questa (1975), 2 reporting Handley and Revel Coles.

18 See Questa (1975), 17 n. 13, again reporting Handley.

19 On χοροῦ and the structure of New Comedy see Sandbach (1973), 12, 12 n. 1.

20 See Handley (1968), 14, 20 n. 12.

21 See Handley (1968), 20 n. 11. The movements of Nicobulus in *Bacchides* go contrary to the principle stated by Handley (1969), 40. See Questa (1969), 209.

22 This is Acidalius' division of the line between speakers. Our oldest Plautine manuscript A apparently does not indicate change of speaker after *is est* and reads *et* between *contra* and *contollam* (likewise the Palatine manuscripts which read *tollam*). The symmetry of the rest of the encounter (see p. 28) and analogy with other such Plautine scenes of meeting strongly recommend the redistribution here adopted: cf. *Aulularia* 813 *congrediar.* :: *contollam gradum*; *Epidicus* 543ff. *haud scio an congrediar astu* . . . :: *hanc congrediar astu*; *Epidicus* 547 *compellabo.* :: *orationis aciem contra conferam*; *Persa* 15 *congrediar* . :: *contra adgredibor.* The intrusion of *et* in AP is explained by Havet (1904), 142f. who, although citing the clinching parallel (*Aulularia* 812f.), recommends a distribution which does not preserve the symmetry.

23 I omit ll. 540–51 which are absent from A and are attested as being absent from other parts of the tradition. Tränkle (1975), 118ff. pointing out internal incoherencies and unplautine diction convincingly argues that the lines are interpolated (for doubts about their authenticity see also Maurach (1976), 482f.). One may add to Tränkle's linguistic arguments the fact that in l. 547 *inimicos . . . in se* is unique in Plautus who elsewhere and frequently uses the dative with *inimicus*. The prepositional usage, however, does have analogies in Plautus (see Adams (1976) 49 and 154 n. 4).

24 Attribution and sense are far from certain here. See Sandbach (1973), ad loc.

25 See Haffter (1934). Such distinctions are not absolutely clear-cut. Some lyric passages display extremely simple diction and high-flown language is to be found in senarii, especially in prologues and in

monologues of boasting slaves (see, as well as Haffter, Löfstedt (1942) 115, (1933), 108f., 305f.).

26 See Sandbach (1973), 36f.

27 See Questa (1969), 192f., 202 who notes that the tone of the senarii (500f.) is also pathetic.

28 See Handley (1968), 17.

29 For this second possibility see Sandbach (1973), ad loc.

30 See Bain (1977), 139, 147, 168, 175.

31 On this fragment see Jocelyn (1967), 321f.

32 See Haffter (1934), 46f.

33 See Bain (1977), 195ff.

34 So Sandbach (1973), ad loc. The reversal of the sequence of entrances also probably entailed a drastic reduction of the monologue.

35 Plautus, *Bacchides* 686, 690, 746f. give us clues as to the content of this scene.

36 See Thierfelder (1975), 97.

37 For 1 cf. *CGF* 282.14ff. (on which see Bain (1977), 159f.). For 2 cf. Menander, *Samia* 406f. (on which see Lowe (1973), 97f.). For 3 cf. Menander, *Samia* 383 (προσιτέον there is spoken by an eavesdropper). The fourth stage is of course exemplified in our *Dis exapaton* passage.

38 This is well observed by Lowe (1973), 98.

39 See Bain (1977), 152, 179 n. 3.

40 On *gradus* as a military term see Jocelyn (1967), 172f. Note the military language in a similar context at *Epidicus* 547 (quoted in n. 22 above).

41 See Wright (1974), 140ff. See Nisbet–Hubbard (1970) on Horace, *Odes* 1.36.

42 See Minar in Minar–Sandbach–Helmbold (1969), 166 n. *a.* for *aduenticia* and *aduentoria*. Plautus, *Bacchides* 94 and Cicero, *Ad Atticum* 4.5.4 give us *uiatica* (see Shackleton Bailey (1964), 104).

43 The passages he collects are something of a mixed bag. For differentiation and classification see Blänsdorf (1976), 715.

44 For one such example (*Pseudolus* 1313ff. based on the ending of *Bacchides*) see Williams (1956), 449. See also Bain (1977), 166f. for a suggestion about *Trinummus* 515ff. Jacques (1968), 221 was the first to drawn attention to the resemblance between our passage and *CGF* 257.23ff. which he regards as a possible source for Plautus.

45 Professor Handley tells me that he does not think much more can be got out of the papyrus than is printed in the OCT.

46 It is interesting to note that the motif is found earlier in the play at *Bacchides* 475 where Mnesilochus claims with truth that Pistoclerus is acting for a friend, but Philoxenus and Lydus do not take him to mean himself.

47 See Pöschl (1973), 18, 34.

48 For discussions see Jacques (1968), 218ff., Del Corno (1975), 17f. and Maurach (1976), 482. Maurach suggests that ἠδίκηκας shows that Sostratos has been deceiving himself up to now: 'Letzten Endes liebt er doch das Mädel und fühlt sich schlimm betrogen.' Possibly this is so, but it is worth noting that great stress is laid earlier in

Bacchides (N.B. ll. 385ff.) on the friendship between the young men and it may well be that we are meant to see that Sostratos while occupied in his mind with 'Bacchis' feels at the same time a deep sense of hurt at what he thinks his friend has done to him. The sight of Moschos brings upon him the sudden feeling of a betrayal of trust. Jacques and Del Corno both stress the importance of the friendship theme in the Menander play. These things would be clearer if the crucial lines were not so fragmentary.

49 Comparable considerations arise elsewhere in Plautus with regard to the behaviour and attitudes of young men in love (cf. particularly *Pseudolus* 122). On Plautus' treatment of such characters see Flury (1968), 72.

50 Maurach (1976), 481f.

51 Mention of him is indicated by τούτου and προήρπασας in l. 19. Sandbach thinks that ἤδη 'στιν οὗτος φροῦδος (l. 18) also refers to him. I believe with Questa (1969), 196 and Del Corno (1975), 15f. that the words form a question not a statement, that they represent a formula of transition from dialogue to monologue, and that they refer to the newly departed Lydos. I take ἤδη to be sarcastic – 'Gone already, has he?' Sandbach's view is conditioned by the register of φροῦδος. He misses one occasion where Menander does use it in the literal sense, Menander, *Dyskolos* 776. It might well be a high-flown, out-of-date word (see, however, Dover (1968) on Aristophanes, *Clouds* 718). If so it could still be used with comic exaggeration.

52 *beneuolens* (l. 553) and *amicus* (l. 557) are synonyms. See Reitzenstein (1912), 17f.

53 So Maurach (1976), 482 f. who notes Plautus' delight in *perplexim lacessere*.

54 Like our passage is *Mercator* 894ff.

55 See Handley (1968), 17 and Del Corno (1975), 17ff.

56 Leo continues in the second half of the sentence by praising Plautus as a translator.

57 Quintilian, *Institutio oratoria* 10.1.99.

58 See Wilamowitz (1925), 169: 'Ich muss behaupten, dass man es treffend gar nicht anders bezeichnen darf als ein Singspiel, opera buffa; man soll Worte brauchen, bei denen man sich etwas denken kann. Komödie trifft nicht zu.'

59 See Handley (1975), 120ff. and Bain (1977), 210ff.

3   FROM POLYPHEMUS TO CORYDON

1 For reasons of space I have had to assume that the reader has to hand a text of the *Eclogues* and the *Idylls*. For bibliography see McKay (1974). I have not noted mere matters of agreement and disagreement. I have found most useful Pfeiffer (1933), Posch (1969) with Schmidt (1972a), Coleman (1977) and Moore-Blunt (1977): the last contains a useful survey of modern opinions on the second *Eclogue*. If I have made explicit my disagreements with the views expressed in Coleman (1977), that is only because his is the standard commentary with

which all readers must now begin their study of the poem. My greatest debt is to Professor Francis Cairns: my approach to the problem of imitation takes as its starting point his insights into the nature of ancient poetry as expressed in his published works and in the course of many discussions. I am also grateful to him for allowing me to read the typescript of his book on Tibullus.

2 The chronology of the *Eclogues* is still highly controversial: for discussion and different views from mine see Coleman (1977), 14–21 and Schmidt (1974).

3 *Eclogue* 3.84–8, 8.11–12. For Pollio see André (1949); Du Quesnay (1977); Nisbet–Hubbard (1978), 7–11 (with additional bibliography).

4 It is commonly denied that *facetum* here refers to wit: for example, by Rose (1942), 24ff. and 226. For a definition of *facetus* see Fordyce (1961), 131–2: incongruity is the essence of the wit of the *Eclogues* as of the *Idylls*. Horace's words are either a reply to *Catalepton* 5.12–14 (*dulces Camenae . . . meas chartas | reuisitote, sed pudenter et raro*) or, less probably, the forger's point of departure.

5 For a recent general account see Wardman (1976).

6 See Fraser (1972) 1.305ff.

7 For a convenient survey of building activities in Rome at this time see MacKendrick (1960), 116ff. Asinius Pollio founded a library (Pliny, *Natural history* 35.10 makes explicit the comparison with the Ptolemies) and built the Atrium Libertatis from the spoils of his campaigns (see Broughton (1952), 388).

8 39: *Eclogues* and Pollio's triumph; 36–35: Horace, *Satires* 1 and Octavian's return from the defeat of Sextus Pompeius; 29: Octavian's triple triumph and L. Varius Rufus, *Thyestes*; Horace, *Epodes* and *Satires* 2; Virgil, *Georgics*; 27: Messalla's triumph and Tibullus 1; 24–23: Horace *Odes* 1–3 and Propertius 3 and Augustus' return from Spain; and so on.

9 Compare Cicero, *De finibus* 1.7 *quamquam si plane sic uerterem Platonem aut Aristotelem, ut uerterunt nostri poetae fabulas, male, credo, mererer de meis ciuibus, si ad eorum cognitionem diuina illa ingenia transferrem.* (Ironical.)

10 Compare, for example, Propertius 3.1.3–4; Horace, *Odes* 3.30.13–14.

11 See, most recently, Williams (1968); Nisbet–Hubbard (1970); Cairns (1972) and, in general, compare Culler (1975).

12 The verb βουκολιάζεσθαι in Theocritus seems to mean 'to sing songs in the manner of herdsmen'. It is coined on analogy with verbs like Δωρίσδειν 'to speak like a Dorian' and παροιμιάζεσθαι 'to speak in proverbs'. By the time of the *Lament for Bion* the bucolic poet is the herdsman (11) and the verb means 'to compose a bucolic poem' (120).

13 For recent discussion of Virgil's general relationship to Theocritus see Muecke (1975); Schmidt (1972).

14 Wilamowitz (1906) is still fundamental: for a convenient summary see Gow (1952), lix sqq.

15 [Theocritus], *Epigrams* 26 and 27. For details of their work see Fraser (1972) 1.474, 2.688–9 (with bibliography).

16 Eight of which are often considered to be spurious: the debate continues.

17 For example, it is tempting to overstate the novelty of Menalcas' song in *Eclogue* 5 until it is recalled that Theocritus wrote on the deification of Berenice (fr. 3 Gow).

18 A chance discovery earlier this century revealed a bucolic precedent for *Eclogue* 6 (Page (1942), 502ff.). Longus' *Daphnis and Chloe* is a treasure-house of bucolic motifs (see, on the relationship of the novel to Hellenistic poetry, Giangrande (1962)), which offers many parallels to apparently novel themes in the *Eclogues*. There is no reason to suppose that he knew Virgil's poems: see Mittelstadt (1970), 215.

19 See Artemidorus [Theocritus], *Epigram* 26. In the *Lament* the refrain of *Idyll* 1 ἄρχετε βουκολικᾶς . . . ἀοιδᾶς becomes ἄρχετε Σικελικαὶ . . . Μοῖσαι and Bion, who imitated more than the bucolic *Idylls*, is simply ὁ βουκόλος (11) and ὁ βούτας (81). See n. 21.

20 The tables contained in Posch (1969), 17–27 are, for all their limitations (see Schmidt (1972a)), invaluable guides.

21 The scholia (on *Idylls* 1–18, 28, 29 and the *Syrinx*) have as their final comment on *Idyll* 18 τέλος τῶν Θεοκρίτου βουκολικῶν: compare the scholion on Apollonius Rhodius 1.1234: Θεόκριτος ἐν τοῖς βουκολικοῖς ἐν τῷ Ὕλᾳ ἐπιγραφομένῳ. Perhaps for some collectors the criterion was the Doric dialect rather than what we would consider bucolic features: at *Lament for Bion* 94–6 ᾠδᾶς βουκολικᾶς and Μοίσας τᾶς Δωρίδος are synonyms; compare Δωρὶς ἀοιδά (12) and Σικελικόν τι λίγαινε καὶ ἁδύ τι βουκολιάζευ (120). For the dialect of *Idyll* 12, which has as its title the peculiar Doric word Ἀίτης and a rustic speaker, see Giangrande (1971), 98–9. The ten *merae rusticae* attributed to Theocritus by Servius (3.3.20–1 Thilo) should not be taken too seriously. The number may well have begun life as an attempt to answer a traditional question of Virgilian scholarship (3.3.15 Thilo): *de eclogis multi dubitant, quae licet decem sint*; compare Philargyrius 3.13.14 Hagen: *quaeri solet, cur non ultra quam X eclogas scripsit. sane sciendum, VII eclogas esse meras rusticas* would be a counter-argument in the same silly debate. Virgil, of course, had no equivalent of dialect for defining the genre, and had to find other means.

22 Their authenticity was apparently never disputed in antiquity: see Gow (1952) 2.170–1, 185–6. It is simplest to assume that Virgil thought them genuine and I have accordingly referred to their author throughout as Theocritus.

23 See Muecke (1975); Schmidt (1972), 57–68.

24 See especially Quintilian 10.2; for a convenient account see Clark (1957), 144–76.

25 For a brief but instructive discussion of Virgilian *aemulatio* see Aulus Gellius, *Noctes Atticae* 13.27(26).

26 Parthenius *quo grammatico in Graecis Vergilius usus est* (Macrobius, *Saturnalia* 5.18). For the type of questions to be considered in preparing an imitation see especially Quintilian 10.2.27.

27 Cicero, *De finibus* 1.10 *debeo . . . iis seruire qui uel utrisque litteris* (i.e. Greek and Latin) *uti uelint uel, si suas habent, illas non magno*

opere desiderent. Cicero does not even contemplate educated Romans who were not able to read Greek fluently: neither does Quintilian; nor should we!

28 Cicero, *De finibus* 1.6 *nostrum iudicium et nostrum scribendi ordinem adiungimus . . . quodsi Graeci leguntur a Graecis, iisdem de rebus alia ratione compositis, quid est cur nostri a nostris non legantur?*

29 Cicero, *De finibus* 1.6 *quid habent cur Graeca anteponant iis quae et splendide dicta sint neque sint conuersa de Graecis?* Compare 1.10.

30 Cicero, *De finibus* 1.7 *locos quidem quosdam, si uidebitur, transferam . . . cum inciderit ut id apte fieri possit.*

31 *Idyll* 8.56, 9.15; compare *Idylls* 1 and 11. The examples given in the following notes are not intended to be exhaustive.

32 *Idyll* 8.56, 9.25 ff., 3.25 ff.

33 *Idyll* 3.2, 8.2 (mountains); 4.56, 1.21, 1.116 (woods).

34 *Idyll* 6.4; compare *Idylls* 1, 7, 10.

35 *Idyll* 1.128ff.; *Idyll* 5.53 (Nymphae); 8.43, 93 (Nais). See Rumpel (1879) s.vv.

36 Amaryllis *Idyll* 3.1, 4.38; Amyntas *Idyll* 7.2; Corydon *Idyll* 4.1, 5.6; Damoetas *Idyll* 6.1; Menalcas *Idyll* 8.9, 9,2; Thestylis *Idyll* 2.1.

37 Cattle, sheep and goats *Idylls* passim; cicada *Idyll* 5.29, 7.138; stag *Idyll* 1.135, lizard *Idyll* 7.21; lioness *Idyll* 3.15, 23.19; wolf *Idyll* 10.30; wild boar *Idyll* 5.23.

38 Columella, *De re rustica* 9.1.1.

39 Attempts to identify the various plants can be found in Coleman (1977). For further discussion and their role in the *Idylls* see Lembach (1970) s.v. ἄνηθον (*anethum*); κύτισος (*cytisus*); δάφνη (*laurus*); κρίνον (*lilium*); μᾶλον (*mala*); νάρκισσος (*narcissus*); μάκων (*papauer*); ἕρπυλλος (*serpyllum*); ἄκανθα (*spineta*); πτελέος (*ulmus*); σχοῖνος (*uncus*); ἴον (*uiola*).

40 For *narcissus* in such catalogues see, for example, *Anthologia Palatina* 5.144, 147; Pfeiffer (1933), 33.

41 For *myrtus* and *laurus* (54) see Ibycus 315 Page; Theocritus, *Epigram* 4.7; *Eclogue* 7.62; Horace, *Odes* 3.4.18–19. Schmidt (1972), 292 n. 283 suggests that the pair may have occurred in Euphorion's *Hyacinthos.*

42 *casia* joins roses and myrtle in Tibullus' underworld for lovers (1.3.61ff.); *caltha* (βούφθαλμον; χρυσάνθεμον) is among the flowers gathered by Proserpina's companions at Ovid, *Fasti* 4.438. Note Pliny, *Natural history* 21.168 *heliochrysum alii chrysanthemum uocant.* ἑλίχρυσος appears at *Idyll* 1.30, 2.78; it was a favourite garland flower: Ibycus 34 Page; Lembach (1970), 171–2.

43 *Idyll* 9.19, 10.54–5.

44 Plautus, *Mostellaria* 39–40; Horace, *Epode* 3.3–4 *edit cicutis alium nocentius. o dura messorum ilia!*; Pseudo-Virgil, *Moretum.*

45 See Lembach (1970), 54; *Idyll* 5.128 αἴγιλον αἶγες ἔδοντι.

46 *hedus* and *edus* are alternative forms of *haedus, ebiscum* of *hibiscum.* The change of *d* to *b* would not worry an ancient etymologist: compare Varro, *De lingua Latina* 5.172, 7.31. Goats were notoriously omnivorous (Eupolis, fr. 14 K) and even humans could eat *hibiscum* (for example, Calpurnius Siculus 4.32). The adjective *uiridi* supports this

view as does the dative with *compellere* (see Servius ad loc.; Nisbet–Hubbard (1970), 288). Contrast Coleman (1977), ad loc.

47 See Rumpel (1879) and Lembach (1970), index s.vv.

48 See Williams (1968), 317–19.

49 *uaccinium* (18, 50) properly denotes a bilberry which has pink flowers. *Eclogue* 2.18 is a condensed translation of *Idyll* 10.28 where the ὑάκινθος is described as μέλας (*nigra*). With *mollia uaccinia* (50) compare *Iliad* 14.348–9 ὑάκινθον . . . μαλακόν. The allusion may be deliberate: for Homeric phrases on the lips of Theocritean herdsmen see, conveniently, Dover (1971), li. Berries would be out of place in either line: contrast Coleman (1977), ad loc.

50 For apples as love-gifts see *Idylls* 2.120, 3.10, 11.10; Foster (1899); Littlewood (1967). At *Idyll* 27.50 'velvet apples' denote a girl's breasts. For *malum*–μῆλον as cheeks, see *OLD* s.v. (6); LSJ s.v. B.II.2. Virgil is alluding to Lucretius 5.888–9: *puerili aeuo florente iuuentas . . . molli uestit lanugine malas.*

51 Compare Horace, *Odes* 1.13.2–3 with Nisbet–Hubbard (1970), ad loc. Theocritus has βράβιλον (*pruna*??) in a different context: see Lembach (1970), 139ff.

52 Isidore, *Origines* 17.7.25 *fructus eius* [sc. *castaneae*] *gemini in modum testiculorum intra folliculum reconditi sunt.* Compare n. 50 and note that female genitals were sometimes called roses (Dover (1971), 136–7) and that roses are another common love-gift, conspicuous by their absence here. κάρυα (*nuces*) are mentioned as food in *Idyll* 9.21.

53 See, for example, Catullus 22.14 *infaceto est infacetior rure.* The rustics in Longus do not even know the name of love (*Daphnis and Chloe* 1.13.5)! See the interesting description of Theocritus by Manilius 2.41–2 *nec siluis siluestre canit perque horrida motus | rura serit dulcis Musamque inducit in aulas.*

54 See Cairns (1975*b*), 79–91. This tradition is best represented by the *Georgics.*

55 The many similarities between *Eclogue* 2 and *Epode* 2 result, at least in part, from the fact that both present an idealized, townsman's view of the countryside.

56 For mime see Page (1942), 336–61; for elegy see Cairns (1969); Hubbard (1974), 149–53.

57 *Idyll* 3.1ff., 10.1ff., 11.11.

58 *Idyll* 5.90ff. and passim; 7.52ff., 96ff.; 12; compare *Idylls* 23, 29, 30.

59 *Idyll* 7.52ff. (Aegeanax?), 20 (Eunica).

60 Compare *Idyll* 1.148, 5.29, 7.138. *raucis* does not mean 'shrill, screeching'; it is the equivalent of ἠχέτης or ἠχήεις (so Moore-Blunt (1977), 38–40): compare *raucae palumbes, Eclogue* 1.57; *rauci cycni, Aeneid* 11.458.

61 *Idyll* 10.26–7; compare Longus 1.13.2, 1.16.4.

62 *Idyll* 7.120–1: note *cadunt*, 18.

63 *Idyll* 5.92–5, 7.120, 10.28–31.

64 *Idyll* 9.15–20, 11.34ff.; compare Longus 1.16.4.

65 *Idyll* 5.106–7; compare *Eclogue* 3.74–5, 7.29–30, 10.65–6. Virgil did not, obviously, consider hunting to be out of place in his pastoral world.

66 Compare *Idyll* 6.1–5, 42–6; 8.55–6; 11.65–6; and 1.3.

67 *Idyll* 1.128–9, 4.29–30, 5.5ff., 8.21ff.; compare Longus 1.28–9.

68 *Idyll* 10.34; 3.10–11, 21ff., 35; 5.96–7, 132ff.; 11.40–1, 56–7; compare Longus 1.15, 3.4.3, 3.15.3, 3.18.2.

69 *Idyll* 3.35.

70 With *Eclogue* 2.45ff. compare Sappho, fr. 2 Lobel–Page (a kletic – i.e. 'summoning' – hymn to Aphrodite). For *huc ades* summoning a deity: Tibullus 1.7.49; Bömer (1958), 14; for anaphora of *tibi* in hymns (*Du-Stil*), see Norden (1913), 150ff. (Anaphora is the repetition of a word at the beginning of successive clauses, phrases, etc.)

71 Servius ad loc.: *tantum honoris habet puero, ut ei dicat etiam numina obscutura.* Contrast Coleman (1977), 103, 108. For *candidus* of a god see *Eclogue* 5.56; *TLL* 3.421.36ff.; for flowers blooming at the arrival of a deity Lucretius 1.7–8; [Homer], *Hymn to Apollo* 133ff.

72 Note, especially, *quoque* (53): the whole countryside and its inhabitants will be honoured by the presence of Alexis. See preceding note.

73 A passage adapted more simply at *Eclogue* 7.53ff. (Alexis). It is difficult to be sure how far Virgil uses names allusively, but Nais occurs only here in Theocritus. I would not go as far as Moore-Blunt (1977), 37f., who uses the original context of the name Thestylis to argue that she is preparing an aphrodisiac for the reapers (36–8): Servius' explanation of why they ate spicy foods seems to me preferable. But the name Amaryllis is clearly used to point up the debt to *Idyll* 3: that seems to be the main function of such allusions.

74 See n. 68; Pfeiffer (1933), 32–4.

75 See Beare (1964), 128–58. The setting of mimes was usually urban.

76 The tendency to classify bucolic as *epos* (Horace, *Satires* 1.10.43–5; Quintilian 10.1.55; Longinus 33.4) must have led to acute awareness of this incongruity. See Kroll (1924), 204: *Mimen im Hexameter sind eigentlich ein Unding.*

77 See Dover (1971), xlv–xlviii. Note the contrived balance of *Eclogue* 2.8–9, 16, 18, 20, 54, 63–4. For repetitions: *nihil . . . nil*, 6–7; *mea . . . me*, 6–7; *nunc etiam*, 8–9; *nonne*, 14–15; *quamuis*, 16; *quam*, 20; *non*, 22; *mecum*, 28–31; *Pana . . . Pan*, 29–31; *Amyntas*, 35, 39; *mihi*, 36–7; *Damoetas*, 37–9; *dixit*, 38–9; *tibi*, 42–6; *et uos . . . et te*, 54; *nec munera . . . nec . . . muneribus*, 55–6; *lupum*, 63–4; *capellam*, 63–4.

78 Rustic metaphors, see n. 63; *exempla* (Amphion, Daphnis, Paris): *Idyll* 3.40ff., 20.33ff. Proverbs (58–9, 70, see Moore-Blunt (1977), 40–1): see Heimgartner (1940); Gow (1952) and Dover (1971), indices s.v. Note Aristotle, *Rhetoric* 2.21.9 (1395a): 'Rustics are especially fond of coining maxims (γνωμοτύποι) and readily produce them.'

79 Compare *Eclogue* 2.6–7 with *Idyll* 3.6–9, 7.119; 2.9 with 7.23; 2.12–13 with 7.138–40; 2.17–18 with 7.121; 2.18 with 10.28–9; 2.36–7 with 4.30, 1.128ff.; 2.63–5 with 10.30–1; 2.68 with 7.56. The more extended allusions will be discussed below.

80 See Cairns (1975) for an attempt to analyse the lyric features of Horace, *Odes* 3.11.

81 For this device see Kroll (1924), 150 with examples.

82 Noted by Robertson (1970–71),10.

83 I owe this point to Professor Cairns.

84 See Quintilian 1.6.34.

85 Virgil has not chosen a new epithet (*crudelis*) because χαρίεσσ'/ *formosus* and λευκά/*candidus* are inapplicable to Alexis: see 16–17. For the (correct) etymology, Alexis–ἀλέξειν, see Varro, *De lingua Latina* 7.82 on Paris whom *pastores nunc Alexandrum uocant* (Ennius, fr. 20 Jocelyn) and Hercules Alexicacos: Virgil twice links Alexis with his namesake Alexander–Paris (26–7, as judge of a beauty contest; 61, explicitly). For Alexis–ἀλέγειν note also *nec munera curat Alexis*, 56, and the fact that the verb ἀλέγειν is always used in the present tense and usually negatived.

86 The verb *contaminare* means properly 'to spoil': see Duckworth (1952), 202–8. Modern scholars use the noun to denote combined imitation of two models, without pejorative overtones. For the technique see Kroll (1924), 171–4. See also above, p. 203, n. 2; below, p. 229, n. 4.

87 See Cairns (1972), 146–7.

88 Date and authorship of this poem are unknown: see Gow (1952), 2.364–5. But there is no good reason for supposing it to be post-Virgilian.

89 For this use of the term 'genre' see below, p. 229 and n. 2. See Cairns (1972) for the fullest modern discussion of the importance of genres in ancient poetry.

90 See Lieberg (1962); Lucretius 4.1183–4.

91 For this aspect of the *Idylls* see, especially, Giangrande (1971).

92 For the genre komos see Copley (1956) with bibliography; Cairns (1972), index s.v.; (1975*a*); (1977*b*); and Pinotti (1977) for a schematized generic analysis of the primary (A) elements and secondary (B) elements (topoi).

93 See n. 109.

94 For this symptom of love see n. 57; Sappho, fr. 102.2 Lobel–Page; Lucretius 4.1124; Longus 1.13.6, 1.17.4.

95 Pinotti (1977), 67 n. 69; Cairns (1972), 210, 254 n. 62.

96 Compare Aristophanes, *Ecclesiazusae* 963; *Idyll* 23; Ovid, *Metamorphoses* 14.698ff.

97 Gifts: Pinotti (1977), 67 n. 67; apples: see n. 50.

98 Pinotti (1977), 65 n. 60: admission.

99 Pinotti (1977), 66 n. 63 (wretchedness); 65 n. 61 (cruelty).

100 Pinotti (1977), 67 n. 67 (garlands).

101 Pinotti (1977), 66 n. 63.

102 Pinotti (1977), 67 n. 66.

103 Pinotti (1977), 67 n. 67.

104 Pinotti (1977), 66 nn. 63 and 65.

105 *Idyll* 11 is identified as a komos by Cairns (1972), 143–7. In what follows I build on his analysis with some minor modifications.

106 Compare Sappho 156 Lobel–Page; Anacreon 488 Page: the point is not noticed by either Gow (1952) or Dover (1971).

107 Plutarch, *Amatorius* 759B.

108 Cairns (1972), 251 n. 11; add Propertius 4.7.15–20.

109 For the komos as part of a marriage-suit Copley (1956), 26–7, quotes only Chariton, *Chaereas and Callirhoe* 1.2.3. But other komasts desire marriage: the goatherd in *Idyll* 3 (see above); Polyphemus in *Idylls* 6 and 11; Iphis in Ovid, *Metamorphoses* 14.698ff.; Vertumnus in the hitherto unidentified komos which includes the Iphis story (*Metamorphoses* 14.623–771). Tibullus alludes to the prospect of living with Delia in two komoi: 1.2.71–2, 1.5.19ff.

110 Pinotti (1977), 68 n. 73.

111 See Gentili (1972); Bonanno (1973).

112 Pinotti (1977), 68 n. 73; Cairns (1972), 85–9; Nisbet–Hubbard (1970), 289–91.

113 On reaction see Cairns (1972), 138–57.

114 For the *renuntiatio amoris* see Cairns (1972), 79–82; also his essay above, pp. 121–41.

115 For *Idyll* 30 as a *renuntiatio amoris* see Cairns (1972), 80–1. The similarities are: love as a disease (30.1) and love as madness (11.72); self-address (30.11ff., 11.72); self-exhortation to a more sensible life (30.14, 11.73); use of proverbs to bolster resolve (30.14ff., 11.73f.). Compare Cairns (1972), 147: 'The best evidence that one *Idyll* of Theocritus is a komos is provided by another *Idyll* which certainly is.' See also Gow (1952) 2.219, 515.

116 Cairns (1972), 80–1; Gow (1952) on *Idyll* 11.76 and 78.

117 For all these elements as topoi of the *renuntiatio amoris* see nn. 115, 167, 168, 170, 171, 174, 175, 177–80, 182.

118 The giggling of the girls should be understood as genuine enticement: it is sexual laughter, not mockery. See the passages collected by Gow (1952), ad loc.; contrast Dover (1971), ad loc. That ancient readers would have been in no doubt that the Cyclops was indeed cured is confirmed by Callimachus, *Epigram* 46 Pfeiffer, where in a clear allusion to *Idyll* 11 Polyphemus is cited as an *exemplum* of one who had found a cure for love in song. Coleman (1977), 107–8, expresses the doubts of the modern reader.

119 See Gow (1952), 2.77.

120 *Anthologia Palatina* 7.100; 12.127, 164, 229.

121 Compare Cicero, *In Pisonem* 89 with Nisbet (1961), ad loc.; Propertius 1.20.52. For *formosum* . . . *ardebat* note *Scholium Veronense* on *Aeneid* 4.149: *formonsum non aliunde dicimus quam a calido, formum enim dicebant antiqui calidum*; Servius on *Aeneid* 8.453: *foruum est calidum unde et formosos dicimus quibus calor sanguinis ex rubore pulchritudinem creat*. Virgil may be hinting at this supposed etymology.

122 *candidus* is contrasted with the sun-burned (*niger*) and Theocritean rustic, Menalcas: compare Longus 1.13.2, 1.16.4, 1.16.5.

123 *Idyll* 7.52ff.; and especially *Idyll* 20.3–4 (quoted by Coleman (1977), 104). For the contrast of town and country see also Longus 2.19, 3.15.1, 4.6.2, 4.37.1.

124 For *ardere* see Pichon (1966), 88–9. With its use here compare Callimachus, fr. 67.2 Pfeiffer. But the construction with the accusative may be a deliberately colloquial touch (compare *Eclogue* 3.1): *OLD* s.v. 7 quotes in addition only Terence, *Phormio* 82; Aulus Gellius 6(7).8.3.

125 This phrase is notoriously difficult. With the transmitted text and if *nec* is taken with *habebat* it must mean 'and he did not know what to hope for': see Gratwick (1973), 10 and (for the difference between *habere quid* and *habere quod* with subjunctive) K–S 2.500. Contrast Cicero, *De senectute* 68 *at senex ne quod speret quidem habet*; Ovid, *Metamorphoses* 13.247 *omnia cognoram nec quod* [edd.: *quid* MN] *specularer habebam*. It is quite clear that this cannot be the meaning here: Corydon is not in any doubt as to the hopelessness of his love (Servius ad loc. *nec spem potiendi habebat*). Emendation has been suggested: *quod*; *qui*; see Gratwick (1973), 10. But, although *nec* obviously links *ardebat* with *habebat*, the negative element could be taken with *speraret* as suggested by my translation: compare, for example, Ovid, *Metamorphoses* 11.493–4 *ipse pauet nec se qui sit status ipse fatetur | scire ratis rector nec quid iubeatue uelitue*. This gives the required sense without emendation, allows *habere quid* its normal meaning and suits the context. So understood the phrase is, like *ardebat*, a description of Corydon's state of mind, not an editorial comment. *Habere quid* for *scire quid* is a colloquialism: *TLL* 6.3.2437.13ff.; *sperare* is a cliché of erotic language: see Pichon (1966), 267: *est confidere aut se amatum iri aut amantem rediturum.*

126 *studium* does not mean passion (*amor*); it denotes an energetic, enthusiastic and persistent application to something or support for a person: Coleman (1977), 92–3.

127 See Enk (1946) for numerous parallels and bibliography; add Orpheus (*Georgics* 4.464ff.; Ovid, *Metamorphoses* 10.76–7). Cicero is a real life example (though not of course an unhappy lover!): *Ad Atticum* 12.13 etc. The most important parallel is with Callimachus' Acontius who 'used to go into the country on any pretext and avoid his father; consequently the more witty of his companions nick-named him Laertes and thought that he had become a farmer; but Acontius did not care about vineyards or mattocks [compare *Eclogue* 2.66–70] and he would only sit beneath oaks or pines and converse with them thus: O trees, would that you had a mind and voice so that you might only say "beautiful Cydippe"' (Aristaenetus, *Epistle* 1.10.53–9 Mazal).

128 See, for example, Plautus, *Mercator* 656–7 *quanto te satiust rus aliquo abire, ibi esse, ibi uiuere | adeo dum illius te cupiditas atque amor missum facit*; Terence, *Eunuchus* 216ff.; *Eclogue* 10.55–61 (*tamquam haec sit nostri medicina furoris*); *Epistula Sapphous* 137 *tamquam nemus antraque prosint*; Horace, *Epode* 2.37–8 *quis non malarum, quas amor curas habet, | haec inter obliuiscitur?*; Ovid, *Remedia* 169ff. with Geisler (1969), 229–35.

129 *narratio* was one of the elementary rhetorical exercises. Its subject could be mythical (like *Idyll* 11) or realistic fiction (like comedy, mime, *Eclogue* 2). It should be *breuis, aperta, probabilis* (Cicero, *De inuentione* 28–9; *lucidam, breuem, ueri similem*, Quintilian 4.2.31). See further Reichel (1909), 51–69; (more briefly but more conveniently) Bonner (1977), 260–3. For examples see Libanius 8.38–58 Foerster.

130 Compare Parthenius, *Erotica pathemata* 4.1 'Alexander, son of Priam, while herding (his flocks) on Mount Ida, fell in love with Oenone, the

daughter of Cebren'; see also *Erotica pathemata* 7, 10, 11, 12, 24, 25, 26; and compare Catullus 64.52–7; Ovid, *Metamorphoses* 4.55–62 (Pyramus and Thisbe).

131 Parallels with *Eclogue* 2.1–5 have been romanized in the translation.

132 See n. 131.

133 It is not necessary at this point to decide on a specific model. For *Idyll* 11 see below. Compare Du Quesnay (1977), 68.

134 A standard feature in Parthenius, *Erotica pathemata* and the *narrationes* of Libanius; compare Phanocles, fr. 1 Powell.

135 I am indebted to Dr J. C. McKeown for reminding me of the vitality of mime in the first century. See nn. 56 and 75.

136 See Copley (1940), 52–61; (1956), 18–19, 134ff., 171.

137 *Idyll* 23.1–3 '*A passionate man loved a cruel youth*, fine in form (*formosum*) but not in ways; he hated his lover and had no tenderness at all' (compare *nec quid speraret habebat*). Virgil probably knew this poem: compare *Eclogue* 8.60 with *Idyll* 23.20 and 5.40–5 with 23.43–8.

138 Gow translates ll. 17–18: 'Yet the remedy he found, and seated on some high rock would gaze seaward and sing thus.' This implies an illogical and otiose sequence of thought: Polyphemus wasted away with love and sang of Galatea; but he found the cure; and he continued to sing his songs of unrequited love! It seems to me better to relate the imperfect ἄειδε to the aorist εὗρε in a different way: he found the cure when he was singing this song. Compare *Idyll* 6.2–4, 35. This makes a specific announcement of the generically sophisticated reaction, for which see Cairns (1972), 147. I would translate 80: 'This was how, you see, Polyphemus shepherded his love as he sang.' Contrast with this view, for example, Coleman (1977), 107–8.

139 See Du Quesnay (1977), 52–75.

140 Contrast Coleman (1977), 92. I do not mean to imply that his song actually is rough and ready, only that *incondita* suggests, in part, 'and he sang in his countrified way': no Roman peasant ever sang like this, as Virgil and his readers would be only too aware. The asymmetry, the disjointedness and the shifts from present to past to future are there to create an impression of strong feeling: the technique is ubiquitous in Hellenistic poetry and the device was recommended by the rhetoricians (for example, Nicolaus 3.490.14ff. Spengel; Menander 3.413.12–15 Spengel) as noted by Pfeiffer (1933), 4–5. For *inconditus* see *OLD* s.v.; *TLL* 7.1.1002.11ff. and note Varro, *Menippean* 363 *homines rusticos in uindemia incondita cantare*; for the sense 'impromptu' see Livy 4.20.2; 5.49.7; 7.38.3 with Ogilvie (1965) on 3.29.5. For *iactare* compare Livy 4.53.11 *inconditi uersus militari licentia iactati*; 7.2.7. In general compare Horace, *Satires* 1.4.8–21 (on Lucilius) and contrast Catullus 95 (on Cinna's *Zmyrna*).

141 Euripides, Fragment 663 Nauck: 'indeed Love teaches (a man to be) a poet, even if he has previously been without a muse'. This was a tag already in Plato, *Symposium* 196e. Compare Ovid, *Remedia* 310 *dole tantum, sponte disertus eris*; *Fasti* 4.109 (among the inventions of Venus) *primus amans carmen uigilatum nocte negata | dicitur ad clausas concinuisse fores*. The theme was also used by Bion, frs 9, 10, 16 Gow.

142 Cicero, *Tusculan disputations* 4.68–76; Lucretius 4.1037ff.; Philodemus, *De musica* 4.6.13–26, 4.15.1–7 Kemke; Neubecker (1956), 32–4, 50–1.

143 Compare Horace, *Epode* 2 and Ovid, *Remedia* 169ff. See Rohde (1914), 541–54, 624; Kier (1933); Vischer (1965); Geisler (1969), 233–44; Nisbet–Hubbard (1970), 215–17; Cairns (1975b). For the delight of boys in hunting see *Aeneid* 4.156–9; 7.477–8, 493–9; 9.590–2 (Ascanius); Tibullus 1.4.49–50 and 4.3.11 with Smith (1913), ad loc.; for the general Roman delight in hunting see Aymard (1951); Geisler (1969), 245–54; Nisbet–Hubbard (1970), 12.

144 This poem too is probably a komos. That the lover narrates in the past tense his rejection rather than leaving it implicit is a formal sophistication. Using a substitute addressee (shepherds, 19) he describes his beauty, his musical abilities; and catalogues mythical precedents for loving a herdsman. He ends with a prayer that she should be forever lonely. See Cairns (1972), 87–9, 218–45; index s.v. 'formal sophistication'.

145 Ovid, *Remedia* 583–4 *tristis eris, si solus eris, dominaeque relictae | ante oculos facies stabit, ut ipsa, tuos*; Servius on *Eclogue* 2.60 *iterum per phantasiam quasi ad praesentem loquitur*; Lucretius 4.1061–2; Horace, *Satires* 1.5.15; Phanocles, fr. 1.6 Powell; *Anthologia Palatina* 12.127.5–8; and compare Aristotle, *Rhetoric* 1.11.11.

146 Catullus 64.132ff.; *Eclogue* 10.42–9; Propertius 1.17, 18.

147 Cairns (1972), 80 (B1).

148 In view of ποησεῖς (*Idyll* 3.9) *coges* (R) is preferable to *cogis* (P): it is at least arguably better sense for Corydon to ask 'Will you force me to die?' (i.e. Now that you know the force of my feelings will you continue to reject me and force me to die?) than for him to ask 'Are you (deliberately??) forcing me to die?'

149 Pinotti (1977), 65 n. 61; Copley (1956), 149 nn. 44–7, 154–5 nn. 25–30.

150 For example, Ovid, *Amores* 1.6.55, 65–6; compare Pinotti (1977), 66 n. 65.

151 Pinotti (1977), 66 n. 64; Cairns (1977b), 330 n. 1.

152 Cairns (1977b), 330 n. 1, 335 n. 1; add Bion, fr. 11.1–6 Gow.

153 Cairns (1977b), 330 n. 3, 331 n. 1; Copley (1956), 145 nn. 7, 10.

154 Moore-Blunt (1977), 38–40.

155 At *Idyll* 11.25–9 (imitated at *Eclogue* 8.37–40), Polyphemus tells of the beginnings of his passion. Since Corydon is treading in Alexis' footsteps ('in the fashionable manner': Moore-Blunt (1977), 38, quoting Aristaenetus 1.41; Meleager, *Anthologia Palatina* 12.84.5), it may be supposed that he saw him on a visit to the mountains, as Polyphemus saw Galatea, but on a hunting expedition with his *dominus* (29; and the orphaned (?) *capreoli*, 41) rather than gathering flowers.

156 Pinotti (1977), 68 n. 73; Copley (1956), 150 nn. 52, 53; 155 n. 33; 160 n. 42; Nisbet–Hubbard (1970), 289–91; *Idyll* 7.105, 119, 121; 23.28–32.

157 Pinotti (1977), 67 n. 69; Cairns (1972), 210, 254 n. 62; add *Idyll* 20.19–29; Ovid, *Metamorphoses* 14.765–9; and for poems as a komast's gifts, *Amores* 3.8.1ff. (another komos).

158 See below. For the poverty of the komast as against the venality of the beloved see Callimachus, fr. 193 Pfeiffer (*Iambus* 3); Horace, *Epode* 11.11ff.; Tibullus 1.2.67–80, 1.5.61–8; Ovid, *Amores* 3.8. Compare Tibullus 1.4.57–72.

159 See *Aeneid* 6.46 with Norden (1927), ad loc.; compare *Anthologia Palatina* 5.167.5–6 (komos); Catullus 34.1–4; 61 and 62 refrain; such 'aretalogies' as [Tibullus] 3.6.13ff. (*Er-Stil*).

160 Pinotti (1977), 68 n. 71; add Ovid, *Amores* 1.6.53 and for the lover's assistant deities see Copley (1956), 149 n. 48.

161 Compare Horace, *Epode* 2; Ovid, *Remedia* 175–96 with Geisler (1969), ad loc.

162 It was conventional wisdom that a mortal should not aspire to marry an immortal: Alcman, *Partheneion* 1.16–19, etc. For the divinity of the beloved see Lieberg (1962): Stroh (1971), 220–1 points out that deification of the beloved is often matched by the slavery of the lover (quoting *Anthologia Palatina* 12.118, 158, 169; Xenophon, *Cyropedia* 5.1.12; Isocrates, *Helen* 56–7).

163 Ovid, *Amores* 1.6.67–70; *Anthologia Palatina* 5.145; Copley (1940), 59–60.

164 Pinotti (1977), 70 n. 69; Copley (1956), 170 n. 19; Cairns (1972), 254 n. 48; *Idyll* 7.123ff.

165 See n. 128.

166 For *renuntiatio amoris* see nn. 114, 115.

167 On self-address see Williams (1968), 461–3; in the *renuntiatio*: Catullus 8.1, 19; Propertius 2.5.13; compare *Anthologia Palatina* 12.117.3; Menander, *Sicyonios* 397ff. Sandbach. See also above, p. 96.

168 Love as madness in the *renuntiatio*: *Anthologia Palatina* 5.112.2; Catullus 8.1; Ovid, *Amores* 3.11; compare Propertius 3.24.9ff.

169 Festus 150 Lindsay: *demens, quod de sua mente decesserit*; Kenney (1971), 140; compare Cicero, *Tusculan disputations* 4.75 (the lover) *maxime autem admonendus est quantus sit furor amoris* (as part of his cure).

170 See Cairns (1972), 81 (B9); compare Homer, *Odyssey* 21.251; Theocritus, *Idyll* 22.159ff.; Lucretius 4.1173; Cicero, *Tusculan disputations* 4.75 *etiam nouo quidam amore ueterem amorem tamquam clauo clauum eiciendum putant*; Martial 1.68.8; Ovid, *Remedia* 451–2 *at tibi, qui fueris dominae male creditus uni, | nunc saltem nouus est inueniendus amor*; 462 *successore nouo uincitur omnis amor*; 475ff.

171 Return to sense: *Anthologia Palatina* 5.112.6, 12.117.4; Catullus 8.8–12; Horace, *Odes* 3.26.1–4; Ovid, *Amores* 3.11; Propertius 3.24.15ff.

172 Servius on *Eclogue* 2.70 *non mirum me esse dementem qui habeo uites semiputatas. nam in sacris dicitur, quod corripiatur furore qui sacrificauerit de uino, quid est de uitibus inputatis.*

173 Coleman (1977), 104; Moore-Blunt (1977), 40–1.

174 See Gow (1952) 2.220; Nisbet–Hubbard (1970), 368ff. for lovers who pursue what flees. In the *renuntiatio*: Catullus 8.10 *nec quae fugit sectare*; Ovid, *Amores* 2.9.9 *sequitur fugientia*. Theocritus has cleverly adapted the hunting image to a milking-time adage to suit the character of Polyphemus.

175 Catullus 8.2; Propertius 2.5.10ff., 19f.

176 There was virtually no natural pasture after the end of June. Elm leaves were especially prized as fodder: see White (1970), 284; Columella, *De re rustica* 6.3.6–7, 7.3.21; Longus 1.21.1, 2.20.2, 3.3.4, 4.38.4.

177 Catullus 8.1; Tibullus 1.9.45ff. and see nn. 168, 171.

178 Cairns (1972), 80 (B3).

179 Tibullus 1.9.11 *muneribus meus est captus puer*; see n. 158; Cairns (1972), 81 (B3, 4).

180 Ovid, *Remedia* 301ff., 677; compare Lucretius 4.1121ff.

181 With *Eclogue* 2.58–9 compare Longus 4.7, where a rejected lover destroys a garden and its flowers 'some of which he trampled under foot like a wild boar'. Contrast 2.6.3 'all the flowers are works of Eros; these plants are his "poems"; through him both rivers run and winds blow'; 2.5.5 (Eros tells Philetas that he has been playing in his garden but) 'Look and see whether any flower stem is trodden down, any stream stirred up.' Both may be drawing on a common source.

182 Cairns (1972), 82.

183 See *Aeneid* 6.466 and Norden (1927), ad loc.

184 Pichon (1966), 157.

185 See Plato, *Phaedrus* 241d ὡς λύκοι ἄρν' ἀγαπῶσιν, ὡς παῖδα φιλοῦσιν ἐρασταί (noted by Robertson (1970–71), 20; Schmidt (1972*a*), 775): Socrates is advising against just such lovers as Corydon. Although formally addressed to Alexis, the lines seem better understood as part of Corydon's attempt to understand the nature of his passion: compare n. 169. Why Virgil has substituted the lioness following the wolf for the crane following the plough is not clear. Servius says: *nam necesse est ut ueniente lupo aduentus agnoscatur leonis*: this could be a guess or a paraphrase; or he may know of a proverb to the effect 'after the wolf, look out for the lion'. It is presumably intended as an 'improvement' on the model and should tie in with the explicit moral: *trahit sua quemque uoluptas*, which is itself a tag from Lucretius 2.258 *ducit quemque uoluptas* and is probably itself proverbial (compare Ovid, *Ars amatoria* 1.749 *curae sua cuique uoluptas*), though criticized in antiquity as inappropriate philosophizing. I can only suggest that the lioness was proverbially lustful: Cassandra refers to Clytemnestra (Aeschylus, *Agamemnon* 1258–9) as 'the two-footed lioness lying with the wolf in the noble lion's absence' (Perret (1961), 33); the lioness is *adulter* at Pliny, *Natural history* 8.107 (hyaena); Solinus 17.11 (panther); Claudian 17.304; Leaena was the name of some famous prostitutes (Gow (1965), 93) and for a position of intercourse (Aristophanes, *Lysistrata* 231 with scholium ad loc.).

186 With *Eclogue* 2.66–7 compare Longus 1.14.1.

187 Ovid, *Remedia* 567–8 *est tibi rure bono generosae fertilis uuae | uinea: ne nascens usta sit uua, time*; Cicero, *Tusculan disputations* 4.74 (the lover) *abducendus etiam est non numquam ad alia studia, sollicitudines, curas, negotia*.

188 See n. 170.

189 See nn. 27–30.

190 See Pfeiffer (1933), 32ff.; note especially *Anthologia Palatina* 5.144, 147; 12.256 (Meleager).

191 I am indebted to Professor Cairns for reminding me of the probable nature of the links between the *Eclogues* and *Longus'* *Daphnis and Chloe*. See nn. 18 and 181.

192 *Pan primum calamos . . . coniungere . . . instituit, Eclogue* 2.32–3.

193 *Eclogue* 2.32–3.

194 *Eclogue* 2.30 *haedorumque gregem . . . compellere*; 31 *canendo*; 46 *Nymphae*; compare also Longus 1.13, 22, 24; 2.23.

195 *Eclogue* 2.32 *calamos cera coniungere pluris*; 36–7 *est mihi disparibus septem compacta cicutis* | *fistula*. Compare Tibullus 2.5.31–2 with Smith (1913), ad loc.

196 *Eclogue* 2.31 *imitabere Pana canendo*; compare Longus 3.23.4 (Earth) μιμεῖται καὶ τὸν συρίττοντα Πᾶνα.

197 *Eclogue* 2.37–8 *fistula, Damoetas dono mihi quam dedit olim,* | *et dixit moriens: 'te nunc habet ista secundum'*; compare Longus 1.28–9.

198 So, for example, Mittelstadt (1970), 215. The matter is still controversial.

199 Perhaps indirectly through Gallus. Philitas of Cos was acknowledged as a master by Theocritus (*Idyll* 7.40) and so could have been imitated by Virgil here with propriety. But his fame rested on his elegies and epigrams, a suitable model for Gallus. The one does not exclude the other.

200 For the Philetas of Longus and Philitas of Cos, see in particular Hubaux (1953). For the relationship of novels to Hellenistic poetry in general, Giangrande (1962).

201 For Gallus see Boucher (1966); Ross (1975); Skutsch (1901).

202 For the rival in the komos see Pinotti (1977), 68 n. 70; Cairns (1977*b*), 334 n. 4; (1972), 255 n. 18 and compare Copley (1956), 53–4, 60–1, 91–112, 159 n. 29. For the *renuntiatio*, Cairns (1972), 80–1. Note that Ovid introduces a rival, Acis, into his imitation of *Idyll* 11 (and *Eclogue* 2), another komos.

203 For *deliciae* see Pichon (1966), 125–6; for *dominus* see Ovid, *Amores* 3.7.11; *Ars* 1.314 and for the much commoner *domina* Pichon (1966), 134.

204 See Hubbard (1974), 12–13 and Schulz-Vanheyden (1969); for the expansion of epigram in general, Cairns (1977*c*); Williams (1968), index s.v. 'epigram'.

205 A view persuasively argued by Luck (1976); compare Grassmann (1966), 34ff., 95f. Luck is inexplicably hesitant about connecting *Epode* 15 with Gallus: see Tränkle (1960), 24.

206 For *Epode* 15 see Cairns (1972), 80–1. *Epode* 11 is one *renuntiatio* (for Lyciscus) including another (for Inachia).

207 Note too the coincidences in (the admittedly commonplace) erotic vocabulary: *Epode* 11.24 *urere* ~ *Eclogue* 2.73 *urit*; 11.8 *et paenitet* ~ 2.34 *nec te paeniteat*; 11.11, 27 ~ 2.16, 46 *candidus*; 11.27 *ardor* ~ 2.1 *ardebat*. For verbal links between *Epode* 11 and *Eclogue* 10 see Luck (1976).

208 For other arguments that Gallus treated *medicina furoris* see Tränkle (1960), 22; Ross (1975), 66ff., 91, 116.

209 The well known similarities between *Eclogues* 2 and 10 may thus be due at least as much to independent imitation of Gallus as to self-imitation.

210 For Orpheus as a subject of Gallus' poetry see Ross (1975), 92ff. (For my reservations about Ross's book, see Du Quesnay (1978).) If Virgil complimented his friend by rehandling the theme in *Georgics* 4, a garbled memory of this may lie behind Servius' story of the *Laudes Galli*. See *Georgics* 4.369 and Propertius 1.12.4 for the River Hypanis, the subject of the sole surviving line of Gallus (on which see Norden (1915), 23 n. 4).

211 For Gallus and Callimachus' *Acontius* see Ross (1975), 72–4, 85–9; Hubbard (1974), 11.

212 The most famous treatment of the Amphion story was Euripides' *Antiope*, which was translated into Latin by Pacuvius (note fr. 2 Warmington *tu cornifrontes pascere armentas soles*). It was perhaps treated by the Hellenistic poets (see Alexander Aetolus, fr. 17 Powell). *Amphioniae lyrae* occur at Propertius 1.9.10 immediately after *Chaoniae columbae* which certainly comes from Gallus (compare Euphorion 48 Powell and *Eclogue* 9.12–13 for the epithet in the sense 'of Dodona'). It may be noted that Propertius 3.2 begins with three exemplary singers: Orpheus, Amphion and *quin etiam, Polypheme, fera Galatea sub Aetna | ad tua rorantis carmina flexit equos* (compare Nonnos 6.300ff.). It is tempting to speculate that this might be a catalogue of Gallan themes!

213 See Skutsch (1956), 198–9; Norden (1957), 116–17; Williams (1968), 317–18.

214 The similarities of *Eclogue* 10.55–60 to Tibullus 1.4.47–50 and to Propertius 1.1.9–16 have been taken to indicate allusion to Gallus in all these passages: see Skutsch (1901), 15; Ross (1975), 85.

215 Propertius 2.34.91–2 and Euphorion 43 Powell (from the *Hyacinthos*, compare *Eclogue* 6.82–6). See Barigazzi (1950), 22; Boucher (1966), 91.

216 Note also: the repeated exclamatory *a*, *Eclogue* 2.60, 69; 6.47, 52; 10.47–9; Ross (1969), 51–2; *quae te dementia cepit*, 2.69; 6.47; *quis enim modus adsit amori*, 2.68 and *ecquis erit modus* 10.28. See n. 209.

217 Contrast, for example, Corydon's *incondita* (2.4) and Gallus' *condita carmina* (10.50–1). Virgil's technique of combining a Greek and a Roman model is well known from *Eclogues* 4, 6, 10 (see Du Quesnay (1977)). In this very early poem it is interesting to find apparently the same technique used less overtly.

218 Cairns (1969), 131–4.

219 Varro, *De lingua Latina* 5.92; note in the same passage his explanation of *diues: diues a diuo qui ut deus nihil indigere uidetur*.

220 Compare *Epode* 2.11–12.

221 Corydon is rejected simply because he is a *rusticus*. There is no need to make him a slave as well.

222 White (1970), 75.

223 Robertson (1970–71), 10–11.

224 Compare Homer, *Odyssey* 4.85–7.

225 See *Eclogue* 3.98–9; Varro, *De re rustica* 2.17.

226 White (1970), 277.

227 Quintilian 12.10.57 *qui cum interrogasset rusticum testem, an Amphionem ⟨nosset⟩, negante eo detraxit aspirationem breuiauitque secundam eius*

nominis syllabam, et ille eum sic optime norat. And he may not have been the mythical Amphion!

228 For *Actaeus* see Bömer (1969), 376: it would, for all its rarity, be familiar to Virgil's readers since it was the first word of Callimachus' *Hecale*. Here it balances *Dircaeus* (Theban) in pointed allusion to Amphion's years of exile. Aracynthus was part of Cithaeron which formed the border between Boeotia and Attica: not unexpectedly it is sometimes Theban (Stephanus Byzantinus s.v. and scholiast on Statius, *Thebaid* 2.239), sometimes Attic (Sextus Empiricus 1.12, who mentions it together with Brilessos, the setting of the *Hecale*). It was associated with Pallas Athene by Rhianus (56 Powell) and Statius (*Thebaid* 2.239).

229 Seneca, *Natural questions* 1(5).17.5. The passage was criticized in antiquity according to Servius and these criticisms may lie behind the imitations at Ovid, *Metamorphoses* 13.840ff.; Calpurnius Siculus 2.88–9; Nemesianus 2.74ff. See also Seneca, *Natural questions* 2(5).1.1. My view is essentially that of Virgil's ancient defenders: see Servius, ad loc.

230 For rustic beauty contests see Longus 1.15–16, 3.24 (where Daphnis awards an apple to Chloe as Paris had to Aphrodite).

231 The beauty of Daphnis at *Eclogue* 5.44 is a mark of his divinity; compare *candidus* 5.56. Contrast the sun-burned beauty of Daphnis which sends Pan into raptures in *Anthologia Palatina* 7.556.

232 For hired helpers at harvest time see White (1970), 347ff.

233 Columella, *De re rustica* 9.1.1. The word is linked with those for goat: *caper, capra, capella* (the gift in *Idyll* 3).

234 See Pfeiffer (1968), 138ff.; Giangrande (1967) and (1970); Schlunk (1974).

235 See Gow (1952), 2.215–16; but I think that Theocritus deliberately made the bears plural. Note that Ovid carefully preserves the point (*Metamorphoses* 13.834).

4 TWO PLAGUES

1 Mauretanians, see Nadeau (1977).

2 It has been argued that *extrinsecus* 1099 means 'from outside this universe' because Lucretius holds that some clouds do come into our universe from outside in 483–94. But this cannot be the explanation of *extrinsecus* here. The decisive argument is drawn from the reprise of this proposition in 1119–22 where the whole context makes it clear that the sky or climate that is inimical to us is creeping in from foreign parts like those listed from 1106, and not from outside the universe.

3 West (1975).

4 West (1973).

5 The paradox is pointed by the etymological connection with *angustus*, cf. *angor aegritudo premens* (Cicero, *TD* 4.18), translating Diog. Laert. 7.112 ἄχθος δὲ λύπην βαρύνουσαν, one sustained image for another.

6 *Sudor et ille quidem morituris frigidus* is odd in two ways: first, in saying

that if the sweat is cold the sufferer is going to die, he includes a terminal symptom amongst his early symptoms; second because it is not at all easy to distinguish cold sweat on a horse from hot sweat. This point about cold sweat is surely not included as a genuine diagnostic symptom, but rather as an intrusion of technical medical lore. Hippocrates, *Aphorism* 4.37, states that cold sweat in acute fever is a sign of death.

7 Dr E. L. Harrison of Leeds University in a letter in June 1978 makes the interesting suggestion that the Virgilian *inventio* of self-lacerating horses may have been prompted by the self-consuming serpents in Lucretius 4.637–9 'ut quod ali cibus est aliis fuat acre uenenum | est itaque ut serpens hominis quae tacta saliuis | disperit ac *sese mandendo conficit ipsa*'.

8 Dutoit (1936).

9 Klepl (1967), particularly pp. 67–9; Commager (1957); Bright (1971).

10 Parry (1969).

5   HORATIAN *IMITATIO* AND *ODES* 2.5

1 *Lesbio* in *Odes* 1.26 and *Aeolium* in *Odes* 3.30, like *Lesboum* in *Odes* 1.1.34, presumably include Sappho (cf. 2.13.24–5; *Epistles* 1.19.28) as well as Alcaeus; and Horace imitated Anacreon, Pindar and Bacchylides besides. In what follows, however, I concentrate on Alcaeus since he is the model to whom Horace himself gives pride of place.

2 Cf. *Epistles* 1.19.8–33.

3 I print without complete confidence Lachmann's conjecture for the MSS' *mihi cumque*; cf. Nisbet–Hubbard (1970), ad loc.

4 *Pythians* 1.1ff., *Olympians* 2.1, *Nemeans* 4.44. Further, Fraenkel (1957), 168f.

5 Notably *Odes* 2.20.1–8, 3.30.6–14.

6 Cf. Commager (1962), 316f. His whole ch. 6 is helpful, if at times fanciful, on Horace's conception of himself as a poet in the *Odes*.

7 This apparent paradox finds moving expression in Homer: see *Iliad* 6.357f., *Odyssey* 1.328–64, 8.572–9.15; and suffering is the stuff of Homeric epic (*Iliad* 1.2, *Odyssey* 1.4 ἄλγεα). Likewise in Virgil, *Georgics* 4, Orpheus' poetry, which charms the underworld and nature, is inspired by sorrow for his dead wife.

8 See Macleod (1977), 367–72, for a fresh attempt to expound this vexed passage.

9 It is true that Horace's friendship with Maecenas is of some importance in the *Epodes*, more straightforwardly in 1 and 9, more wryly and jocularly in 3 and 14; so the picture of the *Epodes* in *Epistles* 1.19 is affected by the conventional view of Archilochus as the poet of invective. But it does also serve to indicate what tendencies are more marked in both *Odes* and *Epodes*.

10 Cairns (1975) has studied *Odes* 3.11 along these lines; the results are illuminating.

11 Hellenistic poetry may sometimes help to change entirely our view of Horace's relationship to his archaic models. Thus the fresh and

convincing interpretation of *Odes* 1.14 by Anderson (1966), which equates the ship with an aging woman, finds support in *Anthologia Palatina* 5.204 (Meleager), cf. 5.44 (Rufinus), 5.161 (Hedylus?). 9.415 (Antiphilus of Byzantium) is also relevant. See also Woodman (1980).

12 This poem seems to be echoed by Lucilius 1041–4 Marx. Two details in Lucilius have analogies in Horace: the word *subigere* and the metaphor of the yoked ox (which is added to that of the horse).

13 Cf. Theocritus 11.72; Virgil, *Eclogues* 2.69; Catullus 51.13; 52.1, 4; 76.5. Further, Williams (1968), 461–3.

14 Sappho 130 Lobel–Page; Alcman 59, Ibycus 6, Anacreon 13, 31, 55, 83 Page.

15 For bibliography on this poem and some parallels for the image of the grapes, see the edition of E. M. Voigt (1971). Two supplements not mentioned there may be worth considering. In l. 6 ἔπαυσέ σ’ (sc. δαίμων) seems better at least than ἔπαυσά σ’: i.e. 'the god' or circumstances, age (ll. 9–10) and troubles (l. 7), have (had?) put a stop to the addressee's 'folly', but he or she still needs admonishing by the poet. In l. 20 ἀκρασίαν seems plausible. The word would be used of sexual incontinence like ἀνοίας in l. 5; and the antithesis καρτε[ρ . . . ἀκρ]ασίαν which presumably results is attractive. The sense would then be something like 'hold out against lust'. Political interpretations have been suggested for this poem. They can hardly be dismissed out of hand when the piece is so fragmentary; but there is nothing which requires such a reading, and the imagery of ll. 9–12 is naturally and conventionally used of beauty and age in individuals. Another Horatian *Ode* (3.15) may represent a comparable story: a woman who insists on making love when too old for it set against a younger one. In that poem the two women are mother and daughter; the same could be true here, if the metaphor of κλᾶμμα ('shoot') may be pressed. Some details also tally: Alcaeus line 7 παυσαι ∼ Horace ll. 2 *fige modum*, 4 *desine*; Alcaeus 9–10 ∼ Horace 4 *maturo . . . propior funeri*; Alcaeus 20 ἀκρ]ασίαν, if that word may be read there, ∼ Horace 2 *nequitiae*. *Odes* 4.13.1–12 represents another story of this kind; there is also a similar metaphor from vegetation there (ll. 6, 9f.).

16 Gow–Page (1965), 2.131, cautiously commend Wilamowitz's interpretation: 'The infant Eros lisps to the soul of Diaulus the love-poems addressed by Philocrates to Antigenes . . . Asclepiades thus pays a compliment to an unknown poet Philocrates, and to a child Diaulus whom he prepares for the courtship which he will pay when the boy is of more suitable age.' This is surely right.

17 Cf. Commager (1962), 253. For *in Venerem ruentis* cf. Livy 3.47.7 'placet pecudum ferarumque ritu promisce in concubitus ruere?'

18 Cf. Reckford (1969), 104f.

19 For an attempt at interpreting this simile in its context see Macleod (1974), 219f.

20 Cf. Quintilian 6.2.2–19.

21 E.g. Demetrius, *On style* 119; Seneca, *Letters* 114.1–21.

22 E.g. 2.1.157–76, 2.2.109–25.

23 Cf. *Ars poetica* 309–18; *Epistles* 1.19.8–18. To represent human character convincingly we need, as well as a knowledge of life, the knowledge of right and wrong which philosophy gives; to imitate models satisfactorily we need to see where their real merit, ethical no less than poetic, lies. On the link between moral and literary imitation see further Macleod (1977), 366–7; note also Plutarch, *Moralia* 26B.

24 See above all *Iliad* 24.522–51; *Odyssey* 1.353–5, 18.130–42.

25 I owe valuable criticisms to Professor Francis Cairns and Professor R. G. M. Nisbet. I am further indebted to Professor Nisbet for showing me the typescript of his and Miss Hubbard's commentary on *Odes* 2.5. Their notes may, of course, be used to supplement my deliberately selective account of the tradition behind the poem.

For some seventeenth-century English poems related to *Odes* 2.5 see Leishman (1966), 165ff. The difference between their 'conscious extravagance and semi-humorous hyperbole' (Leishman, p. 172) and Horatian *ethos* is striking and revealing. Likewise, André Chénier in *Bucoliques* XIII, whose first twelve lines are clearly modelled on *Odes* 2.5, recaptures only the sensuousness of Horace's poem.

6   *IVDICIVM TRANSFERENDI*

1 For Virgil's treatment of his sources in *Aeneid* 2 see Austin (1964), xii–xiv.

2 467–8; Book 2 has more unfinished lines (ten) than any other book of the poem: cf. Austin (1964), 55 and below, n. 42.

3 Heinze (1915), 40, Jackson Knight (1932), 136 = 125; cf. Wistrand (1960), 152 = 358.

4 Heinze (1915), 41 n. 2: 'Da erzählt Aeneas freilich vom Standpunkt der andern aus, aber er kann das ohne Bedenken, indem er sich aufs lebhafteste in ihre Situation versetzt' – though it is really Virgil rather than Aeneas who does this. On the subject of 'uident' in v. 485 see below, n. 55.

5 On the concentration of similes in this part of Book 2 cf. Mountford (1968–69), 33.

6 He is first mentioned, as 'Pelides Neoptolemus', in the list of the Greeks in the Horse at 2.263; the commentators there are so busy with 'primus' that they fail to notice that in giving, as he does here only, to the son of Achilles the patronymic belonging properly to Achilles himself Virgil prepares the ground for the subsequent virtual identification of father and son. For the Homeric picture of Neoptolemus as a mighty warrior see *Odyssey* 11.505–37 (cf. Knauer (1964), 380).

7 Cf. Jackson Knight (1932), 64 = 68 on Virgil's manipulation of the mythological data: Pyrrhus 'must be reserved for the climax of Priam's death' and so cannot kill Coroebus, as he does elsewhere.

8 Cf. Hornsby (1970), 62. Note also the last verse and the last word of our passage: 'tenent Danai qua deficit *ignis*'; and cf. Hornsby ibid. 24.

9 Enjambment is the carrying over of the sense and construction from one verse to the next.

10 Whether this sort of thing is classified as hendiadys ('the resolution of a complex expression into its parts': Moore (1891), 273) or 'theme and variation' must depend on the taste and fancy of the classifier.

11 Bullock-Davies (1970), 139.

12 See the passages cited by Borthwick (1967), 19–20, especially Diomedes, *Ars grammatica* 3 (*GL* 1.475.12–17 K) 'pyrrhius dictus est . . . a Pyrro Achillis filio, qui crebris et citis *exultationibus* bis breuiter prominentem clipeum genibus incumbens et per hunc *hostibus terrorem inmittens* inferebatur . . .'

13 Virgil's commentators do not always notice this sort of thing. Another instance, I suggest, is to be found in Jupiter's speech to Venus in Book 1: 'ueniet lustris labentibus aetas | cum domus Assaraci Pthiam clarasque Mycenas | seruitio premet ac uictis dominabitur Argis' (283–5). This must have been meant to recall Hector's words to Andromache: ἔσσεται ἦμαρ ὅτ᾽ ἄν ποτ᾽ ὀλώλη Ἴλιος ἱρή | καὶ Πρίαμος καὶ λαὸς ἐϋμμελίω Πριάμοιο (*Iliad* 6.448–9), 'A day will come when destruction shall fall on holy Troy, on Priam, and on the people of Priam of the good ashen spear.' 'Seruitio . . . Argis' further recalls Hector's vision (*Iliad* 6.455) of Andromache as a slave 'weaving in Argos at another woman's loom'. Cf. Jocelyn (1977), 357.

14 The commentators generally refer to *Theriaca* 31–4 and 164–7; but cf. Gualandri (1970), 150, citing 128–9 (perhaps of doubtful relevance?) and 137–8; and Borthwick (1976), 204, citing 389–92.

15 The translations of Nicander are those of Gow–Scholfield (1953).

16 ἕρματα Borthwick (1976), 204 n. 32.

17 Aelian, *De natura animalium* 6.4 μέλλοντες δέ τινα ἐλλοχᾶν ἢ ἄνθρωπον ἢ θῆρα τὰς θανατηφόρους ῥίζας ἐσθίουσι καὶ τὰς πόας μέντοι τὰς τοιαύτας. A reference to *Iliad* 23.93–5 follows.

18 The difficulties of interpretation of vv. 471–2 must be considered with this point in mind. Virgil is not reproducing Nicander but exploiting him; Gualandri's ingenious suggestion that 'in lucem' and 'pastus' should be construed together = 'per vedere la luce, per riacquistare la vista' (Gualandri (1970), 151) turns the verse into a nature note. Similarly to read 'timidum' for the disputed 'tumidum' (ibid.) destroys the vital suggestion of lurking menace. Whether snakes really swell when they hibernate (or even whether the ancients thought they did) is neither here nor there; this snake is *tumidus* because it is a symbol, pregnant with evil intent. Cf. Putnam (1965), 27: 'Here at last the latent violence of the snake imagery bursts forth in all its new brilliance.' It is, however, possible that the position of 'in lucem', which has exercised the commentators, owes something to that of ὑπ᾽ ἠελίοιο in Nicander. The best comment is that of Page (1894), 245: 'the words strictly go with the verb of motion *convolvit* 474, but are thrown forward to emphasise the main idea which is that of "light" . . . and the construction is influenced by the idea of an attack, advance, or assault which pervades the whole simile'. Cf. Knox (1950), 394 n. 32.

19 As suggested by Austin (1964), 187 on v. 474.

20 See West (1969), 42 on the central importance of 'the unilateral correspondence in line 473'.

21 As expressed by Richmond (1976), 150. It will not do to maintain that 'the language used by Virgil can be accounted for by the imitation of the Homeric simile . . . and by the reminiscence of the passage in the *Georgics*', etc. It is not merely Virgil's language that has to be 'accounted for'; the critic is concerned with the function of the simile in its context, a context which here includes the whole of the subsequent episode, the character of Neoptolemus, and the part played by him in the Sack.

22 Cf. Schlunk (1974), 36–48.

23 Knox (1950), 394; cf. above, n. 6.

24 Borthwick (1976), 203, citing Pindar, *Olympians* 8.37ff., Lycophron, *Alexandra* 185, 309, 327.

25 Richmond (1976), 150.

26 Borthwick (1967), 19.

27 Cf. Coffey (1961), 66 nn. 26, 27; Knox (1950), 394 n. 35.

28 So applied: *Iliad* 3.33–7 is rather different. Cf. Fränkel (1921), 69.

29 Austin (1964), 186.

30 The phrase 'aggeribus ruptis' may conceivably be a reminiscence of a verse in another torrent-simile (of a rather different kind) at *Iliad* 13.139 ῥήξας ἀσπέτῳ ὄμβρῳ ἀναιδέος ἔχματα πέτρης, 'having with its irresistible flood broken the supports of the stubborn rock'. Cf. Knauer (1964), 380, comparing also *Iliad* 4.452–5, 11.492–5.

31 Thus both similes exemplify a common phenomenon, indebtedness to a Greek original both directly and through a Latin intermediary – in the first case Virgil himself.

32 Austin (1964), 193; cf. also West (1970), 272–5.

33 Cf. Kenney (1971), 24–6.

34 Cf. *OLD* s. vv. *agger* 3b, c; *moles* 3d.

35 Coincidence of the end of a word with the end of a foot. This particular diaeresis after the first dactyl becomes an epic cliché: Winbolt (1903), 13–16.

36 See Jocelyn (1965), 139–42.

37 Norden (1915), 154–8, Ogilvie (1965), 120.

38 Norden (1915), 155.

39 Norden (1915), 155–6. The words 'stratisue ariete muris' make a perfect hexameter ending, but it is hazardous to assume that all such metrical tags in the early books of Livy are verbatim quotations from Ennius: Norden ibid. 157, Walsh (1961), 136–7.

40 For this as a stock ingredient in such descriptions, cf. further Livy 2.33.8 'clamor inde oppidanorum mixtus muliebri puerilique ploratu ad terrorem, *ut solet*, primum ortus . . .'; and the references collected by Woodman (1972), 155–6 and nn.

41 See the parallels cited by the commentators ad loc., but the fact that the idea is not unique to Virgil does not detract from its special appropriateness here, in a context of violent intrusion.

42 One adverse comment must be ventured, if only to elicit a competent defence. The transition from the first part of the description to the second in v. 488b strikes me as not merely abrupt but – for Virgil – inept. The commentators leap valiantly into the breach. 'The epithet . . .

marks the contrast between the patines of bright gold in the serene heaven and the horror upon earth' (Austin (1964), 191); 'notice the contrast between the beauty of the stars in the heavens and the horror of the earthly scene' (Williams (1972), 247). These observations take no account of one fact, which is that the proper setting for this cliché is the open air: see the variations played upon the theme at 2.222, 338, 5.140, 227–8, 451, 9.504, 10.262, 895, 11.192, 745, 878, 12.409, 462, 756–7. Contrast the death of Dido, when 'it clamor *ad alta* | *atria*' (4.665–6); perhaps it was a reminiscence of this passage which led the 'many' irritably reproved by Servius to take 'aurea sidera' = *laquearia*. Be that as it may, I wonder if I am alone in feeling that this half-verse is dubiously appropriate both in sense and in rhythm, and that in this context the rapidity of 'ferit aúrea sídera clámor' gives a curiously facile effect? Contrast the death of Camilla in battle, where the enjambment makes all the difference: 'tum uero immensus surgens ferit aúrea clámor | sídera' (11.832–3). The commentators do not explain and the translators do not render 'tum' in v. 489; is it enumerative = 'next' or equivalent to *praeterea*, or what? Have we here a hitherto undiagnosed example (for so far as I know this suggestion is novel) of a *tibicen*, one of the 'props' inserted by Virgil to shore up incomplete passages (*Vita Donati* 85)? For the possibility that unfinished lines (and hence also *tibicines*) may be the sign of a late rather than an early stage of composition see Mackail (1930), 47.

43 'Der Fall Trojas gipfelt in König Priamos' Tod': Heinze (1915), 39, pointing out that this emphasis was an original inspiration of Virgil's.

44 Cf. Klingner (1967), 416–17.

45 Austin (1964), 198.

46 'furentem | caede Neoptolemum': 'furentem' picks up 'furens' from the previous verse, and the juxtaposition with 'caede' calls attention to the fact that Neoptolemus is now given his real name, 'New War/ Warrior'. In him, the new Achilles, the war itself is reborn.

47 Cf. Wigodsky (1972), 78, noting also the Ennian colouring of 2.241–2 'o patria, o diuum domus Ilium et incluta bello | moenia Dardanidum!' Cf. Austin (1964), 114.

48 See Jocelyn (1967), 248; and on 'the religious aspects of the destruction of the palaces of Eetion and Priam', ibid. 244.

49 Austin (1964), xi. Cf. Büchner (1956), 335: 'Vom 2. Buche wird man ausgehen wenn man die Gestaltungskraft Vergils ermessen will.'

50 Variously defined: e.g. 250–633 (Quinn); 250–558 (Heinze, Duckworth, Williams); 268–633 (Klingner); etc. Questions of structure and centrality are complicated by the incomplete state of the book and more particularly by the problems of the doubtful Helen-episode and the relationship of the account of Priam's murder to the main narrative; on the latter cf. Quinn (1968), 119.

51 Cf. Heinze (1915), 40, Büchner (1956), 326, 330–1, Putnam (1965), 28, Quinn (1968), 118–19, Mountford (1968–69), 33, Camps (1969), 59.

52 For ring-composition in the first episode of the book (Sinon and Laocoon) see the analysis of Quinn (1968), 114–18. It is curious that the

composer of the Helen-episode employed the technique: Murgia (1971), 215–16.

53 But see Duckworth (1962), 21–4 for other Virgilian examples of this 'recessed panel' structure.

54 Wistrand (1960), 153 = 359; cf. Servius ad loc., comparing 7.184.

55 Most commentators have agreed that the whole scene is to be visualized in this way: that is, that the *armati* of v. 485 are the Trojan guard posted at vv. 449–50 (so Servius) and that the subject of 'uident' is the Greeks. The only objection to this interpretation is what is called the change of subject at v. 485, but this does not seem to me a real difficulty. After 'apparet . . . apparent' the third member of the sentence most naturally refers to what else is seen by those to whom these things were visible; any 'change of subject' is syntactical rather than actual. (As Austin remarks, Virgil could have written 'armati apparent', but would that not have overdone the anaphora?) However, Williams (1972), 247 dissents from the general opinion, arguing that 'the imagery of the previous lines requires that the subject of *vident* should be the Trojans inside, Priam and those around him'. I do not understand what is meant by 'imagery' here, and evocation of Priam himself at this point, as distinct from the majesty of his name, is to my mind un-wanted. More recently Fosse (1973), following a suggestion originally made by R. A. Schröder, has suggested that the subject of 'uident' should be understood as 'penetralia'. This to be sure adds point to 'in limine' and accentuates the theme of profane intrusion, but the consequent change of what I have called the 'actual' subject of the sentence seems to me to damage the rhetoric. Artistic considerations, as I argue in the text, are in my view decisively in favour of taking v. 485 as forming part of the moment of vision shared by the reader with the attacking Greeks.

56 Austin (1964), 189. The effect is also assisted by the coincidence of ictus and word-accent: 'apparet domus íntus et átria lónga patéscunt'. Contrast 488b (above, n. 42), where to my ear the effect is hurried and perfunctory.

57 Cf. Page (1894), 246 on 'the pictorial power of the repetition [of "apparet"] and also its pathos, as emphasising the profanation which the venerable palace was suffering'.

58 1.703–4 '. . . famulae, quibus ordine longam | cura penum struere et flammis adolere penatis'; cf. Servius 'ideo domorum secreta dicta "penetralia" aut ab eo quod est penitus aut a penatibus'; Festus p. 231 Lindsay 'Penetralia sunt penatium deorum sacraria.' Modern scholarship confirms this (Ernout–Meillet (1959–60) 496 s.v. *penus*); but ancient etymological doctrine need not be scientifically correct in order to be artistically and rhetorically significant. What matters is what Virgil and his readers believed.

59 Austin (1964), 190.

60 For the possibility that this portion of the passage had not been completely worked up cf. above, n. 42.

61 Bullock-Davies (1970), 141.

62 For a parallel to this scheme, with an element standing outside the

concentric frames to balance the element surrounded by them, one may compare the book of the *Eclogues* (Duckworth (1962), 3).

63 Witness continuing controversy, which there is no need to document here, about, for instance, Propertius' *Monobiblos* and the *Metamorphoses*.

64 The device that was used on the Greek stage to reveal 'an interior scene or the results of actions done in the interior of the building' (Pickard-Cambridge (1946), 120); as happens, for instance, at the end of Sophocles' *Electra*.

65 Wistrand (1960), 153 = 359.

66 Cf. Gransden (1976), 14–15.

67 As Williams (1972), 250 remarks, 'no Roman could read lines 557–8 without thinking of Pompey'. Critics and commentators, however, are notably reluctant to draw conclusions: see, for instance, the non-committal footnote at Quinn (1963), 238, and the silence of Putnam (1965), 98–9. Yet Virgil chose to *end* his account of Priam's death, a focal point in Book 2, as is generally agreed, with this unmistakable allusion. Why? The critic is not entitled to side-step the question.

68 Henry (1878), 252.

69 A reason for not confining the student's literary diet to the first-rate: cf. Kenney (1975), 16–17.

70 This is of course the point of Kipling's parable 'The Ship that found Herself'; it was not intended in the first instance to apply to literature, but Kipling would have been the first to acknowledge the applicability.

71 Johnson (1974), 174–5; on Virgil ibid. 180, and Johnson (1976), passim. For reservations see West (1977).

7 SELF-IMITATION WITHIN A GENERIC FRAMEWORK

Earlier versions of this essay formed the basis of lectures given in 1977 at Portsmouth Polytechnic, the University of Manchester Seminar Topics in Current Research, the Fundación Pastor, Madrid, and the Universities of Valladolid and Salamanca. I am grateful for comments made on those occasions and for the detailed advice of Mr I. M. Le M. Du Quesnay and Dr James McKeown. They do not necessarily share the views expressed here.

1 In this essay 'imitation' and 'self-imitation' are regarded as covering the whole gradation from the most fleeting reference to the most substantial borrowing.

2 I use the word 'genre' not to mean certain forms of literature (e.g. elegy or epic) but certain types of poem (e.g. genethliakon, 'birthday poem'; propemptikon, 'sending off poem'; basilikon, 'praise of a king'; or *renuntiatio amoris*). 'Topoi' are the elements or motifs which recur in examples of any genre. See in general Cairns (1972); also above, p. 44.

3 Cf. Du Quesnay (1977), 55 and n. 213 with addendum 99.

4 The best understood examples of the process are some of Horace's *Odes* where the 'motto' beginning a poem refers to one source but

other source(s) influence the rest of it. Many of the phenomena discussed in Kroll (1924), ch. 9 (Die Kreuzung der Gattungen) also
involve *contaminatio* to some degree. See also Gentili (1977), ch. 1.

5 Cf. Fliedner (1975) on ll. 25f.

6 See the subsequent notes and Giangrande (1977), 177 (on *Selbst-
variation*).

7 For analysis and comparisons cf. Cairns (1972), 145ff., 194ff., 202ff.

8 See Cairns (1973).

9 Cf. Copley (1957), ch. 6; Cairns (1972), 231, 235; Cairns (1979), ch. 7.

10 Cf. Cairns (1972), 173ff., 217; Cairns (1979), chs 5, 6, 7.

11 Cf. Cairns (1979), ch. 5.

12 Cf. Cairns (1977*b*).

13 Cf. Macleod (1974*a*).

14 Cf. Cairns (1977).

15 Cf. Cairns (1977*a*).

16 Cf. Cairns (1978).

17 The *Amores* survives in its second edition, in which Ovid reduced
the original five books of *Amores* to three. It is therefore possible
that 3.11 is historically the earlier poem. On the whole question, and
on the possibility of late poems in *Amores* Bk 1, cf. Cameron (1968).
But this is not really a difficulty for the present study. Ovid arranged
his second edition so that 3.11 came after 2.9, and he therefore must
have intended it to be read after, and as a reworking of, 2.9.

18 For a fuller account of the genre with examples and discussion see
Cairns (1972), 79–82.

19 See Cairns (1972), esp. 226ff.

20 On combination of topoi see Cairns (1972), 112f.

21 The sense of *longa* which agrees with *naualia* is transferred to *pinum*
to suggest *nauis longa* (warship). Such *enallage adiectivi* is common in
Hellenistic poetry. Cf. Giangrande (1977*a*), 514f.

22 *tempus erat* (24) means 'it is high time', i.e. 'it is now time and has been
for some period'. Cf. K–S 1.123, §23.3.

23 Jäger (1967), 148ff.; Lörcher (1975), 18ff. An argument is sometimes
advanced for dividing *Amores* 2.9 based on the alleged preference of
Augustan poets for books with multiples of five poems in them. This
is refuted succinctly by Jäger (1967), 149 n. 86.

24 Mainly derived from Jäger (1967) and Lörcher (1975), loc. cit. but with
extra points added.

25 Cf. Jäger (1967), 151.

26 On reaction cf. Cairns (1972), ch. 6.

27 Unlike Meleager and Ovid, Horace's attitude to his addressee Venus
is friendly and retirement is his sole reason for giving up love.

28 Cf. André (1966), index s.v. *Amor*.

29 Cf. Arnott (1975).

30 Cf. Arnott (1975), 143 and nn. 8f.; Cairns (1979), ch. 8.

31 On ring-composition see Cairns (1979), ch. 8 and the bibliography
there in n. 4.

32 Cf. Jäger (1967), 141ff.; Lörcher (1975), 15ff.; Cairns (1972), 139f.

33 Derived from the works cited above (n. 32).

34 The topoi of *Amores* 3.11 are treated at Cairns (1972), 8off. and the 'reaction' at 138ff. These discussions are assumed in what follows.

35 Jäger (1967), 148 notes the link between the two elegies but does not offer a detailed comparison.

36 Cf. *TLL*, s.v.

37 Cf. Cairns (1979), ch. 7.

38 See *TLL*, s.v. *cornu* IV.

39 Cf. Cairns (1972), 8off.

40 On the latter motifs see most recently Yardley (1973).

41 Cf. Nisbet–Hubbard (1970) on Hor. *Od.* 1.28.28.

42 For *per te* = διὰ σέ see Norden (1913), Indexes III, s.v. Διά;; IV s.v. *per* etc.; Kleinknecht (1967), Index B, s.v. διὰ σέ. On divine power to do opposites cf. Krischer (1968).

43 With *si tamen exaudis* (51) cf. e.g. Virg. *Aen.* 1.603ff.; 2.689ff.; 5.687ff.

44 Cf. Appel (1909), 152; Nisbet–Hubbard (1970), on Hor. *Od.* 1.3.1; 1.28.25.

45 Cf. Nisbet–Hubbard (1970), on Hor. *Od.* 1.9.8; *TLL*, s.v. II.I.B.4.

46 Cf. Smith (1971), on Tib. 1.5.7; *OLD* s.v. 10b.

47 This is a witty substitute for the normal displacement of *te*, on which see Nisbet–Hubbard (1970), on Hor. *Od.* 1.6.2; Smith (1971), on Tib. 1.5.7 *parce tamen, per te furtiui foedera lecti*, which *Am.* 3.11.45 echoes *cum variatione*.

48 Cf. Appel (1909), 78f.

49 *uelis* (50) presumably alludes to the prayer topos that a god can achieve anything by a simple act of will. Cf. Nisbet–Hubbard (1970) on Hor. *Od.* 1.12.31.

50 Cf. Cairns (1972), passim; Krischer (1971), 24ff. (on 'Ersatzmotif'), esp. 35; Du Quesnay (1977), 57; Cairns (1979), ch. 2, n. 43.

51 Cf. Cairns (1979), ch. 6.

52 Cf. Cairns (1979), chs 6, 8.

53 Conveniently collected by Munari (1970), 5off.

54 Cf. Buckland (1908), 652ff.

55 E.g. Sen. *Suas.* 7.3; *Ep.* 70.24; Plin. *Ep.* 1.3.3; 2.10.4; 3.5.4. In two legal texts where *se adserere* is found, quite different questions are under discussion. In *Dig.* 41.14.2.1 the status being aspired to is *ingenuitas*, not *libertas*; in *Dig.* 47.10.11.9 competence to sue under the *actio iniuriarum* is the issue.

56 Cf. *Dig.* 11.4.2.

57 Cf. Cairns (1971*a*).

58 Cf. Cairns (1971).

8   SELF-IMITATION AND THE SUBSTANCE OF HISTORY

This essay was begun at Vandœuvres, Geneva: I am most grateful to the Fondation Hardt for the opportunity of working in that *locus amoenus*. I must express my gratitude also to Ian Du Quesnay, Frank Goodyear and David West, to whose comments and criticisms the present version of this essay owes a great deal.

1 *Caligula* 3.2 '*caesorum clade Variana* ueteres ac dispersas reliquias uno tumulo *humaturus* [sc. Germanicus], *colligere* sua manu et comportare primus adgressus est'. In fact, the episode is briefly mentioned also by Dio, as excerpted by Xiphilinus (57.18.1 'Germanicus . . . *collected* and *buried* the bones of *those who had fallen with Varus*'); but in view of the great similarity of wording, I believe that Dio is here (as elsewhere) deriving his information from Suetonius.

2 Scholars have rightly seen that Tacitus is aiming at a cinematographical view of the site, moving his eye from Varus' camp to the rampart, then to the middle of the plain, and finally to the adjacent woods (see Koestermann (1963), 211). I thus prefer Koehler's *primo* as the first signpost in the sequence 'dein . . . medio campi . . . *adi*acebant . . . lucis propinquis' rather than *prima*, the reading of the MS.

3 Ring-composition in Tacitus has in general not been investigated, but for one elaborate example in *Annals* 4 see Woodman (1972), 150–5. For a rather different view of the structure of the present passage see Soubiran (1964), 62.

4 *qui aderat exercitus* is a key phrase because it illustrates 'the contrast of the living with the dead, the victorious with the slaughtered army, (which) is evidently prominent in the mind of the writer' (Furneaux (1896), 262).

5 Pliny's work is in fact mentioned by name at *Annals* 1.69.2.

6 Since the two passages concern events which are more than fifty years apart and which take place in different areas of the Roman world, I do not think the similarities are to be explained by postulating a common historical source (except in the sense mentioned below, n. 26).

7 Cf. also *Annals* 6.19.2 'iacuit immensa strages . . . dispersi aut aggerati', but the context is different.

8 It does not occur in Lucan 9.789ff. (the aftermath of Pharsalus), a reference which I owe to Professor P. G. Walsh and which is the only comparable passage that I know. The very paucity of such 'visits to battle-fields' in Latin literature is another reason why I do not believe there can have been a common literary prototype from which Livy, Virgil, Lucan and Tacitus all derive: if such a prototype had existed, it would surely have been used more frequently than this.

9 Self-imitation is the term used also by Brakman (1925), 195, whose brief comparison of the two passages (which I had not seen until my essay was completed) goes no further than noting some of the parallels: he was in no way concerned to place the passages in any wider context. The only comment of Koestermann (1963), 210, is 'vgl. das Gegen-stück Hist. II 70', while Heubner (1968), 219 and 242–4, makes no comparison at all between the two passages.

10 The irony has been prepared for by *recentis uictoriae* at the beginning and *quae laeta in praesens* in the middle of the episode.

11 This point emerges from the analysis of the episode by Rademacher (1975), 136–9: it provides additional support for E. Wolff's emendation *facies uiae* (for the MSS' *pars uiae*) in section 2.

12 I am not of course suggesting that *Histories* 2.70 is devoid of Sallustian

phraseology, which is demonstrably not the case (see Heubner (1968), 242–3).

13 Soubiran (1964), 60. For other examples of word-play (paronomasia) on adjacent words see Austin (1964) on *Aeneid* 2.27; for other types of word-play involving changes of vowel-quantity, as here, see Woodman (1977) on Velleius 108.2.

14 Baxter (1972), 255, states that commentators have missed this parallel; but it is in Kuntz (1962), 137.

15 *ora* = 'skulls' seems not to be found before Tacitus except here in Virgil and in a line of Ovid which is also an echo of Virgil (*Heroides* 9.89 'adfixa penatibus ora').

16 Baxter (1972), 256, claims to be the first to spot this parallel; but it is in Koestermann (1963) ad loc. and Soubiran (1964), 62.

17 For Germans as hardly human see Woodman (1977) on Velleius 117.3.

18 For such conventions in general see Syme (1958), 126 with refs in n. 2; for size in particular see Woodman (1977) on Velleius 106.1.

19 The similarity of the night scenes was noted by Wolff (1888) on *Histories* 5.15.1.

20 This striking correspondence was not noted by Norden (1923), 214 n. 1, when he pointed to the general similarity of the two passages. But he was arguing a different case, namely that both passages derive from a common source (the *Bella Germaniae* of the elder Pliny). In fact, the phrase *inter undas* at *Annals* 1.64.2 has seemed so strange to some scholars that they have emended it (*inter umida* Schütz: *inter uda* Polster), while Wellesley (1963), 256, simply declares it to be 'impossible'. (I owe this textual information to Professor Goodyear.)

21 Miller (1959), 189. It is an interesting question why Tacitus varied *Histories* 2.70 when he repeated it at *Annals* 1.61 but did not do the same here. I suspect that in the former case his imagination responded to the challenge of describing a scene which, as we have noted (above, n. 8), was relatively novel, whereas in the present case such a stimulus was absent (battle-scenes were commonplace: see below, n. 39).

22 At this point it is interesting to recall that Bacha (1906) suggested that numerous parts of the *Annals* could be seen as imitations of other parts of the same work and could thus be impugned as unhistorical. It should be clear from my discussion here that Bacha's thesis is by no means as silly as has generally been supposed, and that, if his book is to be dismissed, it is rather because of the unconvincing nature of his examples. (He mentions neither of the cases discussed here.)

23 See Goodyear (1972), 135–6.

24 See Kroll (1924), 382. For three other cases where Tacitus echoes Tiberius' own official words see Woodman (1977), 267–70, on Velleius 129.3; cf. also Miller (1968).

25 This interpretation of Tacitus' *narrative*-technique closely resembles Thucydides' account of his own *speech*-technique at 1.22.1 (as expounded by De Ste Croix (1972), 7–11), namely that there is a core of truth in every Thucydidean speech (ἡ ξυμπᾶσα γνώμη) but that the bulk of each speech is Thucydides' own invention (τὰ δέοντα). The main difficulty for modern scholars, as De Ste Croix remarks (p. 11),

is that 'we can seldom be sure that we know how extensive the ξυμπᾶσα γνώμη is, and therefore we may often not be able to decide how much of a speech . . . is Thucydides' own formulation'. The same applies, *mutatis mutandis*, to Tacitus' narrative.

26 Syme (1958), 176–7, mentions that among the sources available to Tacitus when he composed the *Histories* there were eye-witnesses and monographs on individual battles. If Tacitus used such a source at *Histories* 2.70, then there is a sense in which both that passage and *Annals* 1.61 derive from a 'common historical source' (see above, n. 6).

27 The details of Tacitus' description of Germanicus' visit are still being repeated, without qualification, in modern text-books of ancient history.

28 See Wiseman (1979), ch. 3.

29 I restrict my examples to 'substantive imitation', but we should remember how commonly ancient historians resorted to other types of imitation. One such type is mentioned above (p. 149), but imitation could be used to signal the tradition to which a historian belonged (so Tacitus begins his *Annals* with the same two words as Sallust had begun the historical section (6.1) of his *Catiline*), or it could be a symptom of literary hero-worship (as in the case of Arruntius and his Sallustomania, cf. Seneca, *Letters* 114.17–19), or it was a method whereby an historian demonstrated his superiority to a predecessor (*aemulatio*, cf. Livy, *praefatio* 2 'scribendi arte rudem uetustatem superaturos'; Tacitus, *Agricola* 10.1 'Britanniae situm populosque multis scriptoribus memoratos non [!] in comparationem curae ingeniiue referam'). Besides, all Roman historians will have been taught to imitate passages from the historical classics during their schooldays (cf. e.g. Quintilian 10.1.31–4, 73–5). Since in the ancient world the writing of history was regarded as a literary pursuit little different from the writing of poetry, we should not be surprised that ancient historians resorted to the same literary techniques (such as *imitatio*) as poets.

30 See Charlesworth (1927).

31 See Goodyear (1972), 217–18 and 263 respectively.

32 See Wiseman (1979), ch. 2. On other occasions Livy repeats under a slightly different guise a story he has already told elsewhere: thus Manlius' encounter with a giant Gaul at 7.9.6–10.14 recurs at 7.26.1–9 where Corvinus meets another giant Gaul; and the rape of Lucretia at 1.57–9 recurs, with judicious and appropriate variation, at 3.44–9 (where the lady is called Verginia), 4.9.4 (the Maid of Ardea) and 38.24. 3ff. (the wife of one Ortiagon). On these rapes see Ogilvie (1965), 219–20, 477–8.

33 Thucydides 1.22.4, 2.48.3, 3.82.2. For the correct interpretation of these passages see De Ste Croix (1972), 29–33.

34 E.g. Plato, *Laws* 688c-d; Diodorus 1.1.3; Plutarch, *Sertorius* 1.

35 See Charlesworth (1927) and Martin (1955).

36 Martin (1955), 124.

37 I make this latter point because Borzsák (1968), 486–7, has suggested that Germanicus is an idealized counterpart to the Domitian-like

Vitellius ('Durch einen Vergleich der beiden Inspektionen wird der Unterschied zwischen einem entmenschten Usurpator und einem wirklichen römischen imperator, der zusammen mit seinem Heere die *virtus, humanitas, pietas, disciplina* verkörpert, gehörig veranschaulicht'). While there is of course a general contrast between the motives and behaviour of the two commanders, Tacitus does not seem to me to have taken any measures that would bring the contrast to the attention of his readers. Besides, Tacitus portrays Germanicus in far more ambiguous terms than Borzsák has allowed (see Goodyear (1972), 239–41). Borzsák's is the longest comparison of *Annals* 1.61–2 with *Histories* 2.70 that I have seen, but he mentions none of the verbal parallels and his discussion came to my attention only after my ideas on *Annals* 1.61–5 as a whole has been formulated.

38 Cf. Duris fr. 1 Jacoby; Cicero, *De oratore* 2.59 'delectationis causa . . . legere soleo', *Ad familiares* 5.12.4 'multam etiam casus nostri uarietatem . . . suppeditabunt plenam cuiusdam uoluptatis, quae uehementer animos hominum . . . tenere possit. nihil est enim aptius ad delectationem lectoris quam temporum uarietates fortunaeque uicissitudines . . . [5] expletur animus iucundissima uoluptate'; Vitruvius 5 *praefatio* 1; Pliny, *Letters* 5.8.4.

39 Cf. Cicero, *Orator* 66 '(historia) in qua . . . pugna describitur'; Horace, *Odes* 2.1.17–24; Lucian, *De historia conscribenda* 45.

40 See Goodyear (1972), 30–1.

41 For a full account of this amazing and instructive story see Knightley (1975), 176–7 (whose book should be recommended reading for those who wish to understand how ancient historians worked). The reporter who deceived his newspaper and the public on this occasion assumed (quite rightly) that no one could check his stories on account of the distance involved. The same is even more true of ancient historians (see above, p. 153), who lived in a world where communications were so much more difficult.

9   *LENTE CVRRITE, NOCTIS EQVI*

1 On the Greek antecedents of the motif see Gow–Page (1965), 2.622 (= n. on Meleager 27). Cf. also Antipater of Thessalonica 7 in Gow–Page (1968), 1.16 and 2.26. On the later developments of the motif see Fränkel (1969), 11–17; Robinson (1966), 826.

2 I thus agree with Luck (1969), 159.

3 So Cairns (1972), 178.

4 So Cairns (1972), 137. A kletic hymn is one in which the suppliant calls (Greek καλέω) or summons a god to visit a certain person or locality: see e.g. Nisbet–Hubbard (1970), 343–4.

5 See the excellent analysis of the poem's structure by Elliott (1973–4), 127–32. A *suasoria* was strictly a form of speech or rhetorical exercise in which the speaker 'was required to offer advice to a famous historical (or, occasionally, legendary) personage, or to a body of people, in a critical situation or dilemma' (Bonner (1977), 278): its elements are given by Quintilian 3.7.7–9; 4.2. The *suasoria* was an exercise of which

Ovid was particularly fond (see Seneca, *Controversiae* 2.2.12). On the structure and technique of the *Amores* as a whole see Du Quesnay (1973), 1–48.

6 Cf. Lörcher (1975), 45.

7 Cf. Morgan (1977), 41. Ovid has *omnia perpeterer* at *Heroides* 20.83.

8 Dawn is called φθονερός in Antipater of Thessalonica, *Anthologia Palatina* 5.3. Cf. Chaucer, *Troilus* 3.1454.

9 See Ovid, *Metamorphoses* 4.167–89, which I discuss on pp. 169f., above. Cf. Marlowe, *Hero and Leander* 2.301–6.

10 Cf. Juliet's prayer to night to hasten in *Romeo and Juliet* 3.2, a passage which shows the influence of Ovid.

11 Cf. Luck (1969), 149–80.

12 On the styles of Virgil and Ovid see Kenney (1973), 116–28. Kenney is primarily writing about the *Metamorphoses*, but much of what he says is of wider application.

13 For statistics on Ovid's use of elision and the frequency of dactyls in his hexameters see Platnauer (1951), 37, 72–3.

14 Aphaeresis is the removal of a letter or syllable from the beginning of a word, e.g. *decretumst* for *decretum est.*

15 Cf. Du Quesnay (1973), 29, 'imitation and allusion are among the most sophisticated aspects of Ovid's art'.

16 On Ovid's pentameters see further Wilkinson (1963), 216–17; Barsby (1973), 19–22.

17 Homoeoteleuton occurs when words or clauses have a similar ending (from ὁμοιοτέλευτον); assonance is the close repetition of similar vowel sounds.

18 Cf. Barsby (1973), 135, on the opening of *Amores* 1.12: 'Ovid does not keep the reader long in suspense. The first couplet, having proclaimed that this is a sequel to the preceding poem, immediately announces the failure of Ovid's letter.'

19 1.176. In the second sestiad of this most Ovidian poem Marlowe makes use of the 'premature dawn' motif at 301–6 with an interesting mythological variant at 87–9 (Aurora seems to be in love with the sun-god).

20 It has been said that there is a difficulty in this couplet of Ovid, on the grounds that the sailor, unlike the other workers, does not rest at night and start work at dawn. But the sailor does start to suffer at dawn, and thus serves as a transitional figure linking the nocturnal lover to the diurnal toilers.

21 See (briefly) Robathan (1973), 205; Shannon (1929), xiv ('Chaucer's greatest obligation is to Ovid'), 133–7. For Ovid's influence on medieval writers, see bibliography in Gariepy (1970), 44–5.

22 Boccaccio's *Filocolo* may have suggested the Tithonus–Titan conflation. See Robinson (1966), 826–7.

23 See Leishman (1951), 188–9; Gill (1972), 47–72. Smith (1975), 401, also cites Petrarch, *Canzoni* 188, but this poem is unlike Ovid in tone and Donne does not seem to have used it here.

24 Gardner (1965), 202, compares *Metamorphoses* 2.386–7, but that passage contains no reference to the sun's age: he says he is tired of his endless daily task because of his grief for his son Phaethon.

25 Marlowe, *Jew of Malta* 1.1.37.

26 Ovid does not use metaphysical conceits. When we speak of a poem of Donne as Ovidian (which we may properly do of many of the *Songs and Sonnets* and all the *Elegies*), we are thinking of the poet's persona, tone and attitude to his subject, his addressee and his readers: see Candelaria (1960), 294–7. More than half the stanzas of Donne's *The Bait* have to be omitted in order to produce an 'Ovidian' poem: see Lee (1962), 170–3.

10 PYRAMUS AND THISBE IN SHAKESPEARE AND OVID

 1 Ovid does not give her name. Other sources call her Arsippe or Arsinoe.
 2 Cf. Lucian, *De dea Syria* 14 (Loeb vol. 4).
 3 Cf. Perdrizet (1932), 192–228.
 4 See the discussion in Perry (1967), 153–66.
 5 See Levi (1947), vol. 1, 117–18; vol. 2, pl. xx.
 6 Cf. Ovid, *Amores* 1.5.11.
 7 Paintings are known from the triclinium of Loreius Tiburtinus, the triclinium of Lucretius Fronto, and site ix.5.14. Illustrations of the first will be found in Grant (1962), pl. 76, of the second in Rizzo (1929), pl. 134(a), and of the third in Ward-Perkins and Claridge (1976), pl. 142.
 8 The crudest and most influential statement of this view is given by Lewis (1936), 2–5. A refutation is conducted on a very broad front by Dronke (1965), vol. 1. The presence of romantic love in certain areas of Roman elegy is discussed by Sullivan (1961), 528–36. Further evidence is afforded by the Greek romances.
 9 I believe Klose (1968), 85–6 is right to stand firm on this point.
10 See Callan (1946), 273–4.
11 The hymeneal character of the play suggests it was originally performed in connection with an aristocratic marriage. The names of the couple are not known for certain. See Chambers (1944), 61–7.
12 It seemed worth while to make this point in view of the odd statement in Thomson (1952), 77: 'There is no evidence that he used the Knight's Tale in Chaucer.' See Baldwin (1959), 480–3.
13 The classical reader can get this far for himself, simply by comparing the relevant texts. For a more detailed discussion, however, he will probably need to refer to Baldwin (1968), 109–20.
14 As the available editions do not mention the point or else get it wrong, one should perhaps point out that Hercules did *not* take part in the fight of the Lapiths and Centaurs as described in *Met.* 12.210–535. It is true that in 537ff. Tlepolemus, Hercules' son, complains that his father has not been mentioned in the narrative (595ff. in Golding's translation) – almost as if such a reference might have been expected. This no doubt gave Shakespeare the idea. But in fact Hercules' fight with the Centaurs took place on quite a different occasion and in a different place – viz at the cave of Pholus (Diodorus Siculus 4.12 and

Apollodorus 2.5.4). The words of Tlepolemus are no doubt to be explained as a lead-in to the section on Hercules which follows. This is not the most dexterous of Ovid's links.

15 I owe this point to H. L. Brooks, the editor of the forthcoming Arden edition of *A Midsummer Night's Dream*. He kindly read a draft of this essay and made a number of helpful comments.

16 See Staton (1962–63), 165–78. On the fairies in general see Latham (1930) and Briggs (1959).

17 To use these lines in an attempt to date the play is surely imprudent. Such phenomena are frequently a sign of divine displeasure in Ovid, Seneca, and elsewhere.

18 In view of the reference to Helen in the next line some editors suppose that Pyramus is also dimly thinking of Alexander (Paris). But that seems rather too arcane; it is perhaps better to assume a grosser error, namely that Helen has been confused with Hero.

19 E.g. *The Taming of the Shrew* 3.1.28–9 (= *Heroides* 1.33–4) 'Hic ibat Simois; hic est Sigeia tellus; | Hic steterat Priami regia celsa senis.'

20 E.g. *As You Like It* 3.3.8 'TOUCHSTONE: I am here with thee and thy goats, as the most capricious poet, honest Ovid, was among the Goths' (where 'goats' is taken up semantically by 'capricious' and phonetically by 'Gōths'), and *Loves's Labour's Lost* 4.2.128ff. 'HOLOFERNES: Ovidius Naso was the man . . .'

21 The text of this passage is uncertain. In the first line modern editions (e.g. Arden, New Penguin, Macmillan) follow Q, reading: 'Thisby, the flowers of odious savours sweet –'. This, however, involves a break in the syntax when we reach 'So hath thy breath.' The Cambridge editors thought Shakespeare wrote *a*, which might mean either 'have' or 'of', and so they printed *ha'*. This saves the syntax but *sounds* very unlikely. I have followed Collier, Craig and others, who read 'have'. (Could the corruption not have been aural rather than visual? 'Have' and 'of' are very close phonetically.) The second line is also uncertain. Some print '"Odious"? Odorous!' But the essence of the joke is unaffected.

22 'Courteous wall' probably comes from Golding (95–6): 'we think ourselves in det | For this same piece of courtesie'. In v. 83 Golding had translated Ovid's *tenui rima* by 'crany'; Shakespeare took this over in 3.1.75–6: 'and let him hold his fingers thus, and through the cranny shall Pyramus and Thisbe whisper'. As a final gloss on the v-sign, one might perhaps observe that *tenui rima* is used in an obscene sense by Juvenal (*Sat.* 3.97).

23 The obscene sense of 'stones' is confirmed by Partridge (1968), 192, though he does not mention this instance.

24 The ballad by I. Tomson contained in C. Robinson's *A Handfull of Pleasant Delites* (1584) is printed in Bullough (1957), vol. 1, 409–11. In addition to this Muir (1977), 72–3 mentions an anonymous version of the story in a miscellany entitled *A Gorgeous Gallery of Gallant Inventions*, and a work by Thomas Mouffet *Of the Silkewormes and their Flies*. The latter, Muir believes, was read by Shakespeare in manuscript. See also Furness (1895), 272ff. and Bush (1932), 50.

25 Since Ovid's story purports to explain how the white mulberry turned red, the tree is much more important for him than it is for Shakespeare. A study of its occurrence in vv. 51–2, 89–90, 95, 116, 125–7, 131–2, 158–61, and 165 will show how closely it is associated with the motif of blood. When one thinks of a tree stained with the blood of one who died for love, it is easy to see how in the Middle Ages Pyramus was sometimes regarded as a Christ figure and Thisbe as an allegory of the human soul. About A.D. 1200, for example, the episode was represented amongst the sculptures on Basel cathedral. See Schmitt-von Mühlenfels (1972), 55ff. and pls XI–XIII. The allegory was also elaborated by Petrus Berchorius in the fourteenth century; see Bush (1932), 18. For the devil as a lion, see 1 Peter 5.8.

26 The story need not necessarily entail a knowledge of the white mulberry, but that type was doubtless known to the Greeks in connection with the eastern silk trade.

27 In Ovid Thisbe hides in a cave, but Gower has: 'as a bridd which were in Mue | withinne a buissh sche kepte hire clos' (*Confessio Amantis* 1412f.).

28 Contrast her intentional deception of her parents and servants (*fallere* in v. 85 and *fallit* in v. 94).

29 If the mechanicals play it straight, why do they call the piece a comedy? The relevant passages are (*a*) 1.2.11–13, where Quince gives the title as *The Most Lamentable Comedy and Most Cruel Death of Pyramus and Thisbe*, (*b*) 1.2.14–17, where Bottom calls it 'merry' (though in fact he knows nothing about it), (*c*) 3.1.9, where Bottom says 'There are things in this comedy of Pyramus and Thisbe that will never please', (*d*) 4.2.46, where Bottom hopes the piece will be greeted as 'a sweet comedy', and (*e*) 5.1.56f., where according to the playbill the play is 'A tedious brief scene of young Pyramus and his love Thisbe: very tragical mirth.' To take (*e*) first: Theseus is certainly puzzled by 'tragical mirth'. The explanation given by Philostrate is that the piece is indeed laughable because is it is badly written and performed (in earnest) by incompetent dolts. This patronizing and satirical explanation, however, cannot account for passages (*a*) to (*d*), though it is sometimes said to do so. Are we perhaps to imagine (*a*) that although the writer did not mean it to be funny and knew it did not have a happy ending, he chose that as the title to make his play sound more impressive? (Editors refer us to Preston's *Cambises*: 'a lamentable tragedy mixed full of pleasant mirth' which belonged to the previous generation.) And could it be that in (*b*), (*c*) and (*d*) Bottom, having heard the title, knows the piece is to be a 'comedy' but has no clear idea of what a comedy is? I make the proposal with an amateur's misgivings. Finally, one should perhaps remember that the authorship of the piece is rather obscure and that the script is left conveniently vague (the performance does not tally with the rehearsal).

30 I owe this point to H. L. Brooks.

31 Sidney, *An Apology for Poetry*, ed. G. Shepherd (repr. London 1967), 100. The poet is described as 'making things either better than Nature bringeth forth, or, quite anew, forms such as never were in Nature, as

the Heroes, Demigods, Cyclops, Chimeras, Furies, and such like . . .
Her [Nature's] world is brazen, the poets only [i.e. alone] deliver a
golden.'
32 Plotinus, *Enneads* 5.8.1 (trans. MacKenna) quoted by M. Abrams
(1953), 42. One must also keep in mind the Christian suspicion of
worldly things as coming between the human mind and a higher
reality.

II EPILOGUE

1 Brink (1971), 306.
2 The last two alternatives may in some cases amount to the same thing.
3 It can also happen that a writer's life, as well as his writing, is influenced
by some previous work of literature: see Griffin (1976), 88–9. Keats
seems to have been an example of this (see p. 199).
4 In prose, historiography is such a genre; but we have already noted
that even there the matter is by no means straightforward.
5 Fraenkel (1957), 106–7.
6 Press (1966), 206.
7 Gittings (1954), 5.
8 Gittings (1954), 5. In such a case it is impossible to know for certain
whether a particular influence or borrowing is conscious or not;
the same is true of many other imitative poems, and in general it is
more helpful to be aware of the effect of imitation rather than to puzzle
over whether the writer intended it. On this whole question see, for
example, Lee (1971) and, briefly, Press (1966), 209.
9 See Griffin (1976).
10 See Shipley (1970), s.v. 'imitation'.

ABBREVIATIONS AND
BIBLIOGRAPHY

Note. Scholarly discussions and commentaries are listed under B and throughout the book are referred to by author's name, date, and page number only. Periodical abbreviations generally follow the system used in *L'Année philologique.*

A. ABBREVIATIONS

CGF Austin, C. *Comicorum Graecorum Fragmenta in Papyris Reperta,* Berlin, 1973
GL Keil, H. *Grammatici Latini,* Vols 1–7, Leipzig, 1857
K–S Kühner, R.–Stegmann, C. *Ausführliche Grammatik der lateinischen Sprache,* Vol. 2 *Satzlehre,* parts 1 and 2, 4th edn (reprint), Hanover, 1971
LSJ Liddell, H. G.–Scott, R.–Jones, H. S. *A Greek–English Lexicon,* Oxford, 1961
OCD *Oxford Classical Dictionary,* 2nd edn, Oxford, 1970
OCT Oxford Classical Text(s)
OLD *Oxford Latin Dictionary,* Oxford, 1968–
RE *Paulys Real-Encyclopädie der classischen Altertumswissenschaft,* ed. G. Wissowa et al., Stuttgart, 1893–

B. BIBLIOGRAPHY

Abrams, M. (1953). *The mirror and the lamp.* Oxford
Adams, J. N. (1976). *The text and language of a Vulgar Latin chronicle (Anonymus Valesianus II). BICS* Suppl. 36. London
Anderson, W. S. (1966). 'Horace *Carm.* 1.14: what kind of ship?', *CP* 61.84–98
André, J. (1949). *La vie et l'oeuvre d'Asinius Pollion.* Paris
André, J.-M. (1966). *L'otium dans la vie morale et intellectuelle romaine.* Paris
Appel, G. (1909). *De Romanorum precationibus.* Giessen
Arnott, W. G. (1970). 'Menander: discoveries since the *Dyskolos*', *Arethusa* 3.49–70
 – (1975). 'The modernity of Menander', *G&R* 22.140–55
Austin, R. G. (1964). *P. Vergili Maronis Aeneidos Liber Secundus.* Oxford
 – (1971). *P. Vergili Maronis Aeneidos Liber Primus.* Oxford
Aymard, J. (1951). *Essai sur les chasses romaines.* Paris
Bacha, E. (1906). *Le génie de Tacite.* Brussels–Paris

Bader, B. (1970). 'Der verlorene Anfang der plautinischen *Bacchides*', *RhM* 113.304–23

Bain, D. (1977). *Actors and audience: a study of asides and related conventions in Greek drama*. Oxford

Baldwin, T. W. (1959). *On the literary genesis of Shakespeare's plays*. Urbana
 – (1968). 'The pedigree of Theseus' pups', *Shakespeare-Jahrbuch (W)* 109–20

Barigazzi, A. (1950). 'Euforione e Cornelio Gallo', *Maia* 3.16–25
 – (1966). *Favorino di Arelate: Opere*. Florence

Barsby, J. A. (1973). *Ovid's Amores Book* 1. Oxford

Baxter, R. T. S. (1972). 'Virgil's Influence on Tacitus in Books 1 and 2 of the *Annals*', *CP* 67.246–69

Beare, W. (1964). *The Roman stage*. 3rd edn. London

Blänsdorf, J. (1976). Review of Pöschl (1973), *Gnomon* 48.714–16

Bömer, F. (1958). *P. Ovidius Naso: Die Fasten*. Vol. 2 *Kommentar*. Heidelberg
 – (1969). *P. Ovidius Naso: Metamorphosen Buch I–III: Kommentar*. Heidelberg

Bompaire, J. (1958). *Lucien écrivain*. Paris

Bonanno, M. G. (1973). 'Osservazioni sul tema della "giusta" reciprocità amorosa da Saffo ai comici', *QUUC* 16.110–20

Bonner, S. F. (1977). *Education in Ancient Rome*. London

Borthwick, E. K. (1967). 'Trojan leaps and Pyrrhic dance in Euripides' *Andromache* 1129–41', *JHS* 87.18–23
 – (1976). 'Zoologica Pindarica', *CQ* 26.198–205

Borzsák, S. (1968). *P. Cornelius Tacitus. RE* Suppl. 11.373–511. (Sonderausgabe.) Stuttgart

Boucher, J. P. (1966). *Gaius Cornelius Gallus*. Paris

Brakman, C. (1925), 'Tacitea', *Mnem*. 53.188–97

Briggs, K.M. (1959). *The anatomy of Puck*. London

Bright, D. F. (1971). 'The Plague at Athens and the structure of the *De Rerum Natura*', *Latomus* 30.607–32

Brink, C. O. (1971). *Horace on Poetry II: the Ars poetica*. Cambridge

Broughton, T. R. S. (1952). *The magistrates of the Roman Republic*. Vol. 2. Philological Monographs publ. by the American Philological Association 15

Büchner, K. (1956). *P. Vergilius Maro. Der Dichter der Römer*. Stuttgart

Buckland, W. W. (1908). *The Roman law of slavery*. Cambridge

Bullock-Davies, C. (1970). 'The image of the *limen* in *Aeneid* ii', *G&R* 17.135–41

Bullough, G. (1957). *Narrative and dramatic sources of Shakespeare*. London

Bush, D. (1932). *Mythology and the Renaissance tradition*. London

Cairns, F. (1969). 'Propertius 1.18 and Callimachus, *Acontius and Cydippe*', *CR* 19.131–4
 – (1971). 'Propertius 2.30A and B', *CQ* 21.204–13
 – (1971a). 'Propertius 2.29A', *CQ* 21.455–60
 – (1972). *Generic composition in Greek and Roman poetry*. Edinburgh
 – (1973). 'Catullus' *Basia* poems (5, 7, 48)', *Mnem*. 26.15–22
 – (1975). '*Splendide mendax*: Horace, *Odes* 3.11', *G & R* 22.129–39

– (1975*a*). *Further adventures of a locked-out lover: Propertius 2.17*. Liverpool
– (1975*b*). 'Horace, *Epode* 2, Tibullus 1.1 and rhetorical praise of the countryside', *Museum Philologum Londiniense* 1.79–91
– (1977). 'Horace on other people's love affairs: *Odes* 1.27, 11.4, 1.8, 111.12', *QUUC* 24.121–47
– (1977*a*). 'Horace, *Odes* 111.13 and 111.23', *Ant. Class.* 46.523–43
– (1977*b*). 'Two unidentified komoi of Propertius: 1.3 and 11.29', *Emerita* 45.325–53
– (1977*c*). 'The distaff of Theugenis: Theocritus, *Idyll* 28', in *Papers of the Liverpool Latin Seminar* 1976 (ed. F. Cairns). Arca 2. Liverpool
– (1978). 'The Genre Palinode and three Horatian examples: *Epode* 17, *Odes* 1.16, *Odes* 1.34', *Ant. Class.* 47.546–52
– (1979). *Tibullus: a Hellenistic poet at Rome*. Cambridge
Callan, N. (1946). 'Thyne Owne Book: a note on Chaucer, Gower and Ovid', *Rev. Eng. Stud.* 22.269–81
Cameron, A. (1968). 'The first edition of Ovid's *Amores*', *CQ* 18.320–33
Camps, W. A. (1969). *An introduction to Virgil's Aeneid*. Oxford
Candelaria, F. H. (1960). 'Ovid and the indifferent lovers', *Renaissance News* 13.294–7
Chambers, E. K. (1944). 'The occasion of *A Midsummer-Night's Dream*' in his *Shakespearean gleanings* 61–7. Oxford
Charlesworth, M. P. (1927). 'Livia and Tanaquil', *CR* 41.55–7
Clark, D. L. (1957). *Rhetoric in Greco-Roman education*. New York
Clausen, W. (1970). 'Catullus and Callimachus', *HSCP* 74.85–94
Coffey, M. (1961). 'The subject matter of Virgil's similes', *BICS* 8.63–75
Coleman, R. (1977). *Vergil: Eclogues*. Cambridge
Commager, H. S. (1957). 'Lucretius' interpretation of the plague', *HSCP* 62.105–18
– (1962). *The Odes of Horace: a critical study*. New Haven–London
Conington, J. (1884). *P. Vergili Maronis Opera*. The works of Virgil . . . 11. 4th ed. rev. H. Nettleship. London.
Copley, F. O. (1940). 'The suicide-paraclausithyron: a study of Ps. Theocritus, *Idyll* xx111', *TAPA* 71.52–61
– (1956). *Exclusus Amator*. Philological Monographs publ. by the the American Philological Association 17
Culler, J. (1975). *Structuralist poetics*. London
Del Corno, D. (1975). 'Alcuni aspetti del linguaggio di Menandro', *Studi class. e orientali* 24.13–48
De Ste Croix, G. E. M. (1972). *The origins of the Peloponnesian War*. London
Dorsch, T. S. (1969). *Aristotle, Horace, Longinus: classical literary criticism*. Penguin Classics. Harmondsworth
Dover, K. J. (1968). *Aristophanes Clouds*. Oxford
– (1971). *Theocritus: select poems*. London
Dronke, P. (1965). *Medieval Latin and the rise of the European love-lyric*. Oxford
Duckworth, G. E. (1952). *The nature of Roman comedy*. Princeton
– (1962). *Structural patterns and proportions in Virgil's Aeneid*. Ann Arbor

Bibliography

Du Quesnay, I. M. Le M. (1973). 'The *Amores*' in *Ovid* (ed. J. W. Binns), 1–48. London
- (1977). 'Vergil's Fourth *Eclogue*' in *Papers of the Liverpool Latin Seminar 1976* (ed. F. Cairns). Arca 2. Liverpool
- (1978). Review of Ross (1975), *CR* 28.276–7
Dutoit, E. (1936). *Le thème de l'adynaton dans la poésie antique*. Paris
Eden, P. T. (1975). *A commentary on Virgil: Aeneid VIII*. Leyden
Elliott, A. (1973–74). '*Amores* 1.13: Ovid's art', *CJ* 69.127–32
Enk, P. J. (1946). *Sex. Propertii elegiarum liber I* (*Monobiblos*). Vol. 2. Leyden
Ernout, A.–Meillet, A. (1959–60). *Dictionnaire étymologique de la langue latine*. Vols 1–2. 4th edn. Paris
Fantham, E. (1978). 'Imitation and evolution: the discussion of rhetorical imitation in Cicero, *De Oratore* 2.87–97 and some related problems of Ciceronian theory', *CP* 73.1–16
Flashar, H. (forthcoming). 'Die klassizistische Theorie der Mimesis', *Entretiens sur l'Antiquité classique* 25. Vandoeuvres–Geneva
Fliedner, H. (1975). 'Ohne Liebe ein Gott: Überlegungen zu Ov. am. 2,9,25f.', *Monumentum Chiloniense: Kieler Festschrift für E. Burck* (ed. E. Lefèvre), 432–5. Amsterdam
Flury, P. (1968). *Liebe und Liebessprache bei Menander, Plautus und Terenz*. Heidelberg
Fordyce, C. J. (1961). *Catullus: a Commentary*. Oxford
Fosse, L. M. (1973). 'A note on the interpretation of Vergil, *Aeneid* II 485', *SO* 49.93–4
Foster, B. O. (1899). 'The Symbolism of the apple in classical antiquity', *HSCP* 10.39ff.
Fraenkel, E. (1935). *Naevius. RE* Suppl. 6.622–40.
- (1957). *Horace*. Oxford
- (1960). *Elementi plautini in Plauto* (tr. F. Munari). Florence
Fränkel, H. (1921). *Die homerischen Gleichnisse*. Göttingen
Fraser, P. M. (1972). *Ptolemaic Alexandria*. Vols. 1–3. Oxford
Furneaux, H. (1896). *The Annals of Tacitus*. Vol. 1. 2nd edn. Oxford
Furness, H. H. (1895). *A Midsummer Night's Dream*. Variorum edn. Philadelphia
Gaiser, K. (1970). 'Die plautinischen *Bacchides* und Menanders *Dis Exapaton*', *Philologus* 114.51–87
- (1972). 'Zu Eigenart der römischen Komödie: Plautus and Terenz gegenüber ihren griechischen Vorbildern', *Aufstieg und Niedergang der römischen Welt* (ed. H. Temporini), 1.2.1027–113
Gardner, H. (1965). *John Donne. The elegies and the songs and sonnets*. Oxford
Gariepy, R. J. (1970). 'Recent scholarship on Ovid (1958–68)', *CW* 64.37–56
Geisler, H. J. (1969). *P. Ovidius Naso: Remedia Amoris mit Kommentar zu Vers 1–396*. Berlin
Gentili, B.(1972). 'Il "letto insaziato" di Medea e il tema dell'*Adikia* a livello amoroso nei lirici (Saffo, Teognide) e nella *Medea* di Euripide', *Studi class. e orientali* 21.60–72
- (1977). *Lo spettacolo nel mondo antico*. Bari
Giangrande, G. (1962). 'On the origins of the Greek romance', *Eranos* 60.132–59

-- (1967). '"Arte allusive" and Alexandrian epic poetry', *CQ* 17.85–97
- (1970). 'Hellenistic poetry and Homer', *Ant. Class.* 39.46–77
- (1971). 'Theocritus' Twelfth and Fourth *Idylls*: a study in Hellenistic irony', *QUUC* 12.95–113
- (1977). 'Aphrodite and the oak trees', *Museum Philologum Londiniense* 2.177–86
- (1977a). 'Textual problems in Theocritus *Idyll* XXI', *Ant. Class.* 46.495–522
Gill, R. (1972). '*Musa iocosa mea*: thoughts on the Elegies' in *John Donne: Essays in celebration* (ed. A. J. Smith), 47–72. London
Gittings, R. (1954). *John Keats. The living year.* London
Golding, A. (1567). *Ovid's Metamorphoses* (ed. J. F. Nims, 1965). New York
Goodyear, F. R. D. (1972). *The Annals of Tacitus.* Vol. 1. Cambridge Classical Texts Commentaries 15. Cambridge
Goold, G. P. (1970). 'Servius and the Helen episode', *HSCP* 74.101–68
Gow, A. S. F. (1952). *Theocritus.* Cambridge
- (1965). *Machon.* Cambridge Classical Texts and Commentaries 1. Cambridge
Gow, A. S. F.–Page, D. L. (1965). *The Greek anthology: Hellenistic epigrams.* Vols 1–2. Cambridge
- (1968). *The Greek anthology: The Garland of Philip.* Vols 1–2. Cambridge
Gow, A. S. F.–Scholfield, A. F. (1953). *Nicander: the poems and poetic fragments.* Cambridge
Gransden, K. W. (1976). *Virgil Aeneid Book VIII.* Cambridge
Grant, M. (1962). *Myths of the Greeks and Romans.* London
Grassmann, V. (1966). *Die erotischen Epoden des Horaz.* Zetemata 39. Munich
Gratwick, A. S. (1973). 'Corydon and his prospects', *CR* 23.10
Griffin, J. (1976). 'Augustan poetry and the life of luxury', *JRS* 66.87–105
Gualandri, I. (1970). 'Nota esegetica ad *Eneide* 2,471–472', *Acme* 23.149–51
Haffter, H. (1934). *Untersuchungen zur altlateinische Dichtersprache.* Berlin
- (1967). *Terenz und seine künstlerische Eigenart.* Darmstadt [= *MH* 10 (1953), 1–20 and 73–102]
Handley, E.W. (1968). *Menander and Plautus: a study in comparison.* London [repr. in German in *Die römische Komödie: Plautus und Terenz* (ed. E. Lefevre), Wege der Forschung 236 (Darmstadt, 1973), 249–76]
- (1969). 'The conventions of the comic stage and their exploitation by Menander', *Entretiens sur l'Antiquité classique* 16 (*Ménandre*), 1–42. Vandoeuvres–Geneva
- (1975). 'Plautus and his public: some thoughts in new comedy in Latin', *Plauto e il teatro* (Atti del v. Congressio Internazionale di Studi sul Drama Antico [= *Dioniso* 46]), 117–32. Syracuse
Havet, L. (1904). 'Plautus', *RPh* 28.136–50
Heimgartner, P. G. (1940). *Die Eigenart Theokrits in seinem Sprichwort.* Freiburg
Heinze, R. (1915). *Virgils epische Technik.* 3rd edn. Leipzig–Berlin
Henry, J. (1878). *Aeneidea.* Vol. 2. Dublin
Heubner, H. (1968). *P. Cornelius Tacitus: Die Historien.* Vol. 2 *Zweites Buch.* Heidelberg

Heyne, C. G. (1832). *P. Vergilius Maro.* Vol. 2. 4th edn (cur. G. P. E. Wagner). Leipzig–London

Hornsby, R. A. (1970). *Patterns of action in the Aeneid: an interpretation of Virgil's epic similes.* Iowa City

Hubaux, J. (1953). 'Le dieu Amore chez Properce et chez Longus', *Acad. Roy. de Belgique* (Classe des Lettres et des Sciences Morales et Politiques), sér. 5, 39.263–70

Hubbard, M. (1974). *Propertius.* London

Jackson Knight, W. F. (1932). *Vergil's Troy. Essays on the Second Book of the Aeneid.* Oxford [= *Vergil: epic and anthropology* (London, 1967), 15–134]

Jacques, J.-M. (1968). 'Ménandre inédit: la *Double fourberie* et la *Samienne*', *Bull. de l'Assoc. G. Budé*, n.s. 4.213–39

Jäger, K. (1967). *Zweigliedrige Gedichte und Gedichtpaare bei Properz und in Ovids Amores.* Diss. Tübingen

Jensen, C. (1923). *Philodemus über die Gedichte.* Berlin

Jocelyn, H. D. (1965). 'Ancient scholarship and Virgil's use of Republican Latin poetry II', *CQ* 15.126–44

 – (1967). *The Tragedies of Ennius.* Cambridge Classical Texts and Commentaries 10. Cambridge

 – (1977). 'The ruling class of the Roman Republic and Greek philosophers', *Bull. John Rylands Univ. Library of Manchester* 59.323–66

Johnson, W. R. (1974). 'The emotions of patriotism: Propertius 4.6', *CSCA* 6.151–80

 – (1976). *Darkness visible: a study of Virgil s Aeneid.* Berkeley–Los Angeles–London

Kenney, E. J. (1971). *Lucretius De Rerum Natura Book III.* Cambridge

 – (1973). 'The style of the *Metamorphoses*' in Ovid (ed. J. W. Binns), 116–53. London

 – (1975). *New frameworks for old. The place of literature in the Cambridge classical course.* Cambridge

Kier, H. (1933). *De laudibus vitae rusticae.* Marburg

Kleinknecht, H. (1967). *Die Gebetsparodie in der Antike.* Repr. Hildesheim

Klepl, H. (1967). *Lukrez und Vergil in ihren Lehrgedichten.* Repr. Darmstadt

Klingner, F. (1967). *Virgil. Bucolica, Georgica, Aeneis.* Zurich–Stuttgart

Klose, D. (1968). 'Shakespeare und Ovid', *Shakespeare-Jahrbuch (W)* 72–93

Knauer, G. N. (1964). *Die Aeneis und Homer.* Hypomnemata 7. Göttingen

Knightly, P. (1975). *The first casualty.* London

Knox, B. M. W. (1950). 'The serpent and the flame: the imagery of the Second Book of the *Aeneid*', *AJP* 71.379–400

Koestermann, E. (1963). *Cornelius Tacitus: Annalen.* Vol. 1 *Buch 1–3.* Heidelberg

Krischer, T. (1968). 'Sappho's Ode an Aphrodite', *Hermes* 96.1–14

 – (1971). *Formale Konventionen der homerischen Epik.* Zetemata 56. Munich

Kroll, W. (1924). *Studien zum Verständis der römischen Literatur.* Stuttgart

Kuntz, F. (1962). *Die Sprache des Tacitus.* Munich

Latham, M. C. (1930). *The Elizabethan fairies.* London

Lee, A. G. (1962). 'Tenerorum lusor amorum' in *Critical essays on Roman literature: elegy and lyric* (ed. J. P. Sullivan), 149–80. London
- (1971). *Allusion, parody and imitation*. St John's College Cambridge Lectures. Hull
Leishman, J. B. (1951). *The monarch of wit*. London
- (1966). *The art of Marvell's poetry*. London
Lembach, K. (1970). *Die Pflanzen bei Theokrit*. Heidelberg
Leo, F. (1966). *Plautinische Forschungen: zur Kritik und Geschichte der Komödie*. 2nd edn. Repr. Darmstadt
- (1967). *Geschichte der römischen Literatur*. Vol. 1. Repr. Darmstadt
Levi, D. (1947). *Antioch mosaic pavements*. London
Lewis, C. S. (1936). *The allegory of love*. Oxford
Lieberg, G. (1962). *Puella Divina: die Gestalt der göttlichen Geliebten bei Catull im Zusammenhang der antiken Dichtung*. Amsterdam
Littlewood, A. R. (1967). 'The symbolism of the apple', *HSCP* 72.147–81
Löfstedt, E. (1942, 1933). *Syntactica*. Vols 1² and 2. Lund
Lörcher, G. (1975). *Der Aufbau der drei Bücher von Ovids Amores*. Heuremata 3. Amsterdam
Lowe, J. C. B. (1973). 'Notes on Menander', *BICS* 20.94–103
Luck, G. (1969). *The Latin love elegy*. 2nd edn. London
- (1976). 'An interpretation of Horace's Eleventh *Epode*', *Illinois Classical Studies* 1.122–6
Ludwig, W. (1968). 'The originality of Terence and his Greek models', *GRBS* 9.169–82
Mackail, J. W. (1930). *The Aeneid edited with introduction and commentary*. Oxford
McKay, A. G. (1974). 'Recent work on Virgil. A bibliographical survey, 1964–73', *CW* 68.2–19
MacKendrick, P. (1960). *The mute stones speak*. London
Macleod, C. W. (1974). 'Two comparisons in Sappho', *ZPE* 15.217–20
- (1974a). 'Propertius 2.26', *SO* 51.131–6
- (1977). 'The poet, the critic and the moralist: Horace, *Epistles* 1.19', *CQ* 27.359–76
Marti, H. (1963). 'Terenz 1909–1959', *Lustrum* 8 (Fortsetzung von *Lustrum* 6.114ff.), 5–101
Martin, R. H. (1955). 'Tacitus and the death of Augustus', *CQ* 5.123–8
Maurach, G. (1976). Review of Pöschl (1973), *Gymnasium* 83.479–84
Miller, N. P. (1959). *Tacitus Annals Book* 1. London
- (1968). 'Tiberius speaks', *AJP* 89.1–19
Minar, E. L.–Sandbach, F. H.–Helmbold, W. C. (1969). *Plutarch's Moralia*. Loeb edn. Vol. 9. Cambridge, Mass.
Mittelstadt, M. C. (1970). 'Bucolic-lyric motifs and dramatic narrative in Longus' *Daphnis and Chloe*', *RhM* 113.211–27
Moore, J. L. (1891). 'Servius on the tropes and figures of Vergil', *AJP* 12.267–92
Moore-Blunt, J. (1977). '*Eclogue* 2: Virgil's utilisation of Theocritean motifs', *Eranos* 75.23–42
Morgan, K. (1977). *Ovid's art of imitation*. Mnem. Suppl. 47. Leyden
Mountford, J. (1968–69). 'Tempo and texture in *Aeneid* II', *PVS* 8.26–38

Bibliography

Muecke, F. (1975). 'Virgil and the genre of pastoral', *Aumla* 44.169–80
Muir, K. (1977). *Shakespeare's sources*. 2nd edn. London
Munari, F. (1970). *P. Ovidi Nasonis Amores*. 5th edn. Florence
Murgia, C. E. (1971). 'More on the Helen episode', *CSCA* 4.203–17
Nadeau, J. Y. (1977). 'Ethiopians again', *Mnem.* 30.76–7
Neubecker, A. J. (1956). *Die Bewertung der Musik bei Stoikern und Epikureern: eine Analyse von Philodems Schrift De Musica*. Berlin
Nisbet, R. G. M. (1961). *Cicero: in L. Calpurnium Pisonem Oratio*. Oxford
Nisbet, R. G. M.–Hubbard, M. (1970). *A Commentary on Horace: Odes Book I*. Oxford
 – (1978). *A Commentary on Horace: Odes Book II*. Oxford
de Nonno, M. (1977). 'Le citazione di Prisciano da autori latini nella testimonianza del Vat. Lat. 3313', *RFIC* 105.385–402
Norden, E. (1913). *Agnostos Theos*. Leipzig–Berlin
 – (1915). *Ennius und Vergilius*. Leipzig–Berlin
 – (1923). *Die germanische Urgeschichte in Tacitus' Germania*. 3rd edn. Leipzig–Berlin
 – (1927). *P. Vergilius Maro: Aeneis Buch VI*. 3rd edn. Berlin
Ogilvie, R. M. (1965). *A Commentary on Livy Books 1–5*. Oxford
Page, D. L. (1942). *Select Papyri III: Literary Papyri, Poetry*. Loeb edn. London–Cambridge, Mass.
Page, T. E. (1894). *The Aeneid of Virgil Books I–VI*. London
Parry, A. (1969). 'The language of Thucydides' description of the plague', *BICS* 16.106–18
Partridge, E. (1968). *Shakespeare's bawdy*. London
Perdrizet, P. (1932). 'Légendes babyloniennes dans les *Métamorphoses* d'Ovide', *Rev. hist. relig.* 105.193–228
Perret, J. (1961). *Virgile: les Bucoliques*. Paris
Perry, B. E. (1967). *The ancient romances*. California
Peterson, W. (1891). *M. Fabi Quintiliani . . . Liber Decimus.*. Oxford
Pfeiffer, E. (1933). *Virgils Bukolika: Untersuchungen zum Formproblem*. Stuttgart
Pfeiffer, R. (1968). *History of classical scholarship from the beginnings to the end of the Hellenistic age*. Oxford
Pichon, R. (1966). *Index verborum amatoriorum*. Repr. Hildesheim
Pickard-Cambridge, A. W. (1946). *The theatre of Dionysus at Athens*. Oxford
Pinotti, P. (1977). 'Propert. IV 9: Alessandrinismo e arte allusiva', *GIF* n.s. 8.50–71
Platnauer, M. (1951). *Latin elegiac verse*. Cambridge
Pöschl, V. (1973). *Die neuen Menanderpapyri und die Originalität des Plautus*. SHAW Phil.-hist. Klasse, 4. Abhandlung. Heidelberg
Posch, S. (1969). *Beobachtungen zur Theokritnachwirkung bei Vergil*. Innsbruck–Munich
Press, J. (1966). *The fire and the fountain*. London
Putnam, M. C. J. (1965). *The poetry of the Aeneid*. Cambridge, Mass.–London
Questa, C. (1969). 'Alcune Strutture sceniche di Plauto e Menandro (con osservazioni su *Bacchides* e Δὶς ἐξαπατῶν)', *Entretiens sur l'Antiquité classique* 16 (*Ménandre*), 183–228. Vandoeuvres–Geneva
 – (1975). *T. Maccius Plautus: Bacchides*. 2nd edn. Florence

Quinn, K. (1963). *Latin explorations*. London
- (1968). *Virgil's Aeneid: a critical description*. London
Rademacher, U. (1975). *Die Bildkunst des Tacitus*. Spudasmata 29. Hildesheim-New York
Reckford, K. J. (1969). *Horace*. New York
Reichel, G. (1909). *Quaestiones Progymnasmaticae*. Leopzig
Reiff, A. (1959). *interpretatio, imitatio, aemulatio*. Bonn
Reitzenstein, R. (1912). *Zur Sprache der lateinischen Erotik. SHAW* Phil.-hist. Klasse 12. Heidelberg
Richmond, J. A. (1976). 'Symbolism in Virgil: skeleton-key or will-o'-the-wisp?', *G&R* 23.142–58
Richter, W. (1957). *Vergil: Georgica*. Munich
Rizzo, G. E. (1927). *La pittura ellenistico-romana*. Milan
Robathan, D. (1973). 'Ovid in the Middle Ages' in *Ovid* (ed. J. W. Binns), 191–208. London
Robertson, F. (1970–71). 'Virgil and Theocritus', *PVS* 10.8–23
Rohde, E. (1914). *Der griechische Roman und seine Vorläufer*. Leipzig
Rose, H. J. (1942). *The Eclogues of Virgil*. Berkeley–Los Angeles
Ross, D. O. (1969). *Style and tradition in Catullus*. Cambridge, Mass.
- (1975). *Backgrounds to Augustan poetry: Gallus, elegy and Rome*. Cambridge
Rumpel, J. (1879). *Lexicon Theocriteum*. Stuttgart
Russell, D. A. (1964). *'Longinus' On the Sublime*. Oxford
Russell, D. A.–Winterbottom, M. (1972). *Ancient literary criticism*. Oxford
Sandbach, F. H. (1969). 'Menander's manipulation of language for dramatic purposes', *Entretiens sur l'Antiquité classique* 16 (*Ménandre*), 111–43. Vandœuvres–Geneva
Sandbach (1973) = Gomme, A. W.–Sandbach, F. H. *Menander: a commentary*. Oxford
Schlunk, R. R. (1974). *The Homeric scholia and the Aeneid*. Ann Arbor
Schmidt, E. A. (1972). *Poetische Reflexion: Vergils Bukolik*. Munich
- (1972a). Review of Posch (1969), *Gnomon* 44.771–6
- (1974). *Zur Chronologie der Eklogen Virgils. SHAW* Phil.-hist. Klasse, 6. Abhandlung. Heidelberg
Schmitt-von Mühlenfels, F. (1972). *Pyramus und Thisbe*. Heidelberg
Schulz-Vanheyden, E. (1969). *Properz und das griechische Epigram*. Münster
Shackleton Bailey, D. R. (1964). 'Recensuit et emendavit', *Philologus* 108.102–16
Shannon, E. F. (1929). *Chaucer and the Roman poets*. New York
Shipley, J. T. (1970). *Dictionary of world literary terms*. Revised edn. London
Skutsch, F. (1901). *Aus Vergils Frühzeit*. Leipzig
Skutsch, O. (1956). 'Zu Vergils Eklogen', *RhM* 99.193–201
Smith, K. F. (1971). *The elegies of Albius Tibullus*. Repr. Darmstadt
Soubiran, J. (1964). 'Thèmes et rhythmes d'épopée dans les *Annales* de Tacite', *Pallas* 12.55–79
Staton, W. F. (1962–3). 'Ovidian elements in *A Midsummer Night's Dream*', *Huntington Library Quarterly* 26. 165–78
Steinmetz, P. (1964). 'Gattungen und Epochen der griechischen Literatur in der Sicht Quintilians', *Hermes* 92. 454–66

Stemplinger, E. (1912). *Das Plagiat in der griechischen Literatur*. Leipzig–Berlin

Stroh, W. (1971). *Die römische Liebeselegie als werbende Dichtung*. Amsterdam

Sullivan, J. P. (1961). 'Two problems in Roman love elegy', *TAPA* 92.522–36

Syme, R. (1958). *Tacitus*. Oxford

Thierfelder, A. (1975). 'Su alcuni generi particolari del comico in Plauto', *Plauto e il Teatro* (Atti del v. Congresso Internazionale di Studi sul Drama Antico [= *Dioniso* 46]), 89–109. Syracuse

Thomson, J. A. K. (1952). *Shakespeare and the Classics*. London

Tränkle, H. (1960). *Die Sprachkunst des Properz und die Tradition der lateinischen Dichtersprache. Hermes* Einzelschriften 15. Wiesbaden

– (1975). 'Zu zwei umstrittenen Stellen der plautinischen *Bacchides*', *MH* 32.115–23

Vischer, R. (1965). *Das einfache Leben*. Göttingen

Voigt, E. M. (1971). *Sappho et Alcaeus: Fragmenta*. Amsterdam

Walsh, P. G. (1961). *Livy: his historical aims and methods*. Cambridge

Wardman, A. (1976). *Rome's debt to Greece*. London

Ward-Perkins, J. B. (1976). *Pompeii A.D.* 79. London

Webster, T. B.. L. (1974). *An introduction to Menander*. Manchester

Wellesley, K. (1964). Review of Koestermann (1963), *JRS* 54.255–7

West, D. (1969). 'Multiple-correspondence similes in the *Aeneid*', *JRS* 59.40–9

– (1970). 'Virgilian multiple-correspondence similes and their antecedents', *Philologus* 114.262–75

– (1973). 'Horace's poetic technique in the *Odes*' in *Horace* (ed. C. D. N. Costa), 29–58. London

– 1975). 'Lucretius' methods of argument (3.417–614)', *CQ* 25.94–116

– (1977). Review of Johnson (1976), *THES* 8 July 1977, p. 18

White, K. D. (1970). *Roman farming*. London–Southampton

Wigodsky, M. (1972). *Virgil and early Latin Poetry. Hermes* Einzelschriften 24. Wiesbaden

Wilamowitz-Moellendorff, U. von (1906). *Die Textgeschichte der griechischen Bukoliker*. Berlin

– (1925). *Menander: Das Schiedsgericht*. Berlin

Wilkinson, L. P. (1955). *Ovid recalled*. Cambridge

– (1963). *Golden Latin artistry*. Cambridge

Williams, G. (1956). 'Some problems in the construction of Plautus' *Pseudolus*', *Hermes* 84.424–55

– (1968). *Tradition and originality in Roman poetry*. Oxford

Williams, R. D. (1972). *The Aeneid of Virgil Books* 1–6. London

Winbolt, S. E. (1906). *Latin hexameter verse*. London

Wiseman, T. P. (1979). *Clio's cosmetics*. Leicester

Wistrand, E. (1960). 'Virgil's palaces in the *Aeneid*', *Klio* 38.146–54 [= *Opera Selecta*, Acta Instituti Romani Regni Sueciae, ser. 8, 10 (Stockholm, 1972), 351–60]

Wolff, E. (1888). *Cornelii Taciti Historiarum Libri*. Vol. 2 *Buch III–V*. Berlin

Woodman, A. J. (1972). 'Remarks on the structure and content of Tacitus, *Annals* 4.57–67', *CQ* 22.150–8

– (1977). *Velleius Paterculus: The Tiberian narrative (2.94–131)*. Cambridge Classical Texts and Commentaries 19. Cambridge

–	(1980). 'The craft of Horace in *Odes* 1.14', *CP* (forthcoming)

Wright, J. (1974). *Dancing in chains: the stylistic unity of the Comoedia Palliata*. Papers and Monographs of the American Academy in Rome 25. Rome

Yardley, J. C. (1973). 'Sick-visiting in Roman elegy'. *Phoenix* 27.283–8

SELECT INDEXES

A. GENERAL INDEX

Actaeus 221
adynaton 84–5, 160, 169
aemulatio 10, 234
Alcaeus, Horace's relationship to 89–94
anaphora 42, 72, 161, 211
anthropomorphism 80–8
aphaeresis 163, 236
archaism, linguistic 2–3
'arrangement' 5
asyndeton 19, 203

βουκολιάϑεσθαι 38, 207
bucolics (of Theocritus), defined 208

cacoϑēlia 15
compositio 5
contaminatio 18, 20, 43–4, 67–8, 121, 195, 229–30

dates of publication, often coinciding with patrons' returns from campaign 36, 207
decorum 8
diaeresis 111, 226
Dircaeus 221

eccyclema 118, 229
elision 163
ellipse 72
enjambment 105, 111, 112, 115, 224, 227
etymology 39–40, 44, 64, 106, 116, 209–10, 212, 213, 221, 225, 228

furtum 202

Gallus, C. Cornelius 35, 60–3, 220
giggling (in Theocritus), sexual not mocking 213
golden line 81

hendiadys 225
homoeoteleuton 164, 236
hymnic language 42, 55, 135–6, 160, 211, 217, 231
hysteron proteron 80

imitatio, in the rhetorical schools 38–9, 234; *uitiorum* 15
inconditus 215
'inversion' 76–7
invitations, formulaic language of 29, 205

jokes (in Plautus), of the 'unexpected' type 31

kletic hymn 160, 211, 235
κλοπή 11–13
komos 45, 46–7, 50–1, 53–6, 60, 124, 212–13, 216, 217; as part of marriage suit 213; in Ovid (*Amores* 3.8) 216, (*Metamorphoses* 13.789ff.) 219 (n. 202), (*Metamorphoses* 14.623–771) 213; in Theocritus (*Idyll* 20) 53, 216

laudes Galli 220
lioness (*leaena*), as symbol of lust 218

meetings, formulaic language of 27–8
metaphrasis 201
military language 19–20, 28–9, 126, 129–30, 133, 139, 205
mime 40–1, 42, 49, 210, 211, 215
mimeisthai 3
mimēma 4
mimēsis 1–16

narratio 48, 161, 214
nec quid speraret habebat (Virgil, *Eclogues* 2.2) 214

B. INDEX LOCORUM